D1153119

THE BOOK ®

Ford Fiesta
Service and Repair Manual

I M Coomber and Christopher Rogers

Models covered
All Fiesta models with petrol engines and manual transmission; Hatchback & Van, including XR2 & special/limited editions
957 cc, 1117 cc, 1296 cc, 1392 cc & 1597 cc

Does not cover CTX (automatic) transmission models

(1030 - 224 - 9AA10)

© Haynes Publishing 1997

ABCDE
FGI

3

A book in the **Haynes Service and Repair Manual Series**

ISBN 1 85960 187 1

British Library Cataloguing in Publication Data
A catalogue record for this book is available from the British Library.

Printed by J H Haynes & Co Ltd, Sparkford, Nr Yeovil, Somerset BA22 7JJ, England

Haynes Publishing
Sparkford, Nr Yeovil, Somerset BA22 7JJ, England

Haynes North America, Inc
861 Lawrence Drive, Newbury Park, California 91320, USA

Editions Haynes S.A.
Tour Aurore - La Défense 2, 18 Place des Reflets,
92975 PARIS LA DEFENSE Cedex, France

Haynes Publishing Nordiska AB
Box 1504, 751 45 UPPSALA, Sweden

Contents

LIVING WITH YOUR FORD FIESTA

Roadside Repairs

Weekly Checks

MAINTENANCE

Routine Maintenance and Servicing

Contents

REPAIRS & OVERHAUL

Engine and Associated Systems

Transmission

Brakes and Suspension

Body Equipment

Wiring Diagrams

REFERENCE

Index

Although the Ford Fiesta range of models was first introduced in February 1977, this manual covers the Fiesta range produced from August 1983 until February 1989. As with the earlier models, the New Fiesta is a two-door hatchback with an upward lifting tailgate, but the external and internal features of the new models have been restyled and updated.

The mechanical layout remains similar; with a transverse-mounted engine, separate manual gearbox and integral final drive unit, and front-wheel-drive.

The engine types available are the previously used 957 cc and 1117 cc overhead valve units (which have had design modifications to improve the fuel consumption), and the 1296 cc, 1392 cc and 1597 cc overhead camshaft CVH (Compound Valve Hemispherical head) units which provide good performance coupled with economy. A diesel-engined variant is also available, but this is not included in this manual.

The transmission types available are the four-speed or five-speed manual gearbox with full synchromesh and a central floor-mounted gear-lever.

All models are fitted with disc front brakes and drum rear brakes.

The front suspension is fully independent MacPherson strut type with coil springs and double acting telescopic shock absorbers, whilst the rear suspension is of the five link type with Panhard rod and telescopic double-acting shock absorbers. Certain models have a rear anti-roll bar.

For the home mechanic, the Fiesta is an ideal car to maintain and repair since design features have been incorporated to reduce the actual cost of ownership to a minimum, with the result that components requiring relatively frequent attention (eg the exhaust system) are easily removed.

Your Ford Fiesta manual

The aim of this manual is to help you get the best value from your vehicle. It can do so in several ways. It can help you decide what work must be done (even should you choose to get it done by a garage), provide information on routine maintenance and servicing, and give a logical course of action and diagnosis when random faults occur. However, it is hoped that you will use the manual by tackling the work yourself. On simpler jobs, it may even be quicker than booking the car into a garage and going there twice, to leave and collect it. Perhaps most important, a lot of money can be saved by avoiding the costs a garage must charge to cover its labour and overheads.

The manual has drawings and descriptions to show the function of the various components, so that their layout can be understood. Then the tasks are described and photographed in a clear step-by-step sequence.

References in this manual to "low series" models indicate bottom of the range models such as Base, Popular or L. "High series" indicates upper range models such as Ghia, XR2 and special editions.

Ford Fiesta L

Ford Fiesta XR2

Acknowledgements

Thanks are due to Champion Spark Plug who supplied the illustrations showing spark plug conditions. Certain other illustrations are the copyright of the Ford Motor Company and are used with their permission. Thanks are also due to Sykes-Pickavant Limited, who supplied some of the workshop tools, and to all those people at Sparkford who helped in the production of this manual.

Working on your car can be dangerous. This page shows just some of the potential risks and hazards, with the aim of creating a safety-conscious attitude.

General hazards

Scalding

• Don't remove the radiator or expansion tank cap while the engine is hot.
• Engine oil, automatic transmission fluid or power steering fluid may also be dangerously hot if the engine has recently been running.

Burning

• Beware of burns from the exhaust system and from any part of the engine. Brake discs and drums can also be extremely hot immediately after use.

Crushing

• When working under or near a raised vehicle, always supplement the jack with axle stands, or use drive-on ramps. *Never venture under a car which is only supported by a jack.*
• Take care if loosening or tightening high-torque nuts when the vehicle is on stands. Initial loosening and final tightening should be done with the wheels on the ground.

Fire

• Fuel is highly flammable; fuel vapour is explosive.
• Don't let fuel spill onto a hot engine.
• Do not smoke or allow naked lights (including pilot lights) anywhere near a vehicle being worked on. Also beware of creating sparks
(electrically or by use of tools).
• Fuel vapour is heavier than air, so don't work on the fuel system with the vehicle over an inspection pit.
• Another cause of fire is an electrical overload or short-circuit. Take care when repairing or modifying the vehicle wiring.
• Keep a fire extinguisher handy, of a type suitable for use on fuel and electrical fires.

Electric shock

• Ignition HT voltage can be dangerous, especially to people with heart problems or a pacemaker. Don't work on or near the ignition system with the engine running or the ignition switched on.

• Mains voltage is also dangerous. Make sure that any mains-operated equipment is correctly earthed. Mains power points should be protected by a residual current device (RCD) circuit breaker.

Fume or gas intoxication

• Exhaust fumes are poisonous; they often contain carbon monoxide, which is rapidly fatal if inhaled. Never run the engine in a confined space such as a garage with the doors shut.
• Fuel vapour is also poisonous, as are the vapours from some cleaning solvents and paint thinners.

Poisonous or irritant substances

• Avoid skin contact with battery acid and with any fuel, fluid or lubricant, especially antifreeze, brake hydraulic fluid and Diesel fuel. Don't syphon them by mouth. If such a substance is swallowed or gets into the eyes, seek medical advice.
• Prolonged contact with used engine oil can cause skin cancer. Wear gloves or use a barrier cream if necessary. Change out of oil-soaked clothes and do not keep oily rags in your pocket.
• Air conditioning refrigerant forms a poisonous gas if exposed to a naked flame (including a cigarette). It can also cause skin burns on contact.

Asbestos

• Asbestos dust can cause cancer if inhaled or swallowed. Asbestos may be found in gaskets and in brake and clutch linings. When dealing with such components it is safest to assume that they contain asbestos.

Special hazards

Hydrofluoric acid

• This extremely corrosive acid is formed when certain types of synthetic rubber, found in some O-rings, oil seals, fuel hoses etc, are exposed to temperatures above 400°C. The rubber changes into a charred or sticky substance containing the acid. *Once formed, the acid remains dangerous for years. If it gets onto the skin, it may be necessary to amputate the limb concerned.*
• When dealing with a vehicle which has suffered a fire, or with components salvaged from such a vehicle, wear protective gloves and discard them after use.

The battery

• Batteries contain sulphuric acid, which attacks clothing, eyes and skin. Take care when topping-up or carrying the battery.
• The hydrogen gas given off by the battery is highly explosive. Never cause a spark or allow a naked light nearby. Be careful when connecting and disconnecting battery chargers or jump leads.

Air bags

• Air bags can cause injury if they go off accidentally. Take care when removing the steering wheel and/or facia. Special storage instructions may apply.

Diesel injection equipment

• Diesel injection pumps supply fuel at very high pressure. Take care when working on the fuel injectors and fuel pipes.

⚠ *Warning: Never expose the hands, face or any other part of the body to injector spray; the fuel can penetrate the skin with potentially fatal results.*

Remember...

DO

• Do use eye protection when using power tools, and when working under the vehicle.

• Do wear gloves or use barrier cream to protect your hands when necessary.

• Do get someone to check periodically that all is well when working alone on the vehicle.

• Do keep loose clothing and long hair well out of the way of moving mechanical parts.

• Do remove rings, wristwatch etc, before working on the vehicle – especially the electrical system.

• Do ensure that any lifting or jacking equipment has a safe working load rating adequate for the job.

DON'T

• Don't attempt to lift a heavy component which may be beyond your capability – get assistance.

• Don't rush to finish a job, or take unverified short cuts.

• Don't use ill-fitting tools which may slip and cause injury.

• Don't leave tools or parts lying around where someone can trip over them. Mop up oil and fuel spills at once.

• Don't allow children or pets to play in or near a vehicle being worked on.

The following pages are intended to help in dealing with common roadside emergencies and breakdowns. You will find more detailed fault finding information at the back of the manual, and repair information in the main chapters

If your car won't start and the starter motor doesn't turn

☐ Open the bonnet and make sure that the battery terminals are clean and tight.
☐ Switch on the headlights and try to start the engine. If the headlights go very dim when you're trying to start, the battery is probably flat. Get out of trouble by jump starting (see next page) using a friend's car.

If your car won't start even though the starter motor turns as normal

☐ Is there fuel in the tank?
☐ Is there moisture on electrical components under the bonnet? Switch off the ignition, then wipe off any obvious dampness with a dry cloth. Spray a water-repellent aerosol product (WD-40 or equivalent) on ignition and fuel system electrical connectors like those shown in the photos. Pay special attention to the ignition coil wiring connector and HT leads.

A Check that the spark plug HT leads are securely connected by pushing them onto the plugs.

B Check that the HT leads are securely connected to the distributor

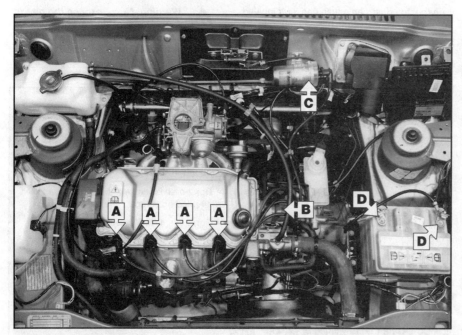

Check that the electrical connections are secure (with the ignition switched off) and spray them with a water dispersant spray like WD40 if you suspect a problem due to damp.

C Check that the HT leads are securely connected to the ignition HT coil (arrowed)

D Check the security and condition of the battery terminals.

Jump starting

Jump starting will get you out of trouble, but you must correct whatever made the battery go flat in the first place. There are three possibilities:

1 *The battery has been drained by repeated attempts to start, or by leaving the lights on.*

2 *The charging system is not working properly (alternator drivebelt slack or broken, alternator wiring fault or alternator itself faulty).*

3 *The battery itself is at fault (electrolyte low, or battery worn out).*

When jump-starting a car using a booster battery, observe the following precautions:

✔ Before connecting the booster battery, make sure that the ignition is switched off.

✔ Ensure that all electrical equipment (lights, heater, wipers, etc) is switched off.

✔ Make sure that the booster battery is the same voltage as the discharged one in the vehicle.

✔ If the battery is being jump-started from the battery in another vehicle, the two vehcles MUST NOT TOUCH each other.

✔ Make sure that the transmission is in neutral (or PARK, in the case of automatic transmission).

1 Connect one end of the red jump lead to the positive (+) terminal of the flat battery

2 Connect the other end of the red lead to the positive (+) terminal of the booster battery.

3 Connect one end of the black jump lead to the negative (-) terminal of the booster battery

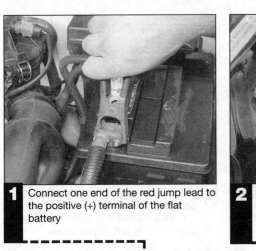

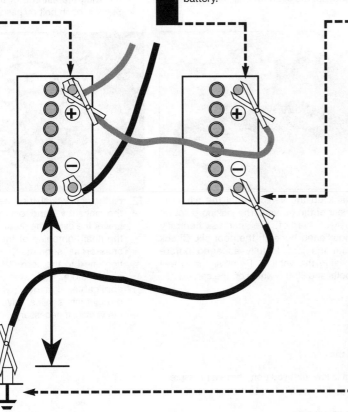

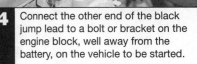

4 Connect the other end of the black jump lead to a bolt or bracket on the engine block, well away from the battery, on the vehicle to be started.

5 Make sure that the jump leads will not come into contact with the fan, drive-belts or other moving parts of the engine.

6 Start the engine using the booster battery, then with the engine running at idle speed, disconnect the jump leads in the reverse order of connection.

Wheel changing

Some of the details shown here will vary according to model. For instance, the location of the spare wheel and jack is not the same on all cars. However, the basic principles apply to all vehicles.

 Warning: Do not change a wheel in a situation where you risk being hit by other traffic. On busy roads, try to stop in a lay-by or a gateway. Be wary of passing traffic while changing the wheel – it is easy to become distracted by the job in hand.

Preparation

☐ When a puncture occurs, stop as soon as it is safe to do so.

☐ Park on firm level ground, if possible, and well out of the way of other traffic.

☐ Use hazard warning lights if necessary.

☐ If you have one, use a warning triangle to alert other drivers of your presence.

☐ Apply the handbrake and engage first or reverse gear.

☐ Chock the wheel diagonally opposite the one being removed – a couple of large stones will do for this.

☐ If the ground is soft, use a flat piece of wood to spread the load under the foot of the jack.

Changing the wheel

1 To remove the spare wheel lift the part of the floor which forms the lid to its housing and then release the wheel retaining stud.

2 The spare wheel is located in the luggage compartment and the jack is stored beneath the spare wheel.

3 Remove the wheel trim, if applicable, for access to the wheel bolts. Prise the trim off using the flat end of the wheelbrace. Slacken each bolt by half a turn.

4 Jack up the vehicle until the wheel is clear of the ground. The jacking point on each side of the car is centrally positioned beneath the door sill. Check that the jack is fully engaged before raising the vehicle. Remove the wheel bolts and lift the wheel off the car.

5 Fit the new wheel, then insert and tighten the bolts by hand only at this stage. Lower the car to the ground and carry out the final tightening of the wheel nuts in criss-cross sequence. Have the nuts tightened to the correct torque as soon as possible. Refit the wheel trim, if applicable. If a new wheel has been brought into service, have it balanced on the vehicle if necessary.

Finally...

☐ Remove the wheel chocks.

☐ Stow the jack and tools in the correct locations in the car.

☐ Check the tyre pressure on the wheel just fitted. If it is low, or if you don't have a pressure gauge with you, drive slowly to the nearest garage and inflate the tyre to the right pressure.

☐ Have the damaged tyre or wheel repaired as soon as possible.

Identifying leaks

Puddles on the garage floor or drive, or obvious wetness under the bonnet or underneath the car, suggest a leak that needs investigating. It can sometimes be difficult to decide where the leak is coming from, especially if the engine bay is very dirty already. Leaking oil or fluid can also be blown rearwards by the passage of air under the car, giving a false impression of where the problem lies.

 Warning: Most automotive oils and fluids are poisonous. Wash them off skin, and change out of contaminated clothing, without delay.

 The smell of a fluid leaking from the car may provide a clue to what's leaking. Some fluids are distinctively coloured. It may help to clean the car carefully and to park it over some clean paper overnight as an aid to locating the source of the leak.
Remember that some leaks may only occur while the engine is running.

Sump oil

Engine oil may leak from the drain plug...

Oil from filter

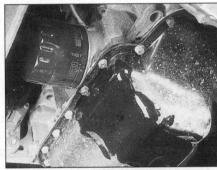

...or from the base of the oil filter.

Gearbox oil

Gearbox oil can leak from the seals at the inboard ends of the driveshafts.

Antifreeze

Leaking antifreeze often leaves a crystalline deposit like this.

Brake fluid

A leak occurring at a wheel is almost certainly brake fluid.

Power steering fluid

Power steering fluid may leak from the pipe connectors on the steering rack.

Front towing eye

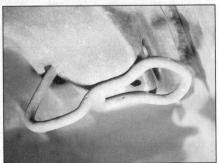

Rear towing eye

Towing

Towing eyes are fitted to the front and rear of the vehicle for attachment of a tow rope **(see illustrations)**.

Always unlock the steering column if being towed by another vehicle. If servo-assisted brakes are fitted, remember that the servo is inoperative if the engine is not running.

Introduction

There are some very simple checks which need only take a few minutes to carry out, but which could save you a lot of inconvenience and expense.

These "Weekly checks" require no great skill or special tools, and the small amount of time they take to perform could prove to be very well spent, for example;

☐ Keeping an eye on tyre condition and pressures, will not only help to stop them wearing out prematurely, but could also save your life.

☐ Many breakdowns are caused by electrical problems. Battery-related faults are particularly common, and a quick check on a regular basis will often prevent the majority of these.

☐ If your car develops a brake fluid leak, the first time you might know about it is when your brakes don't work properly. Checking the level regularly will give advance warning of this kind of problem.

☐ If the oil or coolant levels run low, the cost of repairing any engine damage will be far greater than fixing the leak, for example.

Underbonnet check points

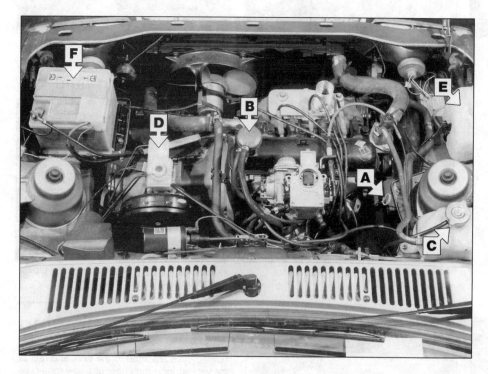

◄ ohv engine

A Engine oil level dipstick

B Engine oil filler cap

C Coolant expansion tank

D Brake fluid reservoir

E Windscreen washer reservoir

F Battery

A *Engine oil level dipstick*

B *Engine oil filler cap*

C *Coolant expansion tank*

D *Brake fluid reservoir*

E *Windscreen washer reservoir*

F *Battery*

Engine oil level

Before you start

✔ Make sure that your car is on level ground.
✔ Check the oil level before the car is driven, or at least 5 minutes after the engine has been switched off.

 If the oil is checked immediately after driving the vehicle, some of the oil will remain in the upper engine components, resulting in an inaccurate reading on the dipstick!

The correct oil

Modern engines place great demands on their oil. It is very important that the correct oil for your car is used (See "Lubricants and Fluids").

Car Care

● If you have to add oil frequently, you should check whether you have any oil leaks. Place some clean paper under the car overnight, and check for stains in the morning. If there are no leaks, the engine may be burning oil *(see "Fault Finding").*

● Always maintain the level between the upper and lower dipstick marks (see photo 3). If the level is too low severe engine damage may occur. Oil seal failure may result if the engine is overfilled by adding too much oil.

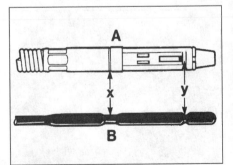

1 The location of the oil level dipstick varies depending on which engine is fitted. Refer to the photos on pages 0•10 and 0•11 for the exact location. Withdraw the dipstick.

3 Note the oil level on the end of the dipstick, which should be between the upper "MAX" mark (X) and lower "MIN" mark (Y). Two types of dipstick are used. Type "A" being of the type used on models with an auxiliary warning system, and "B" being the standard type.

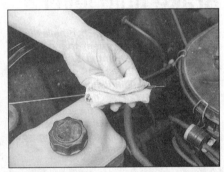

2 Wipe it on a clean rag and re-insert it fully. Withdraw it again and read the oil level relative to the marks on the end of the stick.

4 Oil is added through the filler cap. Pull off the cap and top-up the level; a funnel may help to reduce spillage . Add the oil slowly, checking the level on the dipstick frequently. Avoid overfilling (see "Car Care").

Coolant level

Warning: DO NOT attempt to remove the expansion tank pressure cap when the engine is hot, as there is a very great risk of scalding. Do not leave open containers of coolant about, as it is poisonous.

Car Care

● With a sealed-type cooling system, adding coolant should not be necessary on a regular basis. If frequent topping-up is required, it is likely there is a leak. Check the radiator, all hoses and joint faces for signs of staining or wetness, and rectify as necessary.

● It is important that antifreeze is used in the cooling system all year round, not just during the winter months. Don't top-up with water alone, as the antifreeze will become too diluted.

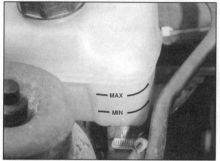

1 The coolant level varies with the temperature of the engine. When the engine is cold, the coolant level should be as shown. When the engine is hot, the level may rise slightly above the "MAX" mark.

2 If topping-up is necessary, **wait until the engine is cold**. Slowly turn the expansion tank cap anti-clockwise to relieve the system pressure. Once any pressure is released, turn the cap anti-clockwise until it can be lifted off.

3 Add a mixture of water and antifreeze through the expansion tank filler neck until the coolant reaches the "MAX" level mark. Refit the cap, turning it clockwise as far as it will go until it is secure.

Brake fluid level

Warning: Brake hydraulic fluid can harm your eyes and damage painted surfaces, so use extreme caution when handling and pouring it.
● **Do not use fluid that has been standing open for some time, as it absorbs moisture from the air which can cause a dangerous loss of braking effectiveness.**

● Make sure that your car is on level ground.
● The fluid level in the master cylinder reservoir will drop slightly as the brake pads wear down, but the fluid level must never be allowed to drop below the 'MIN' mark.

Safety first

● If the reservoir requires repeated topping-up this is an indication of a fluid leak somewhere in the system, which should be investigated immediately.

● If a leak is suspected, the car should not be driven until the braking system has been checked. Never take any risks where brakes are concerned.

1 The "MAX" and "MIN" marks are indicated on the side of the reservoir. The fluid level must be kept between the marks.

2 If topping-up is necessary, first wipe the area around the filler cap with a clean rag, then disconnect the electrical connector before removing the cap.

3 When adding fluid, it's a good idea to inspect the reservoir. The system should be drained and refilled if dirt is seen in the fluid (see Chapter 9 for details). Avoid spilling any fluid on surrounding paintwork.

4 Use only the specified hydraulic fluid; mixing different types of fluid can cause damage to the system. After filling to the correct level, refit the cap securely, to prevent leaks and the entry of foreign matter. Wipe off any spilt fluid.

Screen washer fluid level

Screenwash additives not only keep the winscreen clean during foul weather, they also prevent the washer system freezing in cold weather - which is when you are likely to need it most. Don't top up using plain water as the screenwash will become too diluted, and will freeze during cold weather. On no account use engine antifreeze in the washer system - this could discolour or damage paintwork.

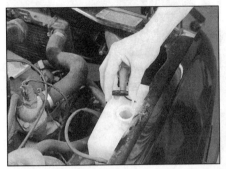

1 The windscreen washer fluid reservoir is located on the right-hand side of the engine compartment.

2 While the rear screen reservoir is stored in the luggage compartment near the spare wheel. The screen washer level can be seen through the reservoir body. If topping-up is necessary, open the cap.

3 When topping-up the reservoir a screenwash additive should be added in the quantities recommended on the bottle.

Electrical system

✔ Check all external lights and the horn. Refer to the appropriate Sections of Chapter 12 for details if any of the circuits are found to be inoperative.

✔ Visually check all wiring connectors, harnesses and retaining clips for security, and for signs of chafing or damage.

HAYNES HiNT *If you need to check your brake lights and indicators unaided, back up to a wall or garage door and operate the lights. The reflected light should show if they are working properly.*

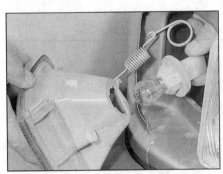

1 If a single indicator light, brake light or headlight has failed it is likely that a bulb has blown and will need to be replaced. Refer to Chapter 12 for details.
If both brake lights have failed, it is possible that the brake light switch above the brake pedal needs adjusting. This simple operation is described in Chapter 9.

2 If more than one indicator light or headlight has failed it is likely that either a fuse has blown or that there is a fault in the circuit (refer to *"Electrical fault-finding"* in Chapter 12).
The fuses are mounted behind the "cubby-hole" located at the lower right-hand side of the facia under a removable cover.

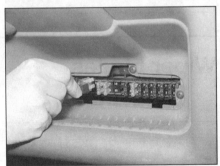

3 To replace a blown fuse, simply pull it out. Fit a new fuse of the same rating, available from car accessory shops.
It is important that you find the reason that the fuse blew - a checking procedure is given in Chapter 12.

Battery

Caution: Before carrying out any work on the vehicle battery, read the precautions given in "Safety first" at the start of this manual.

✔ Make sure that the battery tray is in good condition, and that the clamp is tight. Corrosion on the tray, retaining clamp and the battery itself can be removed with a solution of water and baking soda. Thoroughly rinse all cleaned areas with water. Any metal parts damaged by corrosion should be covered with a zinc-based primer, then painted.

✔ Periodically (approximately every three months), check the charge condition of the battery as described in Chapter 5A.

✔ If the battery is flat, and you need to jump start your vehicle, see *"Roadside Repairs"*.

1 The battery is located on the left-hand side of the engine compartment. The exterior of the battery should be inspected for damage such as a cracked case or cover. If a battery with cell covers has been fitted (rather than the maintenance-free type), periodically check that the cells are covered by about 6 mm of electrolyte. Top-up using distilled or de-ionised water.

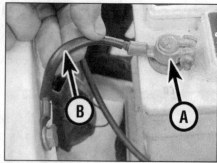

2 Check the tightness of battery clamps (A) to ensure good electrical connections. You should not be able to move them. Also check each cable (B) for cracks and frayed conductors.

HAYNES HiNT

Battery corrosion can be kept to a minimum by applying a layer of petroleum jelly to the clamps and terminals after they are reconnected.

3 If corrosion (white, fluffy deposits) is evident, remove the cables from the battery terminals, clean them with a small wire brush, then refit them. Accessory stores sell a useful tool for cleaning the battery post ...

4 ... as well as the battery cable clamps

Wiper blades

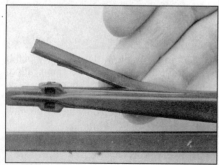

1 Check the condition of the wiper blades; if they are cracked or show any signs of deterioration, or if the glass swept area is smeared, renew them. For maximum clarity of vision, wiper blades should be renewed annually, as a matter of course.

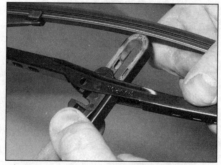

2 To remove a wiper blade, pull the arm fully away from the glass until it locks. Swivel the blade through 90°, press the locking tab(s) with your fingers, and slide the blade out of the arm's hooked end. On refitting, ensure that the blade locks securely into the arm.

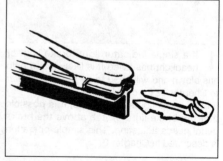

3 To remove the wiper blade rubber (earlier type) from its holder, use your thumb to draw back the rubber insert until the spring clip can be removed, then slide the rubber insert from the blade. Fit the new blade rubber by reversing the removal operation. Refit the blade by sliding it onto the hook on the arm.

Tyre condition and pressure

It is very important that tyres are in good condition, and at the correct pressure - having a tyre failure at any speed is highly dangerous. Tyre wear is influenced by driving style - harsh braking and acceleration, or fast cornering, will all produce more rapid tyre wear. As a general rule, the front tyres wear out faster than the rears. Interchanging the tyres from front to rear ("rotating" the tyres) may result in more even wear. However, if this is completely effective, you may have the expense of replacing all four tyres at once! Remove any nails or stones embedded in the tread before they penetrate the tyre to cause deflation. If removal of a nail does reveal that

the tyre has been punctured, refit the nail so that its point of penetration is marked. Then immediately change the wheel, and have the tyre repaired by a tyre dealer.

Regularly check the tyres for damage in the form of cuts or bulges, especially in the sidewalls. Periodically remove the wheels, and clean any dirt or mud from the inside and outside surfaces. Examine the wheel rims for signs of rusting, corrosion or other damage. Light alloy wheels are easily damaged by "kerbing" whilst parking; steel wheels may also become dented or buckled. A new wheel is very often the only way to overcome severe damage.

New tyres should be balanced when they are fitted, but it may become necessary to re-balance them as they wear, or if the balance weights fitted to the wheel rim should fall off. Unbalanced tyres will wear more quickly, as will the steering and suspension components. Wheel imbalance is normally signified by vibration, particularly at a certain speed (typically around 50 mph). If this vibration is felt only through the steering, then it is likely that just the front wheels need balancing. If, however, the vibration is felt through the whole car, the rear wheels could be out of balance. Wheel balancing should be carried out by a tyre dealer or garage.

Tread Depth - visual check

1 The original tyres have tread wear safety bands (B), which will appear when the tread depth reaches approximately 1.6 mm. The band positions are indicated by a triangular mark on the tyre sidewall (A).

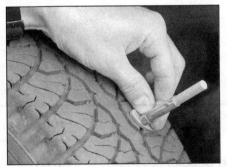

Tread Depth - manual check

2 Alternatively tread wear can be monitored with a simple, inexpensive device known as a tread depth indicator gauge.

Tyre Pressure Check

3 Check the tyre pressures regularly with the tyres cold. Do not adjust the tyre pressures immediately after the vehicle has been used, or an inaccurate setting will result. Tyre pressures are shown on the next page.

4 **Tyre tread wear patterns**

Shoulder Wear

Underinflation (wear on both sides)
Under-inflation will cause overheating of the tyre, because the tyre will flex too much, and the tread will not sit correctly on the road surface. This will cause a loss of grip and excessive wear, not to mention the danger of sudden tyre failure due to heat build-up.
Check and adjust pressures
Incorrect wheel camber (wear on one side)
Repair or renew suspension parts
Hard cornering
Reduce speed!

Centre Wear

Overinflation
Over-inflation will cause rapid wear of the centre part of the tyre tread, coupled with reduced grip, harsher ride, and the danger of shock damage occurring in the tyre casing.
Check and adjust pressures

If you sometimes have to inflate your car's tyres to the higher pressures specified for maximum load or sustained high speed, don't forget to reduce the pressures to normal afterwards.

Uneven Wear

Front tyres may wear unevenly as a result of wheel misalignment. Most tyre dealers and garages can check and adjust the wheel alignment (or "tracking") for a modest charge.
Incorrect camber or castor
Repair or renew suspension parts
Malfunctioning suspension
Repair or renew suspension parts
Unbalanced wheel
Balance tyres
Incorrect toe setting
Adjust front wheel alignment
Note: *The feathered edge of the tread which typifies toe wear is best checked by feel.*

Lubricants and fluids

Engine .... Multigrade engine oil, viscosity range SAE 10W/30 to 10W/50

Cooling system .... Antifreeze to Ford spec SSM-97B-9103-A

Gearbox .... Gear oil, viscosity SAE 80EP, to Ford spec SQM-2C-9008-A

Brake hydraulic system .... Brake fluid to Ford spec SAM-6C-9103-A Amber

Tyre pressures

Tyre pressures (cold) bar (lbf/in^2):	Front	Rear
135 SR 13:		
Normal loading/usage (up to three people)	1.8 (26)	1.8 (26)
Fully laden (normal usage)	2.6 (37)	2.8 (40)
155/70 SR 13:		
Normal loading/usage (up to three people)	1.6 (23)	1.8 (26)
Fully laden (normal usage)	2.1 (30)	2.3 (33)
165/65 SR 13:		
Normal loading/usage (up to three people)	1.6 (23)	1.8 (26)
Fully laden (normal usage)	2.1 (30)	2.3 (33)
185/60 HR 13:		
Normal loading/usage (up to three people)	1.8 (26)	1.8 (26)
Fully laden (normal usage)	2.0 (28)	2.0 (28)

Note: Increase the above pressures by 0.1 bar (1.4 lbf/in^2) for every 10 kph (6 mph) above 160 kph (100 mph) for sustained high speed use.

Chapter 1
Routine maintenance and servicing

Contents

Degrees of difficulty

Easy, suitable for novice with little experience | **Fairly easy,** suitable for beginner with some experience | **Fairly difficult,** suitable for competent DIY mechanic | **Difficult,** suitable for experienced DIY mechanic | **Very difficult,** suitable for expert DIY or professional

Servicing Specifications

Lubricants and fluids

See end of "Weekly checks"

Capacities

Engine oil

With filter:
1.0 and 1.1 OHV	3.25 litres (5.7 Imp pints)
1.3, 1.4 and 1.6 CVH	3.50 litres (6.2 Imp pints)

Without filter:
1.0 and 1.1 OHV	2.75 litres (4.8 Imp pints)
1.3, 1.4 and 1.6 CVH	3.25 litres (5.7 Imp pints)

Cooling system (including heater)
1.0 and 1.1 OHV	5.5 litres (9.7 Imp pints)
1.3 and 1.4 CVH	6.3 litres (11.1 Imp pints)
1.6 CVH	8.0 litres (14.1 Imp pints)

Fuel tank
All models - pre 1985, except XR2	34 litres (7.5 gallons)
XR2	38 litres (8.4 gallons)
All models - 1985 on	40 litres (8.8 gallons)

Gearbox
4-speed	2.8 litres (4.9 Imp pints)
5-speed	3.1 litres (5.5 Imp pints)

Engine

Oil filter type . . . . Champion C104
Valve clearances (only OHV applicable):
  Inlet:
    At operating temperature . . . . 0.22 mm (0.009 in)
    Cold . . . . 0.20 to 0.25 mm (0.008 to 0.010 in)
  Exhaust:
    At operating temperature . . . . 0.59 mm (0.023 in)
    Cold . . . . 0.56 to 0.61 mm (0.022 to 0.024 in)

Cooling system

Drivebelt tension . . . . 4.0 mm (0.16 in) total deflection at the midpoint of the belt's longest run

Fuel system

Air filter element type:
  1.0 and 1.1 (OHV) . . . . Champion W153
  1.3 (CVH) . . . . Champion W127
  1.4 (CVH) . . . . Champion W179
  1.6 (CVH) . . . . Champion W201

Ignition system

Spark plugs:
  Make and type:
    Mechanical system . . . . Champion RS9YCC or RS9YC
    Electronic system . . . . Champion RC7YCC or RC7YC
  Electrode gap:
    RS9YCC and RC7YCC . . . . 0.80 mm (0.032 in)
    RS9YC and RC7YC . . . . 0.75 mm (0.030 in)

Note: *The spark plug gap quoted is that recommended by Champion for their specified plugs listed above. If spark plugs of any other type are to be fitted, refer to their manufacturer's recommendations.*

Contact breaker points gap . . . . 0.40 to 0.50 mm (0.016 to 0.020 in)
Dwell (mechanical ignition):
  Angle . . . . 48° to 52°
  Variation (from idle to 2000 rpm) . . . . 4° maximum
  Overlap (lobe-to-lobe variation) . . . . 3° maximum
Timing (initial):
  1.0 litre OHV (pre 1986) . . . . 12° BTDC
  1.1 litre OHV (pre 1986) . . . . 6° BTDC
Ignition HT lead set:
  Resistance . . . . 30 k ohms maximum per lead
  Type:
    Mechanical system . . . . Champion CLS 8 boxed set
    Electronic system . . . . Champion CLS 9 boxed set

Brakes

Front brake pad friction material minimum thickness . . . . 1.5 mm (0.059 in)
Rear brake shoe friction material minimum thickness . . . . 1.0 mm (0.04 in)

Tyres

Tyre sizes:
Note: *Manufacturers often modify tyre sizes and pressure recommendations. The following is intended as a guide only. Refer to your vehicle handbook or a Ford dealer for the latest recommendations.*
  XR2 . . . . 185/60 HR 13
  Other models . . . . 135 SR 13, 155/70 SR 13 or 165/65 SR 13

Tyre pressures: *See end of "Weekly checks"*

Torque wrench settings

	Nm	lbf ft
Engine oil drain plug	25	18
Radiator coolant drain plug	1.5	1.1
Gearbox oil filler/level plug	27	20
Roadwheel bolts	100	74
Spark plugs:		
OHV engines	13 to 20	10 to 15
CVH engines	27	20
Brake caliper piston housing bolts	23	17

The maintenance intervals in this manual are provided with the assumption that you will be carrying out the work yourself. These are the minimum maintenance intervals recommended by the manufacturer for vehicles driven daily. If you wish to keep your vehicle in peak condition at all times, you may wish to perform some of these procedures more often. We encourage frequent maintenance, because it enhances the efficiency, performance and resale value of your vehicle.

If the vehicle is driven in dusty areas, used to tow a trailer, or driven frequently at slow speeds (idling in traffic) or on short journeys, more frequent maintenance intervals are recommended.

When the vehicle is new, it should be serviced by a factory-authorised dealer service department, in order to preserve the factory warranty.

Every 250 miles (400 km) or weekly
- [ ] Refer to "Weekly checks"

Every 6000 miles (10 000 km) or 6 months - whichever comes sooner
- [ ] Renew engine oil and filter (Section 3)
- [ ] Check brake pads or shoes for wear (front and rear) (Section 4)
- [ ] Check operation of brake fluid level warning indicator (Section 4)
- [ ] Inspect engine bay and underside of vehicle for fluid leaks or other signs of damage (Section 5)
- [ ] Check function and condition of seat belts (Section 6)
- [ ] Check condition and security of exhaust system (Section 7)
- [ ] Check tightness of wheel nuts (Section 8)
- [ ] Check choke adjustment (Section 9)
- [ ] Check idle speed (Section 10)
- [ ] Check mixture adjustment (Section 11)
- [ ] Check spark plugs (Section 12)
- [ ] Check HT leads, distributor cap and ignition circuit (Section 13)
- [ ] Check operation of latches, check straps and locks; lubricate if necessary (Section 14)
- [ ] Check ignition timing and contact breaker gap (dwell angle) (OHV engines) (Section 15)
- [ ] Check operation of throttle damper (where applicable) (Section 16)

Every 12 000 miles (20 000 km) or 12 months - whichever comes sooner
- [ ] Check tightness of battery terminals, clean and neutralise corrosion (Section 17)
- [ ] Check engine valve clearances - OHV engines (Section 18)
- [ ] Check handbrake mechanism (Section 19)
- [ ] Check condition and tension of auxiliary drivebelt (Section 20)

Every 12 000 miles (20 000 km) or 12 months - whichever comes sooner (continued)
- [ ] Renew spark plugs (Section 21)
- [ ] Check gearbox oil level (Section 22)
- [ ] Renew distributor contact breaker points and lubricate distributor - OHV engines (Section 23)
- [ ] Check security and condition of steering and suspension components, gaiters and boots (Section 24)
- [ ] Inspect underbody and panels for corrosion or other damage (Section 25)
- [ ] Inspect brake pipes and hoses (Section 26)
- [ ] Road test (Section 27)
- [ ] Check crankcase ventilation system (Section 28)

Every 24 000 miles (40 000 km) or 2 years - whichever comes sooner
- [ ] Check air cleaner temperature control (Section 29)
- [ ] Renew emission control filter element - CVH engines (Section 30)
- [ ] Renew air cleaner element (Section 31)

Every 36 000 miles (60 000 km) or 3 years - whichever comes sooner
- [ ] Renew brake hydraulic system seals and hoses if necessary (Section 32)
- [ ] Renew brake hydraulic fluid (Section 33)
- [ ] Renew timing belt - CVH engines (Section 34)
- [ ] Check front wheel alignment (Section 35)

Every 2 years, regardless of mileage
- [ ] Renew coolant (Section 36)

1

Engine compartment - OHV

1 Coolant expansion tank
2 Engine oil dipstick
3 Oil filter
4 Ignition coil
5 Brake fluid reservoir
6 Battery
7 Cooling fan
8 Oil filler cap
9 Carburettor (air cleaner removed)
10 Alternator
11 Washer reservoir

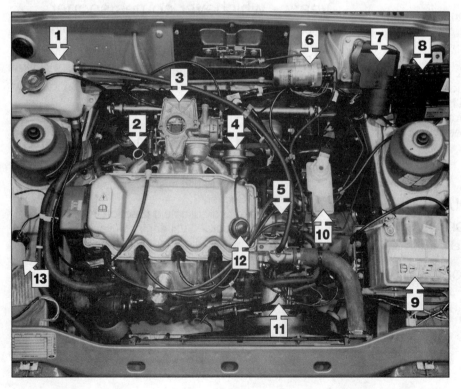

Engine compartment - CVH

1 Coolant expansion tank
2 Engine oil dipstick
3 Carburettor (air cleaner removed)
4 Fuel pump
5 Distributor
6 Ignition coil
7 Windscreen wiper motor
8 Ignition amplifier module
9 Battery
10 Brake fluid reservoir
11 Cooling fan
12 Oil filler cap
13 Washer reservoir

Underside view of car at front - CVH

1 *Suspension arm*
2 *Driveshaft*
3 *Tie-bar*
4 *Alternator*
5 *Sump*
6 *Exhaust*
7 *Starter motor*
8 *Engine/gearbox bearer*
9 *Gearbox*
10 *Disc brake caliper*
11 *Gearchange rod and stabilizer rod*

1

Underside view of car at rear

1 *Rear silencer*
2 *Brake secondary cable*
3 *Fuel tank*
4 *Suspension coil spring*
5 *Shock absorber lower mounting*
6 *Panhard rod*
7 *Anti-roll bar (certain models only)*
8 *Towing eye*
9 *Axle beam*
10 *Exhaust system mounting*
11 *Handbrake adjustment check plunger*
12 *Suspension trailing arm*
13 *Brake pressure control valve*

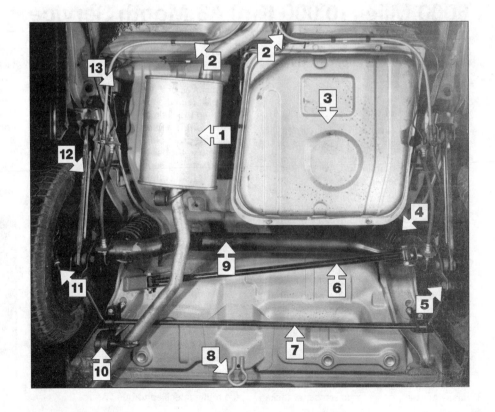

1 Introduction

This Chapter is designed to help the home mechanic maintain his/her vehicle for safety, economy, long life and peak performance.

The Chapter contains a master maintenance schedule, followed by Sections dealing specifically with each task in the schedule. Visual checks, adjustments, component renewal and other helpful items are included. Refer to the accompanying illustrations of the engine compartment and the underside of the vehicle for the locations of the various components.

Servicing your vehicle in accordance with the mileage/time maintenance schedule and the following Sections will provide a planned maintenance programme, which should result in a long and reliable service life. This is a comprehensive plan, so maintaining some items but not others at the specified service intervals, will not produce the same results.

As you service your vehicle, you will discover that many of the procedures can - and should - be grouped together, because of the particular procedure being performed, or because of the close proximity of two otherwise-unrelated components to one another. For example, if the vehicle is raised for any reason, the exhaust can be inspected at the same time as the suspension and steering components.

The first step in this maintenance programme is to prepare yourself before the actual work begins. Read through all the Sections relevant to the work to be carried out, then make a list and gather together all the parts and tools required. If a problem is encountered, seek advice from a parts specialist, or a dealer service department.

2 Intensive maintenance

If, from the time the vehicle is new, the routine maintenance schedule is followed closely, and frequent checks are made of fluid levels and high-wear items, as suggested throughout this manual, the engine will be kept in relatively good running condition, and the need for additional work will be minimised.

It is possible that there will be times when the engine is running poorly due to the lack of regular maintenance. This is even more likely if a used vehicle, which has not received regular and frequent maintenance checks, is purchased. In such cases, additional work may need to be carried out, outside of the regular maintenance intervals.

If engine wear is suspected, a compression test will provide valuable information regarding the overall performance of the main internal components. Such a test can be used as a basis to decide on the extent of the work to be carried out. If, for example, a compression test indicates serious internal engine wear, conventional maintenance as described in this Chapter will not greatly improve the performance of the engine, and may prove a waste of time and money, unless extensive overhaul work is carried out first.

The following series of operations are those most often required to improve the performance of a generally poor-running engine:

Primary operations

a) Clean, inspect and test the battery
b) Check all the engine-related fluids
c) Check the condition and tension of the auxiliary drivebelt
d) Renew the spark plugs
e) Inspect the distributor cap and HT leads - as applicable
f) Check the condition of the air cleaner filter element, and renew if necessary
g) Renew the fuel filter (if fitted)
h) Check the condition of all hoses, and check for fluid leaks
i) Check the idle speed and mixture settings - as applicable

If the above operations do not prove fully effective, carry out the following secondary operations:

Secondary operations

a) Check the charging system
b) Check the ignition system
c) Check the fuel system
d) Renew the distributor cap and rotor arm - as applicable
e) Renew the ignition HT leads - as applicable

6000 Mile (10 000 Km) / 6 Month Service

3 Engine oil and filter renewal

1 Frequent oil and filter changes are the most important preventative maintenance procedures which can be undertaken by the DIY owner. As engine oil ages, it becomes diluted and contaminated, which leads to premature engine wear.

2 Before starting this procedure, gather together all the necessary tools and materials. Also make sure that you have plenty of clean rags and newspapers handy, to mop up any spills. Ideally, the engine oil should be warm, as it will drain better, and more built-up sludge will be removed with it. Take care, however, not to touch the exhaust or any other hot parts of the engine when working under the vehicle. To avoid any possibility of scalding, and to protect yourself from possible skin irritants and other harmful contaminants in used engine oils, it is advisable to wear gloves when carrying out this work. Access to the underside of the vehicle will be greatly improved if it can be raised on a lift, driven onto ramps, or jacked

up and supported on axle stands (see "Jacking and vehicle support"). Whichever method is chosen, make sure that the vehicle remains level, or if it is at an angle, so that the drain plug is at the lowest point.
3 Slacken the drain plug about half a turn **(see illustration)**. Position the draining container under the drain plug, then remove the plug completely. If possible, try to keep the plug pressed into the sump while unscrewing it by hand the last couple of turns. Recover the sealing washer from the drain plug.

 Remove the engine oil drain plug quickly so that the stream of oil runs into the container, not up your sleeve!

4 Allow some time for the old oil to drain, noting that it may be necessary to reposition the container as the oil flow slows to a trickle.
5 After all the oil has drained, wipe off the drain plug with a clean rag. Check the sealing washer for condition, and renew it if necessary. Clean the area around the drain plug opening, and refit the plug. Tighten the plug to the specified torque.

6 Move the container into position under the oil filter.
7 Using an oil filter removal tool if necessary, slacken the filter initially, then unscrew it by hand the rest of the way **(see illustration)**. Empty the oil from the old filter into the container, and discard the filter.
8 Use a clean rag to remove all oil, dirt and sludge from the filter sealing area on the engine. Check the old filter to make sure that the rubber sealing ring hasn't stuck to the engine. If it has, carefully remove it.

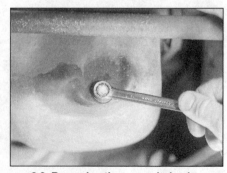

3.3 Removing the sump drain plug

3.7 Removing the engine oil filter with a clamp wrench

9 Apply a light coating of clean engine oil to the sealing ring on the new filter, then screw it into position on the engine. Tighten the filter firmly by hand only - **do not** use any tools. Wipe clean the filter and sump drain plug.

10 Remove the old oil and all tools from under the car, then lower the car to the ground (if applicable).

11 Remove the oil filler cap and withdraw the dipstick. Fill the engine, using the correct grade and type of oil (see *"Lubricants and fluids"* and *"Capacities"* in the Specifications). An oil can spout or funnel may help to reduce spillage. Pour in half the specified quantity of oil first, then wait a few minutes for the oil to fall to the sump. Continue adding oil a small quantity at a time until the level is up to the lower mark on the dipstick. Finally, bring the level up to the upper mark on the dipstick. Insert the dipstick, and refit the filler cap.

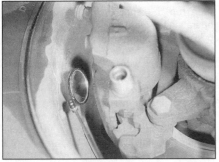

4.2a Using a mirror to check disc brake pads for wear

4.4a Remove the inspection plug from the rear brake backplate . . .

12 Start the engine and run it for a few minutes; check for leaks around the oil filter seal and the sump drain plug. Note that there may be a delay of a few seconds before the oil pressure warning light goes out when the engine is first started, as the oil circulates through the engine oil galleries and the new oil filter, before the pressure builds up.

13 Switch off the engine, and wait a few minutes for the oil to settle in the sump once more. With the new oil circulated and the filter completely full, recheck the level on the dipstick, and add more oil as necessary.

14 Dispose of the used engine oil safely.

4 Front and rear brake pad/shoe check

1 Firmly apply the handbrake, then jack up the front and rear of the car and support it securely on axle stands (see *"Jacking and vehicle support"*).

2 For a quick check, the front brake disc pads can be inspected without removing the front wheels by inserting a mirror between each caliper and roadwheel **(see illustrations)**. If any one pad is worn down to the minimum specified thickness, all four pads (on both front wheels) must be renewed.

3 For a comprehensive check, the brake disc pads should be removed and cleaned. The operation of the caliper can then also be checked, and the condition of the brake discs can be fully examined on both sides. Refer to Chapter 9 for further information.

4.2b Inspect the disc brake pads through the caliper housing aperture

4.4b . . . to check the rear brake linings for wear

4 The rear brake shoe friction material can be inspected for wear without removing the roadwheels. Working beneath the vehicle, prise the plug from the brake backplate and using an inspection lamp or torch, check that the friction material thickness is not less than the minimum given in the Specifications **(see illustrations)**. If any one of the shoes has worn below the specified limit, the shoes must be renewed as an axle set (4 shoes).

5 At the same interval, check the function of the brake fluid level warning light. Chock the wheels, release the handbrake and switch on the ignition. Unscrew and raise the brake fluid reservoir cap whilst an assistant observes the warning light: it should come on as the level sensor is withdrawn from the fluid. Refit the cap.

6 On completion, refit the wheels and lower the car to the ground.

5 Fluid leak check

> **HAYNES HINT** *Leaks in the cooling system will usually show up as white or rust-coloured deposits around the area adjoining the leak.*

1 Visually inspect the engine joint faces, gaskets and seals for any signs of water or oil leaks. Pay particular attention to the areas around the rocker cover, cylinder head, oil filter and sump joint faces. Bear in mind that over a period of time some very slight seepage from these areas is to be expected but what you are really looking for is any indication of a serious leak. Should a leak be found, renew the offending gasket or oil seal by referring to the appropriate Chapter(s) in this manual.

2 Similarly, check the transmission for oil leaks, and investigate and rectify and problems found.

3 Check the security and condition of all the engine related pipes and hoses. Ensure that all cable-ties or securing clips are in place and in good condition. Clips which are broken or missing can lead to chafing of the hoses, pipes or wiring which could cause more serious problems in the future.

4 Carefully check the condition of all coolant, fuel and brake hoses. Renew any hose which is cracked, swollen or deteriorated. Cracks will show up better if the hose is squeezed. Pay close attention to the hose clips that secure the hoses to the system components. Hose clips can pinch and puncture hoses, resulting in leaks. If wire type hose clips are used, it may be a good idea to replace them with screw-type clips.

5 With the vehicle raised, inspect the fuel tank and filler neck for punctures, cracks and

1

other damage. The connection between the filler neck and tank is especially critical. Sometimes a rubber filler neck or connecting hose will leak due to loose retaining clamps or deteriorated rubber.

6 Similarly, inspect all brake hoses and metal pipes. If any damage or deterioration is discovered, do not drive the vehicle until the necessary repair work has been carried out. Renew any damaged sections of hose or pipe.

7 Carefully check all rubber hoses and metal fuel lines leading away from the petrol tank. Check for loose connections, deteriorated hoses, crimped lines and other damage. Pay particular attention to the vent pipes and hoses which often loop up around the filler neck and can become blocked or crimped. Follow the lines to the front of the vehicle carefully inspecting them all the way. Renew damaged sections as necessary.

8 From within the engine compartment, check the security of all fuel hose attachments and pipe unions, and inspect the fuel hoses and vacuum hoses for kinks, chafing and deterioration.

9 Check the condition of all exposed wiring harnesses.

6 Seat belt check

1 Periodically check the belts for fraying or other damage. If evident, renew the belt.

2 If the belts become dirty, wipe them with a damp cloth using a little detergent only.

3 Check the tightness of the anchor bolts and if they are ever disconnected, make quite sure that the original sequence of fitting of washers, bushes and anchor plates is retained.

7 Exhaust system check

With the vehicle raised on a hoist or supported on axle stands (see *"Jacking and vehicle support"*), check the exhaust system for signs of leaks, corrosion or damage and check the rubber mountings for condition and security **(see illustration)**. Where damage or corrosion are evident, renew the system complete or in sections, as applicable, using the information given in Chapter 4.

8 Roadwheel security check

With the wheels on the ground, slacken each wheel bolt by a quarter turn, then retighten it immediately to the specified torque.

7.1 Inspect the exhaust system rubber mounting

9 Choke adjustment check

On models equipped with carburettors of Ford manufacture, refer to Chapter 4, Section 9 and check that the choke is adjusted within the stated parameters.

10 Engine idle speed check

Note: *Refer to the precautions given in Section 1 of Chapter 4 before proceeding.*
Note: *Before carrying out any carburettor adjustments, ensure that the ignition timing and spark plug gaps are set as specified. To carry out this adjustment, an accurate tachometer will be required.*

Ford 1V carburettor

1 Ensure that the air cleaner is correctly fitted, and that all vacuum hoses and pipes are securely connected and free from restrictions, then run the engine until it is at normal operating temperature.

2 With the engine at normal operating temperature, adjust the idle speed screw **(see illustration)** to obtain the specified idle speed, using a tachometer to ensure accuracy.

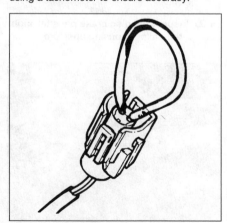

10.3 Temporary bridging wire in cooling fan thermal switch multi-plug

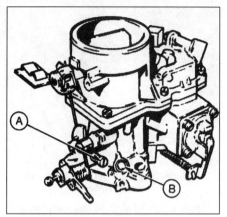

10.2 Ford 1V carburettor idle speed screw (A) and mixture screw (B)

Ford VV carburettor

3 This procedure must be carried out with the radiator cooling fan in operation. To keep the fan running during the adjustment procedure, disconnect the wiring multi-plug from the thermal switch (located in the thermostat housing) and bridge the two contacts in the plug with a short length of wire **(see illustration)**. Disconnect the wire and refit the multi-plug on completion of the adjustments. Make sure that the engine and ignition are switched off when connecting and disconnecting the bridging wire.

4 Ensure that the air cleaner is correctly fitted, and that all vacuum hoses and pipes are securely connected and free from restrictions, then run the engine until it is at normal operating temperature.

5 With the engine at normal operating temperature, connect a tachometer in accordance with the manufacturer's instructions.

6 Start the engine, run it at 3000 rpm for 30 seconds and then let it idle. Turn the idle speed adjusting screw in or out as necessary to bring the speed to that given in the Specifications **(see illustration)**.

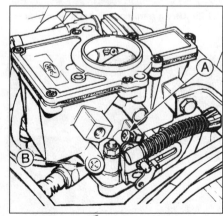

10.6 Ford VV carburettor idle speed screw (A) and mixture screw (B)

Every 6000 miles or 6 months

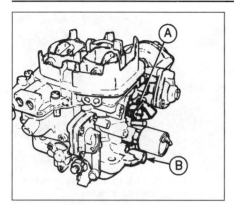

10.7 Weber 2V carburettor idle speed screw (A) and mixture screw (B)

Weber 2V carburettor

7 Refer to the information relating to the Ford 1V carburettor for details, and to the accompanying illustration **(see illustration)** for the adjusting screws. Ensure that the engine fan is operating by pulling the two wires from the sensor, and connecting the wires with a jumper lead.

Weber 2V DFTM

8 Before carrying out this adjustment, ensure that the air cleaner is correctly fitted and that all vacuum hoses and pipes are securely connected and free from restrictions. Run the engine until it is at normal operating temperature.

9 The cooling fan must be kept running during the adjustment procedure. To do this, disconnect the wiring multi-plug from the thermal switch (located in the thermostat housing) and bridge the two contacts in the plug with a short length of wire.

10 Start the engine and turn the idle speed adjustment screw **(see illustration)** to obtain the specified idle speed, using a tachometer to ensure accuracy.

Weber 2V TLD carburettor

11 Refer to the information relating to the Weber 2V DFTM carburettor for details, and to the accompanying illustration **(see illustration)** for the adjusting screws.

Weber (1V) TLM carburettor

12 Before carrying out this adjustment, ensure that the air cleaner is correctly fitted and that all vacuum hoses and pipes are securely connected and free from restrictions. Run the engine until it is at normal operating temperature.

13 Connect a reliable tachometer to the engine in accordance with the manufacturer's instructions.

14 Increase the engine speed to 3000 rpm and hold it at this speed for 30 seconds, then allow it to idle. Adjust the idle speed to within the specified range by turning the idle speed screw **(see illustration)**.

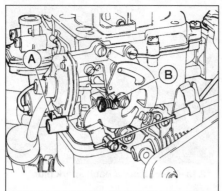

10.10 Weber 2V DFTM carburettor mixture screw (A) and idle speed screw (B)

11 Mixture adjustment check

Note: *Refer to the precautions given in Section 1 of Chapter 4 before proceeding.*

Note: *Before carrying out any carburettor adjustments, ensure that the ignition timing and spark plug gaps are set as specified. To carry out the adjustments an accurate tachometer and an exhaust gas analyser (CO meter) will be required. Adjustment of the idle mixture setting should not be attempted in territories where this may cause a violation of exhaust emission regulations. Where these regulations are less stringent the following procedures may be used.*

Ford 1V carburettor

1 Ensure that the air cleaner is correctly fitted and that all vacuum hoses and pipes are securely connected and free from restrictions, then run the engine until it is at normal operating temperature.

2 Using a small screwdriver, prise out the tamperproof plug (if fitted) over the idle mixture screw.

3 Connect the CO meter and tachometer according to the manufacturer's instructions.

4 Adjust the idle speed to the specified setting.

5 Run the engine at 3000 rpm for 30 seconds to clear the inlet manifold of excess fuel. Repeat this operation every 30 seconds during the adjustment procedure.

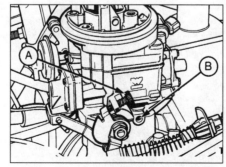

10.14 Weber (1V) TLM carburettor idle speed screw (A) and mixture screw (B)

6 Turn the idle mixture screw in the desired direction to achieve the fastest possible engine speed consistent with smooth, even running or the correct specified CO reading on the meter scale.

7 If necessary, readjust the idle speed setting on completion. Fit a new tamperproof plug to the mixture screw.

Ford VV carburettor

8 This procedure must be carried out with the radiator cooling fan in operation. To keep the fan running during the adjustment procedure, disconnect the wiring multi-plug from the thermal switch (located in the thermostat housing) and bridge the two contacts in the plug with a short length of wire. Disconnect the wire and refit the multi-plug on completion of the adjustments. Make sure that the engine and ignition are switched off when connecting and disconnecting the bridging wire.

9 To adjust the mixture accurately, connect a CO (exhaust gas) analyser and a tachometer in accordance with the manufacturer's instructions.

10 Ensure that the air cleaner is correctly fitted and that all vacuum hoses and pipes are securely connected and free from restrictions, then run the engine until it is at normal operating temperature.

11 Using a thin, sharp screwdriver, prise out the tamperproof plug which covers the mixture screw.

12 Start the engine and run it at 3000 rpm for 30 seconds, then allow it to return to idle. Turn the mixture screw in (weak) or out (rich) until the CO level is within the specified range as indicated on the analysing equipment. The adjustment must be carried out within 30 seconds; otherwise, again increase the engine speed for 30 seconds before continuing with the adjustment.

13 Once the mixture is correct, adjust the idle speed then recheck the mixture.

14 Switch off the engine and remove the tachometer and the exhaust gas analyser. Fit a new tamperproof plug to the mixture screw.

15 In the absence of a suitable exhaust gas analyser, an approximate setting of the mixture screw may be made by turning the screw inwards (engine idling) until the idle speed just begins to drop. Unscrew the screw

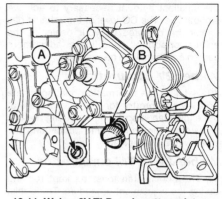

10.11 Weber 2V TLD carburettor mixture screw (A) and idle speed screw (B)

1

the smallest amount necessary to achieve smooth idle. The CO level of the exhaust gas should be checked by your dealer at the earliest opportunity and further adjustment carried out as may be necessary.

Weber 2V carburettor

16 Refer to the information relating to the Ford 1V carburettor for details. Ensure that the engine fan is operating by pulling the two wires from the sensor, and connecting the wires with a jumper lead.

Weber 2V DFTM carburettor

17 The cooling fan must be kept running during the adjustment procedure. To do this, disconnect the wiring multi-plug from the thermal switch (located in the thermostat housing) and bridge the two contacts in the plug with a short length of wire.
18 Ensure that the air cleaner is correctly fitted and that all vacuum hoses and pipes are securely connected and free from restrictions, then run the engine until it is at normal operating temperature.
19 Using a small screwdriver, prise out the tamperproof plug (if fitted) over the idle mixture screw.
20 Connect the CO meter and tachometer according to the manufacturer's instructions.
21 Adjust the idle speed to the correct setting.
22 Run the engine at 3000 rpm for 30 seconds to clear the inlet manifold of excess fuel. Repeat this operation every 30 seconds during the adjustment procedure.
23 Turn the idle mixture screw in the desired direction to achieve the fastest possible engine speed consistent with smooth, even running; or the correct specified CO reading on the meter scale.
24 If necessary, readjust the idle speed setting. Refit the cooling fan multi-plug and fit a new tamperproof plug.

Weber 2V TLD carburettor

25 Refer to the information relating to the Weber 2V DFTM carburettor for details.

Weber (1V) TLM carburettor

26 Ensure that the air cleaner is correctly fitted and that all vacuum hoses and pipes are securely connected and free from restrictions, then run the engine until it is at normal operating temperature.

12.1a Clean around each spark plug . . .

27 With the engine at normal operating temperature, connect a tachometer and exhaust gas analyser in accordance with the manufacturer's instructions.
28 Prise out the tamperproof plug from the mixture screw hole in the throttle valve block.
29 Wait for the radiator cooling fan to operate, then raise the engine speed to 3000 rpm, hold it at this speed for 30 seconds, return to idle and check the exhaust CO level on the exhaust gas analyser. If it is not as specified, turn the mixture screw (clockwise to weaken) and repeat the checking procedure.
30 On completion, fit a new tamperproof plug.

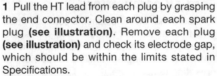

12 Spark plug check

1 Pull the HT lead from each plug by grasping the end connector. Clean around each spark plug **(see illustration)**. Remove each plug **(see illustration)** and check its electrode gap, which should be within the limits stated in Specifications.
2 To adjust the gap, bend the outer electrode with a proper spark plug gapping tool. Recheck the gap using feeler blades or wire gauges **(see illustrations)**.
3 Note that the correct functioning of each plug is vital for the correct running and efficiency of the engine. It is essential that the plugs fitted are appropriate for the engine and the suitable type is specified at the beginning of this Chapter. Spark plug cleaning is rarely

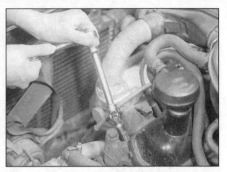
12.1b . . . before using a socket to remove the spark plugs

necessary and should not be attempted unless specialised equipment is available as damage can easily be caused to the firing ends.
4 The appearance of a removed spark plug can give some indication of the condition or state of tune of the engine, but as modern engines run on a weaker fuel/air mixture in order to conform to current emission control regulations, a rather whiter appearance of the spark plug electrode area must be expected than was the case on older cars. As the mixture control is preset during production, a black appearance of the plug electrode will normally be due to oil passing worn piston rings or valve stem oil seals, unless the carburettor has been tampered with.
5 When installing the plugs use a long reach socket, apply a little grease to the threads of the plugs **(see illustration)** and tighten them only to the specified torque wrench setting. Overtightening may damage the plug or its seat.

12.2a Measuring a spark plug electrode gap with a feeler blade

12.2b Measuring a spark plug electrode gap with a wire gauge

12.2c Adjusting a spark plug electrode gap with a special tool

12.5 Lightly grease the spark plug threads before fitting

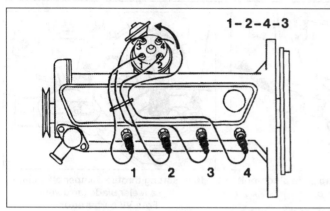

13.2a HT lead connections - OHV engines

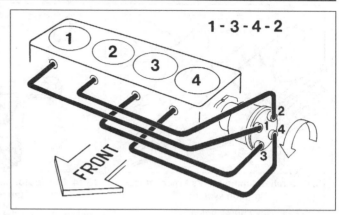

13.2b HT lead connections - CVH engines

13 HT lead, distributor cap and ignition circuit check

1 Clean each HT lead by wiping along its length with a fuel-moistened cloth and inspect it for damage.

2 Note the fitted position of each lead before disconnection **(see illustrations)**. When removing a lead from a spark plug or the HT coil, pull the lead off by its rubber connector **(see illustration)**.

3 The socket contacts on the distributor cap should be cleaned if they appear corroded **(see illustration)**. A smear of petroleum jelly (not grease) applied to the ferrule on the end of the HT lead will help to prevent corrosion.

4 Remove the distributor cap and rotor arm.

5 Examine the rotor arm and inside of the distributor cap . If the contacts are corroded or are excessively burnt, or if the carbon centre contact in the cap is worn away, renew the cap or rotor, as necessary. Check carefully for hairline cracks and signs of arcing. Make sure that the HT leads are reinstalled in their correct firing order.

6 Check that all HT and LT electrical leads are correctly routed and clear of all moving or hot engine components. Ensure that all lead connections are secure and where applicable, protected.

14 Hinge and lock check and lubrication

1 Work around the vehicle, and lubricate the bonnet, door and tailgate hinges with a light machine oil.

2 Lightly lubricate the bonnet release mechanism and exposed sections of inner cable with a smear of grease.

3 Check the security and operation of all hinges, latches and locks, adjusting them where required.

4 Check the condition and operation of the tailgate struts, renewing them if either is leaking or is no longer able to support the tailgate securely when raised.

15 Ignition timing and contact breaker gap (dwell angle) check - OHV engines

Contact breaker gap (dwell angle)

1 Access to the distributor is improved by removing the air cleaner unit.

2 Prise down the distributor cap retaining clips or remove the securing screws, as appropriate. Remove the distributor cap and rotor.

3 Apply a spanner to the crankshaft pulley bolt and turn the crankshaft until the distributor points are fully open, with the heel of the cam follower on the highest point of one of the lobes of the cam.

4 Using feeler blades, check the points gap **(see illustration)**. If the blade is not a sliding fit, release the screw at the fixed contact so that the contact will move and adjust the gap to that specified. Retighten the screw, refit the rotor and cap. Take care not to contaminate the points with oil from the feeler blades.

5 This method of adjustment should be regarded as second best as on modern engines, setting the points gap is usually carried out by measuring the dwell angle.

6 The dwell angle is the number of degrees through which the distributor cam turns during the period between the instants of closure and opening of the contact breaker points. Checking the dwell angle not only gives a more accurate setting of the contact breaker gap, but this method also evens out any variations in the gap which could be caused by pitting of the points, wear in the distributor shaft or its bushes, or difference in height of any of the cam peaks.

7 The dwell angle should be checked with a dwell meter connected in accordance with the maker's instructions. Refer to the Specifications for the correct dwell angle. If the dwell angle is too large, increase the points gap. If it is too small, reduce the gap.

1

13.2c Pull the HT lead connector - not the lead

13.3 Inspect each HT lead end ferrule for corrosion

15.4 Checking the contact breaker points gap using a feeler blade

15.10 Ignition timing marks - mechanical ignition system

A Crankshaft pulley notch
B Timing cover scale

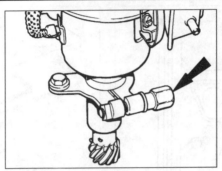

15.14 Distributor clamp plate pinch-bolt (arrowed)

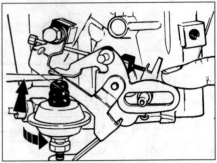

16.5 Setting throttle damper clearance using a feeler blade (arrowed) - Ford VV carburettor

8 The dwell angle should always be adjusted before checking and adjusting the ignition timing, as follows:

Ignition timing

9 Before checking the timing, check and adjust the dwell angle with the engine at normal operating temperature.
10 Increase the contrast of the notch in the crankshaft pulley and the appropriate mark on the timing index (refer to Specifications) by applying quick-drying white paint **(see illustration)**.
11 Connect a timing light (stroboscope) in accordance with the manufacturer's instructions.
12 Start the engine and allow it to idle.
13 Disconnect the vacuum pipe from the distributor and plug the pipe with a piece of rod.
14 If the timing light is now directed at the engine timing marks, the pulley notch will appear to be stationary and opposite the

specified mark on the scale. If the marks are not in alignment, release the distributor clamp pinch-bolt **(see illustration)** and turn the distributor in whichever direction is necessary to align the marks.
15 Retighten the pinch-bolt, switch off the engine, remove the timing light and reconnect the vacuum pipe.
16 It may now be necessary to check and adjust the engine idle speed if the distributor setting has to be varied to any extent.

16 Throttle damper operation check

1 To check the operation of the throttle damper fitted to models equipped with a Ford VV carburettor, proceed as follows:
2 Warm up the engine to normal operating temperature, then switch off. Connect a tachometer in accordance with the manufacturer's instructions. To keep the fan

running during the adjustment procedure, disconnect the wiring multi-plug from the thermal switch (located in the thermostat housing) and bridge the two contacts in the plug with a short length of wire.
3 Start the engine and increase its speed to 3200 ± 150 rpm by means of the idle speed adjustment screw. When the speed has stabilised, switch off the engine.
4 Rotate the secondary throttle lever clockwise to remove any play between the primary and secondary throttle levers, but ensure that the primary lever does not move.
5 Using a feeler blade, unscrew the damper until a clearance of 0.1 to 0.3 mm exists between the damper plunger and the secondary throttle lever **(see illustration)**. Hold the damper in this position and tighten the locknut.
6 Start the engine and return the idle speed to the specified rpm. Disconnect the tachometer and bridging wire, refit the multi-plug, then refit the air cleaner.

12 000 Mile (20 000 Km) / 12 Month Service

17 Battery terminal check

HAYNES HINT *To keep corrosion to a minimum, coat the battery terminals with petroleum jelly or a proprietary anti-corrosive compound.*

⚠ *Warning: Before carrying out any work on the vehicle battery, read through the precautions given in "Safety first!" at the beginning of this manual.*

1 To clean the battery terminals disconnect them, negative earth first, after having first removed the cover (where fitted). Use a wire brush or abrasive paper to clean the terminals. Bad corrosion should be treated

with a solution of bicarbonate of soda, applied with an old toothbrush. Do not let this solution get inside the battery.
2 Coat the battery terminals with petroleum jelly or a proprietary anti-corrosive compound before reconnecting them **(see illustration)**. Reconnect and tighten the positive (live) lead first, followed by the negative (earth) lead. Do not overtighten.

17.2 Protect each battery terminal before reconnection

18 Engine valve clearance check - OHV engines

HAYNES HINT *When checking valve clearances, it will be easier to turn the engine by hand if the spark plugs are removed but take care not to allow dirt to enter the spark plug holes.*

1 This operation should be carried out with the engine cold and the air cleaner, spark plugs and rocker cover removed.
2 Using a ring spanner or socket on the crankshaft pulley bolt, turn the crankshaft in a clockwise direction until No 1 piston is at top dead centre (TDC) on its compression stroke. This can be verified by checking that the pulley and timing cover marks are in

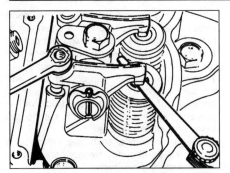

18.5 Adjusting a valve clearance - OHV

5 The clearances for the inlet and exhaust valves are different (see Specifications). Use a feeler blade of the appropriate thickness to check each clearance between the end of the valve stem and the rocker arm. The blade should be a stiff sliding fit. If it is not, turn the adjuster bolt with a ring spanner. These bolts are of stiff thread type and require no locking nut. Turn the bolt clockwise to reduce the clearance and anti-clockwise to increase it **(see illustration)**.

6 Refit the rocker cover, spark plugs and air cleaner on completion of adjustment.

19 Handbrake check

19.5 Handbrake adjustment indicator plunger

Pre-September 1985 models

1 Adjustment of the handbrake is normally automatic by means of the self-adjusting mechanism working on the rear brake shoes.
2 However, due to cable stretch, checking of the handbrake adjustment is recommended. Adjustment must be carried out if the movement of the lever becomes excessive (more than six notches). Proceed as follows:
3 Chock the front wheels then fully release the handbrake.
4 Raise and support the vehicle at the rear with safety stands.
5 On adjustment check that the plunger protrudes from each rear brake backplate **(see illustration)**, their respective length of movement indicating the handbrake adjustment condition. Before checking their movement (stroke) length, firmly apply the footbrake to ensure that the automatic adjuster mechanism is fully actuated.
6 Now check the plunger stroke movement. If the total movement of both sides added

together is between 0.5 and 3.0 mm then adjustment is satisfactory. This should give three to six clicks (notches) of handbrake application movement. If there is no measurable plunger movement or if the total measurement exceeds that specified adjust as follows.
7 Loosen the handbrake cable locknut, then rotate the adjuster sleeve **(see illustration)** so that the plungers can just rotate and the total movement of both plungers is as specified above.
8 Hand tighten the locknut against the sleeve so that two engagement clicks are felt, then further tighten another two clicks using a suitable wrench.

Models from September 1985

9 Proceed as above, noting that since September 1985 a locking pin has been fitted to the cable adjuster abutment bracket to lock the adjuster sleeve and locknut together.
10 Should it be necessary to adjust the cable, the locking pin must be removed by pulling it out using pliers **(see illustration)**. After adjustment a new nylon locking pin must be used and can be fitted by carefully tapping it into place.

alignment and that the valves of No 4 cylinder are rocking. When the valves are rocking, this means that the slightest rotation of the crankshaft pulley in either direction will cause one rocker arm to move up and the other to move down.

3 Numbering from the thermostat housing end of the cylinder head, the valves are identified as follows:

Valve No	Cylinder no
1 - Exhaust	1
2 - Inlet	1
3 - Exhaust	2
4 - Inlet	2
5 - Exhaust	3
6 - Inlet	3
7 - Exhaust	4
8 - Inlet	4

4 Adjust the valve clearances by following the sequence given in the following table. Turn the crankshaft pulley 180° (half a turn) after adjusting each pair:

Valves rocking	Valves to adjust
7 and 8	1 (Exhaust), 2 (Inlet)
5 and 6	3 (Exhaust), 4 (Inlet)
1 and 2	7 (Exhaust), 8 (Inlet)
3 and 4	5 (Exhaust), 6 (Inlet)

1

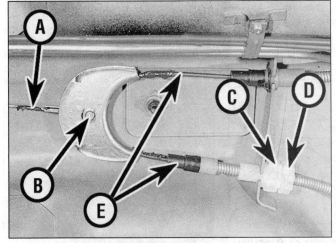

19.7 Handbrake cable assembly

A Primary cable   C Adjuster sleeve   E Secondary cable
B Equaliser   D Locknut

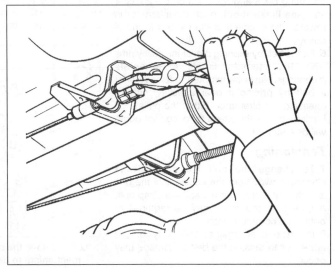

19.10 Removing the handbrake cable adjuster locking pin

20.2 Auxiliary drivebelt tension checking point - OHV

20 Auxiliary drivebelt check

Inspection

1 Check the full length of the drivebelt for cracks and deterioration. It will be necessary to turn the engine in order to check that portion of the drivebelt is in contact with the pulleys.

2 Check that the total deflection of the auxiliary drivebelt is 4.0 mm at the mid point of its longest run **(see illustration)**.

3 Note that if the belt is too slack, it will slip and soon become glazed or burnt and the coolant pump (OHV) and alternator will not perform correctly, with consequent overheating of the engine and low battery charge. If the belt is too tight, the bearings in the alternator and/or coolant pump will soon be damaged.

4 If necessary, renew or tension the belt as follows:

Renewal

5 To remove a belt, slacken the alternator mounting bolts and the bolts on the adjuster link **(see illustration)**, push the alternator in towards the engine and slip the belt from the pulleys.

6 Fit the belt by slipping it over the pulley rims while the alternator is still loose on its mountings. Never be tempted to remove or fit a belt by prising it over a pulley without releasing the alternator. Either the pulley will be damaged or the alternator or coolant pump will be distorted.

Tensioning

7 To change the belt tension, pull the alternator away from the engine until the belt is fairly taut and nip up the adjuster strap bolt. A little trial and error may be required to obtain the correct tension.

8 Do not lever against the body of the alternator to tension the belt or damage may occur.

9 Recheck the tension of the drivebelt after the engine has been run for ten minutes.

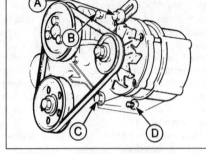
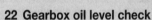

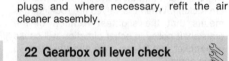

20.5 Alternator adjuster and mounting bolts - OHV

A *Adjuster link clamp bolt*
B *Adjuster link-to-block bolt*
C *Lower front mounting bolt*
D *Lower rear mounting bolt*

21 Spark plug renewal

HAYNES HiNT *Number each HT lead using sticky tape or paint before removal so as to avoid confusion when refitting.*

1 The correct functioning of the spark plugs is vital for the correct running and efficiency of the engine. It is essential that the plugs fitted are of the type appropriate for the engine.

2 Make sure that the ignition is switched off before inspecting the HT leads to see if they carry their cylinder numbers - if not, number each lead using sticky tape or paint.

3 Where necessary, for improved access, remove the air cleaner assembly.

4 Disconnect the leads from the plugs by pulling on the connectors, not the leads.

5 Clean the area around each spark plug using a small brush, then using a plug spanner (preferably with a rubber insert),

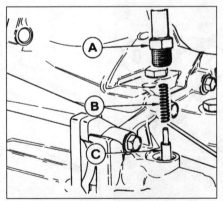

22.0 Remove the selector shaft locking mechanism to drain the gearbox oil

A *Selector shaft   B Spring*
    cap nut   C Interlock pin

unscrew and remove the plugs. Cover each exposed spark plug hole with a clean rag to prevent the ingress of any foreign matter.

6 Before fitting new spark plugs, check that the threaded connector sleeves are tight.

7 Check the electrode gap of each plug with a feeler blade of the specified thickness and if necessary, bend the outer electrode with a proper spark plug gapping tool to set the gap to the specified clearance.

8 Coat the threads of each plug with suitable anti-seize compound, taking care not to contaminate the electrodes.

9 Screw in the spark plugs by hand, then tighten them to the specified torque. *Do not exceed the torque figure.*

10 Push the HT leads firmly onto the spark plugs and where necessary, refit the air cleaner assembly.

22 Gearbox oil level check

Caution: Gearbox oil can foam when hot and give a false level reading. Allow the gearbox to cool before checking the oil level.

Note: *Regular oil changing is not specified by the manufacturers but the gearbox oil can be drained if necessary (prior to removal of the unit or after traversing a flooded road for example) by removing the selector shaft locking mechanism (see illustration).*

1 The following procedure should be adopted when checking the oil level on all gearbox types.

2 Ensure that the car is standing on level ground and the gearbox is cool.

3 Unscrew the filler plug from the front face of the gearbox. The plug is of socket-headed type and a suitable key will be required for removal **(see illustration)**.

4 With the plug removed, check the oil level. To do this accurately, make up an oil level check dipstick from a short length of welding rod or similar material. Make a 90° bend in the rod, then mark the downward leg in 5 mm increments. The dipstick is then inserted through the filler plug orifice so that the unmarked leg rests flat on the plug orifice

22.3 Gearbox oil filler plug location (arrowed)

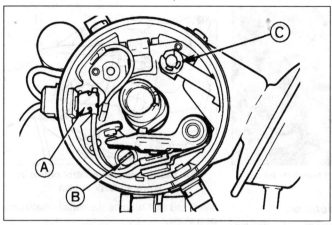

23.3 Contact breaker points removal

A LT lead connector   C Vacuum advance strut
B Securing screw   circlip

24.3 Inspect the steering rack bellows

threads, with the marked leg dipped in the oil. Withdraw the dipstick and read off the level of oil.

5 On gearboxes manufactured up to August 1985 the oil level must be maintained between 5 and 10 mm below the lower edge of the filler plug hole.

6 On gearboxes manufactured from September 1985 onwards the oil level must be maintained between 0 and 5 mm below the lower edge of the filler plug hole.

7 To determine the date of gearbox manufacture, locate the aluminium build code tag which will be attached to one of the gearbox housing retaining bolts. The gearbox part number is stamped on the tag and if the last letter of the part number suffix is a "D", then the gearbox is of the early type. If the last letter of the suffix is an "E", then the gearbox is of the later type.

8 Top-up the gearbox with the specified type of oil if necessary until the level is correct for the gearbox type (see *"Lubricants and fluids"*). Take care not to overfill the unit as this can lead to excessive heat build-up, increased leakage and impaired gear changing.

9 On completion, refit the filler plug.

23 Contact breaker point renewal and distributor lubrication - OHV engines

1 If necessary, remove the air cleaner assembly to allow ready access to the distributor. Identify and disconnect the leads from the spark plugs, prise down the distributor cap clips or remove the screws, and place the cap and leads to one side.

2 Remove the rotor arm.

3 Pull off the contact breaker LT lead from the points **(see illustration)**.

4 Unscrew and remove the screw from the fixed contact arm. Take great care not to drop the screw into the interior of the distributor: if necessary, cover the openings in the

baseplate with rag before starting to remove the screw.

5 With the screw removed, lift out the contact breaker assembly.

6 Fit and adjust the new contact breaker set, leaving the securing screw loose until the gap has been set.

7 Apply a little high melting-point grease to the distributor cam. (Grease may be supplied with the new contact breaker set.)

8 Refit the rotor arm and the distributor cap and reconnect the spark plug leads in their previously noted location.

9 Check and adjust the dwell angle and the ignition timing.

24 Steering and suspension security check

1 Check the shock absorbers by bouncing the vehicle up and down at each corner in turn. When released, it should come to rest within one complete oscillation. Continued movement, or squeaking and groaning noises from the shock absorber suggests that renewal is required.

2 With the weight of the vehicle on its roadwheels, inspect all of the suspension

24.4 Apply leverage to check for excessive balljoint wear

flexible bushes for wear and check the torque wrench settings of all bolts and nuts.

3 Raise and support the vehicle. Examine all steering and suspension components for wear, damage and fluid leakage. Pay particular attention to dust covers and gaiters **(see illustration)**, which if renewed promptly when damaged can save further damage to the component protected.

4 At the same intervals, check the front suspension lower arm balljoints for wear by levering up the arms **(see illustration)**. Balljoint free movement must not exceed 0.5 mm. The track rod end balljoints can be checked in a similar manner, or by observing them whilst an assistant rocks the steering wheel back and forth. If the lower arm balljoint is worn, the complete lower arm must be renewed.

5 Wheel bearings can be checked for wear by spinning the relevant roadwheel. Any roughness or excessive noise indicates worn bearings, which must be renewed, as no adjustment is possible. It is unlikely that any wear will be evident unless the vehicle has covered a very high mileage. It should be noted that it is normal for the bearings to exhibit slight endfloat, which is perceptible as wheel rock at the wheel rim.

25 Underbody inspection

1 Except on vehicles with a wax-based underbody protective coating, have the whole of the underframe of the vehicle steam-cleaned, engine compartment included, so that a thorough inspection can be carried out to see what minor repairs and renovations are necessary.

2 Steam-cleaning is available at many garages and is necessary for the removal of the accumulation of oily grime which sometimes is allowed to become thick in

1

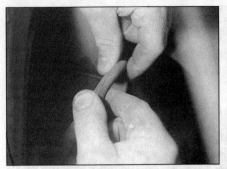

26.1 Bend flexible brake hoses to check for splitting and decay

28.3 Oil filler cap and breather hoses

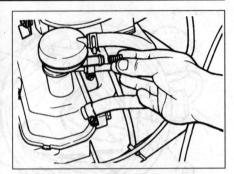

28.4 Clean emission control orifice in solvent - OHV shown

certain areas. If steam-cleaning facilities are not available, there are some excellent grease solvents available, which can be brush-applied; the dirt can then be simply hosed off.

3 After cleaning, position the vehicle over a pit, or raise it at front and rear on ramps or axle stands (see *"Jacking and vehicle support"*).

4 Using a strong light, work around the underside of the vehicle, inspecting it for corrosion or damage. If either is found, refer to Chapter 11 for details of repair.

26 Brake pipe and hose check

1 Periodically inspect the rigid brake pipes for rust and other damage, and the flexible hoses for cracks, splits or "ballooning" **(see illustration)**. Have an assistant depress the brake pedal (ignition on) and inspect the hose and pipe unions for leaks. Renew any defective item without delay.

27 Road test

Instruments and electrical equipment

1 Check the operation of all instruments and electrical equipment.

2 Make sure that all instruments read correctly, switch on all electrical equipment in turn to check that it functions properly.

Steering and suspension

3 Check for any abnormalities in the steering, suspension, handling or road "feel".

4 Drive the vehicle, and check that there are no unusual vibrations or noises.

5 Check that the steering feels positive, with no excessive "sloppiness", or roughness, and check for any suspension noises when cornering, or when driving over bumps.

Drivetrain

6 Check the performance of the engine, clutch, transmission and driveshafts.

7 Listen for any unusual noises from the engine, clutch and transmission.

8 Make sure that the engine runs smoothly when idling, and that there is no hesitation when accelerating.

9 Where applicable, check that the clutch action is smooth and progressive, that the drive is taken up smoothly, and that the pedal travel is not excessive. Also listen for any noises when the clutch pedal is depressed.

10 Check that all gears can be engaged smoothly, without noise, and that the gear lever action is not abnormally vague or "notchy".

Check the operation and performance of the braking system

11 Make sure that the vehicle does not pull to one side when braking, and that the wheels do not lock prematurely when braking hard.

12 Check that there is no vibration through the steering when braking.

13 Check that the handbrake operates correctly, without excessive movement of the

lever, and that it holds the vehicle stationary on a slope.

14 Test the operation of the brake servo unit as follows. With the engine off, depress the footbrake four or five times to exhaust the vacuum. Start the engine, holding the brake pedal depressed. As the engine starts, there should be a noticeable "give" in the brake pedal as vacuum builds up. Allow the engine to run for at least two minutes, and then switch it off. If the brake pedal is depressed now, it should be possible to detect a hiss from the servo as the pedal is depressed. After about four or five applications, no further hissing should be heard, and the pedal should feel considerably firmer.

28 Crankcase ventilation system check

1 Inspect the crankcase ventilation system for blockage or damage. A blocked hose can cause a build-up of crankcase pressure, which in turn can cause oil leaks.

2 Inspect each hose for distortion, perishing and correct routing.

3 Clean the oil filler cap with solvent and check that the vent hose connections are not blocked **(see illustration)**.

4 Clean the emission control orifice located in the oil filler assembly with solvent **(see illustration)**.

24 000 Mile (40 000 Km) / every 2 years

29 Air cleaner temperature control check

Note: *A vacuum pump will be required for this check if the heat sensor or diaphragm unit is at fault.*

1 The air cleaner temperature control unit can be checked for operation whilst the engine is cold. Look into the air inlet spout and check that the air control flap valve is in the shut position **(see illustration)**.

2 Now start the engine and allow it to idle. The flap valve should open fully to allow the warm air to be drawn into the cleaner unit from the exhaust manifold ducting. As the engine warms up to its normal operating temperature the flap valve should progressively close to allow cooler air to enter the cleaner unit.

3 If the valve is stuck in the shut position, check the vacuum lines for condition and security. If these are in order, then the heat sensor or diaphragm unit is at fault. Proceed as follows:

4 Detach the diaphragm-to-heat sensor vacuum pipe (at the sensor end) and connect up a vacuum pump to the diaphragm. Pump and apply a vacuum up to 100 mm of mercury and retain this whilst checking the air flap.

5 If the flap opens, the heat sensor is defective and must be renewed, but if it remains shut then the diaphragm or control flap is faulty.

6 Disconnect the vacuum pump and reconnect the vacuum pipe to the sensor unit.

30 Emission control filter element renewal - CVH engines
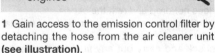

1 Gain access to the emission control filter by detaching the hose from the air cleaner unit **(see illustration)**.

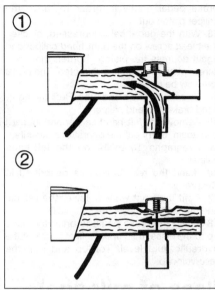

29.1 Air cleaner inlet sensor and diaphragm flap valve operating modes
1 Sensor cold   2 Sensor hot

2 Withdraw the used filter and fit a new item. Ensure that the hose is securely reconnected.

31 Air cleaner element renewal

1 Renew the air cleaner element by first removing the air cleaner unit lid. To do this, undo and remove the retaining screws and prise free the lid from the retaining clips around its periphery **(see illustration)**.

2 Remove and discard the paper element and wipe out the air cleaner casing **(see illustration)**.

3 Place the new element in position and refit the lid.

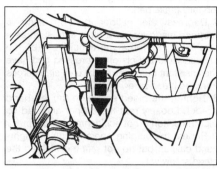

30.1 Detach hose downwards for access to crankcase emission filter in air cleaner body

31.1 Remove the air cleaner lid securing screws . . .

31.2 . . . to expose the air cleaner element

1

36 000 Mile (60 000 Km) / every 3 years

32 Brake hydraulic system seal and hose renewal
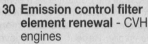

If in doubt as to the condition of any of the brake system seals and hoses, then renew defective items whilst referring to the relevant Sections of Chapter 9.

33 Brake hydraulic fluid renewal

1 An assistant and bleeding equipment will be needed. A considerable quantity of hydraulic fluid will be required - probably about 2 litres.

2 Slacken the front wheel nuts. Raise and support the front of the vehicle and remove the front wheels.

3 Remove the hydraulic fluid reservoir cap.

4 Open both front bleed screws one full turn. Attach one bleed tube to each screw, placing the free end of each tube in a jar.

5 Pump the brake pedal to expel fluid from the bleed screws. Pause after each upstroke to allow the master cylinder to refill.

6 When air emerges from both bleed screws, stop pumping. Detach the left-hand caliper without disconnecting it and remove the inboard brake pad.

7 Depress the caliper piston, using a purpose-made tool or a blunt item such as a tyre lever, to force more fluid out of the caliper. Hold the piston depressed and have the assistant pump the pedal until air emerges from the bleed screw again.

8 Tighten the bleed screw on the left-hand caliper. Loosely refit the caliper and pad so that the piston is not accidentally ejected.

9 Repeat the purging operation on the right-hand caliper, but do not refit it or tighten the bleed screw yet.

10 Fill the reservoir with fresh hydraulic fluid. Position the bleed jar for the right-hand caliper at least 300 mm above the level of the bleed screw.

11 Have the assistant pump the brake pedal until fluid free of bubbles emerges from the bleed screw. Tighten the bleed screw at the end of a downstroke.

12 Place a piece of wood in the caliper jaws to limit piston travel. Keep your fingers clear of the piston. Have the assistant depress the brake pedal gently in order to move the caliper piston out.

13 With the pedal held depressed, slacken the bleed screw on the right-hand caliper and again depress the piston. Tighten the bleed screw when the piston is retracted. The pedal can now be released.

14 Disconnect the bleed tube. Refit the right-hand brake pad and caliper.

15 Remove the left-hand caliper and inboard pad again. Carry out the operations described in paragraphs 10 to 14 on the left-hand caliper.

16 Bleed the rear brakes as described in Chapter 9.

17 Refit the front wheels, lower the vehicle and tighten the wheel nuts.

18 Pump the brake pedal to bring the pads up to the discs, then make a final check of the hydraulic fluid level. Top-up and refit the reservoir cap.

34 Timing belt renewal - CVH engines

Timing belt renewal is recommended for CVH engines. Refer to Chapter 2, Part B for the appropriate renewal procedure.

35 Front wheel alignment check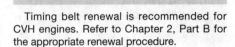

Due to the need for precision equipment to accurately measure the small angles of the steering and suspension settings appertaining to front wheel alignment, it is preferable to leave this work to a specialist. However, if you wish to check front wheel alignment yourself, refer to the information given in Chapter 10.

Every 2 years (regardless of mileage)

36 Engine coolant renewal

Draining

1 It is preferable to drain the system when the coolant is cold. If it must be drained when hot, release the pressure cap very slowly having first covered it with a cloth to avoid any possibility of scalding.

2 Set the heater control to maximum heat position.

3 Place a container under the radiator and release the bottom hose or, where fitted, unscrew the radiator drain plug and allow the system to drain into the container **(see illustrations)**.

Flushing

4 Provided the coolant is of the specified type, then no flushing should be necessary.

5 Where the system has been neglected

however, and rust or sludge is evident at draining, then the system should be flushed through with a cold water hose inserted into the thermostat housing (thermostat removed) until the water flows clean from the disconnected bottom hose and the radiator. If, after a reasonable period, the water still does not run clear the radiator can be flushed with a good proprietary cleaning agent.

6 In severe cases, the drain plug on the cylinder block of OHV models can be unscrewed to assist sludge removal and flushing **(see illustration)**. On CVH models there is no drain plug on the cylinder block so you will need to detach the bottom hose.

7 If the radiator is suspected of being clogged, remove it and reverse flush it with a cold water hose. The normal coolant flow is from left to right (from the thermostat housing to the radiator) through the matrix and out of the opposite side.

8 When the coolant is being changed, it is recommended that the overflow pipe is disconnected from the expansion tank and

the coolant drained from the tank. If the interior of the tank is dirty, remove it and thoroughly clean it out. Evidence of oil within the expansion tank may indicate a leaking cylinder head gasket.

Refilling

9 Reconnect the radiator and expansion tank hoses, and refit the cylinder block drain plug (OHV), or connect the bottom hose (CVH), as applicable.

10 Using the specified antifreeze (see *"Lubricants and fluids"*), fill the system via the expansion tank, until the coolant level reaches the "maximum" mark. Allow time for air in the system to bubble through and add more coolant if necessary. Repeat until the level does not drop and refit the cap.

11 Start the engine and run it to normal operating temperature. Once it has cooled, check and carry out any final topping-up to the expansion tank.

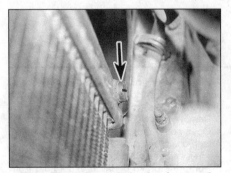
36.3a The radiator drain plug (arrowed)

36.3b The radiator bottom hose clamp

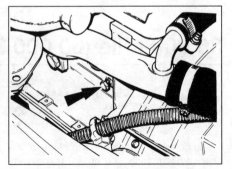
36.6 The cylinder block drain plug (arrowed) - OHV

Chapter 2 Part A:
OHV engine repair procedures

Contents

Degrees of difficulty

Easy, suitable for novice with little experience	Fairly easy, suitable for beginner with some experience	Fairly difficult, suitable for competent DIY mechanic 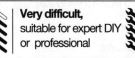	Difficult, suitable for experienced DIY mechanic	Very difficult, suitable for expert DIY or professional

Specifications

General

Engine type	Four-cylinder, overhead valve, water-cooled	
	1.0 litre	**1.1 litre**
Firing order (No 1 at timing cover end)	1-2-4-3	1-2-4-3
Bore	73.96 mm	73.96 mm
Stroke	55.70 mm	64.98 mm
Cubic capacity	957 cc	1117 cc
Compression ratio	8.5 : 1	9.5 : 1
Compression pressure at starter speed	9.5 to 11.5 kgf/cm²	13.3 to 15.3 kgf/cm²
Idle speed (rpm)	750 to 850	750 to 850
Maximum continuous engine speed (rpm)	5950	5450
Engine output (DIN)	33 kW at 5750 rpm	37 kW at 5000 rpm
Engine torque (DIN)	6.9 kgf m at 3700 rpm	8.4 kgf m at 2700 rpm

Cylinder block

Number of main bearings	3
Cylinder bore diameter:	
Standard (1)	73.940 to 73.950 mm
Standard (2)	73.950 to 73.960 mm
Standard (3)	73.960 to 73.970 mm
Standard (4) and service	73.970 to 73.980 mm
Oversizes:	
0.5	74.500 to 74.510 mm
1.0	75.000 to 75.010 mm
Main bearing bore:	
Standard	60.623 to 60.636 mm
Oversize	61.003 to 61.016 mm
Camshaft bearing bore:	
Standard	42.888 to 42.918 mm
Oversize	43.396 to 43.420 mm
Central main bearing width (less thrustwashers)	22.04 to 22.10 mm

Crankshaft

Endfloat	0.072 to 0.285 mm
Main journal diameter:	
Standard	56.990 to 57.000 mm
Yellow dot	56.980 to 56.990 mm
0.254 undersize	56.726 to 56.746 mm
0.508 undersize	56.472 to 56.492 mm
0.762 undersize	56.218 to 56.238 mm

2A

Crankshaft (continued)

Main bearing shell width .... 21.2 to 21.6 mm
Main bearing shell play .... 0.009 to 0.046 mm
Crankpin (big-end) diameter:
    Standard .... 42.99 to 43.01 mm
    0.254 undersize .... 42.74 to 42.76 mm
    0.508 undersize .... 42.49 to 42.51 mm
    0.762 undersize .... 42.24 to 42.26 mm
Thrustwasher thicknesses:
    Standard .... 2.80 to 2.85 mm
    Oversize .... 2.99 to 3.04 mm

Camshaft

Number of bearings 3
Camshaft bearing diameter .... 39.615 to 39.635 mm
Bearing bush inside diameter .... 39.662 to 39.682 mm
Camshaft thrust plate thickness .... 4.457 to 4.508 mm
Camshaft endfloat .... 0.062 to 0.193 mm
Cam lift:
    Inlet valve .... 5.300 mm
    Exhaust valve .... 5.300 mm
Cam length (heel to toe):
    Inlet .... 32.288 to 32.516 mm
    Exhaust .... 32.615 to 32.846 mm

Pistons

Diameter:
    Standard (1) .... 73.910 to 73.920 mm
    Standard (2) .... 73.920 to 73.930 mm
    Standard (3) .... 73.930 to 73.940 mm
    Standard (4) .... 73.940 to 73.950 mm
    Standard service .... 73.930 to 73.955 mm
    0.5 oversize .... 74.460 to 74.485 mm
    1.0 oversize .... 74.960 to 74.985 mm
Piston-to-bore clearance .... 0.015 to 0.050 mm
Piston ring gap (fitted):
    Top and 2nd rings .... 0.25 to 0.45 mm
    Bottom ring .... 0.20 to 0.40 mm
Bottom (oil control) ring gap position .... In line with gudgeon pin
2nd ring gap position .... 90° to oil control ring gap
Top ring gap position .... 180° to oil control ring gap

Gudgeon pins

Pin length .... 54.6 to 55.4 mm
Pin diameters:
    White .... 20.622 to 20.625 mm
    Red .... 20.625 to 20.628 mm
    Blue .... 20.628 to 20.631 mm
    Yellow .... 20.631 to 20.634 mm
Connecting rod interference at 21°C (70°F) .... 0.013 to 0.045 mm
Pin-to-piston interference at 21°C (70°F) .... 0.005 to 0.011 mm

Connecting rods

Big-end bore diameter .... 46.685 to 46.705 mm
Small-end bore diameter .... 20.589 to 20.609 mm
Bearing shell inside diameter (fitted):
    Standard .... 43.016 to 43.050 mm
    0.254 undersize .... 42.768 to 42.802 mm
    0.508 undersize .... 42.518 to 42.552 mm
    0.762 undersize .... 42.268 to 42.302 mm
    1.016 undersize .... 42.018 to 42.052 mm
Journal-to-bearing shell clearance .... 0.006 to 0.060 mm

Cylinder head

Valve seat angle (inlet and exhaust) .... 45°
Valve seat width (inlet and exhaust) .... 1.20 to 1.75 mm
Lower correction angle (inlet and exhaust) .... 30°
Upper correction angle (inlet and exhaust) .... 80°
Upper correction angle - service cutter .... 75°
Valve stem bore (inlet and exhaust):
    Standard .... 7.907 to 7.938 mm
    0.381 oversize .... 8.288 to 8.319 mm

Valves

Clearances	See Servicing Specifications in Chapter 1
Tappet diameter	13.081 to 13.094 mm
Tappet clearance in cylinder block	20.25 to 20.75 mm
Valve spring free length (inlet and exhaust)	42 mm
Valve lift (excluding clearance) (inlet and exhaust)	8.367 mm

Valve head diameter:
Inlet	32.89 to 33.15 mm
Exhaust	29.01 to 29.27 mm

Valve stem diameter:

Inlet valves:
Standard	7.868 to 7.886 mm
0.076 oversize	7.944 to 7.962 mm
0.381 oversize	8.249 to 8.267 mm

Exhaust valves:
Standard	7.846 to 7.864 mm
0.076 oversize	7.922 to 7.940 mm
0.381 oversize	8.227 to 8.245 mm

Valve stem-to-guide clearance:
Inlet	0.021 to 0.070 mm
Exhaust	0.043 to 0.092 mm

Valve timing:
Inlet valve opens	14° BTDC
Inlet valve closes	46° ABDC
Exhaust valve opens	65° BBDC
Exhaust valve closes	11° ATDC

Lubrication system

Minimum oil pressure at 80°C (175°F)	0.6 kgf/cm^2 at 750 rpm
Warning light operates at	0.32 to 0.53 kgf/cm^2
Relief valve opening pressure	2.41 to 2.75 kgf/cm^2

Oil pump clearances:
Outer rotor-to-housing	0.14 to 0.26 mm
Inner-to-outer rotor	0.051 to 0.127 mm
Rotors-to-cover endfloat	0.025 to 0.06 mm

Torque wrench settings

	Nm	lbf ft
Main bearing cap bolts	95	70
Connecting rod (big-end) bolts	31	23
Rear oil seal retainer bolts	18	13
Flywheel bolts	68	50
Chain tensioner bolts	8	6
Camshaft thrust plate bolts	4	3
Camshaft sprocket bolts	19	14
Timing cover bolts	10	7
Coolant pump bolts	10	7
Crankshaft pulley bolt	54	40
Coolant pump pulley bolts	10	7
Starter motor bolts	41	30
Fuel pump bolts	18	13
Oil pump bolts	19	14
Sump drain plug	25	18
Sump fixing bolts:		
Stage 1	8	6
Stage 2	11	8
Stage 3	11	8
Oil pressure sender	15	11
Coolant temperature sender	15	11
Rocker shaft pedestal bolts	42	31
Cylinder head bolts:		
Stage 1	15	11
Stage 2	48	35
Stage 3	88	65
Stage 4 (after 15 minutes delay)	109	80
Rocker cover screws	4	3
Exhaust manifold nuts and bolts	16	12
Inlet manifold nuts and bolts	19	14
Carburettor flange nuts	19	14
Thermostat housing cover bolts	19	14
Spark plugs	19	14
Engine-to-transmission bolts	41	30
Transmission oil filler plug	25	18

2A

1 General information

The engine is of an overhead valve type based upon the "Kent" design used in many earlier Ford models. It is mounted transversely at the front of the vehicle together with the transmission to form a combined power train.

The engine is a water-cooled, four-cylinder in-line type, having overhead valves operated by tappets, pushrods and rocker arms. The camshaft is located within the cylinder block and chain-driven from the crankshaft. A gear on the camshaft drives the oil pump and the distributor, whilst a cam operates the fuel pump lever.

The cylinder head is of crossflow type, having the exhaust manifold mounted on the opposite side to the inlet manifold. The crankshaft runs in three main bearings, with endfloat controlled by semi-circular thrustwashers located on either side of the centre main bearing.

The oil pump is mounted externally on the cylinder block just below the distributor, and the full-flow type oil filter is screwed directly into the oil pump.

2 Operations possible without removing engine from vehicle

1 The following work can be carried out without having to remove the engine:
a) Cylinder head - removal and refitting
b) Valve clearances - adjustment
c) Sump - removal and refitting
d) Rocker gear - overhaul
e) Crankshaft front oil seal - renewal
f) Pistons/connecting rods - removal and refitting
g) Engine mountings - renewal
h) Oil filter - removal and refitting
i) Oil pump - removal and refitting

3 Operations only possible with engine removed from vehicle

1 The following work should be carried out only after the engine has been removed from the vehicle.
a) *Crankshaft main bearings - renewal
b) Crankshaft - removal and refitting
c) **Flywheel - removal and refitting
d) **Crankshaft rear oil seal - renewal
e) Camshaft - removal and refitting
f) Timing gears and chain - removal and refitting

2 Although it is possible to undertake the job marked * without removing the engine, and those marked ** by removing the transmission, such work is not recommended and is unlikely to save much time over that required to withdraw the complete engine/transmission.

4 Cylinder head - removal and refitting

Removal

1 If the engine is in the vehicle, carry out the preliminary operations described in paragraphs 2 to 15.
2 Open the bonnet and fit protective covers to the front wing upper surfaces.
3 Disconnect the battery earth strap. It is as well to remove the battery, so that no metal objects are placed across its terminals.
4 Remove the air cleaner unit.
5 Drain the cooling system. Note that the coolant should have an antifreeze solution mix and can be used again, so drain into a suitable container for re-use.
6 Disconnect the hoses from the thermostat housing.
7 Detach the choke cable.
8 Release the throttle cable from the carburettor operating lever by moving the spring clip and removing the bracket fixing bolt (see illustration).
9 Disconnect the fuel and vacuum pipes from the carburettor.
10 Disconnect the breather hose from the inlet manifold.
11 On vehicles with servo-assisted brakes, disconnect the vacuum hose from the inlet manifold.
12 Disconnect the HT leads from the spark plugs.
13 Disconnect the electrical leads from the temperature sender unit, inlet manifold, carburettor and radiator fan thermal switch.
14 Unbolt and remove the heated air box from the exhaust manifold (where fitted) (see illustration).
15 Disconnect the exhaust downpipe from the manifold by unbolting the connecting flanges. Support the exhaust system at the front end.
16 Pull free and remove the oil filler cap with breather hoses.
17 Extract the four screws and remove the rocker cover.
18 Unscrew and remove the four fixing bolts and lift away the rocker shaft assembly from the cylinder head.

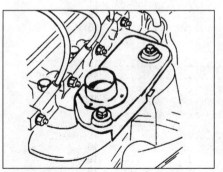

4.14 Heated air box on exhaust manifold

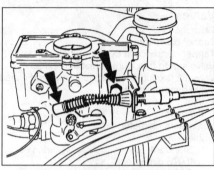

4.8 Disconnect the throttle cable and bracket

19 Withdraw the pushrods, keeping them in their originally fitted sequence. A simple way to do this is to punch holes in a piece of card and number them 1 to 8 from the thermostat housing end of the cylinder head (see illustration).
20 Remove the spark plugs.
21 Unscrew the cylinder head bolts progressively in the reverse order to that given for tightening. Remove the cylinder head.

> **HAYNES HINT** Tap a stuck cylinder head free with a wooden mallet. Do not insert a lever into the head joint as this may damage the mating faces.

Refitting

Caution: Never use jointing compound when refitting the cylinder head and gasket.

22 Before refitting the cylinder head, remove every particle of carbon, old gasket and dirt from the mating surfaces of the cylinder head and block. Do not let the removed material drop into the cylinder bores or waterways: if it does, remove it. Normally, when a cylinder head is removed, the head is decarbonised and the valves ground in to remove all traces of carbon.
23 Clean the threads of the cylinder head bolts and mop out oil from the bolt holes in the cylinder block. In extreme cases, screwing a bolt into an oil-filled hole can cause the block to fracture due to hydraulic pressure.

4.19 Withdraw the pushrods

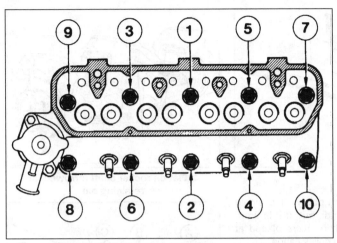

4.27 Cylinder head bolt tightening sequence

4.29 Refit the rocker shaft assembly - engaging the adjuster balls into the pushrod caps (sockets)

24 If there is any doubt about the condition of the inlet or exhaust gaskets, unbolt the manifolds and fit new ones to perfectly clean mating surfaces.

25 Locate a new cylinder head gasket on the cylinder block, making quite sure that the bolt holes, coolant passages and lubrication holes are correctly aligned.

26 Lower the cylinder head carefully into position on the block.

27 Screw in all the bolts finger tight and then tighten them in four stages, in the sequence shown (see illustration) to the specified torque.

28 Refit the pushrods in their original order.

29 Lower the rocker shaft assembly into position, making sure that the rocker adjusting screws engage in the sockets at the ends of the pushrods (see illustration).

30 Screw in the rocker pedestal bolts finger tight. At this stage, some of the rocker arms will be applying pressure to the ends of the valve stems and some of the rocker pedestals will not be in contact with the cylinder head. The pedestals will be pulled down, however, when the bolts are tightened to the specified torque, which should now be done.

31 Adjust the valve clearances.

32 Refit the rocker cover. If the gasket is in anything but perfect condition, renew it.

33 Fit the oil filler cap and breather hose and the spark plugs. Tighten these to the specified

torque. They are of tapered seat type, no sealing washers being used.

34 Connect the exhaust downpipe and fit the heated air box.

35 Reconnect all electrical leads, vacuum and coolant hoses.

36 Reconnect the cables. Refit the battery (if removed) and reconnect the battery terminals.

37 Fit the air cleaner.

38 Refill the cooling system.

5 Valve clearances - adjustment

Refer to Chapter 1, Section 18.

6 Sump - removal and refitting

Removal

1 Disconnect the battery earth lead and drain the engine oil.

2 Unbolt and withdraw the starter motor. Support the motor to avoid straining the electrical wiring.

3 Unbolt and remove the clutch cover plate.

4 Extract the sump securing bolts and remove the sump. If it is stuck, prise it gently with a screwdriver, but do not use excessive leverage. If it is very tight, cut round the gasket joint using a sharp knife.

Refitting

5 Before refitting the sump, remove the front and rear sealing strips and gaskets. Clean the mating surfaces of the sump and cylinder block.

6 Stick new gaskets into position on the block using thick grease to retain them, then install new sealing strips into their grooves so that they overlap the gaskets (see illustration).

7 Before offering up the sump, check that the gap between the sump and oil baffle is between 2.0 and 3.8 mm (see illustration).

8 Screw in the sump bolts and tighten in three stages to the specified torque (see illustration):

Stage 1 - in alphabetical order
Stage 2 - in numerical order
Stage 3 - in alphabetical order

9 It is important to follow this procedure in order to provide sealing against oil leakage.

10 Refit the clutch cover plate and the starter motor and reconnect the battery.

11 Refill the engine with the correct grade and quantity of oil.

2A

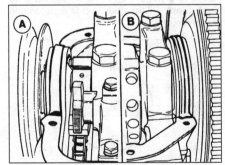

6.6 Sump gaskets and sealing strips
A Timing cover end   B Flywheel end

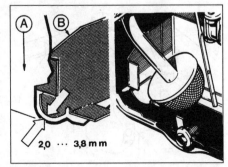

6.7 Sump-to-baffle plate must be as shown
A Sump   B Baffle

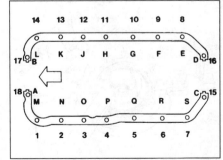

6.8 Sump retaining bolt tightening sequence - arrow indicates front of engine

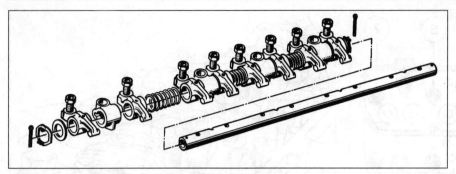

7.3 Rocker components

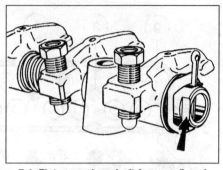

7.4 Flat on rocker shaft (arrowed) and retaining pin

7 Rocker gear - dismantling and reassembly

1 With the rocker assembly removed, extract the split pin from one end of the rocker shaft.
2 Take off the spring and plain washers from the end of the shaft.
3 Slide off the rocker arms, support pedestals and coil springs, keeping them in their originally fitted order **(see illustration)**. Clean out the oil holes in the shaft.
4 Apply engine oil to the rocker shaft before reassembling and make sure that the flat on the end of the shaft is to the same side as the rocker arm adjuster screws **(see illustration)**. This is essential for proper lubrication of the components.
5 If a new rocker shaft is being fitted, check that the end plug is located correctly **(see illustration)**.

8 Crankshaft front oil seal - renewal

1 Disconnect the battery earth cable.
2 Slacken the alternator mounting and adjuster bolts and after pushing the alternator in towards the engine, slip off the drivebelt.
3 Unscrew and remove the crankshaft pulley bolt. To prevent the crankshaft turning while the bolt is being released, jam the teeth of the starter ring gear on the flywheel after removing the clutch cover plate or starter motor for access.

4 Remove the crankshaft pulley. This should come out using the hands but, if it is tight, prise it carefully with two levers placed at opposite sides under the pulley flange.
5 Using a suitable claw tool, prise out the defective seal and wipe out the seat **(see illustration)**.
6 Install the new seal using a suitable distance piece, the pulley and its bolt to draw it into position. If it is tapped into position, the seal may be distorted or the timing cover fractured.
7 When the seal is fully seated, remove the pulley and bolt, apply grease to the seal rubbing surface of the pulley, install it and tighten the securing bolt to the specified torque.
8 Refit the clutch cover or starter motor.
9 Fit and tension the drivebelt and reconnect the battery.

9 Pistons/connecting rods - removal and refitting

Removal

1 Remove the cylinder head and the sump. Do not remove the oil pick-up filter or pipe, which is an interference fit.
2 Note the location numbers stamped on the connecting rod big-ends and caps, and to which side they face **(see illustration)**. No 1 assembly is nearest the timing cover and the assembly numbers are towards the camshaft side of the engine.

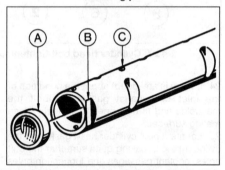

7.5 Rocker shaft front end plug (A), flat (B) and oil hole (C)

3 Turn the crankshaft by means of the pulley bolt until the big-end cap bolts for No 1 connecting rod are in their most accessible position. Unscrew and remove the bolts and the big-end cap complete with bearing shell. If the cap is difficult to remove, tap it off with a plastic-faced hammer.
4 If the bearing shells are to be used again, keep the shell taped to its cap.
5 Feel the top of the cylinder bore for a wear ridge. If one is detected, it should be scraped off before the piston/rod is pushed out of the top of the cylinder block. Take care when doing this not to score the cylinder bore surfaces.
6 Push the piston/connecting rod out of the block, retaining the bearing shell with the rod if it is to be used again.
7 Repeat the operations on the remaining piston/rod assemblies.

Refitting

8 To install a piston/rod assembly, have the piston ring gaps staggered as shown **(see illustration)**. Oil the rings and fit a piston ring compressor.

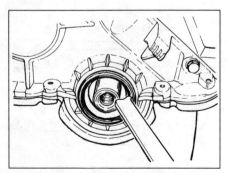

8.5 Prising out the crankshaft front oil seal

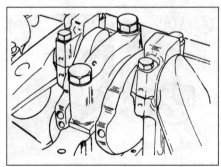

9.2 Connecting rod big-end numbers

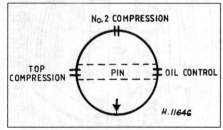

9.8 Piston ring end gap positioning diagram

9 Oil the cylinder bores.

10 Wipe out the bearing shell seat in the connecting rod and insert the shell.

11 Lower the piston/rod assembly into the cylinder bore until the base of the piston ring compressor stands squarely on the top of the block **(see illustration)**.

12 Check that the directional arrow on the piston crown faces towards the timing cover end of the engine and then apply the wooden handle of a hammer to the piston crown. Strike the head of the hammer sharply to drive the piston into the cylinder bore.

13 Oil the crankpin and draw the connecting rod down to engage with the crankshaft. Check that the bearing shell is still in position in the connecting rod.

14 Wipe the bearing shell seat in the big-end cap clean and insert the bearing shell.

15 Fit the cap, screw in the bolts and tighten to the specified torque.

16 Repeat the operations on the remaining pistons/connecting rods.

17 Refit the sump and the cylinder head. Refill with oil and coolant.

---

10 Oil filter and pump - removal and refitting

Removal

1 The oil pump is externally mounted on the rearward facing side of the crankcase **(see illustration)**.

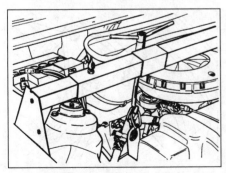

10.1 Oil filter and pump unit

11.1 Typical engine support bar

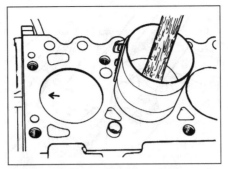

9.11 Installing a piston/connecting rod

2 Using a suitable removal tool (strap wrench or similar), unscrew and remove the oil filter cartridge and discard it.

3 Unscrew the three mounting bolts and withdraw the oil pump from the engine **(see illustration)**.

4 Clean away the old gasket.

Refitting

5 If a new pump is being fitted, it should be primed with engine oil before installation. Do this by turning its shaft while filling it with clean engine oil.

6 Locate a new gasket on the pump mounting flange, insert the pump shaft and bolt the pump into position.

7 Oil the rubber sealing ring of a new filter and screw it into position on the pump, using hand pressure only, not the removal tool.

8 Top-up the engine oil to replenish any lost during the operations.

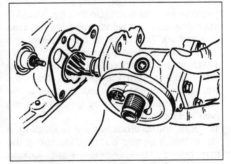

10.3 Removing the oil pump

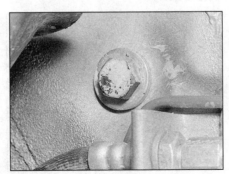

11.2 Right-hand engine mounting side retaining bolt

---

11 Engine/transmission mountings - removal and refitting

1 The engine mountings can be removed if the weight of the engine/transmission is first taken by one of the three following methods:
  a) *Support the engine under the sump using a jack and a block of wood.*
  b) *Attach a hoist to the engine lifting lugs.*
  c) *Make up a bar with end pieces which will engage in the water channels at the sides of the bonnet lid aperture. Using an adjustable hook and chain connected to the engine lifting lugs, the weight of the engine can be taken off the mountings (see illustration).*

Right-hand engine mounting

2 Unscrew and remove the mounting side bolt from under the right-hand wheel arch, just to the rear of and above the brake hose bracket **(see illustration)**.

3 Unscrew and remove the mounting retaining nut and washer from the suspension strut cup retaining plate.

4 Undo the three bolts securing the mounting unit to the cylinder block (working from underneath). The mounting unit and bracket can then be lowered from the engine.

5 Unbolt and remove the mounting from its support bracket.

Engine bearer and mountings

6 Unscrew and remove the two nuts securing each mounting (front and rear) to the engine bearer.

7 Support the engine bearer, then undo and remove the four retaining bolts from the floorpan, two at the front and two at the rear **(see illustration)**.

8 Unscrew the retaining nut to disconnect the rubber mounting from the transmission support.

All mountings

9 Refitting of all mountings is a reversal of removal. Make sure that the original sequence of assembly of washers and plates is maintained.

10 Do not fully tighten all mounting bolts until they are all located. As the mounting bolts and nuts are tightened, check that the mounting rubbers do not twist.

2A

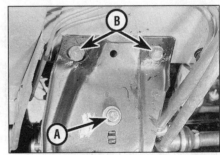

11.7 Engine bearer (rear end) showing mounting retaining nut (A) and retaining bolts to floor (B)

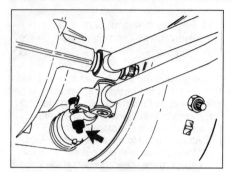

12.16 Gearchange rod clamp bolt (arrowed)

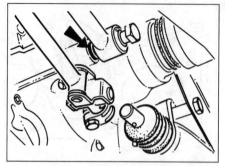

12.17 Gearchange stabilizer rod connection - arrow indicates washer location

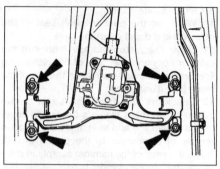

12.19 Gearshift housing unit-to-floor nuts (arrowed)

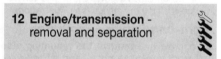

12 Engine/transmission - removal and separation

Caution: After removing the engine, keep it upright until the sump has been removed to prevent sludge from entering the engine internals.

Removal

1 This procedure entails lowering the engine and gearbox, and removing the unit from beneath the car. For this reason, certain items of equipment are necessary. A suitable engine hoist should be employed to lower the engine. A more difficult alternative would be to use a good trolley jack. Secondly, if an inspection pit is not available, four strong axle jacks capable of supporting the weight of the car, must be used. In addition, a willing friend will make the procedure easier.

2 Select 4th gear, or reverse gear on 5-speed models, to make gearshift adjustment easier on reassembly.

3 Open and remove the bonnet.

4 Disconnect the battery leads.

5 Drain the engine coolant.

6 Remove the radiator and thermo-electric fan unit.

7 To drain any remaining coolant within the engine, undo and remove the cylinder block drain plug from the left-hand side at the front (exhaust manifold face) and drain the remaining coolant into a suitable container.

8 Disconnect the crankcase ventilation hoses and remove the air cleaner unit.

9 Unclip and disconnect the heater hoses from the inlet manifold connection and the lateral coolant pipe.

10 Refer to Section 4 and proceed as described in paragraphs 7 to 15 inclusive.

11 Disconnect the wiring connections from the alternator, the carburettor, the inlet manifold, the oil pressure switch, the reversing light switch and the engine oil dipstick (if applicable). Undo the securing bolt and disconnect the engine earth strap.

12 Disconnect the speedometer drive cable at the gearbox end.

13 Disconnect the clutch cable from the release lever and gearbox support.

14 Raise and support the vehicle on safety stands at the front and rear, ensuring that, when raised, the vehicle is level and there is sufficient clearance to lower and remove the engine and transmission from underneath.

15 Disconnect the starter motor leads.

16 Disconnect the gearchange rod from the gearbox selector shaft. Do this by releasing the clamp bolt and withdrawing the rod **(see illustration)**. Tie the rod to the stabilizer and then unhook the tension spring.

17 Unscrew the single bolt and disconnect the stabilizer from the gearbox. Note the washer which is located between the stabilizer trunnion and the gearbox casing **(see illustration)**.

18 Drain the gearbox. As no drain plug is fitted, this is carried out by unscrewing the cap nut on the selector shaft locking assembly. Take care not to lose the locking pin and spring.

19 Undo and remove the four nuts retaining the gearshift housing unit to the floor **(see illustration)**. Rotate the shift rod and stabilizer 180° and support them by tying them up with a length of cord or wire.

20 Unscrew and remove the pivot bolt and nut from the inboard end of the left side front suspension lower arm **(see illustration)**, then remove the bolt which secures the balljoint at the outboard end of the lower arm to the stub axle carrier. An Allen key can be used to prevent the bolt turning while the nut is unscrewed.

21 The left-hand driveshaft must now be released from the transmission. Do this by inserting a lever between the inboard constant velocity (CV) joint and the transmission **(see illustration)**. With an assistant pulling the roadwheel outwards, strike the lever hard with the hand. Note that a quantity of oil will be released when the driveshaft is removed so have a container ready.

22 Tie the driveshaft up to the steering rack housing to prevent strain to the CV joints.

23 Restrain the differential pinion cage to prevent the cage from turning, using a plastic plug or similar. Failure to do this may make reconnection of the driveshafts difficult.

24 Remove the three retaining bolts and detach the tie-bar on the right-hand side, complete with mounting bracket, from the crossmember **(see illustration)**.

25 Release the inboard and outboard ends of the front suspension lower arm on the right-hand side of the vehicle, as described for the left-hand side.

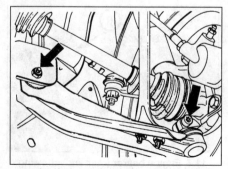

12.20 Front suspension lower arm pivot bolt and nut locations

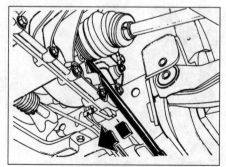

12.21 Driveshaft removal from gearbox

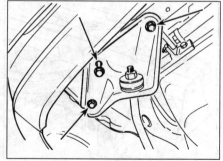

12.24 Tie-bar mounting bolts (arrowed). Note that XR2 variant differs

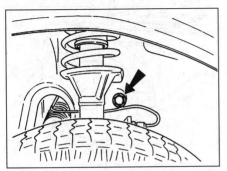

12.28a Engine mounting bolt under right-hand wheel arch

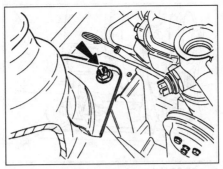

12.28b Engine mounting nut on right-hand suspension strut retaining plate (arrowed)

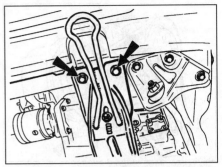

12.28c Engine bearer retaining bolts - front

26 Disconnect the right-hand driveshaft, as previously described for the left-hand one.

27 Connect a suitable hoist to the engine, preferably using a spreader bar and connecting lifting hooks to the engine: lifting lugs provided.

28 With the weight of the engine and transmission just supported, disconnect the engine and transmission mountings at the points shown **(see illustrations)**.

29 Unbolt the engine mounting (complete with coolant hose support bracket, where applicable) from the side-member and from the wing apron panel.

30 Carefully lower the engine/transmission and withdraw it from under the car. To ease the withdrawal operation, lower the engine/transmission onto a crawler board or a sheet of substantial plywood placed on rollers or lengths of pipe.

Separation

31 Unscrew and remove the starter motor bolts and remove the starter.

32 Unbolt and remove the clutch cover plate from the lower part of the clutch bellhousing.

33 Unscrew and remove the bolts from the clutch bellhousing-to-engine mating flange.

34 Withdraw the transmission from the engine. Support its weight so that the clutch assembly is not distorted while the input shaft is still in engagement with the splined hub of the clutch driven plate.

13 Engine - dismantling

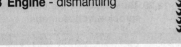

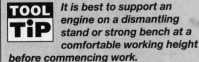
It is best to support an engine on a dismantling stand or strong bench at a comfortable working height before commencing work.

1 The need for dismantling will have been dictated by wear or noise in most cases. Although there is no reason why only partial dismantling cannot be carried out to renew such items as the timing chain or crankshaft

rear oil seal, when the main bearings or big-end bearings have been knocking, and especially if the vehicle has covered a high mileage, then it is recommended that a complete strip down is carried out and every engine component examined.

2 Position the engine so that it is upright on a bench or other convenient working surface. If the exterior is very dirty it should be cleaned before dismantling using paraffin and a stiff brush or a water-soluble solvent.

3 Remove the coolant pipe from the side of the engine by disconnecting the hose clips and the securing bolt **(see illustration)**.

4 If not already done, drain the engine oil.

5 Remove the dipstick and unscrew and discard the oil filter.

6 Disconnect the HT leads from the spark plugs, release the distributor cap and lift it away complete with leads.

7 Unscrew and remove the spark plugs.

8 Disconnect the breather hose from the inlet manifold and remove it complete with the oil filler cap.

9 Disconnect the fuel and vacuum pipes from the carburettor and unbolt and remove the carburettor.

10 Unbolt the thermostat housing cover and remove it, together with the thermostat.

11 Remove the rocker cover.

12 Remove the rocker shaft assembly (four bolts).

13 Withdraw the pushrods, keeping them in their originally fitted order.

14 Remove the cylinder head, complete with manifolds.

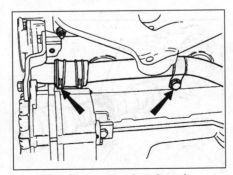

13.3 Engine lateral coolant pipe connections (arrowed)

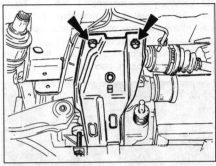

12.28d Engine bearer retaining bolts - rear

15 Remove the bolt that holds the distributor clamp plate to the cylinder block and withdraw the distributor.

16 Unbolt and remove the fuel pump **(see illustration)**.

17 Remove the oil pump.

18 Pinch the two runs of the coolant pump drivebelt together at the pump pulley to prevent the pulley rotating and release the pulley bolts.

19 Release the alternator mounting and adjuster link bolts, push the alternator in towards the engine and remove the drivebelt **(see illustration)**.

20 Unbolt the alternator bracket and remove the alternator **(see illustration)**.

21 Unbolt and remove the coolant pump **(see illustration)**.

2A

13.16 Unbolt and remove the fuel pump

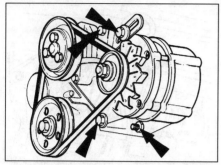

13.19 Alternator retaining and drivebelt adjustment bolts

13.20 Alternator mounting bracket

13.21 Unbolt and remove the coolant pump

22 Unscrew the crankshaft pulley bolt. To do this, the flywheel starter ring gear will have to be jammed to prevent the crankshaft from turning **(see illustration)**.
23 Remove the crankshaft pulley. If this does not pull off by hand, carefully use two levers

behind it placed at opposite points.
24 Place the engine on its side and remove the sump. Do not invert the engine at this stage, or sludge and swarf may enter the oilways.
25 Unbolt and remove the timing chain cover **(see illustration)**.

26 Take off the oil slinger from the front face of the crankshaft sprocket **(see illustration)**.
27 Slide the chain tensioner arm from its pivot pin on the front main bearing cap **(see illustration)**.
28 Unbolt and remove the chain tensioner.
29 Bend back the lockplate tabs from the camshaft sprocket bolts and unscrew and remove the bolts **(see illustration)**.
30 Withdraw the sprocket complete with timing chain.
31 Unbolt and remove the camshaft thrust plate **(see illustration)**.
32 Rotate the camshaft until each cam follower (tappet) has been pushed fully into its hole by its cam lobe.
33 Withdraw the camshaft, taking care not to damage the camshaft bearings **(see illustration)**.
34 Withdraw each of the cam followers, keeping them in their originally fitted sequence by marking them with a piece of numbered tape or using a box with divisions **(see illustration)**.

13.22 Unscrew the crankshaft pulley retaining bolt

13.25 Remove the timing chain cover

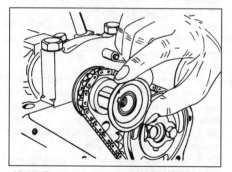

13.26 Removing the crankshaft oil slinger

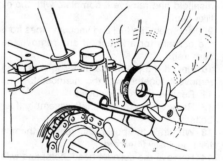

13.27 Sliding off the chain tensioner arm

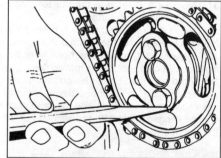

13.29 Bending back the camshaft sprocket bolt locktabs

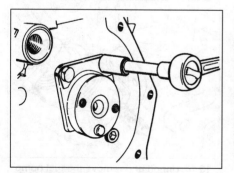

13.31 Unbolting the camshaft thrust plate

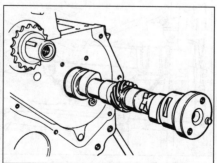

13.33 Withdrawing the camshaft

13.34 Lift out the cam followers (tappets), using a valve grinding tool

13.37 Connecting rod and big-end cap markings (arrowed)

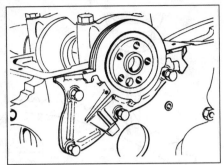

13.44 Crankshaft rear oil seal retainer

35 From the front end of the crankshaft, draw off the sprocket using a two-legged extractor.

36 Check that the main bearing caps are marked F (Front), C (Centre) and R (Rear). The caps are also marked with an arrow which indicates the timing cover end of the engine, a point to remember when refitting the caps.

37 Check that the big-end caps and connecting rods have adjacent matching numbers facing towards the camshaft side of the engine. Number 1 assembly is nearest the timing chain end of the engine. If any markings are missing or indistinct, make some of your own with quick-drying paint **(see illustration)**.

38 Unbolt and remove the big-end bearing caps. If the bearing shell is to be used again, tape the shell to the cap.

39 Now check the top of the cylinder bore for a wear ridge. If one can be felt, it should be removed with a scraper before the piston/rod is pushed out of the cylinder.

40 Remove the piston/rod by pushing it out of the top of the block. Tape the bearing shell to the connecting rod.

41 Remove the remaining three piston/rod assemblies in a similar way.

42 Unbolt the clutch pressure plate cover from the flywheel. Unscrew the bolts evenly and progressively until spring pressure is relieved, before removing the bolts. Be prepared to catch the clutch driven plate as the cover is withdrawn.

43 Unbolt and remove the flywheel. It is heavy, do not drop it. If necessary, the starter ring gear can be jammed to prevent the flywheel rotating. There is no need to mark the fitted position of the flywheel to its mounting flange as it can only be fitted one way. Take off the adapter plate (engine backplate).

44 Unbolt and remove the crankshaft rear oil seal retainer **(see illustration)**.

45 Unbolt the main bearing caps. Remove the caps, tapping them off if necessary with a plastic-faced hammer. Retain the bearing shells with their respective caps if the shells are to be used again, although unless the engine is of low mileage this is not recommended.

46 Lift the crankshaft from the crankcase and lift out the upper bearing shells, noting the thrustwashers either side of the centre

bearing. Keep these shells with their respective caps, identifying them for refitting to the crankcase if they are to be used again.

47 With the engine now completely dismantled, each component should be examined, as described in the following Section before reassembling.

14 Engine - examination and renovation

1 Clean all components using paraffin and a stiff brush, except the crankshaft, which should be wiped clean and the oil passages cleaned out with a length of wire.

2 Never assume that a component is unworn simply because it looks all right. After all the effort which has gone into dismantling the engine, refitting worn components will make the overhaul a waste of time and money. Depending on the degree of wear, the overhauler's budget and the anticipated life of the vehicle, components which are only slightly worn may be refitted, but if in doubt it is always best to renew.

Crankshaft, main and big-end bearings

3 The need to renew the main bearing shells or to have the crankshaft reground will usually have been determined during the last few miles of operation when perhaps a heavy knocking has developed from within the crankcase or the oil pressure warning lamp has stayed on, denoting a low oil pressure probably caused by excessive wear in the bearings.

4 Even without these symptoms, the journals and crankpins on a high mileage engine should be checked for out-of-round (ovality) and taper. For this a micrometer will be needed to check the diameter of the journals and crankpins at several different points around them. A motor factor or engineer can do this for you. If the readings show that either out-of-round or taper is present, then the crankshaft should be reground by your dealer or engine reconditioning company to accept the undersize main and big-end shell bearings which are available. Normally, the company doing the regrinding will supply the necessary undersize shells.

5 If the crankshaft is in good condition, it is wise to renew the bearing shells as it is almost certain that the original ones will have worn. This is often indicated by scoring of the bearing surface or by the top layer of the bearing metal having worn through to expose the metal underneath.

6 Each shell is marked on its back with the part number. Undersize shells will have the undersize stamped additionally on their backs.

7 Standard size crankshafts having main bearing journal diameters at the lower end of the tolerance range are marked with a yellow spot on the front balance weight. You will find that with this type of crankshaft, a standard shell is fitted to the seat in the crankcase but a yellow colour-coded shell to the main bearing cap.

8 If a green spot is seen on the crankshaft then this indicates that 0.254 mm undersize big-end bearings are used in place of the standard diameter.

Cylinder bores, pistons, rings and connecting rods

9 Cylinder bore wear will usually have been evident from the smoke emitted from the exhaust during recent operation of the vehicle on the road, coupled with excessive oil consumption and fouling of spark plugs.

10 Engine life can be extended by fitting special oil control rings to the pistons. These are widely advertised and will give many more thousands of useful mileage without the need for a rebore, although this will be inevitable eventually. If this remedy is decided upon, remove the piston/connecting rods and fit the proprietary rings in accordance with the manufacturer's instructions.

11 Where a more permanent solution is decided upon, the cylinder block can be rebored by your dealer or engineering works, or by one of the mobile workshops which now undertake such work. The cylinder bore will be measured both for out-of-round and for taper to decide how much the bores should be bored out. A set of matching pistons will be supplied in a suitable oversize to suit the new bores.

12 Due to the need for special heating and installing equipment for removal and refitting of the interference type gudgeon pin, the removal and refitting of pistons to the connecting rods is definitely a specialist job, preferably for your Ford dealer.

13 The removal and refitting of piston rings is however well within the scope of the home mechanic. Do this by sliding two or three old feeler blades round behind the top compression ring so that they are at equidistant points. The ring can now be slid up the blades and removed. Repeat the removal operations on the second compression ring and then the oil control ring. This method will not only prevent the rings from dropping onto empty grooves as they are withdrawn, but it will also avoid ring breakage.

2A

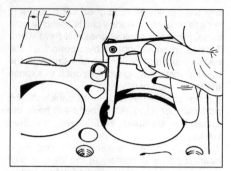

14.14 Checking a piston ring end gap

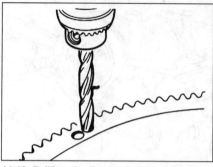

14.19 Drilling the flywheel starter ring gear

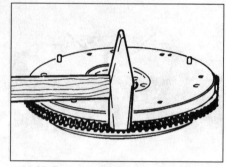

14.20 Removing the ring gear from the flywheel

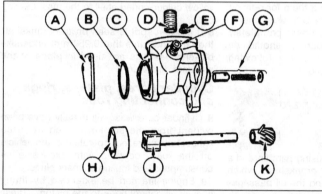

14.24a Oil pump components

A *Cover*	E *Filter (relief valve)*
B *O-ring*	F *Plug*
C *Pump body*	G *Relief valve*
D *Threaded insert*	
H *Outer rotor*	
J *Inner rotor*	
K *Drive pinion*	

14.24b Check the oil pump rotor-to-body clearance at (a) and the inner-to-outer rotor clearance at (b)

14 Even when new piston rings have been supplied to match the pistons, always check that they are not tight in their grooves and also check their end gaps by pushing them squarely down their particular cylinder bore and measuring with a feeler blade **(see illustration)**. Adjustment of the end gap can be made by careful grinding to bring it within the specified tolerance.

15 If new rings are being fitted to an old piston, always remove any carbon from the grooves beforehand. The best tool for this job is the end of a broken piston ring. Take care not to cut your fingers, piston rings are sharp. The cylinder bores should be roughened with fine glass paper to assist the bedding-in of the new rings.

Timing sprockets and chain

16 The teeth on the timing sprockets rarely wear, but check for broken or hooked teeth even so.

17 The timing chain should always be renewed at time of major engine overhaul. A worn chain is evident if, when supported horizontally at both ends, it takes on a deeply bowed appearance.

18 Finally check the rubber cushion on the tensioner spring leaf. If grooved or chewed up, renew it.

Flywheel

19 Inspect the starter ring gear on the flywheel for wear or broken teeth. If evident, the ring gear should be renewed in the following way. Drill the ring gear with two holes, approximately 7 or 8 mm diameter and offset as shown **(see illustration)**. Make sure that you do not drill too deeply or you will damage the flywheel.

20 Tap the ring gear downward off its register and remove it **(see illustration)**.

21 Place the flywheel in the household refrigerator for about an hour and then heat the new ring gear to between 260 and 28°C in

14.25 Oil pump O-ring seal must be renewed (arrowed)

a domestic oven. Do not heat it above 290°C or its hardness will be lost.

22 Slip the ring onto the flywheel and gently tap it into position against its register. Allow it to cool without quenching.

23 The clutch friction surface on the flywheel should be checked for grooving or tiny hair cracks, the latter being caused by overheating. If these conditions are evident, it may be possible to surface grind the flywheel provided its balance is not upset. Otherwise, a new flywheel will have to be fitted - consult your dealer about this.

Oil pump

24 The oil pump should be checked for wear by unbolting and removing the cover plate and checking the following tolerances **(see illustrations)**.

a) *Outer rotor-to-pump body gap*
b) *Inner rotor-to-outer rotor gap*
c) *Rotor endfloat (use a feeler blade and straight-edge across pump body)*

Use feeler blades to check the tolerances and if they are outside the specified values, renew the pump.

25 If the pump is serviceable, renew the O-ring and refit the cover **(see illustration)**.

Oil seals and gasket

26 Renew the oil seals on the timing cover and the crankshaft rear retainer as a matter of routine at time of major overhaul. Oil seals are cheap, oil is not! Use a piece of tubing as a removal and installing tool. Apply some grease to the oil seal lips and check that the small tensioner spring in the oil seal has not been displaced by the vibration caused during fitting of the seal.

27 Renew all the gaskets by purchasing the appropriate "de-coke", short or full engine set. Oil seals may be included in the gasket sets.

Crankcase

28 Clean out the oilways with a length of wire or by using compressed air. Similarly clean the coolant passages. This is best done by flushing through with a cold water hose. Examine the crankcase and block for stripped threads in bolt holes; if evident, thread inserts can be fitted.

29 Renew any core plugs which appear to be leaking or which are excessively rusty.

30 Cracks in the casting may be rectified by specialist welding, or by one of the cold metal key interlocking processes available.

Camshaft and bearings

31 Examine the camshaft gear and lobes for damage or wear. If evident a new camshaft must be purchased, or one which has been built-up such as are advertised by firms specialising in exchange components.

32 The bearing internal diameters should be checked against the Specifications if a suitable gauge is available: otherwise, check for movement between the camshaft journal and the bearing. Worn bearings should be renewed by your dealer.

33 Check the camshaft endfloat by temporarily refitting the camshaft and the thrust plate.

Cam followers

34 It is seldom that the cam followers wear in their bores, but it is likely that after a high mileage, the cam lobe contact surface will show signs of a depression or grooving.

35 Where this condition is evident, renew the cam followers. Grinding out the wear marks will only reduce the thickness of the hardened metal of the cam follower and accelerate further wear.

Cylinder head and rocker gear

36 The usual reason for dismantling the cylinder head is to decarbonise and to grind in the valves. Reference should therefore be made to the next Section, in addition to the dismantling operations described here. First remove the manifolds.

37 Using a standard valve spring compressor, compress the spring on No 1 valve (valve nearest the timing cover). Do not overcompress the spring or the valve stem may bend. If it is found that, when screwing

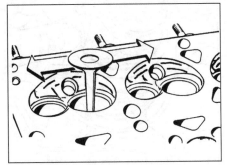

14.42 Checking valve in guide for wear

down the compressor tool, the spring retainer does not release from the collets, remove the compressor and place a piece of tubing on the retainer so that it does not impinge on the collets and strike the end of the tubing a sharp blow with a hammer. Refit the compressor and compress the spring.

38 Extract the split collets and then gently release the compressor and remove it.

39 Remove the valve spring retainer, the spring and the oil seal.

40 Withdraw the valve.

41 Repeat the removal operations on the remaining seven valves. Keep the valves in their originally fitted sequence by placing them in a piece of card which has holes punched in it and numbered 1 to 8 (from the timing cover end).

42 Place each valve in turn in its guide so that approximately one third of its length enters the guide. Rock the valve from side to side **(see illustration)**. If there is any more than an imperceptible movement, the guides will have to be reamed (working from the valve seat end) and oversize stemmed valves fitted. If you do not have the necessary reamer (tool 71-042 or 21-043), leave this work to your Ford dealer.

43 Examine the valve seats. Normally, the seats do not deteriorate but the valve heads are more likely to burn away, in which case new valves can be ground in. If the seats require re-cutting, use a standard cutter available from most accessory or tool stores or consult your motor engineering works.

44 Renewal of any valve seat which is cracked or beyond recutting is definitely a job for your dealer or motor engineering works.

45 If the cylinder head mating surface is suspected of being distorted due to persistent leakage of coolant at the gasket joint, then it can be checked and surface ground by your dealer or motor engineering works. Distortion is unlikely under normal circumstances with a cast iron head.

46 Check the rocker shaft and rocker arms pads which bear on the valve stem end faces for wear or scoring, also for any broken coil springs. Renew components as necessary. If the valve springs have been in use for 50 000 miles (80 000 km) or more, they should be renewed.

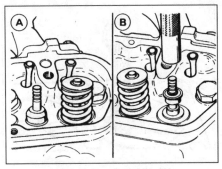

14.47 Valve stem oil seals
A Exhaust valve type   B Inlet valve type

47 Reassemble the cylinder head by first fitting new valve stem oil seals **(see illustration)**. Install No 1 valve (lubricated) into its guide and fit the valve spring with the closer coils to the cylinder head, followed by the spring retainer. Compress the spring and engage the split collets in the cutout in the valve stem. Hold them in position while the compressor is gently released and removed.

48 Repeat the operations on the remaining valves, making sure that each valve is returned to its original guide or if new valves have been fitted, into the seat into which it was ground.

49 On completion, support the ends of the cylinder head on two wooden blocks and strike the end of each valve stem with a plastic or copper-faced hammer; just a light blow to settle the components.

2A

15 Cylinder head and pistons - decarbonising

1 With the cylinder head removed, the carbon deposits should be removed from the combustion spaces using a scraper and a wire brush fitted into an electric drill. Take care not to damage the valve heads, otherwise no special precautions need be taken as the cylinder head is of cast iron construction.

2 Where a more thorough job is to be carried out, the cylinder head should be dismantled so that the valves may be ground in and the ports and combustion spaces cleaned, brushed and blown out after the manifolds have been removed.

3 Before grinding-in a valve remove the carbon and deposits completely from its head and stem. With an inlet valve, this is usually quite easy, simply scraping off the soft carbon with a blunt knife and finishing with a wire brush. With an exhaust valve the deposits are very much harder and those on the head may need a rub on coarse emery cloth to remove them. An old woodworking chisel is a useful tool to remove the worst of the head deposits.

4 Make sure that the valve heads are really clean, otherwise the rubber suction cup of the grinding tool will not stick during the grinding-in operations.

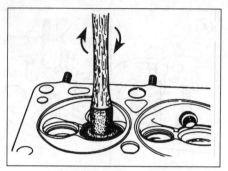

15.6 Grinding-in a valve

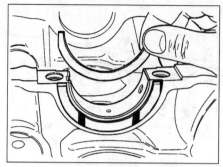

16.4a Crankshaft endfloat half thrustwashers

16.4b Fit the upper main bearing shell (with lubrication groove) and the thrustwashers (centre bearing)

5 Before starting to grind in a valve, support the cylinder head so that there is sufficient clearance under for the valve stem to project fully without being obstructed.

6 Take the first valve and apply a little coarse grinding paste to the bevelled edge of the valve head. Insert the valve into its guide and apply the suction grinding tool to its head **(see illustration)**. Rotate the tool between the palms of the hands in a back-and-forth rotary movement until the gritty action of the grinding-in process disappears. Repeat the operation with the fine paste and then wipe away all traces of grinding paste and examine the seat and bevelled edge of the valve. A matt silver mating band should be observed on both components, without any sign of black spots. If some spots do remain, repeat the grinding-in process until they have disappeared. A drop or two of paraffin applied to the contact surfaces will increase the speed of grinding-in, but do not allow any paste to run down into the valve guide. On completion, wipe away every trace of grinding paste using a paraffin-moistened cloth.

7 Repeat the operations on the remaining valves, taking care not to mix up their originally fitted sequence.

8 Reassemble the valves to the cylinder head.

9 An important part of the decarbonising operation is to remove the carbon deposits from the piston crowns. To do this, turn the crankshaft so that two pistons are at the top of their stroke and press some grease between these pistons and the cylinder walls. This will prevent carbon particles falling down into the piston ring grooves. Stuff rags into the other two bores.

10 Cover the oilways and coolant passages with masking tape and then using a blunt scraper remove all the carbon from the piston crowns. Take care not to score the soft alloy of the crown or the surface of the cylinder bore.

11 Rotate the crankshaft to bring the other two pistons to TDC and repeat the operations.

12 Wipe away the circle of grease and carbon from the cylinder bores.

13 Clean the top surface of the cylinder block by careful scraping.

16 Engine - reassembly

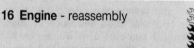

1 With everything clean, commence reassembly by oiling the bores for the cam followers and inserting them fully in their original sequence.

2 Lubricate the camshaft bearings and insert the camshaft from the timing cover end of the engine.

3 Fit the thrust plate and tighten the fixing bolts to the specified torque. The endfloat will already have been checked, as described in Section 14.

4 Wipe clean the main bearing shell seats in the crankcase and fit the shells, noting that the lower shells do not have the lubrication groove. Using a little grease, stick the semi-circular thrustwashers on either side of the centre bearing so that the oil grooves are visible when the washers are installed **(see illustrations)**.

5 Check that the Woodruff key is in position on the front end of the crankshaft and tap the crankshaft sprocket into place using a piece of tubing.

6 Oil the bearing shells and lower the crankshaft into the crankcase.

7 Wipe the seats in the main bearing caps and fit the bearing shells into them. Install the caps so that their markings are correctly positioned **(see illustration)**.

8 Screw in the cap bolts and tighten evenly to the specified torque.

9 Now check the crankshaft endfloat. Ideally a dial gauge should be used, but feeler blades are an alternative if inserted between the face of the thrustwasher and the machined surface of the crankshaft balance weight after having prised the crankshaft first in one direction and then the other **(see illustration)**. Provided the thrustwashers at the centre bearing have been renewed, the endfloat should be with the specified tolerance. If it is not, oversize thrustwashers are available (see Specifications).

10 Rotate the crankshaft so that the timing mark on its sprocket is directly in line with the centre of the crankshaft sprocket mounting flange.

11 Engage the camshaft sprocket within the timing chain and then engage the chain around the teeth of the crankshaft sprocket. Push the camshaft sprocket onto its mounting flange. The camshaft sprocket bolt holes should now be in alignment with the tapped holes in the camshaft flange and both sprocket timing marks in alignment **(see illustration)**. Turn the camshaft as necessary

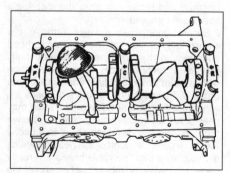

16.7 Main bearing cap markings

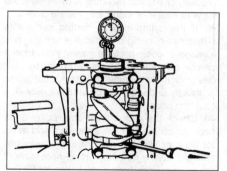

16.9 Checking the crankshaft endfloat using the dial gauge method

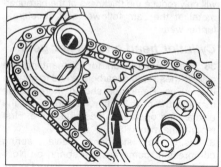

16.11 Crankshaft and camshaft sprocket timing marks (arrowed)

16.12 Secure the camshaft sprocket retaining bolts with the tab washer

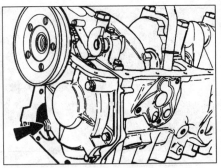

16.15 Bolt (arrowed) which secures timing cover and coolant pump

16.16 Refit the crankshaft rear oil seal retainer - note new gasket

to achieve this, also withdraw the camshaft sprocket and reposition it within the loop of the chain. This is a "trial and error" operation which must be continued until exact alignment of bolt holes and timing marks is achieved.

12 Screw in the sprocket bolts to the specified torque and bend up the tabs of a new lockplate **(see illustration)**.

13 Bolt the timing chain tensioner into position, retract the tensioner cam spring and then slide the tensioner arm onto its pivot pin. Release the cam tensioner so that it bears upon the arm.

14 Fit the oil slinger to the front of the crankshaft sprocket so that its convex side is against the sprocket.

15 Using a new gasket, fit the timing cover which will already have been fitted with a new oil seal. One fixing bolt should be left out at this stage as it also holds the coolant pump **(see illustration)**. Grease the oil seal lips and fit the crankshaft pulley. Tighten the pulley bolt to the specified torque.

16 Using a new gasket, bolt the crankshaft rear oil seal retainer into position. Tighten the bolts to the specified torque **(see illustration)**.

17 Locate the engine adapter (back) plate on its dowels and then fit the flywheel **(see illustration)**.

18 Screw in and tighten the flywheel bolts to the specified torque. To prevent the flywheel turning, the starter ring gear can be jammed or a piece of wood placed between a crankshaft balance weight and the inside of the crankcase.

19 Install and centralise the clutch.

20 The pistons/connecting rods should now be installed. Check to ensure that with the piston crown arrow pointing to the timing cover end of the engine, the oil hole in the connecting rod is on the left as shown **(see illustration)**. Oil the cylinder bores.

21 Install the pistons/connecting rods.

22 Fit the sump.

23 Fit the oil pressure sender unit, if removed.

24 Turn the crankshaft until No 1 piston is at TDC (crankshaft pulley and timing cover marks aligned) and fit the oil pump complete with new gasket and a new oil filter.

25 Using a new gasket, fit the fuel pump. If the insulating block became detached from

the crankcase during removal, make sure that a new gasket is fitted to each side of the block.

26 Fit the coolant pump using a new gasket.

27 Fit the cylinder head.

28 Refit the pushrods in their original sequence, and the rocker shaft.

29 Adjust the valve clearances and refit the rocker cover using a new gasket.

30 Fit the inlet and exhaust manifolds using new gaskets and tightening the nuts and bolts to the specified torque.

31 Refit the carburettor using a new flange gasket and connect the fuel pipe from the pump.

32 Screw in the spark plugs and the coolant temperature switch (if removed).

33 Refit the thermostat and the thermostat housing cover.

34 Fit the pulley to the coolant pump pulley flange.

35 Fit the alternator and the drivebelt and tension the belt.

36 Refit the distributor.

37 Refit the distributor cap and reconnect the spark plug HT leads.

38 Bolt on and connect the coolant pipe to the side of the cylinder block.

39 Fit the breather pipe from the oil filler cap to the inlet manifold and fit the cap.

40 Check the sump drain plug for tightness. A new seal should be fitted at regular intervals to prevent leakage. Refit the dipstick.

41 Refilling with oil should be left until the engine is installed in the vehicle.

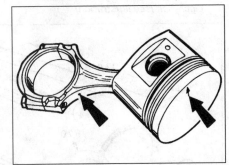

16.20 Piston-to-connecting rod relationship. Lubrication hole and piston crown mark (arrowed) must align as shown

16.17 Locate the engine backplate over the two dowels (arrowed)

17 Engine/transmission - reconnection and refitting

2A

⚠️ *Warning: Before starting a newly installed engine, make a final check to ensure that all engine components have been reconnected and that no rags or tools have been left in the engine bay.*

1 This is a direct reversal of the removal and separation from the transmission. Take care not to damage the engine ancillary components and body panels when raising the unit into position.

Reconnection

2 Reconnection of the engine and transmission is a reversal of separation but if the clutch has been dismantled, check that the driven plate has been centralised, and that the pressure plate bolts are tightened to the specified torque (see Chapter 6).

3 Locate the engine bearer and mountings and tighten the attachment bolts and nuts.

Refitting

4 First check that the engine sump drain plug is tight and that the gearbox cap nut (removed to drain the oil) is refitted, together with its locking pin and spring.

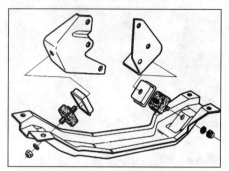

17.5 Engine bearer and mountings

17.13 Connect the gearbox stabilizer rod

17.16a Sliding the clamp onto the gearbox selector shaft

5 Manoeuvre the engine/transmission under the vehicle and attach the lifting hoist. Raise the engine carefully until the engine mounting stud is engaged in the suspension strut retaining plate and the engine bearer is in contact with the floorpan. Align the engine bearer with the retaining bolt holes then fit and tighten the bolts. When tightening the bolts check that the mounting rubbers are not being twisted **(see illustration)**.

6 Refit the transmission bearer to the rubber insulator, fit the right-hand mounting retaining nut and washer, the side-mounted bolt and washer (under the wheel arch) and tighten.

7 With the engine and transmission fully secured, release the lifting hoist and remove it.

8 If some sort of plug was used to prevent the differential pinion cage from turning, remove the plug now. If a plug was not used, insert a finger in the driveshaft hole and align the cage ready to receive the driveshaft. If this is not done, the driveshaft cannot engage with the splined pinion gear. Use a new snap-ring and reconnect the right-hand driveshaft to the transmission by having an assistant apply pressure on the roadwheel. Check that the snap-ring has locked in position.

9 Relocate the right-hand tie-bar and bracket to the crossmember and refit the retaining bolts.

10 Reconnect the right-hand lower suspension arm. Tighten the bolts.

11 Refit the driveshaft and suspension lower arm to the opposite side in a similar way to that just described.

12 Rotate the gearchange housing back through 180° then loosely attach it to the floor panels with the retaining bolts.

13 Reconnect the transmission stabilizer rod, making sure to insert the washer between the rod and the transmission case **(see illustration)**.

14 Check that the gearchange rod is still in 4th (4-speed gearbox) or reverse (5-speed gearbox).

15 Tighten the gearbox housing-to-floor attachment bolts.

16 Check that the contact faces of the gearchange rod and selector shaft are free of grease then reconnect them and adjust as follows, according to gearbox type:

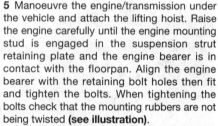

17.16b Gear lever locked in selector housing by pin (arrowed)

Four-speed gearbox - pre 1987 models

a) *Pull downwards on the gearchange rod and slip it onto the selector shaft which projects from the transmission. The clamp should be loose on the gearchange rod* **(see illustration)**.

b) *Using a 3.5 mm diameter rod or pin, insert it as shown and pull the gear lever downwards to lock it in the selector slide. When inserting the rod, point up upward to feel the cut-out in the gear lever before prising it downwards* **(see illustration)**. *Now turn your attention to the gearbox.*

c) *Using a pin or rod, inserted into the hole in the end of the projecting selector shaft, turn the shaft clockwise to its stop and retain it in this position with a strong rubber band. Now tighten the clamp pinch-bolt* **(see illustration)**.

17.16c Tightening the gearchange rod clamp bolt

d) *Remove the locking pins.*

Four-speed gearbox - post February 1987 models

a) *Set the gearchange lever inside the car to 2nd gear.*

b) *Free the control rod (which runs from the floor lever) from the selector rod at the transmission, by unscrewing the clamp bolt.*

c) *Make up a stepped rod similar to the one shown* **(see illustration)**. *This can be achieved by pushing a piece of welding rod through a length of plastic tubing.*

d) *Insert the tool into the left-hand side of the mechanism housing under the car, and feel the point of the tool engage in the hole in the lever arm. Fit the O-ring or heavy rubber band as shown* **(see illustration)**.

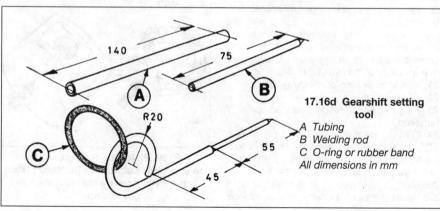

17.16d Gearshift setting tool
A Tubing
B Welding rod
C O-ring or rubber band
All dimensions in mm

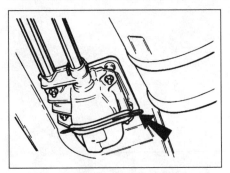

17.16e Setting tool in place - 4-speed gearbox

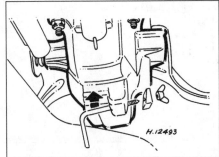

17.16f Hold gear lever in position with lock tool

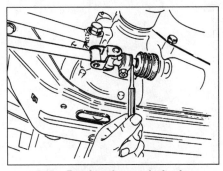

17.16g Retain selector shaft when tightening clamp bolt

e) With 2nd gear correctly engaged, reconnect the control rod to the selector rod by tightening the clamp bolt. Remove the stepped tool.

f) Select each gear in turn to confirm that the linkage has been correctly set.

Five-speed gearbox - pre 1987 models

a) Use a lock tool similar to that shown, pull the gear lever down in its selector gate reverse gear position and set the tool to hold it against the stop (see illustration).

b) Insert a suitable rod or drift into the hole in the selector shaft, rotate the shaft clockwise until it is felt to be against the stop then push it into the gearbox and retain it in this position while tightening the gearchange rod clamp bolt. Remove the drift and lock tool (see illustration).

Five-speed gearbox - post February 1987 models

a) Set the gearchange lever inside the car to 4th gear.

b) Release the control rod (which runs from the floor lever) from the selector rod at the transmission by unscrewing the clamp bolt.

c) Insert a rod (3.5 mm diameter) into the left-hand side of the mechanism housing under the car (see illustration).

d) With the 4th gear correctly engaged, reconnect the control rod to the selector rod by tightening the clamp bolt. Remove the temporary rod.

e) Select each gear in turn to confirm that the linkage has been correctly set.

17 Refit the clutch housing cover plate and secure with retaining bolts.

18 Refit the starter motor and reconnect its wiring.

19 Reconnect the engine earth strap underneath also the reversing light lead.

20 Refit the exhaust system and bolt the downpipe to the manifold. Refit the heated air box which connects with the air cleaner.

21 Reconnect the clutch operating cable.

22 Reconnect the electrical leads, the fuel pipe, the brake vacuum hose and the speedometer cable.

23 Reconnect the throttle cable and the heater hoses.

24 Reconnect the radiator coolant hoses.

25 Fill up with engine oil, gearbox oil and coolant, then reconnect the battery.

26 Refit the bonnet, bolting the hinges to their originally marked positions.

27 Fit the air cleaner and reconnect the hoses and the air cleaner inlet spout.

28 Once the engine is running, check the dwell angle, timing, idle speed and mixture adjustment.

29 If a number of new internal components have been installed, run the vehicle at restricted speed for the first few hundred miles to allow time for the new components to bed in. It is also recommended that with a new or rebuilt engine, the engine oil and filter are changed at the end of the running-in period.

2A

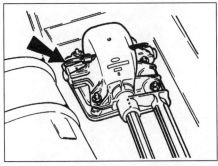

17.16h Setting tool in place - 5-speed gearbox

Chapter 2 Part B:
CVH engine repair procedures

Contents

Degrees of difficulty

Easy, suitable for novice with little experience	**Fairly easy,** suitable for beginner with some experience	**Fairly difficult,** suitable for competent DIY mechanic 	**Difficult,** suitable for experienced DIY mechanic 	**Very difficult,** suitable for expert DIY or professional 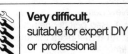

Specifications

1.3 and 1.6 litre engines

General

Engine type .... Four-cylinder, overhead cam, water-cooled. Compound Valve Hemispherical head (CVH)

	1.3 litre	**1.6 litre**
Code	JPC	LUB
Firing order (No 1 at timing cover end)	1-3-4-2	1-3-4-2
Bore	79.96 mm	79.96 mm
Stroke	64.52 mm	79.52 mm
Cubic capacity	1296 cc	1597 cc
Compression ratio	9.5 : 1	9.5 : 1
Compression pressure at starter speed	11.2 to 14.8 kgf/cm²	11.2 to 14.8 kgf/cm²
Maximum continuous engine speed (rpm)	6450	6300

Cylinder block

Number of main bearings 5
Cylinder bore diameter:
  Standard (1) .... 79.94 to 79.95 mm
  Standard (2) .... 79.95 to 79.96 mm
  Standard (3) .... 79.96 to 79.97 mm
  Standard (4) .... 79.97 to 79.98 mm
  Oversize (A) .... 80.23 to 80.24 mm
  Oversize (B) .... 80.24 to 80.25 mm
  Oversize (C) .... 80.25 to 80.26 mm
Main bearing shell inner diameter:
  Standard .... 58.011 to 58.038 mm
  Undersize 0.25 .... 57.761 to 57.788 mm
  Undersize 0.50 .... 57.511 to 57.538 mm
  Undersize 0.75 .... 57.261 to 57.288 mm

Crankshaft

Main bearing journal diameter:
  Standard .... 57.98 to 58.00 mm
  Undersize 0.25 .... 57.73 to 57.75 mm
  Undersize 0.50 .... 57.48 to 57.50 mm
  Undersize 0.75 .... 57.23 to 57.25 mm

Crankshaft (continued)

Main bearing running clearance .... 0.011 to 0.058 mm
Thrustwasher thickness:
    Standard .... 2.301 to 2.351 mm
    Oversize .... 2.491 to 2.541 mm
Crankshaft endfloat .... 0.09 to 0.30 mm
Crankpin (big-end) diameter:
    Standard .... 47.89 to 47.91 mm
    Undersize 0.25 .... 47.64 to 47.66 mm
    Undersize 0.50 .... 47.39 to 47.41 mm
    Undersize 0.75 .... 47.14 to 47.16 mm
    Undersize 1.00 .... 46.89 to 46.91 mm
Big-end bearing running clearance .... 0.006 to 0.060 mm

Camshaft

Number of bearings 5
Belt tension:
    Setting up (torque wrench on camshaft sprocket):
        1.3 litre (colour code blue) .... 6.0 to 6.5 kgf m
        1.6 litre (colour code yellow) .... 4.5 to 5.0 kgf m
    Final setting (using Ford tool 21-113):
        Used belt .... 4 to 5 on scale
        New belt .... 10 to 11 on scale
Note: *A used belt is one which has been in use for more than 30 minutes.*
Camshaft thrust plate thickness .... 4.99 to 5.01 mm
Cam lift:
    1.3 litre .... 5.79 mm
    1.6 litre .... 6.09 mm
Cam length (heel to toe):
    Inlet:
        1.3 litre .... 38.305 mm
        1.6 litre .... 38.606 mm
    Exhaust:
        1.3 litre .... 37.289 mm
        1.6 litre .... 37.590 mm
Camshaft bearing diameter:
    1 .... 44.75 mm
    2 .... 45.00 mm
    3 .... 45.25 mm
    4 .... 45.40 mm
    5 .... 45.75 mm
Camshaft endfloat .... 0.05 to 0.15 mm

Pistons and piston rings

Diameter:
    Standard 1 .... 79.910 to 79.920 mm
    Standard 2 .... 79.920 to 79.930 mm
    Standard 3 .... 79.930 to 79.940 mm
    Standard 4 .... 79.940 to 79.950 mm
    Standard service .... 79.930 to 79.955 mm
    Oversize 0.29 .... 80.210 to 80.235 mm
    Oversize 0.50 .... 80.430 to 80.455 mm
Piston-to-bore clearance:
    Production .... 0.020 to 0.040 mm
    Service .... 0.010 to 0.045 mm
Ring gap positions (when fitted) .... 120° apart
Piston ring gap:
    Compression .... 0.30 to 0.50 mm
    Oil control .... 0.4 to 1.4 mm

Gudgeon pin

Pin diameter:
    White .... 20.622 to 20.625 mm
    Red .... 20.625 to 20.628 mm
    Blue .... 20.628 to 20.631 mm
    Yellow .... 20.631 to 20.634 mm
Play in piston .... 0.005 to 0.011 mm
Interference fit in connecting rod .... 0.013 to 0.045 mm

Connecting rod

Big-end bore diameter	50.890 to 50.910 mm
Small-end bore diameter	20.589 to 20.609 mm
Big-end bearing shell inside diameter:	
Standard	47.916 to 47.950 mm
Undersize 0.25	47.666 to 47.700 mm
Undersize 0.50	47.416 to 47.450 mm
Undersize 0.75	47.166 to 47.200 mm
Undersize 1.00	46.916 to 46.950 mm
Big-end bearing running clearance	0.006 to 0.060 mm

Cylinder head

Valve seat angle	45°
Valve seat width	1.75 to 2.32 mm
Maximum cylinder head distortion permissible:	
Over distance of 26	0.04 mm
Over distance of 156	0.08 mm
Over full length	0.15 mm
Facing head mating surface	0.30 mm
Minimum combustion chamber depth (after refacing)	19.60 mm

Valves - general

	1.3 litre	1.6 litre
Inlet valve opens	13° BTDC	8° BTDC
Inlet valve closes	28° ABDC	36° ABDC
Exhaust valve opens	30° BBDC	34° BBDC
Exhaust valve closes	15° ATDC	6° ATDC
Valve lift:		
Inlet	9.56 mm	10.09 mm
Exhaust	9.52 mm	10.06 mm
Valve spring free length	47.2 mm	47.2 mm

Inlet valve

Length	134.54 to 135.00 mm
Head diameter	41.9 to 42.1 mm
Stem diameter:	
Standard	8.025 to 8.043 mm
Oversize 0.2	8.225 to 8.243 mm
Oversize 0.4	8.425 to 8.443 mm
Valve stem-to-guide clearance	0.020 to 0.063 mm

Exhaust valve

Length:	
1.3 engine	131.17 to 131.63 mm
1.6 engine	131.57 to 132.03 mm
Head diameter:	
1.3 engine	33.9 to 34.1 mm
1.6 engine	36.9 to 37.1 mm
Valve stem diameter:	
Standard	7.999 to 8.017 mm
Oversize 0.2	8.199 to 8.217 mm
Oversize 0.4	8.399 to 8.417 mm
Valve stem-to-guide clearance	0.046 to 0.089 mm

Lubrication system

Minimum oil pressure at 80°C (175°F):	
At 750 rpm	1.0 kgf/cm²
At 2000 rpm	2.8 kgf/cm²
Oil pump type	Gear, driven by crankshaft
Oil pump clearances:	
Gear type pump:	
Outer rotor-to-housing	0.069 to 0.140 mm
Inner rotor-to-housing	0.070 to 0.165 mm
Rotor-to-cover endfloat	0.028 to 0.078 mm
Rotor type pump:	
Outer rotor-to-housing	0.060 to 0.190 mm
Inner-to-outer rotor	0.050 to 0.180 mm
Rotor-to-cover endfloat	0.014 to 0.100 mm

Torque wrench settings

	Nm	lbf ft
Main bearing cap bolts	95	70
Big-end bearing cap bolts	30	22
Oil pump mounting bolts	10	7
Oil pump pick-up tube bolt to block	20	15
Oil pump pick-up to pump	12	9
Oil pump cover	8 to 12	6 to 9
Sump (with one-piece gasket)	5 to 8	4 to 6
Rear oil seal carrier bolts	10	7
Sump bolts	10	7
Flywheel	85	63
Crankshaft pulley bolt	110	81
Cylinder head bolts:		
Stage 1	25	18
Stage 2	55	40
Stage 3	Tighten further 90°	Tighten further 90°
Stage 4	Tighten further 90°	Tighten further 90°
Camshaft thrust plate bolts	12	9
Camshaft sprocket bolt	55	41
Belt tensioner bolts	18	13
Coolant pump bolts	8	6
Rocker arm studs in head	21	15
Rocker arm nuts	27	20
Rocker cover screws	8	6
Timing cover screws	8	6
Exhaust manifold bolts	16	12
Inlet manifold bolts	18	13
Carburettor mounting bolts	20	15
Thermostat housing bolts	8	6
Spark plugs	27	20
Engine-to-transmission bolts	41	30
Transmission oil filler plug	25	18
Fuel pump nuts	14 to 18	10 to 13
Oil pressure switch	18 to 22	13 to 16

1.4 litre engine

The Specifications are the same as for the 1.3 litre CVH engine, except for the following:

General

Code	FUA/FUB
Bore	77.24 mm
Stroke	74.30 mm
Cubic capacity	1392 cc
Maximum continuous engine speed	6200 rpm

Cylinder block

Cylinder bore diameter:	
Standard (1)	77.220 to 77.230 mm
Standard (2)	77.230 to 77.240 mm
Standard (3)	77.240 to 77.250 mm
Standard (4)	77.250 to 77.260 mm
Oversize (A)	77.510 to 77.520 mm
Oversize (B)	77.520 to 77.530 mm
Oversize (C)	77.530 to 77.540 mm
Oversize 0.29	77.525 to 77.535 mm
Oversize 0.50	77.745 to 77.755 mm

Pistons and piston rings

Diameter:	
Standard (1)	77.190 to 77.200 mm
Standard (2)	77.200 to 77.210 mm
Standard (3)	77.210 to 77.220 mm
Standard (4)	77.220 to 77.230 mm
Standard service	77.210 to 77.235 mm
Oversize (A)	77.480 to 77.490 mm
Oversize (B)	77.490 to 77.500 mm
Oversize (C)	77.500 to 77.510 mm
Oversize 0.29	77.490 to 77.515 mm
Oversize 0.50	77.710 to 77.735 mm

Cylinder head

Minimum combustion chamber depth (after refacing)	17.40 mm

Valve timing

Inlet valve opens	15° ATDC
Inlet valve closes	30° ABDC
Exhaust valve opens	28° BBDC
Exhaust valve closes	13° BTDC

Inlet valves

Length	136.29 to 136.75 mm
Head diameter	39.90 to 40.10 mm
Stem diameter:	
Standard	8.025 to 8.043 mm
Oversize 0.2	8.225 to 8.243 mm
Oversize 0.4	8.425 to 8.443 mm

Exhaust valves

Length	132.97 to 133.43 mm
Head diameter	33.90 to 34.10 mm
Stem diameter:	
Standard	7.999 to 8.017 mm
Oversize 0.2	8.199 to 8.217 mm
Oversize 0.4	8.399 to 8.417 mm

Lubrication system

Oil pump type	Rotor, driven by crankshaft
Oil pump clearances:	
Outer rotor-to-housing	0.060 to 0.190 mm
Inner-to-outer rotor	0.050 to 0.180 mm
Rotor-to-cover endfloat	0.014 to 0.100 mm

1 General information

This engine, designated CVH (Compound Valve angle, Hemispherical combustion chamber) can be described in more conventional terms as a four-cylinder overhead camshaft (OHC) engine. It is mounted, together with the transmission, transversely at the front of the vehicle and transmits power through open driveshafts to the front roadwheels.

The engine is available in three capacities; 1.3, 1.4 and 1.6 litre. The 1.4 litre engine being introduced to replace the 1.3 litre unit during early 1986.

The crankshaft is supported in five main bearings within a cast iron crankcase. The cylinder head is of light alloy construction, supporting the overhead camshaft in five bearings. These bearings cannot be renewed and, in the event of wear occurring, the complete cylinder head must be changed. The fuel pump is mounted on the side of the cylinder head and is driven by a pushrod from an eccentric cam on the camshaft.

The cam followers are of the hydraulic type, which eliminates the need for valve clearance adjustment and also ensures that valve timing is always correct. With this type of follower, if the engine has been standing idle for a period of time, or after overhaul, when the engine is started up valve clatter may be heard. This is a normal condition and will gradually disappear within a few minutes of starting up

as the cam followers are pressurised with oil.

The distributor is driven from the rear (flywheel) end of the camshaft.

The coolant pump is mounted on the timing belt end of the cylinder block and is driven by the toothed belt.

A gear type oil pump is mounted on the timing belt end of the cylinder block and is driven by a gear on the front end of the crankshaft.

A full-flow oil filter of throw-away type is located on the side of crankcase nearer the front of the vehicle.

2 Operations possible without removing engine from vehicle

The following work can be carried out without having to remove the engine:
a) Timing belt - renewal
b) Camshaft oil seal - renewal
c) Camshaft - removal and refitting
d) Crankshaft front oil seal - renewal*
e) Sump - removal and refitting
f) Piston/connecting rod - removal and refitting
g) Engine/transmission mountings - removal and refitting

*Note: Replacement of the crankshaft front oil seal with the engine in situ is made difficult by restricted access. Accurate fitting of the new seal in this position will only be possible using Ford special tool number 21-093 (or a similar fabricated distance piece) used, together with the crankshaft timing belt pulley retaining bolt,

to draw the new seal into position against the stop. In view of this, partial removal of the engine and transmission may well be necessary to renew this seal.

3 Operations only possible with engine removed from vehicle

The following work should be carried out only after the engine has been removed:
a) Crankshaft main bearings - renewal
b) Crankshaft - removal and refitting
c) *Flywheel - removal and refitting
d) ** Crankshaft rear oil seal - renewal
e) *Oil pump - removal and refitting

Although it is possible to undertake those operations marked * without removing the engine, and those marked ** by removing the transmission, such work is not recommended and is unlikely to save much time over that required to withdraw the complete engine/transmission.

4 Timing belt - inspection, removal and refitting

Inspection

1 This operation will only normally be required at the specified timing belt renewal intervals (see Chapter 1), or for removal of the coolant pump.

2B

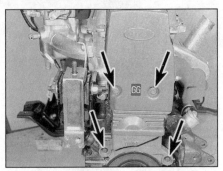

4.4a Undo the four retaining bolts (arrowed) to remove the timing cover - 1-piece type

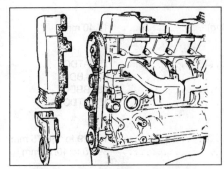

4.4b The 2-piece timing belt cover

2 Disconnect the battery earth lead.

3 Release the alternator mounting and adjuster link bolts, push the alternator in towards the engine and slip the drivebelt from the pulleys.

4 On earlier models, unscrew the four retaining bolts and remove the timing belt cover **(see illustration)**. Note that a two-piece cover has been progressively introduced on all later models **(see illustration)**. The upper half of the cover is visually similar to the earlier one-piece type and can be removed after undoing the two retaining bolts. To withdraw the lower half it will first be necessary to remove the crankshaft pulley after which the two retaining bolts can then be undone and the cover removed.

5 The timing belt can now be inspected for signs of excessive wear or damage; if found, the belt must be renewed. If the belt is

4.7a Camshaft sprocket timing mark

4.7b Align the crankshaft sprocket with its timing mark

damaged or has worn prematurely, a check must be made to find the cause. There are three main causes of timing belt failures and these are as follows:

a) If some of the teeth have sheared off and some are badly worn, check the surface of the crankshaft pulley teeth for signs of damage or defects and renew the pulley, if necessary.

b) If some belt teeth have sheared off and others are cracked at their roots, then this indicates an excessive torque loading on the belt, and the water pump, distributor, timing belt tensioner wheel and the camshaft must be checked for freedom of movement. In the case of the camshaft the rockers must be removed when checking it for freedom of rotation. Renew or repair as necessary before renewing the timing belt.

c) If some teeth have sheared from the belt whilst others are undamaged, the belt will have jammed in the belt pulley or the engine has possibly been over-revved. Check the items mentioned in (b) and renew as necessary.

Note: On 1.4 and 1.6 litre engines, an improved timing belt was introduced in 1988 (part no. 1653887) together with a modified tensioner pulley of larger diameter (part no. 6182891). If the belt is to be renewed, then the modified pulley must also be renewed.

Removal

6 To remove the timing belt, proceed as follows:

4.7c One method of jamming the flywheel ring gear . . .

7 Using a ring or socket spanner on the crankshaft pulley bolt, turn the crankshaft until the timing mark on the camshaft sprocket is opposite the TDC mark on the cylinder head and the small projection on the crankshaft belt sprocket front flange is in alignment with the TDC mark on the oil pump casing. Remove the starter, jam the flywheel ring gear and unbolt and remove the crankshaft pulley **(see illustrations)**.

8 Slacken the bolts which secure the belt tensioner and using a large screwdriver, prise the tensioner to one side to relieve spring tension on the belt. (Some tensioners do not incorporate a spring.) Temporarily retighten the bolts.

9 If the original belt is to be refitted, mark it for direction of travel and also the exact tooth positions on all three sprockets.

10 Slip the timing belt from its sprockets.

Refitting

11 Refit by reversing the removal operations, but before engaging the belt to the camshaft and crankshaft sprockets, check that they are set to TDC as previously described. Adjust the position of the sprockets slightly if necessary, but avoid any excessive movement of the sprockets while the belt is off, as the piston crowns and valve heads may make contact, with consequent damage to both components.

12 Engage the timing belt with the teeth of the crankshaft sprocket (slip the sprocket off the crankshaft if necessary to avoid kinking the belt), and then pull the belt vertically upright on its right-hand run. Keep it taut and engage it with the teeth of the camshaft sprocket. Check that the positions of the crankshaft and camshaft sprockets have not altered.

13 Wind the belt around the camshaft sprocket, around and under the tensioner idler pulley and over the coolant pump sprocket (no set position for this) **(see illustration)**.

14 Loosen the tensioner retaining bolts by half a turn each to allow the tensioner to snap into position against the timing belt.

15 With the crankshaft locked in position at TDC, fit a 41 mm socket and torque wrench onto the camshaft sprocket hexagon and apply an anti-clockwise torque in accordance

4.7d . . . another method of jamming the flywheel ring gear

with the settings given in the Specifications. Whilst applying this torque setting to the camshaft, simultaneously tighten the tensioner retaining bolts, right-hand then left-hand bolt, to their specified torque wrench setting. This is an initial setting up procedure only - the belt tension should be checked with Ford tool 21-113: therefore the car will have to be taken to a dealer as soon as possible **(see illustration)**.

16 Refit the crankshaft pulley, the retaining bolt and washer, and tighten to the specified torque wrench setting **(see illustration)**.

17 Refit the belt cover, refit and adjust the drivebelt, and reconnect the battery.

5 Camshaft oil seal - renewal

1 Disconnect the battery earth lead.
2 Release the timing belt from the camshaft sprocket.
3 Pass a bar through one of the holes in the camshaft sprocket to anchor the sprocket while the retaining bolt is unscrewed. Remove the sprocket.
4 Using a suitable tool, hooked at its end, prise out the oil seal **(see illustration)**.
5 Apply a little grease to the lips of the new seal and draw it into position using the sprocket bolt and a suitable distance piece **(see illustration)**.
6 Refit the sprocket, tightening the bolt to the specified torque wrench setting. Thread-

4.13 Timing belt correctly located

locking compound should be applied to the threads of the bolt.
7 Refit and tension the timing belt.
8 Reconnect the battery.

6 Camshaft - removal and refitting

Removal

1 Disconnect the battery earth lead.
2 Disconnect the crankcase ventilation hose from the inlet manifold and the rocker cover.
3 Extract the two larger screws from the lid of the air cleaner, raise the air cleaner, disconnect the hoses and remove the cleaner.
4 Disconnect the pipes and remove the windscreen washer fluid reservoir from the engine compartment.
5 Disconnect the HT leads from the spark plugs, then remove the distributor cap and secure it to the left-hand side of the engine compartment.
6 Unscrew the three bolts and withdraw the distributor from the cylinder head. Note that the distributor body is marked in relation to the cylinder head.
7 Unbolt and remove the fuel pump, complete with coil spring. Withdraw the insulating spacer and operating pushrod.
8 Unbolt the throttle cable bracket at the carburettor and then disconnect the cable by sliding back the spring clip.
9 Remove the timing belt cover-to-cylinder head attachment bolts.

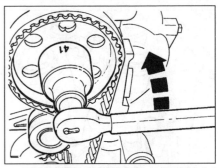
4.15 Method used to initially tension the timing belt

4.16 Crankshaft pulley, bolt and washer

10 Remove the rocker cover **(see illustration)**.
11 Unscrew the securing nuts and remove the rocker arms and guides **(see illustration)**. Keep the components in their originally installed sequence by marking them with a piece of numbered tape or by using a suitably sub-divided box.
12 Withdraw the hydraulic cam followers, again keeping them in their originally fitted sequence **(see illustration)**.
13 Slacken the alternator mounting and adjuster link bolts, push the alternator in towards the engine and slip the drivebelt from the pulleys.
14 Unbolt and remove the timing belt cover and turn the crankshaft to align the timing mark on the camshaft sprocket with the one on the cylinder head.

2B

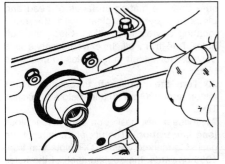
5.4 Removing the camshaft oil seal

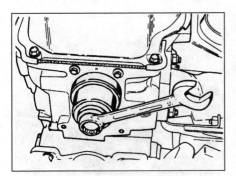
5.5 Installing the camshaft oil seal

6.10 Remove the rocker cover

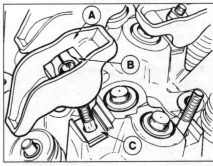
6.11 Rocker arm components

A Rocker arm   *C Spacer plate*
B Guide

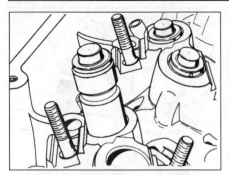

6.12 Withdrawing a cam follower

6.16 Method used to loosen the camshaft sprocket bolt

6.17a Unscrewing the camshaft thrust plate bolts

15 Slacken the bolts on the timing belt tensioner, lever the tensioner against the tension of its coil spring (if fitted) and retighten the bolts. With the belt now slack, slip it from the camshaft sprocket.

16 Pass a rod or large screwdriver through one of the holes in the camshaft sprocket to lock it and unscrew the sprocket bolt **(see illustration)**. Remove the sprocket.

17 Extract the two bolts and pull out the camshaft thrust plate **(see illustrations)**.

18 Carefully withdraw the camshaft from the distributor end of the cylinder head **(see illustration)**.

Refitting

19 Refitting the camshaft is a reversal of removal, but observe the following points.

20 Lubricate the camshaft bearings before inserting the camshaft into the cylinder head.

21 It is recommended that a new oil seal is always fitted after the camshaft has been installed. Apply thread-locking compound to the sprocket bolt threads.

22 Fit and tension the timing belt.

23 Oil the hydraulic cam followers with hypoid type transmission oil before inserting them into their original bores.

24 Refit the rocker arms and guides in their original sequence, use new nuts and tighten to the specified torque. It is essential that before each rocker arm is installed and its nut tightened, the respective cam follower is positioned at its lowest point (in contact with cam base circle). Turn the camshaft (by means of the crankshaft pulley bolt) as necessary to achieve this.

25 Use a new rocker cover gasket. Do not forget to refit the timing belt cover bolts.

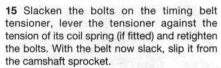

7 Cylinder head - removal and refitting

Removal

1 Disconnect the battery earth lead.

2 Remove the air cleaner and detach the connecting hoses.

3 Drain the cooling system.

4 Disconnect the coolant hoses from the thermostat housing.

6.17b Lifting out the camshaft thrust plate

5 Disconnect the coolant hoses from the automatic choke (if necessary).

6 Disconnect the throttle cable from the carburettor.

7 Disconnect the fuel pipe from the fuel pump.

8 Disconnect the vacuum servo pipe from the inlet manifold.

9 Disconnect the leads from the coolant temperature sender, the ignition coil, and the anti-run-on (anti-diesel) solenoid valve at the carburettor.

10 Unbolt the exhaust downpipe from the manifold by unscrewing the flange nuts. Support the exhaust pipe by tying it up with wire.

11 Release the alternator mounting and adjuster link bolts, push the alternator in towards the engine and slip the drivebelt from the pulleys.

12 Unbolt and remove the timing belt cover.

13 Slacken the belt tensioner bolts, lever the tensioner to one side against the pressure of the coil spring (if fitted) and retighten the bolts.

14 With the timing belt now slack, slip it from the camshaft sprocket.

15 Disconnect the leads from the spark plugs and unscrew and remove the spark plugs.

16 Remove the rocker cover.

17 Unscrew the cylinder head bolts, progressively and in the reverse sequence to that given for tightening. Discard the bolts, as new ones must be used at reassembly.

18 Remove the cylinder head complete with manifolds. Use the manifolds, if necessary, as levers to rock the head from the block. Do not attempt to tap the head sideways off the

6.18 Withdrawing the camshaft

block, as it is located on dowels, and do not attempt to lever between the head and the block, or damage will result.

Refitting

19 Before installing the cylinder head, make sure that the mating surfaces of head and block are perfectly clean with the head locating dowels in position. Clean the bolt holes free from oil. In extreme cases it is possible for oil left in the holes to crack the block.

20 Turn the crankshaft to position No 1 piston about 20 mm (0.8 in) before it reaches TDC.

21 Place a new gasket on the cylinder block **(see illustration)**. The upper surface of the gasket is marked OBEN-TOP. Note that from 1986 onwards, the configuration of the holes on the cylinder head gasket have been changed from the earlier type and a different

7.21a Locate the new cylinder head gasket

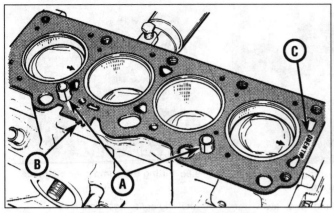

7.21b Cylinder head gasket details

A *Locating dowels*
B *Gasket identification teeth*
  (1.4 litre version shown)
C *Top mark*

7.22a Refit the cylinder head

2B

gasket is used for each size of engine. Identification is by teeth on the rear facing edge of the gasket, as shown **(see illustration)**, according to engine type as follows:

1.6 litre   4 teeth
1.4 litre   2 teeth

22 Locate the cylinder head on its dowels **(see illustration)** and install and tighten the new cylinder head bolts, tightening them in four stages (see Specifications). After the first two stages, the bolt heads should be marked with a spot of quick-drying paint so that the paint spots all face the same direction. Now tighten the bolts (Stage 3) through 90° (quarter turn) followed by a further 90° (Stage 4). Tighten the bolts at each stage only in the sequence shown **(see illustration)** before going on to the next stage. If all the bolts have been tightened equally, the paint spots should now all be pointing in the same direction.
23 Fit the timing belt.
24 Refitting and reconnection of all other components is a reversal of dismantling.
25 Refill the cooling system.

8 Crankshaft front oil seal - renewal

Note: *If replacing the oil seal with the power unit in situ, first refer to the cautionary notes concerning its renewal in Section 2.*
1 Disconnect the battery earth lead.
2 Release the alternator mounting and adjuster link bolts, push the alternator in towards the engine and slip the drivebelt from the pulleys.
3 Unbolt and remove the timing belt cover and by using a spanner or socket on the crankshaft pulley bolt, turn the crankshaft until the timing mark on the camshaft sprocket is in alignment with the mark on the cylinder head.
4 Unbolt and withdraw the starter motor so that the flywheel ring gear can be jammed with a cold chisel or other suitable device and the crankshaft pulley unbolted and removed.
5 Slacken the belt tensioner bolts, lever the tensioner to one side and retighten the bolts.

With the belt slack, it can now be slipped from the sprockets. Before removing the belt note its original position on the sprockets (mark the teeth with quick-drying paint), also its direction of travel.
6 Pull off the crankshaft sprocket. If it is tight, use a two-legged extractor.
7 Remove the dished washer from the crankshaft, noting that the concave side is against the oil seal.
8 Using a hooked tool, prise out the oil seal from the oil pump housing **(see illustration)**.
9 Grease the lips of the new seal and press it into position using the pulley bolt and a distance piece made from a piece of tubing.
10 Fit the thrustwasher (concave side to oil seal), the belt sprocket and the pulley to the crankshaft.
11 Fit and tension the timing belt.
12 Fit the timing belt cover.
13 Refit and tension the alternator drivebelt.
14 Remove the starter ring gear jamming device, refit the starter motor and reconnect the battery.

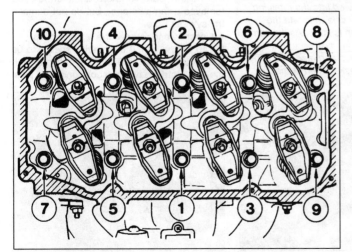

7.22b Cylinder head bolt tightening sequence

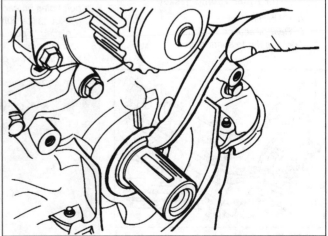

8.8 Extracting the oil seal from the oil pump housing

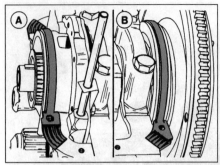

9.8a Sump front (A) and rear (B) sealing strip locations - 4-piece type

9.8b Sump gasket to overlap sealing strip - 4-piece type

9.8c Fitting the sump over a 4-piece gasket

9 Sump - removal and refitting

Removal

1 Disconnect the battery earth lead.
2 Drain the engine oil.
3 Unbolt and remove the starter motor.
4 Unbolt and remove the cover plate from the clutch housing.
5 Unscrew the plastic timing belt guard from the front end of the engine (two bolts).
6 Unscrew the sump securing bolts progressively and remove them.

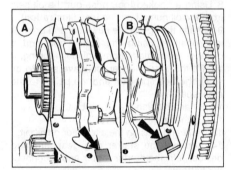

9.9a Sealing compound application area for 1-piece sump gasket

A Oil pump joint
B Rear oil seal carrier joint
Apply sealer to shaded area

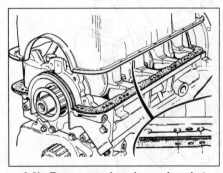

9.9b Ensure spacing pips and gasket holes (inset) engage when fitting modified sump and 1-piece gasket

7 Remove the sump and peel away the gaskets and sealing strips.

Refitting

8 On the earlier four-piece gasket arrangement, make sure that the mating surfaces of the sump and block are clean, then fit new end sealing strips into their grooves and stick new side gaskets into position using thick grease. The ends of the side gaskets should overlap the seals. Offer up the sump, taking care not to displace the gaskets and insert the securing bolts **(see illustrations)**. Tighten the bolts in two stages to the final torque given in the Specifications. Fit the timing belt guard.
9 In April 1985, a modified sump and one-piece sump gasket were introduced to improve sealing in the region of the oil pump and rear oil seal carrier- to-cylinder block joints. Removal and refitting procedures are essentially the same as for the earlier four-piece gasket arrangement but note the following when refitting:
a) *The gasket should be fitted dry but jointing compound should be applied to the oil pump and rear oil seal carrier-to-cylinder block joints as shown* **(see illustration)**.
b) *To aid installation , it is helpful if a few studs can be screwed into the retaining bolt holes on each side to locate the gasket as the sump is fitted. As the sump is placed in position make sure that the spacing pips in the sump face locate in the holes in the gasket, then fit the*

retaining bolts finger tight **(see illustration)**. *Remove the studs and fit the rest of the bolts.*
c) *Tighten the bolts evenly in two stages to the specified torque.*
Note that the one-piece gasket can be fitted to earlier engines provided that it is used in conjunction with the modified sump.
10 Refit the cover plate to the flywheel housing **(see illustration)**.
11 Refit the starter motor.
12 Fill the engine with oil and reconnect the battery.

10 Pistons/connecting rods - removal and refitting

Removal

1 Remove the sump and the cylinder head.
2 Check that the connecting rod and cap have adjacent numbers at their big-end to indicate their position in the cylinder block (No 1 nearest timing cover end of engine) **(see illustration)**.
3 Bring the first piston to the lowest point of its throw by turning the crankshaft pulley bolt and then check if there is a wear ridge at the top of the bore. If there is, it should be removed using a scraper, but do not damage the cylinder bore.
4 Unscrew and remove the big-end bolts.
5 Tap off the cap. If the bearing shell is to be used again, make sure that it is retained with the cap. Note the two cap positioning roll pins.

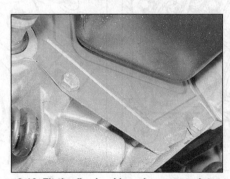

9.10 Fit the flywheel housing cover plate

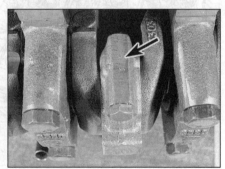

10.2 Connecting rod and big-end cap matching numbers (arrowed)

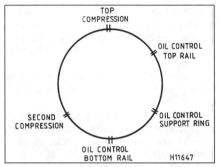

10.8 Piston ring end gap positioning

10.10 Fit the bearing shell to the connecting rod

10.12 Installing a piston/connecting rod assembly

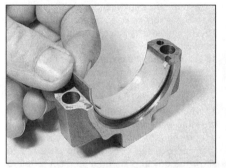

10.14 Fit the bearing shell to the big-end cap

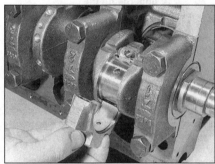

10.15a Fit the big-end cap . . .

10.15b . . . and tighten the retaining bolts

6 Push the piston/rod out of the top of the block, again keeping the bearing shell with the rod if the shell is to be used again.

7 Repeat the removal operations on the remaining piston/rod assemblies.

Refitting

8 To refit a piston/rod assembly, have the piston ring gaps staggered as shown **(see illustration)**. Oil the rings and apply a piston ring compressor. Compress the piston rings.

9 Oil the cylinder bores.

10 Wipe clean the bearing shell seat in the connecting rod and insert the shell **(see illustration)**.

11 Insert the piston/rod assembly into the cylinder bore until the base of the piston ring compressor stands squarely on the top of the block.

12 Check that the directional arrow on the piston crown faces towards the timing cover end of the engine, then apply the wooden handle of a hammer to the piston crown. Strike the head of the hammer sharply to drive the piston into the cylinder bore and release the ring compressor **(see illustration)**.

13 Oil the crankpin and draw the connecting rod down to engage with the crankshaft. Make sure the bearing shell is still in position.

14 Wipe the bearing shell seat in the big-end cap clean and insert the bearing shell **(see illustration)**.

15 Fit the cap, screw in the bolts and tighten them to the specified torque **(see illustrations)**.

16 Repeat the operations on the remaining pistons/connecting rods.

17 Refit the sump and the cylinder head.

18 Refill the engine with oil and coolant.

11 Engine/transmission mountings - removal and refitting

Refer to Chapter 2A, Section 11.

12 Oil filter - renewal

1 The oil filter is of throw-away, screw-on cartridge type, mounted on the right-hand side of the crankcase.

2 Renewal is described in Chapter 1, Section 3.

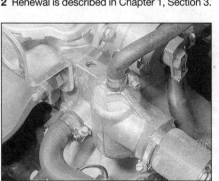

13.1a Thermostat housing hose connections

13 Engine/transmission - removal and separation

2B

Note: *Proceed as described for the OHV engine in Chapter 2A, Section 12 but note the following differences:*

1 A lateral coolant pipe is not fitted to the side of the cylinder block on the CVH variants but the heater hoses must be disconnected from the thermostat housing and distribution **(see illustrations)**.

2 When disconnecting the driveshafts, disregard paragraphs 20 to 26 as they can be detached by undoing the socket-head bolts. These can be loosened using a 6mm Allen key.

3 Disconnect the right-hand shaft just to the right of the intermediate shaft support

13.1b Radiator bottom hose and distribution piece

13.6a Attach engine support sling to points indicated (arrowed)

13.6b Engine and gearbox assembly lowered onto trolley for removal from underneath the car

bracket. Remove the bolts, together with the link washers, and detach the shaft, but do not let it hang freely; support it by suspending with a suitable length of wire. The right-hand intermediate shaft can be left in position during removal of the engine/transmission.

4 Disconnect the inner end of the left-hand driveshaft by unscrewing and removing the socket-head bolts and three link washers. Suspend the driveshaft with wire. Note that there is no need to disconnect the steering track-rod balljoint and lower suspension arm pivot or tie-rod to enable the engine/transmission to be removed and refitted.

5 Remove the intermediate shaft once the engine/transmission is removed, to allow for their subsequent separation.

6 Support and lower the engine/transmission **(see illustrations)**.

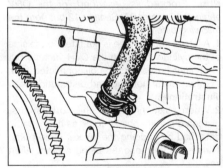

14.12 Crankcase ventilation hose attachment

14 Engine - dismantling

1 The need for dismantling will have been dictated by wear or noise in most cases. Although there is no reason why only partial dismantling cannot be carried out to renew such items as the oil pump or crankshaft rear oil seal, when the main bearings or big-end bearings have been knocking, and especially if the vehicle has covered a high mileage, it is recommended that a complete strip-down be carried out and every engine component examined.

2 Unbolt and remove the engine bearer and mountings. Position the engine so that it is upright and safely chocked on a bench or other convenient working surface. If the exterior of the engine is very dirty it should be cleaned before dismantling, using paraffin and a stiff brush or a water-soluble solvent.

3 Remove the alternator, the mounting bracket and exhaust heat shield, and the adjuster link.

4 Disconnect the heater hose from the coolant pump.

5 Drain the engine oil and remove the filter.

6 Jam the flywheel starter ring gear to prevent the crankshaft from turning and unscrew the crankshaft pulley bolt. Remove the pulley.

7 Unbolt and remove the timing belt cover.

8 Slacken the two bolts on the timing belt tensioner, lever the tensioner against its spring pressure and tighten the bolts to lock it in position.

9 With the belt now slack, note its running direction and mark the mating belt and sprocket teeth with a spot of quick-drying paint. This is not necessary if the belt is being renewed.

10 Disconnect the spark plug leads and remove the distributor cap complete with HT leads.

11 Unscrew and remove the spark plugs.

12 Disconnect the crankcase ventilation hose from its connector on the crankcase **(see illustration)**.

13 Remove the rocker cover **(see illustration)**.

14 Unscrew the cylinder head bolts in the reverse order to tightening and discard them. New bolts must be used at reassembly.

15 Remove the cylinder head, complete with manifolds.

16 Turn the engine on its side. Do not invert it as sludge in the sump may enter the oilways. Remove the sump bolts, withdraw the sump and peel off the gaskets and sealing strips.

17 Remove the bolts from the clutch pressure plate in a progressive manner until the pressure of the assembly is relieved and then remove the cover, taking care not to allow the driven plate (friction disc) to fall to the floor.

18 Unbolt and remove the flywheel. The bolt holes are offset so it will only fit one way.

19 Remove the engine adapter plate.

20 Unbolt and remove the crankshaft rear oil seal retainer **(see illustration)**.

21 Unbolt and remove the timing belt tensioner and take out the coil spring. (This spring is not used on all models) **(see illustration)**.

22 Unbolt and remove the coolant pump.

23 Remove the belt sprocket from the crankshaft using the hands or, if tight, a two-legged puller. Take off the dished washer.

24 Unbolt the oil pump and pick-up tube and remove them as an assembly.

25 Unscrew and remove the oil pressure switch **(see illustration)**.

26 Turn the crankshaft so that all the pistons are half-way down the bores, and feel if a wear ridge exists at the top of the bores. If so, scrape the ridge away, taking care not to damage the bores.

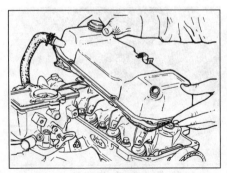

14.13 Lift the rocker cover clear

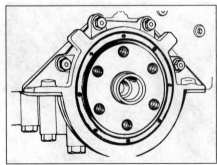

14.20 Crankshaft rear oil seal retainer

14.21 Remove the timing belt tensioner

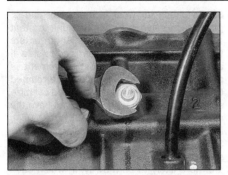

14.25 Unscrew the oil pressure switch

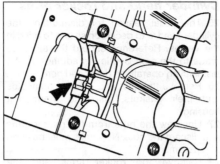

14.34 Crankcase ventilation baffle (arrowed)

27 Inspect the big-end and main bearing caps for markings. The main bearings should be marked 1 to 5 with a directional arrow pointing to the timing cover end. The big-end caps and connecting rods should have adjacent matching numbers. Number 1 is at the timing cover end of the engine. Make your own marks if necessary.

28 Unscrew the bolts from the first big-end cap and remove the cap. The cap is located on two roll pins, so if the cap requires tapping off make sure that it is not tapped in a sideways direction.

29 Retain the bearing shell with the cap if the shell is to be used again.

30 Push the piston/connecting rod out of the top of the cylinder block, again retaining the bearing shell with the rod if the shell is to be used again.

31 Remove the remaining pistons/rods in a similar way.

32 Remove the main bearing caps, keeping the shells with their respective caps if the shells are to be used again. Lift out the crankshaft.

33 Take out the bearing shells from the crankcase, noting the semi-circular thrustwashers on either side of the centre

bearing. Keep the shells identified as to position in the crankcase if they are to be used again.

34 Prise down the spring arms of the crankcase ventilation baffle and remove it from inside the crankcase just below the ventilation hose connection **(see illustration)**.

35 The engine is now completely dismantled and each component should be examined before reassembling.

 15 Engine - examination and renovation

Crankshaft bearings, cylinder bores and pistons

1 Refer to paragraphs 1 to 15 of Section 14, Chapter 2A. The information applies equally to the CVH engine, except that standard sized crankshafts are unmarked and the following differences in the piston rings should be noted.

2 The top rings are coated with molybdenum. Avoid damaging the coating when fitting the rings to the pistons.

3 The lower (oil control) ring must be fitted so that the manufacturer's mark is towards the piston crown, or the groove towards the gudgeon pin. Take care that the rails of the oil control ring abut without overlapping.

Timing sprockets and belt

4 It is very rare for the teeth of the sprockets to wear, but attention should be given to the tensioner idler pulley. It must turn freely and smoothly, be ungrooved and without any shake in its bearing. Otherwise renew it.

5 Always renew the coil spring (if fitted) in the tensioner. If the engine has covered 50 000 miles (80 000 km) then it is recommended that a new belt be fitted, even if the original one appears in good condition.

Flywheel

6 Refer to the information given in Section 14, Chapter 2A.

Oil pump

7 From 1986 onwards the previously used gear type oil pump has been superseded by a new low friction rotor type pump **(see illustrations)**.

8 The examination and renovation procedures are the same for each type of pump.

9 Wear limit tolerances are supplied for both pump types and the clearances can be checked with a feeler blade as follows.

10 Measure the inner-to-outer rotor clearance by inserting the feeler blade between the peak of one of the inner rotor gear teeth or lobes, and the outer rotor.

11 Measure the outer rotor-to-housing clearance by inserting the feeler blade between the outer rotor and the pump body wall.

12 Measure the rotor to cover endfloat by placing a straight edge across the pump body face and inserting a feeler blade between the straight edge and the rotors.

 2B

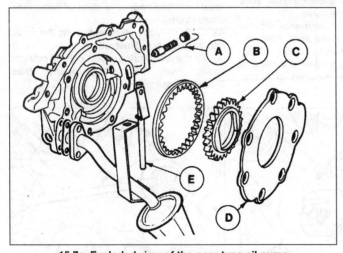

15.7a Exploded view of the gear type oil pump

A Relief valve
B Driven gear
C Drive gear
D Cover plate
E Oil return pipe

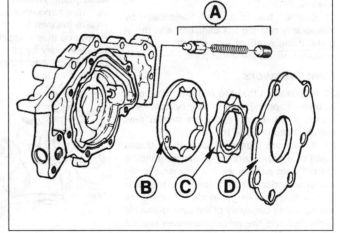

15.7b Exploded view of the rotor type oil pump

A Pressure relief valve
B Outer rotor
C Inner rotor
D Oil pump cover

13 If any of the measured clearances are outside the tolerances given in the Specifications, renew the pump. Note that the rotor type pump can only be fitted to post-1986 engines due to the modified drive slot on the front of the crankshaft.

Oil seals and gaskets

14 Renew the oil seals in the oil pump and in the crankshaft rear oil seal retainer as a matter of routine at time of major overhaul. It is recommended that the new seals should be drawn into these components using a nut and bolt and distance pieces, rather than tapping them into position, to avoid distortion of the light alloy castings.

15 Renew the camshaft oil seal after the camshaft has been installed.

16 Always smear the lips of a new oil seal with grease, and check that the small tensioner spring in the oil seal has not been displaced during installation.

17 Renew all gaskets by purchasing the appropriate engine set, which usually includes the necessary oil seals.

Crankcase

18 Refer to the information given in Section 14, Chapter 2A.

Camshaft and bearings

19 Examine the camshaft gear and lobes for damage or wear. If evident, a new camshaft must be purchased, or one which has been built-up, such as are advertised by firms specialising in exchange components.

20 The bearing internal diameters in the cylinder head should be checked against the Specifications if a suitable gauge is available, otherwise check for movement between the camshaft journal and the bearing. If the bearings are proved to be worn, then a new cylinder head is the only answer as the bearings are machined directly in the cylinder head.

21 Check the camshaft endfloat by temporarily refitting the camshaft and thrust plate. If the endfloat exceeds the specified tolerance, renew the thrust plate.

Cam followers

22 It is seldom that the hydraulic type cam followers (tappets) wear in their cylinder head bores. If the bores are worn then a new cylinder head is called for.

23 If the cam lobe contact surface shows signs of a depression or grooving, grinding out the wear surface will not only remove the hardened surface of the follower but may also reduce its overall length to a point where the self-adjusting capability of the cam follower is exceeded and the valve clearances are not taken up, with consequent noisy operation.

24 The cam follower cannot be dismantled for renewal of individual components. In the event of excessive wear or damage, it should be renewed.

Cylinder head and rocker arms

25 The usual reason for dismantling the cylinder head is to decarbonise and to grind in the valves. Reference should therefore be made to the next Section in addition to the dismantling operations described here.

26 Remove the inlet and exhaust manifolds and their gaskets, also the thermostat housing.

27 Unscrew the nuts from the rocker arms and discard the nuts. New ones must be fitted at reassembly.

28 Remove the rocker arms and the hydraulic cam followers, keeping them in their originally fitted sequence. Keep the rocker guide and spacer plates in order.

29 The camshaft need not be withdrawn but if it is wished to do so, first remove the thrust plate and take the camshaft out from the rear of the cylinder head.

30 The valve springs should now be compressed. A standard type of compressor will normally do the job, but a forked tool (Part No 21-097) can be purchased or made up to engage on the rocker stud using a nut and distance piece to compress it **(see illustration)**.

31 Compress the valve spring and extract the split collets. Do not overcompress the spring, or the valve stem may bend. If it is found when screwing down the compressor tool that the spring retainer does not release from the collets, remove the compressor and place a piece of tubing on the retainer so that it does not impinge on the collets and place a small block of wood under the head of the valve. With the cylinder head resting flat down on the bench, strike the end of the tubing a sharp blow with a hammer. Refit the compressor and compress the spring.

32 Extract the split collets and then gently release the compressor and remove it.

33 Remove the valve spring retainer, the spring and the valve stem oil seal **(see illustration)**. Withdraw the valve.

34 Valve removal should commence with No 1 valve (nearest timing cover end). Keep the valves and their components in their originally installed order by placing them in a piece of card which has holes punched in it and numbered 1 to 8.

35 To check for wear in the valve guides, place each valve in turn in its guide so that approximately one third of its length enters the guide. Rock the valve from side to side. If any more than the slightest movement is possible, the guides will have to be reamed (working from the valve seat end) and oversize stemmed valves fitted. If you do not have the necessary reamer (Tool No 21-071 to 21-074), leave this work to your Ford dealer.

36 Examine the valve seats. Normally the seats do not deteriorate but the valve heads are more likely to burn away, in which case new valves can be ground in. If the seats require recutting, use a standard cutter, available from most accessory or tool stores.

37 Renewal of any valve seat which is cracked or beyond recutting is definitely a job for your dealer or motor engineering works.

38 If the rocker arm studs must be removed for any reason, a special procedure is necessary. Warm the upper ends of the studs with a blow-lamp flame (not a welder) before unscrewing them. Clean out the cylinder head threads with an M10 tap and clean the threads of oil or grease. Discard the old studs and fit new ones, which will be coated with adhesive compound on their threaded portion. Screw in the studs without pausing, otherwise the adhesive will start to set and prevent the stud seating.

39 If the cylinder head mating surface is suspected of being distorted, it can be checked and surface ground by your dealer or motor engineering works. Distortion is possible with this type of light alloy head if the bolt tightening method is not followed exactly, or if severe overheating has taken place.

40 Check the rocker arm contact surfaces for wear. Renew the valve springs if they have been in service for 50 000 miles (80000 km) or more.

41 Commence reassembly of the cylinder head by fitting new valve stem oil seals **(see illustrations)**.

42 Oil No 1 valve stem and insert the valve into its guide **(see illustration)**.

43 Fit the valve spring (closer coils to cylinder head), then the spring retainer **(see illustrations)**.

15.30 Special valve spring compressing tool

15.33 Valve stem oil seal can be prised free

15.41a Using a socket to install a valve stem oil seal

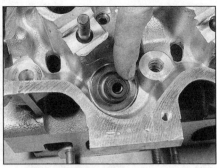
15.41b Valve stem oil seal fitted

15.42 Insert a valve into its guide

15.43a Locate the valve spring . . .

15.43b . . . and the valve spring retainer

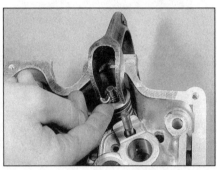
15.44 Compress the spring and insert the split collet

44 Compress the spring and engage the split collets in the cut-out in the valve stem **(see illustration)**. Hold them in position while the compressor is gently released and removed.
45 Repeat the operations on the remaining valves, making sure that each valve is returned to its original guide or, if new valves have been fitted, into the seat into which it was ground.
46 Once all the valves have been fitted, support the ends of the cylinder head on two wooden blocks and strike the end of each valve stem with a plastic or copper-faced hammer, just a light blow to settle the components.
47 Fit the camshaft (if removed) and a new oil seal.
48 Smear the hydraulic cam followers with hypoid type transmission oil and insert them into their original bores **(see illustration)**.

49 Fit the rocker arms with their guides and spacer plates, use new nuts and tighten to the specified torque. It is important that each rocker arm is installed only when its particular cam follower is at its lowest point (in contact with the cam base circle) **(see illustrations)**.
50 Refit the exhaust and inlet manifolds and the thermostat housing, using all new gaskets.

16 Cylinder head and pistons - decarbonising

Refer to the procedure given in Chapter 2A, whilst noting that the cylinder head is of light alloy construction and thus avoiding the use of a rotary (power-driven) wire brush.

15.48 Inserting a hydraulic cam follower

15.49a Fitting a rocker arm spacer plate

15.49b Fit the rocker arm and guide

15.49c Tighten the rocker arm nut

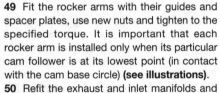
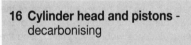

2B

17.1 Crankcase ventilation baffle

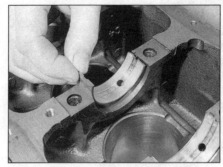

17.2 Main bearing upper shell fitting

17.3 Locate the crankshaft thrustwasher

17.4 Install the crankshaft

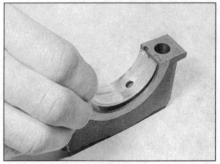

17.5a Fit the bearing shells to the main bearing caps . . .

17.5b . . . then fit the caps . . .

17 Engine - reassembly

1 With everything clean and parts renewed where necessary, commence reassembly by inserting the ventilation baffle into the crankcase. Make sure that the spring arms engage securely **(see illustration)**.
2 Insert the bearing half shells into their seats in the crankcase, making sure that the seats are perfectly clean **(see illustration)**.
3 Stick the semi-circular thrustwashers on either side of the centre bearing with thick grease. Make sure that the oil channels face outwards **(see illustration)**.
4 Oil the bearing shells and carefully lower the crankshaft into position **(see illustration)**.
5 Insert the bearing shells into the main

bearing caps, making sure that their seats are perfectly clean. Oil the bearings and install the caps to their correct numbered location and with the directional arrow pointing towards the timing belt end of the engine **(see illustrations)**.
6 Tighten the main bearing cap bolts to the specified torque.
7 Check the crankshaft endfloat. Ideally a dial gauge should be used, but feeler blades are an alternative if inserted between the face of the thrustwasher and the machined surface of the crankshaft balance web, having first prised the crankshaft in one direction and then the other **(see illustration)**. Provided the thrustwashers at the centre bearing have been renewed, the endfloat should be within specified tolerance. If it is not, oversize thrustwashers are available (see Specifications).

8 The pistons/connecting rods should now be installed. Although new pistons will have been fitted to the rods by your dealer or supplier with the piston crown arrow or cast nipple in the piston oil cut-out pointing towards the timing belt end of the engine, the F mark on the connecting rod or the oil ejection hole in the rod big-end is as shown **(see illustration)**.
9 Oil the cylinder bores and install the pistons/connecting rods.
10 Fit the oil pressure switch and tighten.
11 Before fitting the oil pump, action must be taken to prevent damage to the pump oil seal from the step on the front end of the crankshaft. First remove the Woodruff key and then build up the front end of the crankshaft

17.5c . . . ensuring that they are positioned correctly according to their markings

17.7 Check crankshaft endfloat using a feeler blade

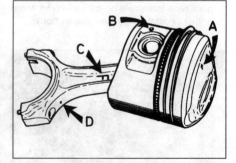

17.8 Piston/connecting rod orientation

A Arrow points towards timing belt end
B Cast nipple position
C Cast F mark on connecting rod
D Oil ejection hole

17.11 Tape the front end of the crankshaft to protect the oil pump seal when fitting

17.13 Oil pump ready for fitting

17.14 Insert the crankshaft Woodruff key

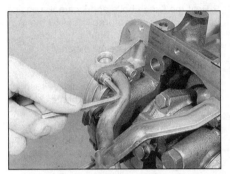

17.15 Fit the oil pump pick-up tube retaining bolts

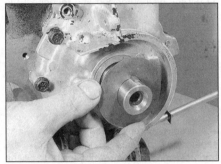

17.16 Locate the thrustwasher . . .

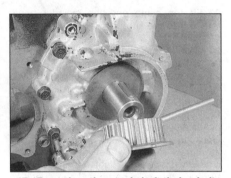

17.17 . . . then the crankshaft timing belt sprocket

2B

17.18 Fit the coolant pump

using adhesive tape to form a smooth inclined surface to permit the pump seal to slide over the step without turning back its lip or displacing the seal spring during installation **(see illustration)**.

12 If the oil pump is new, pour some oil into it before installation in order to prime it and rotate its driving gear a few turns.

13 Align the pump gear flats with those on the crankshaft and install the oil pump, complete with new gasket **(see illustration)**. Tighten the bolts to the specified torque.

14 Remove the adhesive tape and tap the Woodruff key into its groove **(see illustration)**.

15 Bolt the oil pump pick-up tube into position **(see illustration)**.

16 To the front end of the crankshaft, fit the dished thrustwasher (belt guide) so that its concave side is towards the pump **(see illustration)**.

17 Fit the crankshaft belt sprocket. If it is tight, draw it into position using the pulley bolt and a distance piece. Make sure that the belt retaining flange of the sprocket is towards the front of the crankshaft and the nose of the

shaft has been smeared with a little grease before fitting **(see illustration)**.

18 Install the coolant pump using a new gasket **(see illustration)** and tightening the bolts to the specified torque.

19 Fit the timing belt tensioner and its coil spring (where fitted). Lever the tensioner fully against the spring pressure and temporarily tighten the bolts.

20 Using a new gasket, bolt on the rear oil seal retainer, which will have been fitted with a new oil seal and the seal lips greased **(see illustration)**.

21 Engage the engine adapter plate on its locating dowels and then offer up the flywheel. It will only go on in one position as it has offset holes **(see illustrations)**. Insert new bolts and tighten to the specified torque. The bolts are pre-coated with thread sealant.

22 Fit the clutch and centralise it.

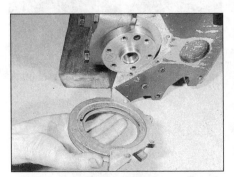

17.20 Locate the crankshaft rear oil seal and retainer

17.21a Locate the engine adapter plate . . .

17.21b . . . followed by the flywheel

17.24a Refit the exhaust manifold . . .

17.24b . . . and hot air ducting

17.24c Engine lift hook is fitted with the inlet manifold

23 Fit the sump and the cylinder head, referring to the appropriate Sections of this Chapter.

24 Refit the manifolds **(see illustrations)**.

25 Install and tension the timing belt.

26 Using a new gasket, fit the rocker cover. Tighten the cover retaining bolts to the specified torque.

27 Reconnect the crankcase ventilation hoses between the rocker cover and the crankcase.

28 Screw in a new set of spark plugs, correctly gapped, and tighten to the specified torque - this is important. If the specified torque is exceeded, the plugs may be impossible to remove.

29 Fit the timing belt cover.

30 Fit the crankshaft pulley (if not done already) and tighten the bolt to the specified torque while the flywheel ring gear is locked to prevent it from turning.

31 Smear the sealing ring of a new oil filter with a little grease, and screw it into position using hand pressure only.

32 Install the engine mounting brackets, if removed **(see illustration)**.

33 Refit the ancillaries. The alternator bracket and alternator, the fuel pump, the thermostat housing and the distributor.

34 Fit the distributor cap and reconnect the HT leads.

35 Check the tightness of the oil drain plug and insert the dipstick.

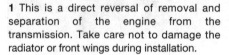

18 Engine/transmission - reconnection and refitting

1 This is a direct reversal of removal and separation of the engine from the transmission. Take care not to damage the radiator or front wings during installation.

Reconnection

2 Check that the clutch driven plate has been centralised and that the pressure plate bolts are tightened to the specified torque (see Chapter 6).

3 Make sure that the engine adapter plate is correctly located on its positioning dowels.

4 Smear the splines of the transmission input shaft with a little grease and then, supporting the weight of the transmission, connect it to the engine by passing the input shaft through the splined hub of the clutch plate until the transmission locates on the dowels.

5 Refit the flange bolts and locate the engine bearer and mounting brackets with the stay rod **(see illustrations)**. Tighten the bolts.

6 Refit the intermediate driveshaft.

Refitting

7 The refitting procedures are similar to those given for the OHV engines in Chapter 2A.

8 Once the engine/transmission is raised and the mountings are secured, the lift sling can be disconnected and the driveshaft reconnected. Insert the driveshaft securing bolts, together with the link washers, and tighten them to their specified torque wrench setting (see Chapter 8).

9 Reconnect the gearchange rod and stabilizer rod, adjusting them as described in Section 17 of Chapter 2A.

10 Once the engine is running, check the timing, idle speed and mixture adjustment.

11 If a number of new internal components have been installed, run the vehicle at a restricted speed for the first few hundred miles to allow time for the new components to bed in. It is also recommended that, with a new or rebuilt engine, the engine oil and filter be changed at the end of the running-in period.

17.32 Engine mounting unit - right-hand rear

18.5a Engine/gearbox bearer mounting bracket and stay rod

18.5b Opposing engine/gearbox mounting bracket

Chapter 3
Cooling, heating and ventilation systems

Contents

Degrees of difficulty

Easy, suitable for novice with little experience	**Fairly easy,** suitable for beginner with some experience	**Fairly difficult,** suitable for competent DIY mechanic	**Difficult,** suitable for experienced DIY mechanic	**Very difficult,** suitable for expert DIY or professional

3

Specifications

System type . . . . Radiator with expansion tank, belt-driven coolant pump and electric radiator fan. Semi-pressurised system on 1.0 and 1.1 litre engines; fully pressurised on 1.3, 1.4 and 1.6 litre engines

Radiator
Type . . . . Crossflow, fin on tube
Pressure cap rating . . . . 0.9 kgf/cm²

Thermostat
Type . . . . Wax
Opening temperature . . . . 85° to 89°C (185° to 192°F)
Fully open temperature . . . . 99° to 102°C (210° to 216°F)

Coolant pump
Type . . . . Centrifugal with vee belt drive (OHV) or driven from toothed timing belt (CVH)
Drivebelt tension . . . . 4.0 mm total deflection at centre of longest run

Torque wrench settings

	Nm	lbf ft
Coolant pump bolts	8	6
Radiator mounting bolts	8	6
Thermostat housing bolts:		
OHV	19	14
CVH	8	6
Coolant pump pulley bolts (OHV)	8	6
Fan shroud-to-radiator bolts	8	6
Fan motor-to-shroud nuts	4	3
Radiator drain plug	1.5	1.1

1 General information and precautions

General information

The cooling system on all models consists of a radiator, a coolant pump, a thermostat and an electrically-operated radiator fan. The system is pressurised and incorporates an overflow container. The system used on the OHV engine differs from that used on the CVH engine in layout and location of components. The coolant pump on the OHV engine is driven by the alternator drivebelt, while the pump on the CVH engines is driven by the toothed timing belt.

The cooling system operates in the following way. When the coolant is cold, the thermostat is shut and coolant flow is restricted to the cylinder block, cylinder head, inlet manifold and the vehicle interior heater matrix. As the temperature of the coolant rises the thermostat opens, allowing initially partial and then full circulation of the coolant through the radiator. If the vehicle is in forward motion then the inrush of air cools the coolant as it passes across the radiator. If the coolant temperature rises beyond a predetermined level, due for example to ascending a gradient or being held up in a traffic jam, then the electric fan will cut in to supplement normal cooling.

The expansion tank is of the degas type and the necessary pressure/vacuum relief valve is incorporated in the tank cap.

Precautions

Warning: Antifreeze mixture is poisonous. Keep it out of reach of children and pets. Wash splashes off skin and clothing with plenty of water. Wash splashes off vehicle paintwork to avoid discolouration.

Antifreeze/water mixture must be renewed at the specified intervals to preserve its anti-corrosive properties. In climates where antifreeze protection is unnecessary, a corrosion inhibitor may be used instead - consult a Ford dealer. Never run the engine for long periods with plain water as coolant. Only use the specified antifreeze as inferior brands may not contain the necessary corrosion inhibitors, or may break down at high temperatures. Antifreeze containing methanol is to be avoided, as the methanol evaporates.

Warning: Take particular care when working under the bonnet with the engine running, or ignition switched on, on vehicles fitted with a temperature-controlled radiator cooling fan. As the coolant temperature rises the fan may suddenly actuate so make sure that ties, clothing, hair and hands are away from the fan. Remember that the coolant temperature will continue to rise for a short time after the engine is switched off.

2 Cooling system - draining, flushing, refilling

Refer to Chapter 1, Section 36.

3 Thermostat - removal, testing and refitting

Removal

1 Drain the cooling system.
2 Loosen the retaining clips and detach the degas and radiator top hoses from the thermostat housing. On the CVH engine, also detach the heater hoses.
3 Disconnect the lead from the thermal switch on the thermostat housing **(see illustration)**.
4 Unscrew and remove the retaining bolts, then lift clear the thermostat housing **(see illustration)**.
5 Prise free and lift out the thermostat, noting its orientation. On the CVH engine, detach the circlip to allow the thermostat to be removed together with its O-ring **(see illustrations)**.

Testing

6 To test the thermostat, first check that in a cold condition its valve plate is closed. Suspend it in a pan of water and gradually heat the water **(see illustration)**. At, or near boiling, the valve plate should be fully open. A more accurate

3.3 Disconnect the fan thermal switch lead - OHV

3.4 Thermostat housing and retaining bolts - CVH

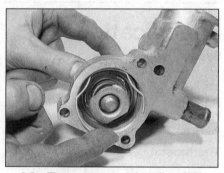

3.5a Thermostat retaining clip - CVH

3.5b Remove the thermostat . . .

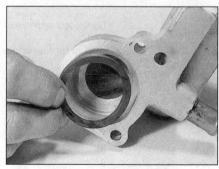

3.5c . . . and seal ring - CVH

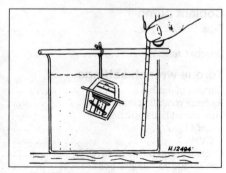

3.6 Thermostat checking method

3.7 Thermostat refitted (CVH) with new hoses and clips

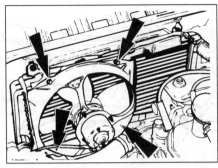

4.2 Radiator fan wiring connector (A) and wire retaining clip (B)

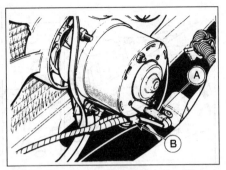

4.3 Radiator fan shroud securing bolts (arrowed)

assessment of the opening and closing points of the thermostat can be made if a thermometer is placed in the water and results compared with the temperatures given in the Specifications. Check that the thermostat closes again as the water cools down.

Refitting

7 Refitting is a reversal of removal. Always use a new gasket and apply a little jointing compound to the threads of the thermostat housing bolts before screwing them in. Use new hoses and clips where necessary **(see illustration)**.

4 Radiator fan - removal and refitting

1 Disconnect the battery.
2 Pull the wiring connector plug from the rear of the fan motor and unclip the wiring from the fan cowl **(see illustration)**.
3 Unscrew the two fan retaining bolts from the base of the cowl, followed by the two upper bolts **(see illustration)**.
4 Carefully lift the fan assembly from the engine compartment, taking care not to damage the radiator.
5 If removing the fan from the motor shaft, first mark their relative fitted positions to ensure correct realignment on assembly.
6 Extract the retaining clip and take off the fan from the motor shaft.
7 Unscrew the three nuts and separate the motor from the shroud.

8 Reassembly and refitting are reversals of the removal and dismantling operations.

5 Radiator - removal, repair and refitting

Removal

1 Drain the cooling system. Retain the coolant if it is fit for further service.
2 Release the retaining clips and disconnect all the hoses from the radiator **(see illustrations)**.
3 Disconnect the wiring plug from the rear of the radiator fan motor.
4 Unscrew and remove the two mounting bolts **(see illustration)** and carefully lift the radiator, complete with cowl and fan, from the engine compartment. The base of the radiator is held in place by lugs.

Repair

5 If the purpose of removal was to thoroughly clean the radiator, first reverse flush it with a cold water hose. The normal coolant flow is from left to right (from the thermostat housing to the radiator) through the matrix and out of the opposite side.
6 If the radiator fins are clogged with dirt, remove it with a soft brush or blow compressed air from the rear of the radiator. It is recommended that the fan assembly is first removed. In the absence of a compressed air line, a strong jet from a water hose may provide an alternative method of cleaning.

7 If the radiator is leaking, it is recommended that a reconditioned or new one is obtained from specialists. In an emergency, minor leaks from the radiator can be cured by using a radiator sealant. If the radiator, due to neglect, requires the application of chemical cleaners, follow the manufacturer's instructions precisely and appreciate that there is an element of risk in the use of most de-scaling products, especially in a system which incorporates alloy and plastic materials.

Refitting

8 Refit the radiator by reversing the removal operations, but make sure that the rubber lug insulators at its base are in position.
9 Refill the system.

6 Coolant pump - removal and refitting

OHV engine

Removal

1 Drain the cooling system.
2 Release the coolant pump pulley bolts now while the drivebelt is still in position. Any tendency for the pulley to turn as the bolts are unscrewed can be restrained by depressing the top run of the belt.
3 Release the alternator mounting and adjuster link bolts, push the alternator in towards the engine and slip the drivebelt from the coolant pump pulley.

3

5.2a Disconnect the radiator top hose . . .

5.2b . . . the bottom hose and expansion tank hose

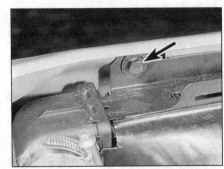

5.4 Radiator left-hand mounting bolt (arrowed)

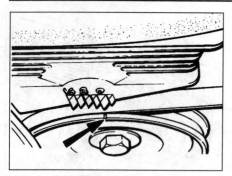

6.12 Timing marks - CVH

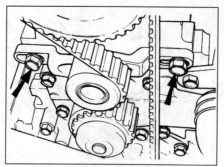

6.16 Slacken the timing belt tensioner bolts (arrowed)

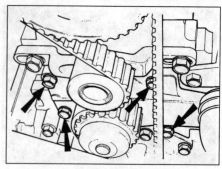

6.19 Coolant pump unit retaining bolts (arrowed)

4 Disconnect the coolant hose from the pump. Remove the previously slackened pulley bolts and take off the pulley.
5 Unbolt the coolant pump and remove it.
6 Peel away the old gasket from the engine block and clean the surface.
7 No provision is made for repair and if the pump is leaking or noisy it should be renewed.

Refitting

8 Refitting is a reversal of removal. Use a new gasket, smeared with jointing compound, and apply the same compound to the threads of the fixing bolts. Tighten the bolts to the specified torque.
9 Adjust the drivebelt tension and refill the cooling system.

CVH engine

Removal

10 Drain the cooling system.
11 Release the alternator mountings and adjuster strap bolt, push the alternator in towards the engine and slip the drivebelt from the pulley.
12 Apply a spanner to the crankshaft pulley bolt and turn the crankshaft until the notch on the pulley is opposite the TDC mark on the belt cover scale **(see illustration)**.
13 Remove the timing belt cover. Note that on engines fitted with the later type two-piece cover, it is not possible to remove the cover lower half unless the crankshaft pulley is removed first. However, if the two lower cover retaining bolts are removed, the cover can be moved away from the engine sufficiently for the pump to be removed and refitted with the cover still in place.
14 Check that the camshaft and the crankshaft sprockets are aligned with their timing marks. This will prove that No 1 piston is at top dead centre, not No 4 piston. If the marks are not aligned, turn the crankshaft through another complete turn.
15 Using a spot of quick-drying paint, mark the teeth of the belt and their notches on the sprockets so that the belt can be re-engaged in its original position in relation to the sprocket teeth.
16 Slacken the belt tensioner bolts **(see illustration)** and slide the tensioner to relieve the tautness of the belt, then slip the belt from

the crankshaft sprocket tensioner pulley and the coolant pump sprocket.
17 Release the clamps and disconnect the hoses from the coolant pump.
18 Remove the timing belt tensioner.
19 Unscrew the four bolts and remove the coolant pump from the engine cylinder block **(see illustration)**.
20 No provision is made for repair and if the pump is leaking or noisy it must be renewed.

Refitting

21 Clean away the old gasket and ensure that the mating surfaces of the pump and block are perfectly clean.
22 Position a new gasket (on the cylinder block) which has been smeared both sides with jointing compound. Offer up the coolant pump, screw in the bolts and tighten to the specified torque.
23 Fit the belt tensioner, but with the mounting bolts only screwed in loosely.
24 Reconnect and tension the timing belt.
25 Refit the timing belt cover.
26 Fit the alternator drivebelt and tension it.
27 Reconnect the coolant hoses to the pump and the bottom hose to the radiator.
28 Fill the cooling system.

---

7 Drivebelt - removal, refitting and tensioning

Refer to Chapter 1, Section 20.

---

8 Expansion tank - removal and refitting

⚠️ *Warning: If the cooling system is hot, release the pressure cap slowly having covered it with a cloth to avoid any possibility of scalding.*

1 Position a suitable container beneath the expansion (degas) tank then loosen the tank hoses and drain the coolant from the tank.
2 Disconnect the overflow pipe from the filler neck on the expansion tank.

3 Unscrew and remove the retaining screw and withdraw the expansion tank.
4 Refit in the reverse order to removal and top-up the cooling system.

---

9 Heater controls - adjustment

1 The heater control cables are adjusted from the control unit.
2 Move the controls to their top and bottom stops to set the adjustment. When moving the controls to the stop positions, a considerable amount of resistance will be felt.

---

10 Heater controls - removal and refitting

Base and L models

1 Disconnect the battery earth lead.
2 From inside the vehicle, remove the dash lower trim panel on each side (left and right). The panels are secured by tags and clips.
3 Remove the retaining screws and withdraw the upper steering column shroud.
4 Withdraw the ashtray from the facia panel.
5 Pull free and remove the heater and ventilation control knobs **(see illustration)**.

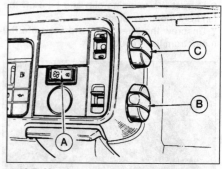

10.5 Heating and ventilation controls - Base and L models

Left-hand drive shown
A Two-stage fan switch
B Temperature control
C Air distribution control

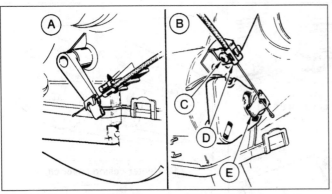

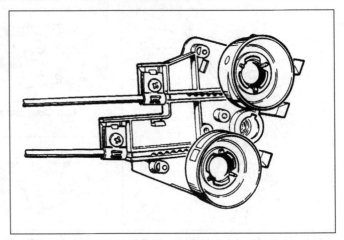

**10.8 Heater control cable connections (to heater casing) -
Base and L models**

A Left side connection
B Right side connection
C Outer cable clamp screw
D Plate nut
E Clip

10.9 Control unit and cable connections - Base and L models

6 Unscrew and remove the two screws from the lower section of the instrument cluster bezel then withdraw the bezel upper section from the guide slots. Lift it clear of the control unit at the side.
7 Detach the switch lead connectors at the rear of the bezel.
8 At the heater casing remove the cable clamp screws and unclip the control cables **(see illustration)**.

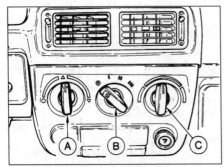

**10.13 Heating and ventilation controls -
Ghia and XR2 models**

A Air distribution control
B Three-stage fan switch
C Temperature control

9 Disconnect the control unit lights, then unscrew and remove the control unit, withdrawing complete with the Bowden cables **(see illustration)**.
10 Refitting is a reversal of the removal procedure. On completion adjust the controls.

Ghia and XR2 models

11 Disconnect the battery earth lead.
12 Working inside the vehicle, remove the dash lower trim panel on each side (left and right). The panels are secured with clips and tags.
13 Pull and withdraw the control knobs from the three rotary switches on the control unit **(see illustration)**.
14 Unscrew and remove the four screws securing the control unit bezel and the control unit screws **(see illustrations)**. Carefully withdraw the control unit from the crash padding.
15 Disconnect the control cables from the heater unit casing by loosening the clamp screws and unclipping the cables.
16 Partially withdraw the control unit (with cables) from under the crash pad so that the fan control switch lead can be detached, then fully remove the control unit.
17 This control unit type can be dismantled by bending back the four securing lugs using

a suitable screwdriver and then removing the cover. To release the Bowden cables, unscrew their clamp screws and disengage the cables from the toothed band guides **(see illustration)**. The pivots and toothed band guides can then be removed from the baseplate of the control unit.
18 Refit in the reverse order to removal and adjust the controls.

**11 Heater blower motor -
removal and refitting**

1 Disconnect the battery earth lead.
2 Undo and remove the six screws securing the bonnet lock mounting plate and then position the plate (and bonnet lock) to one side.
3 Reach through the plate aperture and detach the lead connector from the fan motor, also detach the earth lead.
4 Bend back the two retaining clips and disengage the fan unit.
5 Rotate and remove the fan; pulling it out through the aperture in the cowl panel.

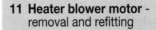

3

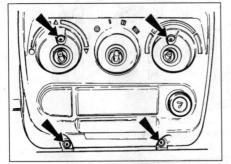

**10.14a Control unit bezel retaining screws
(arrowed) - Ghia and XR2 models**

**10.14b Control unit retaining screws
(arrowed) - Ghia and XR2 models**

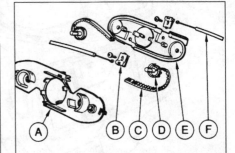

**10.17 Control unit components -
Ghia and XR2 models**

A Cover
B Plate nut
C Toothed belt
D Pivot
E Baseplate
F Cable

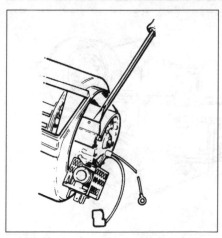

11.6 Heater fan motor retaining clamp

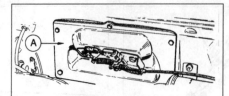

12.6 Cowl panel cover plate (A)

12.7 Fan motor wiring connector (B)

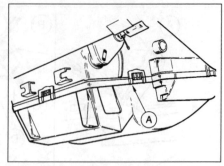

12.10 Heater casing cover clips (A)

6 Disconnect the fan cover then, using a screwdriver, lift the motor securing clamp **(see illustration)** and remove the motor.
7 Refitting is a reversal of the removal procedure.

12 Heater - removal and refitting

Removal

1 Disconnect the battery earth lead.
2 To minimise the coolant loss, move the heater controls to the warm position then drain the engine coolant; saving it for re-use by emptying into a suitable container.
3 Working within the engine compartment, disconnect the coolant hoses from the heater pipe stubs at the rear bulkhead. Raise the ends of the hoses to minimise loss of any remaining coolant in the hoses.
4 The heater matrix will still contain coolant and should be drained by blowing into the

upper heater pipe stub and catching the coolant which will be ejected from the lower one.
5 Remove the cover plate and gasket from around the heater pipe stubs. This is held to the bulkhead by two self-tapping screws.
6 Undo and remove the six screws retaining the cowl panel cover place in position **(see illustration)**. Move the cover plate and bonnet lock to one side, out of the way.
7 Reach through the cover plate aperture and detach the lead connector from the fan motor **(see illustration)**.
8 Working inside the vehicle, remove the dash lower trim panels from both sides. The panels are held in position by clips and tags.
9 Disconnect the control cables from the heater casing and the flap arms.
10 Using a suitable screwdriver, unclip the cover from the heater unit **(see illustration)**, lower the cover, together with the heater matrix and remove rear end from the guide. The heater matrix can now be fully removed, but take care not to spill any remaining coolant over trim and carpets.

11 Disconnect the air distribution ducts from the heater case on the left- and right-hand sides.
12 Undo the two retaining nuts and lower the heater case unit to enable it to be withdrawn sideways from underneath the facia padding. Note that on models fitted with a central console it is first necessary to detach and remove the radial fan and console before the heater can be withdrawn.

Refitting

13 Refitting is a reversal of removal. Check that the heater casing seal to the cowl is in good order, otherwise renew it. Adjust the heater controls on completion.
14 Top-up the cooling system and reconnect the battery.

13 Heater - dismantling and reassembly

1 Use a sharp knife to cut through the casing gaskets in line with the casing half-joint flanges **(see illustration)**.
2 Unclip and separate the half-casings **(see illustration)**.
3 Lift out the electric motor and fan unit.

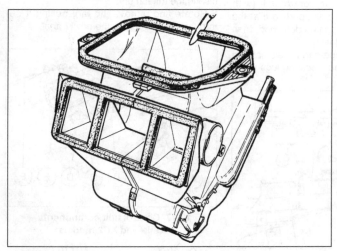

13.1 Cut the heater casing seal gasket

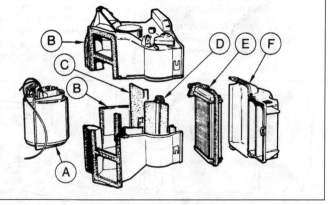

13.2 Heater casing components

A Fan
B Half-casings
C Temperature control valve
D Air distributor valve
E Matrix
F Cover

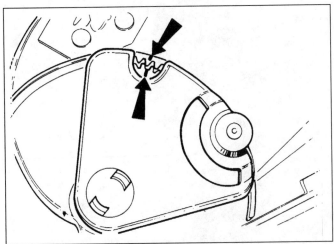

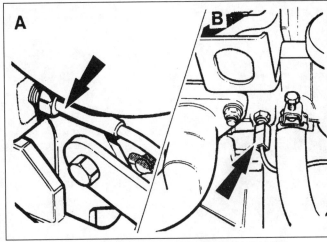

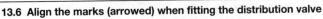

13.6 Align the marks (arrowed) when fitting the distribution valve

14.3 Coolant temperature gauge sender unit location
A OHV engine   B CVH engine

4 If not already removed, unclip the retainers securing the matrix cover, withdraw the cover and lift the matrix from its heater case mounting.
5 The temperature and air distribution control valves can be removed by twisting them and pressing from the casing half.
6 Reassembly is a reversal of the removal procedure. When refitting the air distribution valve, rotate the operating lever so that the window and valve markings align. The valve can only be fitted in this position **(see illustration)**.

14 Coolant temperature gauge sender unit - removal and refitting

1 Should the coolant temperature gauge give incorrect readings (overheating or overcooling indicated, with no apparent accompanying symptoms), then the temperature gauge sender unit may be at fault, and should be renewed as follows.
2 Depressurise the cooling system by removing and refitting the radiator or expansion tank cap, taking precautions against scalding if the engine is still warm.
3 Disconnect the electrical lead, and unscrew

the sender unit from the cylinder head **(see illustration)**. Be prepared for some loss of coolant - this should be negligible.
4 Smear the threads of the new sender unit with sealant, and screw into place. Refit the electrical lead, ensuring that a good metal-to-metal contact is obtained.
5 Top-up the coolant level, and run the engine until normal operating temperature is reached (radiator fan cuts in and out). Check for correct gauge operation and also for leaks from the sender unit. No reading may indicate a poor connection at the sender unit - clean the terminals thoroughly.
6 When the engine has cooled down, top-up the coolant level again if necessary.

3

Chapter 4
Fuel and exhaust systems

Contents

Degrees of difficulty

Easy, suitable for novice with little experience	Fairly easy, suitable for beginner with some experience	Fairly difficult, suitable for competent DIY mechanic	Difficult, suitable for experienced DIY mechanic	Very difficult, suitable for expert DIY or professional

Specifications

System type . . . .   Rear-mounted fuel tank, mechanical fuel pump, thermostatically-controlled air cleaner and Ford or Weber carburettor

Fuel grade requirement
1.0 litre . . . .   91 Octane (2-star)
1.1, 1.3, 1.4 and 1.6 litre . . . .   97 Octane (4-star)
Note: *See Section 1 for information on use of unleaded fuel.*

Fuel pump
Type . . . .   Mechanical diaphragm type, camshaft driven, non-repairable

Air cleaner
Heat sensor rating . . . .   26 to 30°C (79 to 86°F)

Carburettor applications
Ford 1V . . . .   1.0 litre (pre 1986)
Ford VV . . . .   1.1 and 1.3 litre
Weber 2V . . . .   1.6 litre (pre 1987)
Weber 2V DFTM . . . .   1.4 litre
Weber 2V TLD . . . .   1.6 litre (1987-on)
Weber (1V) TLM . . . .   1.0 litre (1986-on)

Ford 1V carburettor

Idle speed	800 rpm
Idle mixture setting (CO level)	1.25%
Fast idle speed (manual choke)	1400 rpm
Float level setting	29 mm
Accelerator pump stroke	2.0 mm
Choke plate pull-down	3.5 mm
Main jet	112

Ford VV carburettor

Idle speed (fan on)	750 to 850 rpm
Idle mixture setting (CO level)	1 to 2%

Weber 2V carburettor

Idle speed	775 to 825 rpm
Idle mixture setting (CO level)	1.0 to 1.50%
Fast idle speed (on high cam)	2675 to 2725 rpm
Float level setting	34.5 to 35.5 mm
Vacuum pull-down	5.2 to 5.8 mm
Choke phasing	1.5 to 2.5 mm
Main jet	115/125
Air jet	160/150
Emulsion tube	F30/F30
Idle jet	50/60

Weber 2V DFTM carburettor

Idle speed (fan running)	750 to 850 rpm
Idle mixture setting (CO level)	1.25 to 1.75%
Float height	7.5 to 8.5 mm
Throttle kicker speed	1250 to 1350 rpm
Choke fast idle	2600 to 2800 rpm
Choke vacuum pull-down	2.7 to 3.2 mm

	Primary	Secondary
Venturi diameter	21 mm	23 mm
Main jet	102	125
Air correction jet	200	165
Emulsion tube	F22	F60
Idle jet	42	60

Weber 2V TLD carburettor

Idle speed (fan running)	750 to 850 rpm
Idle mixture setting (CO level)	1.25 to 1.75%
Float height	30.5 to 31.5 mm
Choke vacuum pull-down	4.0 to 5.0 mm
Choke fast idle	1850 to 1950 rpm

	Primary	Secondary
Venturi diameter	21 mm	23 mm
Main jet	117	127
Emulsion tube	F105	F71
Air correction jet	185	125

Weber (1V) TLM carburettor

Idle speed	775 to 825 rpm
Idle mixture setting (CO level)	1.20 to 1.30%
Float height	29.0 to 31.0 mm
Choke fast idle	3100 to 3300 rpm
Venturi diameter	22
Main jet	112
Air correction jet	220

Torque wrench settings

	Nm	lbf ft
Exhaust manifold flange	35 to 40	26 to 30
Exhaust connecting flange	38 to 45	28 to 33
Carburettor flange nuts:		
Ford	19	14
Weber	20	15
Fuel pump	18	13

1 General information and precautions

General information

The fuel system is composed of four basic components. These are the fuel tank with level indicator, the fuel pump, the carburettor and its controls, and the air cleaner. A basic emission control system is fitted.

The fuel tank is located under the floorpan beneath the rear seats. The filler neck protrudes through the left-hand side of the vehicle, while the combined outlet pipe and fuel level indicator sender unit is located on the right-hand side of the tank. A ventilation or breather pipe is located on the top of the tank.

The fuel pump on all models is a mechanical diaphragm type being driven from the camshaft. On OHV models it is mounted on the side of the cylinder block whilst on CVH models it is mounted on the side of the cylinder head and is actuated by a pushrod. The fuel pumps on both models are fully sealed units and no servicing or repairs are possible.

On all models the air cleaner unit is of the disposable paper element type with an integral thermostatic air inlet control. The thermostatic unit ensures that the air inlet temperature is in accordance with that required, the warm air being drawn from a heat box mounted directly across the exhaust manifold: cool air being drawn through the inlet in the engine compartment. The thermostat within the air cleaner body opens or closes an air control flap valve to regulate the air inlet temperature as required.

Precautions

Fuel

⚠️ **Warning: Many of the procedures given in this Chapter involve the disconnection of fuel pipes and system components which may result in some fuel spillage. Before carrying out any operation on the fuel system, refer to the precautions given in the "Safety first" Section at the beginning of this manual and follow them implicitly. Petrol Is a highly dangerous and volatile substance, and the precautions necessary when handling it cannot be over stressed.**

Use of unleaded fuel

The continuous use of 95 RON unleaded fuel is dependent upon whether the engine is fitted with hardened valve seats. 957 cc and 1117 cc engines built up until the end of January 1986 have "VG" or "CL" stamped on the flywheel end of the cylinder head if they can be run continuously on unleaded fuel. 957 cc and 1117 cc engines built from February

1986 and 1296 cc engines built from October 1985 are all suitable for continuous operation on unleaded fuel. CVH engines built up to the end of 1984 which are suitable for continuous use with unleaded fuel have "LPG" stamped on the cylinder head above No 1 cylinder exhaust port. Later CVH engines are all suitable for continuous operation on unleaded fuel.

Any vehicles which do not come into the foregoing categories may still be run on unleaded fuel, provided that every fourth tankful is of leaded fuel. It is also possible that the ignition timing may need to be retarded to eliminate pinking. For ignition timing values for use with unleaded fuel, see Specifications, Chapter 5.

Tamperproof adjustment screws

Certain adjustment points in the fuel system (and elsewhere) are protected by "tamperproof" caps, plugs or seals. The purpose of such tamperproofing is to discourage adjustment by unqualified operators. In some EEC countries (though not yet in the UK) it is an offence to drive a vehicle with missing or broken tamperproof seals. Before disturbing a tamperproof seal, satisfy yourself that you will not be breaking local or national anti-pollution regulations by doing so. Fit a new seal when adjustment is complete when this is required by law.

Do not break tamperproof seals on a vehicle which is still under warranty.

Work procedures

When working on fuel system components, scrupulous cleanliness must be observed, and care must be taken not to introduce any foreign matter into fuel lines or components. Carburettors in particular are delicate instruments, and care should be taken not to disturb any components unnecessarily. Before attempting work on a carburettor, ensure that the relevant spares are available. Full overhaul procedures for carburettors have not been given in this Chapter, as complete strip-down of a carburettor is unlikely to cure a fault which is not immediately obvious, without introducing new problems. If persistent problems are encountered, it is recommended that the advice of a Ford dealer

3.2 Air cleaner unit underside connections

or carburettor specialist is sought. Most dealers will be able to provide carburettor re-jetting and servicing facilities, and if necessary it should be possible to purchase a reconditioned carburettor of the relevant type.

2 Air cleaner element - renewal

Refer to Chapter 1, Section 31.

3 Air cleaner - removal and refitting

1 Undo and remove the two screws from the centre section of the cover. On 1.0 litre models also undo the support bracket screw.
2 The air cleaner assembly can now be lifted off the carburettor sufficiently far to be able to disconnect the vacuum hose, the crankcase (flame trap) emission hose and the air inlet duct **(see illustration)**.
3 Refit in the reverse order to removal.

4 Fuel pump - testing, removal and refitting

Testing

1 On OHV engines, the fuel pump is mounted on the cylinder block and is actuated by a lever which is in direct contact with an eccentric cam on the camshaft.
2 On CVH engines, the pump is mounted on the cylinder head and is actuated by a pushrod from an eccentric cam on the camshaft.
3 The fuel pump may be quite simply tested by disconnecting the fuel inlet pipe from the carburettor and placing its open end in a container.
4 Disconnect the LT lead from the negative terminal of the ignition coil to prevent the engine firing.
5 Actuate the starter motor. Regular well-defined spurts of fuel should be seen being ejected from the open end of the fuel inlet pipe.
6 Where this is not evident and yet there is fuel in the tank, the pump is in need of renewal. The pump is a sealed unit and cannot be dismantled or repaired.

Removal

7 To remove the pump, disconnect and plug the fuel inlet and outlet hoses at the pump and then unbolt it from the engine **(see illustrations)**.
8 Retain any insulating spacers and remove and discard the flange gaskets.
9 On CVH engines, withdraw the pushrod.

4

Refitting

10 Refitting is a reversal of removal, but use new flange gaskets. If crimped type hose clips were used originally, these will have been destroyed when disconnecting the fuel hoses. Renew them with conventional nut and screw or plastic ratchet type clips.

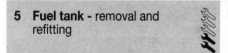

5 Fuel tank - removal and refitting

Removal

1 Disconnect the battery earth lead.
2 Using a length of flexible tubing, syphon as much fuel out of the tank as possible. Ensure adequate ventilation.
3 Jack up the rear of the car and suitably support it for access beneath.
4 Disconnect the flexible hoses from the sender unit.
5 Disconnect the electrical leads from the sender unit **(see illustration)**.
6 While supporting the weight of the tank, unscrew and remove the four retaining nuts with flat washers **(see illustration)**.
7 Remove the tank (and guard, where applicable), leaving the fuel filler pipe in position.
8 If it is necessary to remove the sender unit, this can be unscrewed from the tank using the appropriate Ford tool. Alternatively a suitable C-spanner can probably be used.
9 Taking care not to damage the sealing washer, prise out the tank-to-filler pipe seal.

Refitting

10 Refit the filler pipe seal, using a new seal if there is any doubt about the condition of the old one.
11 Refit the sender unit using a new seal as the original one will almost certainly be damaged.

4.7a Detaching hoses from fuel pump - CVH

12 The remainder of the refitting procedure is the reverse of removal.

6 Fuel tank - cleaning and repair

 Warning: A fuel tank must be repaired professionally. On no account attempt to weld or solder a fuel tank yourself as this will result in an explosion.

1 Remove the fuel tank from the vehicle.
2 If the tank contains sediment or water, it may be cleaned out using two or three rinses with paraffin. Shake vigorously using several changes of paraffin, but before doing so remove the sender unit. Allow the tank to drain thoroughly.
3 If removal of the tank was carried out in order to mend a leak, have it repaired professionally; radiator repairers will usually do this. To remove all trace of vapour requires several hours of steaming out.

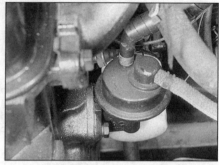

4.7b Fuel pump - OHV

7 Throttle cable - removal, refitting and adjustment

Removal

1 Disconnect the earth lead from the battery.
2 From inside the car, detach and remove the lower dash trim panel on the driver's side.
3 Pull the grommet from the pedal **(see illustration)**, pull the inner cable through and unhook it from the pedal.
4 Using a suitable punch, knock out the bulkhead grommet. This will destroy the grommet, and release the outer cable.
5 Remove the air cleaner to gain access to the carburettor cable connection.
6 Slide the clip from the inner cable end and prise off the cable from the throttle shaft ball **(see illustration)**.
7 Using a suitable screwdriver, carefully prise out the cable retaining clip. Depress the four pegs on the retainer, and pull the retainer from the mounting bracket.

Refitting

8 Refitting is the reverse of this procedure.

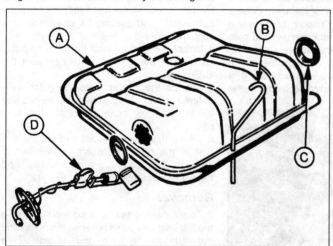

5.5 Fuel tank components

A Tank
B Ventilation hose
C Fuel filler pipe seal
D Sender unit

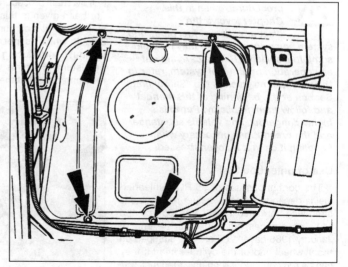

5.6 Fuel tank retaining nuts

Adjustment

9 With the air cleaner removed, jam the pedal in the fully open position using a suitable length of wood against the seat or a heavy weight.

10 Wind back the adjusting sleeve at the carburettor until the carburettor linkage is just in the fully open position **(see illustration)**.

11 Release the pedal, then check to ensure that full throttle can be obtained.

12 Refit the air cleaner.

8 Throttle pedal - removal and refitting

Removal

1 Disconnect the earth lead from the battery.

2 From inside the car, unclip and remove the lower dash trim panel on the driver's side.

3 Pull back the insulation panel and carpet from around the pedal.

4 Pull the grommet from the pedal, pull the inner cable through and unhook it from the pedal.

5 Unscrew and remove the pedal shaft bracket-to-bulkhead retaining bolt **(see illustration)**.

6 On right-hand drive models, unscrew and remove the single retaining nut from under the wheel arch. On left-hand drive models this nut will be found on the engine side of the bulkhead. Remove the pedal.

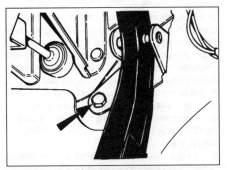

8.5 Pedal unit-to-bulkhead bolt

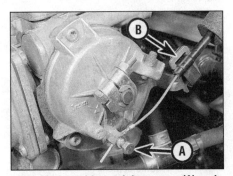

9.3 Choke cable retaining screw (A) and outer cable clip (B)

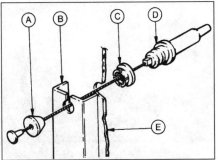

7.3 Throttle cable location at the pedal end

A Inner cable locating grommet
B Pedal shaft
C Outer cable locating grommet
D Outer cable
E Bulkhead

Refitting

7 Refitting is the reverse of this procedure, after which the throttle cable adjustment should be checked.

9 Choke cable (Ford carburettors) - removal, refitting and adjustment

Removal

1 Disconnect the earth lead from the battery.

2 Remove the air cleaner.

3 Undo the screw securing the inner choke cable and carefully prise out the spring clip retaining the outer cable **(see illustration)**.

4 From inside the car, undo the single retaining screw and detach the cable switch mounting shroud **(see illustration)**.

5 Prise free the choke cable control knob retaining clip and withdraw the knob.

6 Extract the retaining bezel and pull the mounting shroud clear. Pull the cable and withdraw it through the engine compartment side of the bulkhead.

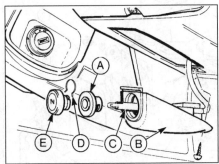

9.4 Choke control knob components

A Bezel   D Clip
B Shroud   E Knob
C Switch lever

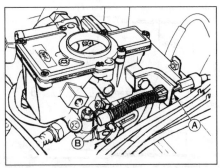

7.6 Throttle cable retaining clip (A) and linkage connection (B) to throttle shaft ball

7.10 Throttle cable adjusting sleeve (arrowed)

Refitting

7 Refit in the reverse order of removal, but adjust as described below according to carburettor type.

Adjustment

Ford 1V carburettor

8 Withdraw the choke knob to provide a clearance of 37 mm between the bezel and the knob **(see illustration)**. If possible, make up a spacer to fit between the knob and bezel to maintain this distance.

9 Working at the carburettor end of the cable, measure and make a mark 22 mm from the end of the inner cable using a pencil or tape.

4

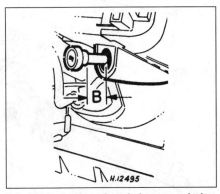

9.8 Choke knob-to-bezel clearance during cable adjustment
B = 37 mm (1.45 in)

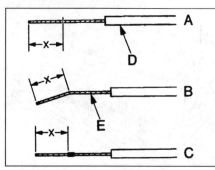

9.9 Choke cable end types

A Plain cable   D Outer cable
B Cable with kink   E Inner cable
C Cable with ferrule X = 22 mm (0.866 in)

Some models have a kink or are fitted with a ferrule at this distance **(see illustration)**.

10 Insert the cable through its location clamp so that the distance mark (kink or ferrule) butts against the inner cable clamp **(see illustration)**. Hold the clamp bolt with a spanner and tighten the retaining screw **(see illustration)**.

11 Firmly pull on the outer cable to position the choke operating lever against the full choke stop (A in photo 9.10b) then secure the outer cable in the retaining clip.

9.10a Locate the ferrule against clamp (arrowed) . . .

12 With the operating lever held against the full choke stop, check that the spacer is still in position between the choke knob and bezel (or distance is as specified in paragraph 8).

13 Remove the spacer and check that the choke fully opens and closes using the choke knob.

Ford VV carburettor

14 Proceed as given in paragraphs 8 to 13 inclusive, but check that a small clearance (1.0 mm) exists between the choke operating lever and the off stop when the lever is released (in the off position).

9.10b . . . and tighten retaining screw. Also shown is the fuel choke stop (A)

10 Carburettors (all types) - dismantling and reassembly

1 A complete strip-down of a carburettor is unlikely to cure a fault which is not immediately obvious without introducing new problems. If persistent carburation problems are encountered, it is recommended that the advice of a Ford dealer or specialist is sought. Most dealers will be able to provide carburettor re-jetting and servicing facilities and if necessary, it should be possible to buy a reconditioned carburettor of the relevant type.

2 If it is decided to go ahead and service a carburettor, check the cost and availability of spare parts before commencement. Obtain a carburettor repair kit, which will contain the necessary gaskets, diaphragms and other renewable items.

3 When working on carburettors, scrupulous cleanliness must be observed and care must be taken not to introduce any foreign matter into components. Carburettors are delicate instruments and care should be taken not to disturb any components unnecessarily.

4 Referring to the relevant exploded view of the carburettor **(see illustrations)**, remove each component part whilst making a note of its fitted position. Make alignment marks on linkages etc.

5 Reassemble the carburettor in the reverse order to dismantling, using new gaskets, O-rings etc. Be careful not to kink any diaphragms.

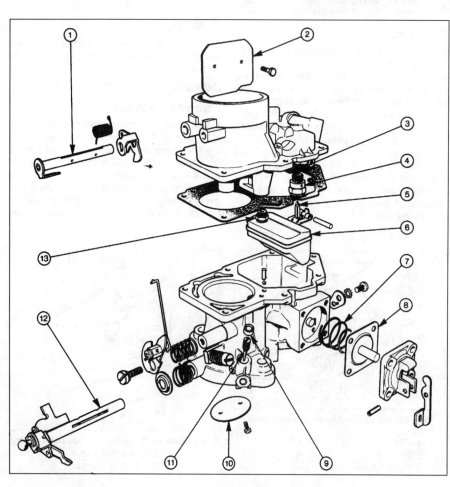

10.4a Ford 1V carburettor components

1 Choke spindle
2 Choke plate
3 Fuel inlet filter
4 Needle valve housing
5 Needle valve
6 Float
7 Pump return spring
8 Accelerator pump diaphragm
9 Tamperproof plug
10 Throttle plate
11 Mixture screw
12 Throttle spindle
13 Main jet

Note: Some carburettors may have an anti-dieseling valve (idle cut-off) fitted

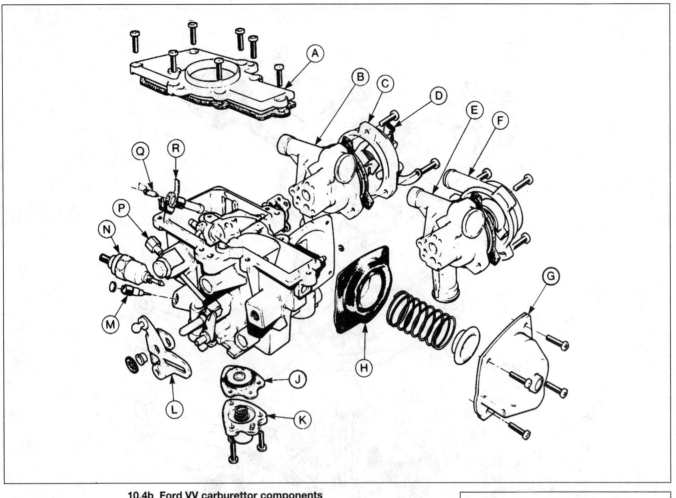

10.4b Ford VV carburettor components

A Top cover
B Manual choke
C Lever housing
D Choke cable bracket
E Auto-choke*
F Bi-metal housing*
G Control diaphragm cover
H Control diaphragm
J Accelerator pump diaphragm

K Accelerator pump cover
L Progressive throttle cam
M Mixture screw
N Anti-dieseling valve
P Idle speed screw
Q Needle valve
R Float bracket
* Certain overseas models only (manual choke
for UK models)

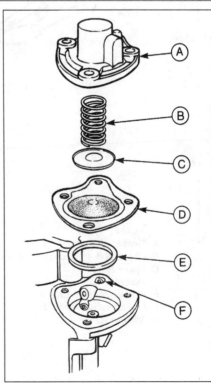

**10.4c Ford VV carburettor -
modified accelerator pump**

A Pump cover   D Diaphragm
B Spring   E Spacer
C Metal plate   F Vacuum passage

4

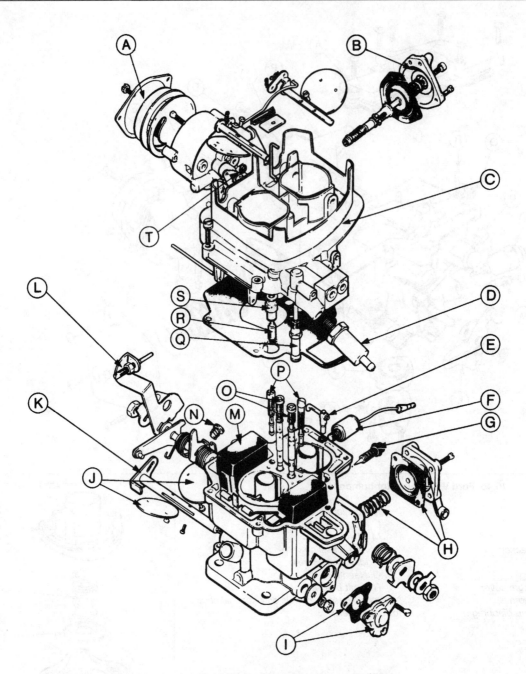

10.4d Weber 2V carburettor components

A Electric choke housing
B Choke pull-down diaphragm unit
C Upper body
D Inlet filter
E Accelerator discharge tube
F Anti-dieseling solenoid
G Mixture screw

H Accelerator pump unit
I Power valve diaphragm unit
J Throttle plates
K Secondary throttle spindle
L Fast idle adjuster
M Float
N Idle speed adjusting screw

O Combined emulsion tube, air
  correction and main jets
P Idle jets
Q Fuel return correction
R Needle valve
S Needle valve housing
T Rubber seal

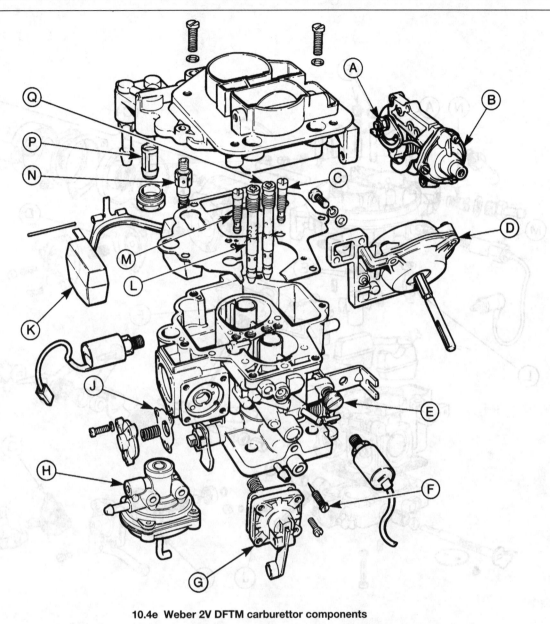

10.4e Weber 2V DFTM carburettor components

A Manual choke unit
B Choke vacuum pull-down
C Secondary idle jet
D Secondary venturi vacuum unit
E Idle speed adjustment screw

F Idle mixture adjustment screw
G Accelerator pump assembly
H Throttle kicker
J Power valve diaphragm
K Float

L Primary emulsion tube
M Primary idle jet
N Needle valve
P Fuel inlet filter
Q Secondary emulsion tube

4

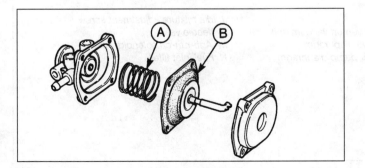

**10.4f Weber 2V DFTM carburettor -
throttle kicker assembly**
A Return spring
B Diaphragm

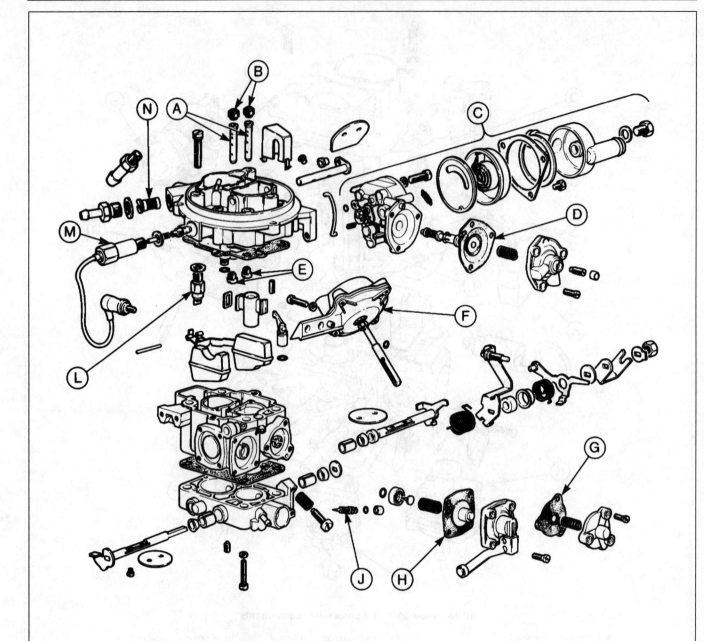

10.4g Weber 2V TLD carburettor components

A Emulsion tubes
B Air correction jets
C Automatic choke assembly
D Choke vacuum pull-down diaphragm

E Main jets
F Secondary venturi vacuum unit
G Power valve diaphragm
H Accelerator pump diaphragm

J Idle mixture adjustment screw
L Needle valve
M Anti-run-on solenoid valve
N Fuel inlet filter

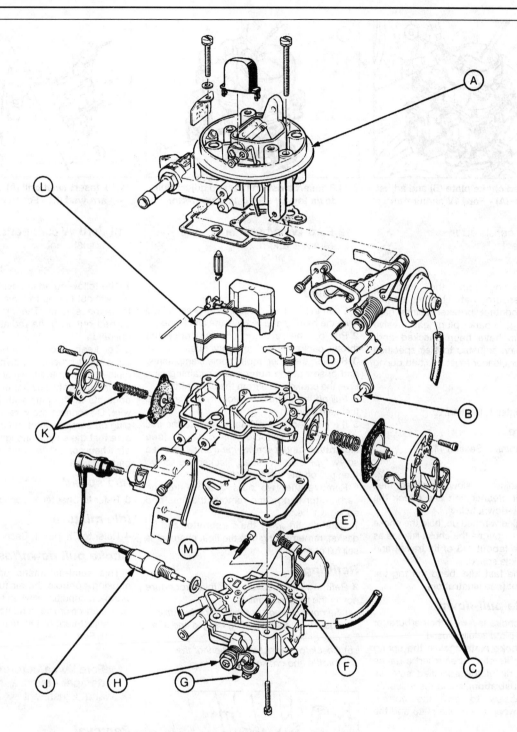

10.4h Weber (1V) TLM carburettor components

A Upper body (top cover)
B Choke mechanism
C Accelerator pump
D Accelerator pump discharge tube

E Idle speed screw
F Throttle valve block
G Fast idle speed screw
H Throttle valve plate spindle

J Anti-run-on solenoid valve
K Power valve assembly
L Float
M Mixture screw

4

11.6 Hold open choke plate (B) and adjust fast idle tag (A) - Ford 1V carburettor

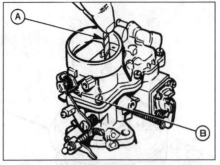

11.8 Insert twist drill (A) and adjust pull down tag (B) - Ford 1V carburettor

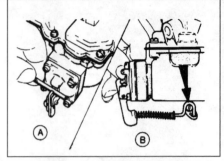

11.10 Insert twist drill (A) and bend U-link - arrowed (B) - Ford 1V carburettor

11 Ford 1V carburettor - adjustment

1 Before carrying out the following adjustments ensure that all other engine variables ie. contact breaker points gap, ignition timing, spark plug gap, valve clearances etc, have been checked and, where necessary, adjusted to their specified settings. The air cleaner must be fitted during adjustments.

Idle speed

2 Refer to Chapter 1, Section 10.

Idle mixture

3 Refer to Chapter 1, Section 11.

Fast idle

4 Check and adjust the slow idle speed, then remove the air cleaner unit and check the choke plate pull-down, below.
5 With the engine warmed up, hold the choke plate fully open, operate the choke linkage as far as possible (about 1/3 of its travel) and check the fast idle speed.
6 To adjust the fast idle, bend the tag the required amount **(see illustration)**.

Choke plate pull-down

7 Rotate the choke lever on the carburettor until the choke plate is fully closed.
8 Open the choke plate against the spring pressure up to its stop, then insert a gauge rod or twist drill of the specified size, as shown **(see illustration)**. Bend the adjusting tag as necessary to give the correct dimension between the choke plate and the carburettor.

Accelerator pump stroke

9 Unscrew the throttle speed screw until it clears the linkage.
10 Depress the accelerator pump diaphragm plunger fully and then check the clearance between the end of the plunger and the operating lever **(see illustration)** using a gauge rod or twist drill of the specified skew.
11 If necessary, bend the operating rod at the U-bend to give the correct clearance. Reset the idle speed.

12 Ford 1V carburettor - removal and refitting

Removal

1 Open the bonnet, disconnect the earth lead from the battery and remove the air cleaner.
2 Pull off the retaining clip and prise the throttle cable off the throttle lever ball.
3 Slacken the inner choke cable clamp screw and prise out the outer cable retaining clip. Free the choke cable from the carburettor.
4 Pull off the distributor vacuum pipe and the fuel vent pipe.
5 If a crimped type clamp is fitted to the fuel inlet pipe, it should be cut off **(see illustration)** and a screw type clamp fitted. If a screw type clamp is fitted, slacken the screw, then pull off the fuel feed pipe.
6 Remove the two nuts that secure the carburettor flange and remove the nuts and spring washers.
7 Carefully lift away the carburettor and its gasket, remembering that the float chamber is still full of petrol.

Refitting

8 Refitting is the reverse of this procedure noting the following points:
a) Remove all traces of the old carburettor gasket, clean the mating flanges and fit a new gasket.
b) Check for correct adjustment of the throttle and choke cables.

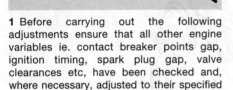

12.5 Cutting off a crimped type fuel hose clip

13 Ford VV carburettor - adjustment

1 The following adjustments can be carried out without having to remove the carburettor from the engine. The procedure must be carried out with the radiator cooling fan in operation.
2 To keep the fan running during the adjustment procedure, disconnect the wiring multi-plug from the thermal switch (located in the thermostat housing) and bridge the two contacts in the plug with a short length of wire. Disconnect the wire and refit the multi-plug on completion of the adjustments. Make sure that the engine and ignition are switched off when connecting and disconnecting the bridging wire.

Idle speed

3 Refer to Chapter 1, Section 10.

Idle mixture

4 Refer to Chapter 1, Section 11.

Choke pull down/fast idle

5 This semi-automatic unit in the choke housing controls the air fuel mixture under warm-up conditions, when the engine is under light load or cruise conditions. The checking and adjustment of this unit is best entrusted to your Ford dealer.

14 Ford VV carburettor throttle damper - removal, refitting and adjustment

Removal

1 Certain later models are fitted with a throttle damper mounted on a bracket on the side of the carburettor to allow progressive closure of the throttle linkage **(see illustration)**.
2 To remove the damper, remove the air cleaner, slacken the locknut and remove the damper from its bracket.

Refitting

3 Refit the damper by screwing it into place in the bracket, then adjust the unit as follows.

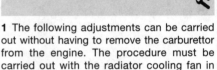

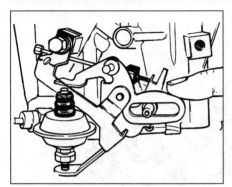

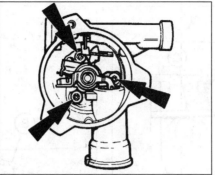

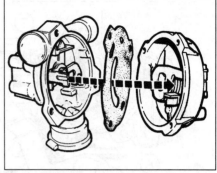

14.1 Throttle damper arrangement -
later model Ford VV carburettor

15.4 Choke unit retaining screws -
Ford VV carburettor

15.6 Choke lever housing fitting details -
Ford VV carburettor

Adjustment

4 Refer to Chapter 1, Section 16.

15 Ford VV carburettor manual choke unit - removal and refitting

Removal

1 Disconnect the battery negative lead.
2 Remove the air cleaner.
3 Remove the retaining clip, slacken the clamp bolt and disconnect the choke cable from the linkage and support bracket.
4 Using a Torx type key or socket bit, undo the three screws and detach the lever housing from the choke unit (see illustration).
5 Undo the three Torx screws and detach the choke unit from the carburettor.

Refitting

6 Refitting is the reverse sequence to removal, but use new gaskets between the choke unit and carburettor, and between the lever housing and choke unit. Ensure that the latter is positioned as shown (see illustration) and make sure that the spring-loaded arm in the lever housing locates over the linkage in the choke unit.
7 Reconnect the choke cable and refit the air cleaner, then reconnect the battery.

16 Ford VV carburettor - removal and refitting

Removal

1 Remove the air cleaner.
2 Disconnect the choke cable from the operating lever on the choke housing.
3 Pull off the electrical lead from the anti-run-on valve on the carburettor.
4 Disconnect the distributor vacuum pipe.
5 Disconnect the throttle cable by pulling the spring clip to release the end fitting from the ball-stud and then unscrewing the cable bracket fixing bolt.
6 Disconnect and plug the fuel inlet hose from the carburettor. If crimped type hose clips are used, cut them off and fit screw type clips at reassembly.
7 Unscrew the two carburettor mounting flange nuts and lift the carburettor from the inlet manifold. Remove the idle speed screw if necessary for access to the nut.

Refitting

8 Refitting is a reversal of removal, but make sure that a new flange gasket is used on perfectly clean mating surfaces.
9 Reconnect and adjust the choke cable.

17 Weber 2V carburettor - adjustment

Idle speed/mixture

1 Refer to Chapter 1, Sections 10 and 11 according to model.

Fast idle

2 Open the bonnet and remove the air cleaner.
3 Run the engine until the normal running temperature is reached. Hold the throttle partly open, then close the choke plates by hand and release the throttle (see illustration).
4 The throttle mechanism will hold the choke mechanism at the fast idle position. Release the choke plates, which should return to the open position.
5 If the choke plates do not fully open, then either the engine has not fully warmed up, or the electric choke is faulty.
6 Without touching the throttle, start the engine and check the fast idle speed against the figure given in the Specifications.
7 To adjust the fast idle speed, slacken the locknut and screw the adjuster (see illustration) in or out as required.
8 Tighten the locknut and refit the air cleaner.

4

17.3 Choke pull-down/fast idle setting - Weber 2V carburettor
A Hold choke plate shut   B Hold throttle partly open

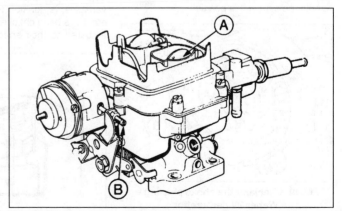

17.7 Fast idle adjustment showing choke plates open (A) and fast
idle adjustment screw (B) - Weber 2V carburettor

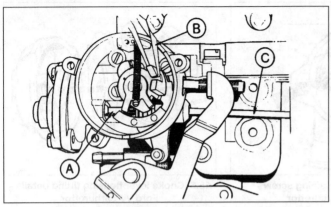

17.11 Hold choke open with a rubber band (B) and push the diaphragm rod (A) with a small screwdriver (C) - Weber 2V carburettor

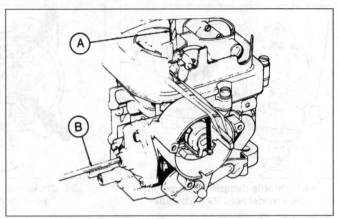

17.12 Insert a twist drill (A) and adjust pull-down (B) - Weber 2V carburettor

Vacuum pull-down

9 With the air cleaner removed, pull the wire off the electric choke.
10 Remove the three retaining screws and lift off the automatic choke outer housing with the bi-metallic spring. Lift off the internal heat shield.
11 Fit an elastic band to the choke plate lever, and position it to hold the choke plates closed **(see illustration)**. Open the throttle to allow the choke plates to close fully.
12 Using a suitable screwdriver, push the choke diaphragm open, then measure the clearance between the choke plate and the carburettor body, using a gauge rod or twist drill of the specified size **(see illustration)**.
13 To adjust the opening, remove the plug and screw the adjusting screw in or out as required.
14 Adjust the choke phasing, as shown below.
15 Refit the heat shield and the choke housing. Reconnect the electric choke wire and the air cleaner.

Choke phasing

16 Adjust the vacuum pull-down as shown above.
17 Hold the throttle partly open, and position the fast idle adjusting screw on the centre step of the fast idle cam. Release the throttle to hold the cam in this position.

18 Push the choke plates down until the cam jams against the fast idle screw **(see illustration)**.
19 Measure the clearance between the choke plate and the carburettor body, using a gauge rod or twist drill of the specified size.
20 Bend the tag **(see illustration)** as required, to give the correct clearance.
21 Refit the heat shield and the choke housing. Reconnect the electric choke wire and the air cleaner.

18 Weber 2V carburettor - removal and refitting

The procedure is very similar to that described for the Ford 1V carburettor, except that the manual choke cable is replaced by an electric choke wire and four nuts are used to secure the unit to the manifold.

19 Weber 2V DFTM carburettor - adjustment

1 Before carrying out the following adjustments ensure that all other engine variables, ie, ignition timing, spark plug gap, etc, have been checked and where necessary adjusted to their specified settings. The air

cleaner must be fitted, the engine must be at normal operating temperature and the radiator cooling fan must be running.
2 To keep the fan running during the adjustment procedure, disconnect the wiring multi-plug from the thermal switch (located in the thermostat housing) and bridge the two contacts in the plug with a short length of wire.

Idle speed

3 Refer to Chapter 1, Section 10.

Idle mixture

4 Refer to Chapter 1, Section 11.

Fast idle

5 Adjust the engine idle speed and mixture settings, then switch off the engine. Leave the tachometer connected from the previous operation.
6 Undo the four bolts securing the air cleaner to the carburettor, disconnect the hot and cold air inlet hoses and lift off the air cleaner. Position the air cleaner clear of the carburettor, but leave the crankcase breather hoses and the vacuum supply hose connected.
7 Pull the choke knob fully out and start the engine.
8 Using a finger on the linkage lever as shown **(see illustration)**, hold the choke plate open and note the fast idle speed.

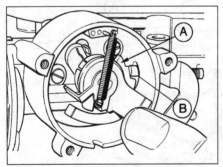

17.18 Checking the choke phasing - Weber 2V carburettor

A Fast idle cam
B Fast idle adjuster screw

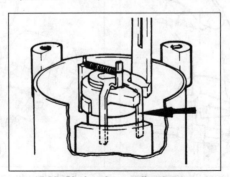

17.20 Choke phase adjusting tag (arrowed) - Weber 2V carburettor

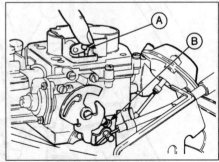

19.8 Fast idle speed adjustment - Weber 2V DFTM carburettor

A Choke valve plate held open
B Fast idle adjustment screw

9 If adjustment is necessary turn the fast idle adjusting screw until the specified speed is obtained.

10 On completion refit the air cleaner and disconnect the tachometer.

Throttle kicker

11 Remove the air cleaner. Plug the vacuum supply from the manifold.

12 Have the engine at normal operating temperature with a tachometer connected in accordance with the manufacturer's instructions.

13 With the engine running and the idle speed and mixture correctly adjusted, manually operate the throttle kicker by lifting the operating lever upwards. Note the increase in engine speed.

14 If the increased speed is outside the figure given in the Specifications, remove the tamperproof plug from the top of the kicker body and adjust the unit to give the specified speed.

15 Remove the tachometer and refit the air cleaner on completion.

20 Weber 2V DFTM carburettor - removal and refitting

Removal

1 Disconnect the battery negative lead.

2 Remove the air cleaner.

3 Disconnect the electrical leads at the solenoids **(see illustrations)**.

20.3a Electrical connections - Weber 2V DFTM carburettor

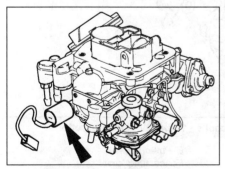

20.3b Back bleed solenoid - Weber 2V DFTM carburettor

4 Disconnect the vacuum pipe at the carburettor outlet.

5 Disconnect the throttle cable by releasing the spring clip securing the end fitting to the ball-stud on the linkage, and then unscrewing the cable bracket fixing bolts.

6 Release the choke cable from the linkage lever and move the bracket, with both cables attached, to one side.

7 Disconnect the fuel inlet and return hoses, noting their respective positions, and plug them after removal. If crimped type clips are used, cut them off and use new screw type clips when refitting.

8 Undo the four mounting flange nuts and washers and withdraw the carburettor from the manifold.

Refitting

9 Refitting is the reversal of removal, but use a new flange gasket and ensure that the mating surfaces are perfectly clean. Reconnect the choke and throttle cables and refit the air cleaner, then adjust the idle speed and mixture settings.

21 Weber 2V TLD carburettor - adjustment

1 Before carrying out the following adjustments ensure that all other engine variables, ie, ignition timing, spark plug gap, etc, have been checked and where necessary adjusted to their specified settings. The air cleaner must be fitted, the engine must be at normal operating temperature and the radiator cooling fan must be running.

2 To keep the fan running during the adjustment procedure, disconnect the wiring multi-plug from the thermal switch (located in the thermostat housing) and bridge the two contacts in the plug with a short length of wire.

Idle speed

3 Refer to Chapter 1, Section 10.

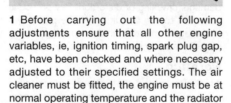

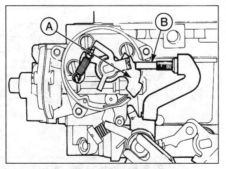

21.7 Fast idle speed adjustment - Weber 2V TLD carburettor

A Fast idle cam
B Fast idle adjusting screw positioned on third step of cam

Idle mixture

4 Refer to Chapter 1, Section 11.

Fast idle

5 Remove the air cleaner.

6 Have the engine at normal operating temperature with a tachometer connected in accordance with the manufacturer's instructions.

7 With the engine stopped, open the throttle linkage slightly by hand and close the choke plate until the fast idle adjusting screw lines up with the third (middle) step of the fast idle cam **(see illustration)**. Release the throttle so that the fast idle screw rests on the cam. Release the choke plate.

8 Without touching the throttle pedal, start the engine by just turning the key.

9 Note the fast idle speed and if adjustment is necessary, turn the fast idle adjusting screw until the specified speed is obtained.

10 On completion refit the air cleaner and disconnect the tachometer.

Automatic choke unit

11 Remove the air cleaner.

12 Release any pressure in the cooling system by loosening the pressure cap on the expansion tank (protect the hands using a cloth if the engine is hot), then disconnect the water inlet and outlet hoses at the automatic choke unit. Clamp the hoses or position them with their ends facing upwards to minimise coolant leakage.

13 Undo the three screws and detach the choke bi-metal coil housing, followed by the internal heat shield.

14 Fit a rubber band to the choke plate lever, open the throttle to allow the choke plate to close, and then secure the band to keep the plate closed.

15 Using a screwdriver, push the diaphragm open to its stop and measure the clearance between the lower edge of the choke plate and the air horn, using a twist drill or other gauge rod **(see illustration)**. Where the clearance is outside that specified, remove the tamperproof plug from the diaphragm housing and turn the screw, now exposed, in or out as necessary.

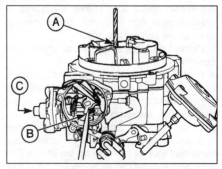

21.15 Choke vacuum pull-down adjustment - Weber 2V TLD carburettor

A Twist drill
B Diaphragm held fully open
C Adjusting screw

4

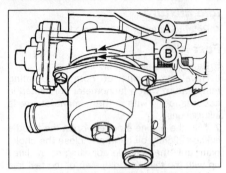

21.19 Bi-metal coil housing and choke body alignment marks - Weber 2V TLD carburettor

A *Dot punch mark*
B *Choke alignment mark on housing*

16 Fit a new diaphragm housing tamperproof plug and remove the rubber band.
17 Refit the heat shield, making sure that the locating peg is correctly engaged in the notch in the housing.
18 Place the bi-metal coil housing in position, with the coil engaged with the slot in the choke lever which projects through the cut-out in the heat shield.
19 Screw in the retaining screws finger tight, and then rotate the housing to set the housing mark opposite the dot punch mark on the choke body **(see illustration)**. Secure the housing.
20 Reconnect the hoses and refit the air cleaner.
21 Check and if necessary top-up the cooling system.

22 Weber 2V TLD carburettor automatic choke unit - removal and refitting

Removal

1 Remove the air cleaner.
2 Release any pressure in the cooling system by loosening the pressure cap, then detach the water inlet and outlet hoses at the automatic choke unit. Clamp the hoses or position them with their ends facing upwards to minimise coolant leakage.
3 Disconnect the lead at the anti-run-on valve solenoid.
4 Disconnect the fuel supply and return hoses at the carburettor. If crimped type hose clips are used, cut them off and use screw type clips at reassembly.
5 Undo the six carburettor upper body retaining screws and remove the upper body. Note that four of the screws are of the Torx type and a suitable key or socket bit will be needed for their removal.
6 With the upper body removed, undo the three screws and remove the choke bi-metal coil housing followed by the internal heat shield **(see illustration)**.

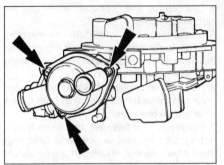

22.6 Choke bi-metal coil housing retaining screws - Weber 2V TLD carburettor

7 Undo the three screws securing the choke housing to the upper body **(see illustration)**, disconnect the link rod and remove the choke housing.
8 Undo the three screws and remove the vacuum pull-down housing cover, then withdraw the spring, diaphragm and operating rod assembly.
9 Make a note of the exact position of the choke mechanism return and tension springs, then undo the nut and remove the connecting rod, levers and link from the choke housing **(see illustration)**.
10 Clean and inspect all the parts for wear, damage, cracking or distortion. Pay particular attention to the condition of the pull-down diaphragm and the choke housing O-ring seal. Renew any parts as necessary.

Refitting

11 Reassemble the choke mechanism connecting rod, levers, link and springs. Secure the assembly with the retaining nut.
12 Locate the vacuum pull-down diaphragm and operating rod in the choke housing and with the diaphragm lying flat on the housing face, refit the cover and secure with the three screws.

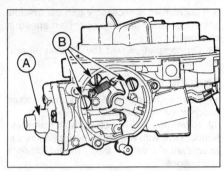

22.7 Vacuum pull-down housing (A) and choke housing retaining screws (B) - Weber 2V TLD carburettor

13 Locate the O-ring seal on the choke housing, then connect the housing to the link rod.
14 Position the housing on the carburettor upper body and secure with the three screws.
15 Refit the upper body to the carburettor.
16 Before refitting the bi-metal coil housing, adjust the vacuum pull-down (see unit adjustment), then fit the coil housing.

23 Weber 2V TLD carburettor - removal and refitting

Removal

1 Disconnect the battery negative lead.
2 Remove the air cleaner.
3 If the engine is still hot, depressurise the cooling system by carefully releasing the pressure cap.
4 Disconnect the coolant inlet and outlet hoses at the automatic choke and clamp or plug their ends to prevent coolant loss.
5 Disconnect the throttle cable by releasing the spring clip securing the end fitting to the ball-stud, then unscrewing the cable bracket fixing bolts.

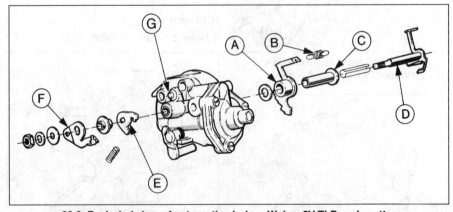

22.9 Exploded view of automatic choke - Weber 2V TLD carburettor

A *Operating link*
B *Fast idle cam return spring*
C *Spindle sleeve*
D *Connecting rod and lever*
E *Pull-down link*
F *Actuating lever*
G *O-ring seal*

6 Disconnect the fuel inlet and return hoses, noting their respective positions, and plug them after removal. If crimped type clips are used, cut them off and use screw type clips when refitting.

7 Disconnect the fuel inlet and return hoses.

8 Disconnect the electrical lead at the anti-run-on valve solenoid.

9 Using a suitable Torx type key or socket bit, unscrew the four mounting through-bolts from the top of the carburettor and remove the unit from the manifold (see illustration).

Refitting

10 Refitting is the reverse sequence to removal but use a new flange gasket and ensure that the mating faces are perfectly clean. On completion, top-up the cooling system and check the idle speed and mixture settings.

24 Weber (1V) TLM carburettor - adjustment

Idle speed

1 Refer to Chapter 1, Section 10.

Idle mixture

2 Refer to Chapter 1, Section 11.

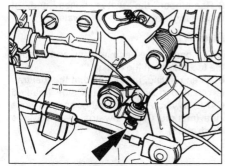

24.4 Fast idle adjustment screw - Weber (1V) TLM carburettor

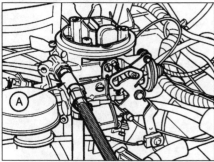

25.4 Fuel supply and return hose arrangement with calibrated T-piece - Weber (1V) TLM carburettor
A Fuel supply hose

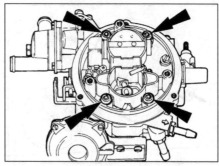

23.9 Carburettor mounting through-bolts - Weber 2V TLD carburettor

Fast idle

3 Have the engine at normal operating temperature with a reliable tachometer connected in accordance with the manufacturer's instructions, and the air cleaner removed.

4 Hold the choke valve plate fully open with the fingers, and then operate the choke lever on the carburettor. If the engine fast idle speed is not as specified, turn the fast idle screw (see illustration). This will be sealed with liquid sealant, and the screw should be locked in a similar manner on completion of adjustment.

25 Weber (1V) TLM carburettor - removal and refitting

Removal

1 Disconnect the battery negative lead.
2 Remove the air cleaner.

3 Release the cooling system pressure cap and then disconnect the coolant hoses from the carburettor. Tie the ends of the hoses up as high as they will go to avoid loss of coolant.

4 Disconnect and plug the fuel hose (see illustration).

5 Disconnect the electrical lead from the fuel cut-off solenoid valve.

6 Disconnect the vacuum and vent hoses from the carburettor.

7 Disconnect the throttle and choke operating cables.

8 Remove the four screws (two Torx type) and lift the carburettor from the inlet manifold.

Refitting

9 When refitting the carburettor, use a new flange gasket and adjust the choke cable to the correct setting.

26 Exhaust and inlet manifolds - removal and refitting

Refer to Chapter 2 for removal and refitting of the manifolds.

27 Exhaust system - renewal and repair

Renewal

1 The exhaust system fitted to all models is of two-piece construction but there are three different system types fitted, according to model type (see illustration).

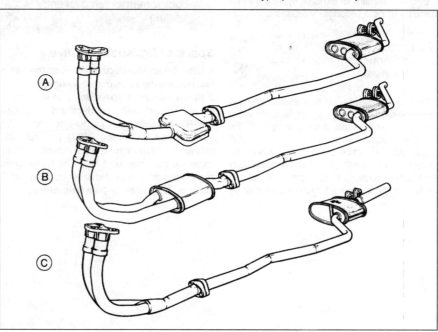

27.1 Exhaust systems
A OHV models   B CVH models   C XR2 models

4

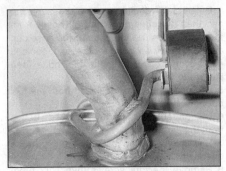

27.3 Exhaust system flexible hanger

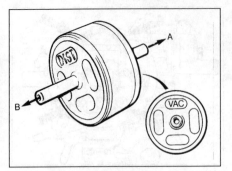

29.2 Spark sustain valve is marked for direction of fitting

A to PVS   *B to distributor*

29.8 Fuel trap is marked for direction of fitting

2 The system can be renewed in sections, as coupling sleeves are supplied so that an old section can be cut out and a new one inserted without the need to renew the entire system at the same time.

3 It is recommended, when working on an exhaust system, that the complete assembly be removed from under the vehicle by releasing the downpipe from the manifold and unhooking the flexible suspension hangers **(see illustration)**.

4 Assemble the complete system, but do not fully tighten the joint clips until the system is back in the vehicle. Use a new exhaust manifold/flange gasket and check that the flexible mountings are in good order.

5 Set the silencer and expansion box in their correct attitudes in relation to the rest of the system before finally tightening the joint clips.

6 Check that with reasonable deflection in either direction, the exhaust does not knock against any adjacent components.

Repair

7 Effective repairs to exhaust system can be made by using a proprietary repair kit.

28 Emission control components - maintenance and testing

1 In view of the special test equipment and procedures there is little that can be done in the way of maintenance and testing for the emissions control system. In the event of a suspected malfunction of the system, check the security and condition of all vacuum and electrical connections then, if applicable, refer to the following paragraphs for further information.

2 In addition, whenever working on any of these systems, make a careful note of any electrical or vacuum line connections before removing, to ensure correct refitting.

Positive crankcase ventilation (PCV)

3 Remove all the hoses and components of the system and clean them in paraffin or petrol. Ensure that all hoses are free from any obstruction and are in a serviceable condition. Where applicable, similarly clean the crankcase breather cap and shake it dry. Renew parts as necessary then refit them to the car.

Thermostatically-controlled air cleaner

4 Refer to Chapter 1, Section 29.

29 Emission control components - removal and refitting

Spark delay/sustain valve

1 Disconnect the vacuum lines at the valve and remove the valve from the engine.

2 When refitting a spark delay valve it must be positioned with the black side (marked CARB) towards the carburettor and the coloured side (marked DIST) towards the distributor. When refitting a spark sustain valve the side marked VAC must be towards the carburettor and the side marked DIST towards the distributor **(see illustration)**.

Ported vacuum switch

3 Remove the filler cap from the expansion tank to reduce pressure in the cooling system. If the engine is hot, remove the cap slowly using a rag to prevent scalding.

4 Disconnect the vacuum lines and, if necessary, the water hoses, then unscrew the valve from the inlet manifold or adapter.

5 When refitting the valve, note that the vacuum line from the carburettor is connected to the middle outlet on the PVS, the vacuum line from the spark delay valve (where fitted) is connected to the outlet nearest to the threaded end of the PVS, and the vacuum line from the spark sustain valve is connected to the outlet furthest from the threaded end of the PVS.

6 Reconnect the water hoses and, if necessary, top-up the cooling system.

Fuel trap

7 Disconnect the vacuum lines and remove the fuel trap from the engine.

8 When refitting, make sure that the fuel trap is positioned with the black side (marked CARB) towards the carburettor and the white side (marked DIST) towards the PVS **(see illustration)**.

Chapter 5 Part A:
Mechanical ignition system

Contents

Degrees of difficulty

Easy, suitable for novice with little experience	**Fairly easy,** suitable for beginner with some experience	**Fairly difficult,** suitable for competent DIY mechanic	**Difficult,** suitable for experienced DIY mechanic	**Very difficult,** suitable for expert DIY or professional 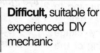

Specifications

General
System type	Battery, (negative earth) coil and distributor with contact breaker
Firing order	1-2-4-3 (No 1 at timing cover end)

Ignition timing (initial)
1.0 litre (pre-1986)	12° BTDC
1.1 litre (pre-1986)	6° BTDC

Ignition timing (initial) for use with unleaded fuel
1.0 models up to 2/86*	12° BTDC
1.0 models from 2/86 to 8/86	12° BTDC
1.1 models up to 2/86*	2° BTDC
1.1 models from 2/86-on	2° BTDC

Fill with leaded fuel every 4th tankful

Distributor
Make	Bosch with drive by gear on camshaft
Automatic advance method	Mechanical and vacuum control
Rotation	Anti-clockwise (viewed from cap)
Condenser capacity	0.20 ± 15% microfarad
Contact breaker points gap	0.40 to 0.50 mm
Dwell angle	48° to 52°
Dwell variation (from idle to 2000 rpm)	4° maximum
Dwell overlap (lobe-to-lobe variation)	3° maximum

Advance characteristics* at 2000 rpm (engine) no load:	**Mechanical**	**Vacuum**	**Total**
1.0 litre (pre-1986)	-1.0° to 4.0°	6° to 12°	5° to 16°
1.1 litre (pre-1986)	3° to 9°	13° to 21°	16° to 30°

Crankshaft degrees; initial advance not included

Spark plugs
Spark plugs	See Chapter 1 Specifications

Coil
Type	Low voltage with 1.5 ohm ballast resistor
Output	23 kV (minimum)
Secondary resistance	5000 to 9000 ohms

Torque wrench settings
	Nm	lbf ft
Spark plugs	13 to 20	10 to 15
Distributor clamp pinch-bolt	4	3
Distributor clamp plate bolt	10	7

1 General information and precautions

General information

A conventional ignition system is used on the 1.0 and 1.1 litre OHV models marketed in the UK before 1986. The system consists of a coil, a distributor with mechanical contact breaker, a ballast resistor and spark plugs. The distributor is mounted on the cylinder block and is driven from a skew gear on the camshaft. It incorporates both mechanical and vacuum advance capability.

The coil is mounted on the bulkhead panel and is of the oil-filled type. The ballast resistor is a grey coloured wire, built into the loom which runs between the ignition switch and the coil. Its purpose is to limit the battery voltage to the coil during normal running to seven volts. During starting, the ballast resistor is bypassed to give full battery voltage at the coil to facilitate quick starting of the engine.

The spark plugs are of small diameter and require a long reach 16 mm (⅝ in AF) socket to remove them instead of a conventional spark plug spanner; they are of the taper seat type.

The HT leads are of suppressed type, of carbon cored construction. Always pull them from the spark plugs by gripping the terminal rubber insulator, not the cable itself. The leads are numbered, No 1 being at the spark plug nearest the timing cover end of the engine.

Precautions

Warning: The HT voltage generated by an ignition system is extremely high, and in certain circumstances could prove fatal. Take care to avoid receiving electric shocks from the HT side of the ignition system. Do not handle HT leads, or touch the distributor or coil when the engine is running. If tracing faults in the HT circuit, use well insulated tools to manipulate live leads.

It is necessary to take extra care when working on the electrical system to avoid damage to semi-conductor devices and to avoid the risk of personal injury. In addition to the precautions given in the "Safety first!" Section at the beginning of this manual, take note of the following points when working on the system.

Always remove rings, watches, etc before working on the electrical system. Even with the battery disconnected, capacitive discharge could occur if a component live terminal is earthed through a metal object. This could cause a shock or nasty burn.

Do not reverse the battery connections. Components could be irreparably damaged.

If the engine is being started using jump leads and a slave battery, connect the batteries positive to positive and negative to negative. This also applies when connecting a battery charger.

Never disconnect the battery terminals, or alternator multi-plug connector, when the engine is running.

The battery leads and alternator multi-plug must be disconnected before carrying out any electric welding on the car.

Never use an ohmmeter of the type incorporating a hand cranked generator for circuit or continuity testing.

Before disconnecting any wiring, or removing components, always ensure that the ignition is switched off.

After working on ignition system components, ensure that all wiring is correctly reconnected before reconnecting the battery or switching on the ignition.

2 Spark plugs, HT leads and distributor cap - inspection and servicing

Refer to Chapter 1, Sections 12, 13 and 21.

3 Contact breaker gap - adjustment

Refer to Chapter 1, Section 15.

4 Contact breaker points - renewal

Refer to Chapter 1, Section 23.

5 Ignition timing - checking and adjustment

Refer to Chapter 1, Section 15.

6 Distributor advance - checking

1 A secondary use of a timing light is to check that the centrifugal and vacuum advance functions of the distributor are working.
2 The tests are not precise, as would be the case if sophisticated equipment were used, but will at least indicate the serviceability of the unit.
3 With the engine idling, timing light connected and vacuum pipe disconnected and plugged, increase the engine speed to 2000 rpm and note the approximate distance which the pulley mark moves out of alignment with the mark on the scale.

4 Reconnect the vacuum pipe to the distributor and repeat the test when for the same increase in engine speed, the alignment differential of the timing marks should be greater than previously observed. Refer to the Specifications for typical figures.
5 A further check of the vacuum advance can be made by removing the distributor cap after the engine has been switched off, disconnecting the distributor vacuum pipe at its suction end, and sucking the pipe. The suction should be sufficient to move the distributor baseplate slightly.
6 If these tests do not prove positive renew the vacuum unit.
7 Some models are equipped with a spark delay/sustain valve in the vacuum line from carburettor to distributor, the purpose of which is to delay vacuum advance under certain part throttle conditions. If such a valve is suspected of malfunctioning, it should be tested by substitution, or taken to a Ford dealer for specialised checking. The main effect of the valve is to reduce exhaust emission levels and it is unlikely that malfunction would have a noticeable effect on engine performance.
8 If a ported vacuum switch (PVS) is fitted in the vacuum line, its purpose is to bypass the spark sustain valve when normal engine operating temperature (as sensed by the temperature of the coolant flowing round the inlet manifold) has been reached.

7 Distributor - removal and refitting

Removal

1 Remove the air cleaner unit.
2 Disconnect the leads from the spark plugs, remove the distributor cap and place the cap with the leads to one side.
3 Disconnect the LT lead from the coil negative terminal and disconnect the distributor vacuum pipe.
4 Using a ring spanner or socket on the crankshaft pulley bolt, turn the crankshaft until No 1 piston is at TDC. Verify this by checking that the timing cover mark is aligned with the notch on the crankshaft pulley and that the rotor arm (contact end) is pointing to the No 1 spark plug lead contact in the distributor cap when fitted. Do not turn the crankshaft again until after the distributor has been refitted.
5 Mark the position of the rotor arm on the rim of the distributor body **(see illustration)**.
6 Mark the position of the distributor body in relation to the cylinder block.
7 Remove the bolt which holds the distributor clamp plate to the cylinder block, do not remove the distributor by releasing the clamp pinch-bolt.
8 Withdraw the distributor.

Refitting

9 To install the original distributor, hold it over its hole in the cylinder block so that the mark

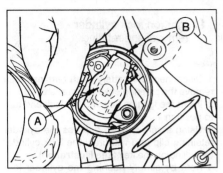

7.5 Rotor arm (A) with rim alignment mark (B)

made before removal is aligned with the one on the cylinder block (No 1 piston still at TDC).

10 When the distributor is installed, the meshing of the drive and driven gears will cause the rotor arm to rotate in an anti-clockwise direction. This must be anticipated by positioning the rotor arm a few degrees in advance of its final marked position.

11 Install the distributor and check that the rotor arm and distributor body marks are aligned with the marks made before removal. Tighten the clamp plate bolt.

12 If the distributor was removed without marking its position, or if a new distributor is being fitted, install the distributor in the following way.

13 Set No 1 piston to TDC. To do this, remove No 1 spark plug and place the finger over the plug hole. Turn the crankshaft pulley bolt until compression can be felt, which indicates that No 1 piston is rising on its firing stroke. Continue turning until the timing marks for TDC are in alignment.

14 Hold the distributor over its hole in the cylinder block so that the vacuum unit is aligned with the engine oil dipstick guide tube.

15 Set the rotor arm to anticipate its rotation as the gears mesh on installation, remembering that the arm will turn in a clockwise direction and should take up a final position with its contact end opposite No 1 spark plug lead contact (as if the distributor cap is fitted).

16 Release the clamp plate pinch-bolt and install the distributor. Check that the body and rotor arm are correctly positioned, then swivel the clamp plate as necessary to be able to screw in the clamp plate bolt. Tighten the clamp plate pinch-bolt.

17 Fit the distributor cap and reconnect the HT and LT leads.

18 Check the timing and then reconnect the vacuum pipe to the distributor.

8 Distributor vacuum unit - renewal

1 This will normally only be required if a new unit is to be fitted because a fault has been diagnosed in the old one.

2 Remove the distributor cap and the rotor arm. Disconnect the vacuum pipe from the unit.

3 Extract the circlip which holds the vacuum advance actuating rod to the pivot post.

4 Extract the two screws which hold the unit to the distributor body, tilt the unit downwards to release the actuating rod from the pivot post and then withdraw the unit.

5 Fitting is a reversal of removal, but apply a little grease to the pivot post. Fitting may be made easier if the distributor baseplate is rotated slightly with the fingers.

9 Condenser - renewal

1 If the condenser is suspected of being faulty, it may be removed and a new one fitted without having to remove the distributor.

2 Release the HT leads from the spark plugs, take off the distributor cap and place the cap and the leads to one side. Remove the rotor arm.

3 Disconnect the LT lead from the coil negative terminal.

4 Mark the position of the distributor body in relation to the clamp plate and then release the clamp plate pinch-bolt.

5 Turn the distributor approximately 120° in **a** clockwise direction to expose the condenser and extract its securing screw. Pull off its lead connecting block and remove the condenser.

6 Fitting is a reversal of removal.

7 Check the ignition timing on completion.

10 Distributor - overhaul

1 Dismantling of the distributor should not be taken beyond the renewal of components described in earlier Sections of this Chapter **(see illustration)**.

2 Internal components are not supplied as spares. In the event of severe wear having taken place, obtain a new or reconditioned unit.

5A

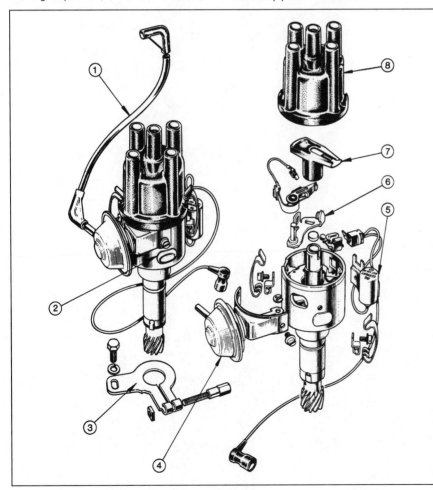

10.1 Bosch distributor showing components which are renewable

1 *Vacuum supply pipe*
2 *Distributor unit*
3 *Distributor clamp*
4 *Vacuum unit*
5 *Condenser*
6 *Contact breakers*
7 *Rotor arm*
8 *Distributor cap*

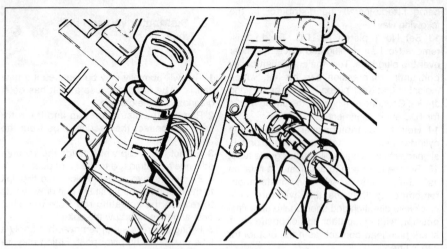

11.3 Ignition lock cylinder removal

11 Ignition lock cylinder - removal and refitting

1 Disconnect the battery earth terminal, then remove the steering column lower shroud.
2 Insert the ignition key into the lock and turn to position 1.
3 Using a screwdriver, depress the cylinder retaining clip and withdraw the lock cylinder by pulling on the key **(see illustration)**.
4 Refit by simply pushing the cylinder into position with the key held in position 1.
5 It should be noted that the steering column lock and tube are a combined unit and the lock cannot be renewed separately.

Chapter 5 Part B:
Electronic ignition system

Contents

Degrees of difficulty

Easy, suitable for novice with little experience	**Fairly easy,** suitable for beginner with some experience	**Fairly difficult,** suitable for competent DIY mechanic	**Difficult,** suitable for experienced DIY mechanic	**Very difficult,** suitable for expert DIY or professional 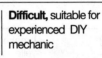

Specifications

General

System type	Battery, (negative earth), coil and distributor (breakerless electronic ignition) incorporating electronic module

Firing order:
OHC	1-2-4-3 (No 1 at timing cover end)
CVH	1-3-4-2 (No 1 at timing cover end)

Ignition timing (initial)

1.0 litre (2/86 to 8/86)	12° BTDC at idling speed
1.0 litre (8/86-on)	10° BTDC at idling speed
1.1 litre (1986-on)	6° BTDC at idling speed
1.3 and 1.4 litre	12° BTDC

Ignition timing (initial) for use with unleaded fuel

1.0 models from 8/86	10° BTDC
1.1 models from 2/86	2° BTDC
1.3 models up to 12/84*	8° BTDC
1.3 models from 12/84	8° BTDC
1.4 models up to 1/87	8° BTDC
1.4 models from 1/87	8° BTDC
1.6 models up to 12/84*	8° BTDC
1.6 models from 12/84	8° BTDC

*Fill with leaded fuel every 4th tankful

Distributor

Make:
OHV engines	Bosch
CVH engines	Bosch or Lucas
Type	Breakerless

Automatic advance method:
1.0 and 1.1 litre (1986-on)	Mechanical and vacuum
1.4 litre	Mechanical and vacuum
All other models	ESC module

Drive:
1.0 and 1.1 litre (1986-on)	Skew gear on camshaft
All other models	Dog on camshaft
Rotation	Anti-clockwise (viewed from top)
Dwell angle	Non-adjustable (governed by module)

Advance characteristics (total) at 2000 rpm (engine speed):
1.0 litre (1986-on)	5° to 15°
1.1 litre (1986-on)	16° to 28°
1.3 litre	18° to 34°
1.4 litre	18° to 30°
1.6 litre	17° to 30.2°

Spark plugs	See Chapter 1 Specifications

Coil

Type	High output breakerless ignition coil
Output (open circuit condition):	
1.0 and 1.1 litre (1986-on)	30 kV (minimum)
1.4 litre	30 kV (minimum)
All other models	25 kV (minimum)
Primary resistance:	
1.0 and 1.1 litre (1986-on)	1.13 to 1.33 ohms
All other models	0.72 to 0.88 ohms
Secondary resistance:	
1.0 and 1.1 litre (1986-on)	3500 to 6500 ohms
1.4 litre	4500 to 8600 ohms
All other models	4000 to 7000 ohms

Torque wrench settings

	Nm	lbf ft
Spark plugs	27	20
Distributor mounting bolts	7	5

1 General information and precautions

General information

Pre-1986 models

The electronic system fitted to Fiesta models manufactured before 1986 consists of a breakerless distributor driven from the end of the camshaft, an electronic amplifier module mounted on the bulkhead on the left-hand side, and a high output type ignition coil fitted next to the amplifier module on the bulkhead.

The breakerless distributor is of Bosch manufacture and is distinguishable from conventional systems by its blue distributor cap. The unit has no mechanical contact breaker or condenser, these components being replaced by a trigger wheel, a trigger coil and a stator. The action of the distributor is to provide a pulse to the electronic module which in turn actuates the ignition coil to ignite the fuel/air mixture via the HT leads and spark plugs.

The electronic amplifier module is a sealed unit located on the left-hand side of the engine compartment bulkhead. The function of the module is to sense the trigger pulse from the distributor and amplify its voltage sufficiently to operate the module's output transistor. On receipt of this amplified voltage the module shuts off the ignition coil primary circuit allowing HT voltage to build up within the coil in the conventional manner and fire the appropriate spark plug via the distributor and HT leads. On completion of the firing cycle the primary circuit is then switched on again by the module and the cycle is repeated for the next cylinder.

The ignition coil operates on conventional principles but with a higher output voltage. The unit is rated at 8 volts and is supplied via a ballast resistor wire during normal running. When starting the engine the ballast resistor wire is bypassed and the coil receives full battery voltage. The coil used on electronic breakerless systems is distinguished by a yellow label on the case.

The spark plugs used are the copper cored resistor type with a metric thread form. Only this type of plug is suitable for use in the electronic ignition system.

Repair and overhaul operations should be limited to those described in this Chapter as only the distributor cap, rotor arm, and HT leads are available as repair parts, all other items are sealed and only renewable as complete units. Should a fault in the system develop or be suspected, the advice of your dealer should be sought. Fault diagnosis procedures are lengthy and must follow a systematic approach using sophisticated test equipment. For these reasons fault diagnosis and repair are considered to be beyond the scope of the average owner.

1986 models onwards

From 1986 onwards, all Fiesta models are fitted with breakerless electronic ignition systems. 1.6 litre CVH models retain the same basic system as described above for the pre 1986 models, except that the electronic module is integral with the distributor. 1.0 and 1.1 litre OHV and 1.4 litre CVH models are equipped with a new system also incorporating an electronic module integral with the distributor. The new system operates in the following way.

The ignition system is divided into two circuits, low tension (primary) and high tension (secondary). The low tension circuit consists of the battery, ignition switch, primary coil windings, electronic amplifier module and the signal generating system inside the distributor. The signal generating system comprises the trigger coil, trigger wheel, stator, permanent magnets and stator pick-up. The high tension circuit consists of the secondary coil windings, the heavy ignition lead from the centre of the distributor cap to the coil, the rotor arm and the spark plug leads and spark plugs.

When the system is in operation, low tension voltage is changed in the coil into high tension voltage by the action of the electronic amplifier module in conjunction with the signal generating system. As each of the trigger wheel teeth pass through the magnetic field created around the trigger coil in the distributor, a change in the magnetic field force (flux) is created which induces a voltage in the trigger coil. This voltage is passed to the electronic amplifier module which switches off the ignition coil primary circuit. This results in the collapse of the magnetic field in the coil which generates the high tension voltage. The high tension voltage is then fed via the carbon brush in the centre of the distributor cap to the rotor arm. The voltage passes across to the appropriate metal segment in the cap and via the spark plug lead to the spark plug where it finally jumps the spark plug gap to earth.

The distributor used on the electronic ignition system of OHV engines is of Bosch manufacture, whereas on CVH engines either a Bosch or Lucas unit may be used. Although the components of the signal generating system differ between the Bosch and Lucas distributors, the principles of operation of both are as just described. The distributor is driven by a skew gear from the camshaft on the OHV engine and by an offset dog on the end of the camshaft on CVH engines.

The ignition advance is a function of the distributor and is controlled both mechanically and by a vacuum-operated system. The mechanical governor mechanism consists of two weights which move out from the distributor shaft as the engine speed rises due to centrifugal force. As they move outwards they rotate the trigger wheel relative to the distributor shaft and so advance the spark. The weights are held in position by two light springs and it is the tension of the springs which is largely responsible for correct spark advancement.

The vacuum control consists of a diaphragm, one side of which is connected via a small bore hose to the carburettor, and the other side to the distributor. Depression in the inlet manifold and carburettor, which varies with engine speed and throttle position, causes the diaphragm to move, so moving the baseplate and advancing or retarding the spark. A fine degree of control is achieved by a spring in the diaphragm assembly. Additionally, one or more vacuum valves and temperature sensitive control valves may be incorporated in the vacuum line between inlet manifold or carburettor and the distributor. These control the duration of the vacuum felt at the distributor and are part of the vehicle emission control systems.

Precautions

General

It is necessary to take extra care when working on the electrical system to avoid damage to semi-conductor devices (diodes and transistors), and to avoid the risk of personal injury. In addition to the precautions given in the *"Safety first!"* Section at the beginning of this manual, take note of the following points when working on the system:

Always remove rings, watches, etc before working on the electrical system. Even with the battery disconnected, capacitive discharge could occur if a component live terminal is earthed through a metal object. This could cause a shock or nasty burn.

Do not reverse the battery connections. Components such as the alternator or any other having semi-conductor circuitry could be irreparably damaged.

If the engine is being started using jump leads and a slave battery, connect the batteries positive to positive and negative to negative. This also applies when connecting a battery charger.

Never disconnect the battery terminals, or alternator multi-plug connector, when the engine is running.

The battery leads and alternator multi-plug must be disconnected before carrying out any electric welding on the car.

Never use an ohmmeter of the type incorporating a hand cranked generator for circuit or continuity testing.

Ignition and engine management systems

 Warning: The HT voltage generated by an electronic ignition system is extremely high, and in certain circumstances could prove fatal. Take care to avoid receiving electric shocks from the HT side of the ignition system. Do not handle HT leads, or touch the distributor or coil when the engine is running. If tracing faults in the HT circuit, use well insulated tools to manipulate live leads.

Engine management modules are very sensitive components, and certain precautions must be taken to avoid damage to the module when working on a vehicle equipped with an engine management system as follows.

When carrying out welding operations on the vehicle using electric welding equipment, the battery and alternator should be disconnected.

Although underbonnet-mounted modules will tolerate normal underbonnet conditions, they can be adversely affected by excess heat or moisture. If using welding equipment or pressure washing equipment in the vicinity of the module, take care not to direct heat, or jets of water or steam at the module. If this cannot be avoided, remove the module from the vehicle, and protect its wiring plug with a plastic bag.

Before disconnecting any wiring, or removing components, always ensure that the ignition is switched off.

On models with underbonnet-mounted modules, do not run the engine with the module detached from the body panel, as the body acts as an effective heat sink, and the module may be damaged due to internal overheating.

Do not attempt to improvise fault diagnosis procedures using a test lamp or multimeter, as irreparable damage could be caused to the module.

After working on ignition/engine management system components, ensure that all wiring is correctly reconnected before reconnecting the battery or switching on the ignition.

On some early Bosch distributors it is possible that with the distributor cap removed, if the engine is cranked, the cap securing clips may fall inward and jam the trigger wheel/vane, knocking it out of alignment. If this happens, the distributor will have to be renewed as the trigger wheel/vane cannot be repositioned. Care should therefore be taken not to crank the engine with the distributor cap removed. Later distributors have redesigned clips which eliminate the problem.

Ignition coil

The LT connections to the coil used with electronic ignition cannot be confused as the terminals are of different size. **Never** fit a coil from a conventional ignition system into an electronic ignition system otherwise the amplifier module may be damaged.

2 Spark plugs, HT leads and distributor cap - inspection and servicing

 Warning: Never remove spark plugs from a CVH engine when it is hot.

1 In general, the same information applies as is made in Section 2 of Chapter 5A. Note, however, that a different type of plug is used and that its electrode gap and tightening torque are different (see Chapter 1 Specifications).
2 Only remove plugs from the CVH engine when it is warm or cold - never when it is hot.
3 Note that the firing order on the CVH engine is different from the OHV engine.

3 Distributor - removal and refitting

Pre-1986 models

Removal

1 The distributor is precisely positioned for optimum ignition timing during production and marked accordingly with a punch mark on the distributor mounting flange and the cylinder head (see illustration).
2 Disconnect the HT leads from the spark plugs.
3 Disconnect the wiring harness multi-plug from the distributor.
4 Release the distributor cap retaining clips, lift off the cap and position it, with the HT leads, to one side (see illustration).
5 Unscrew and remove the two distributor flange mounting bolts and withdraw the distributor from the cylinder head.
6 Check the distributor spindle for side-to-side movement. If excessive movement is found, the distributor must be renewed as it is not possible to obtain individual components for overhaul.

Refitting

7 Before refitting the distributor, check the condition of the oil seal beneath the mounting flange and renew it if necessary.

5B

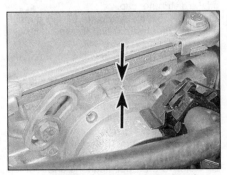

3.1 Distributor and cylinder head alignment marks (arrowed)

3.4 Distributor cap removal

3.15 Ignition timing marks - pre 1986

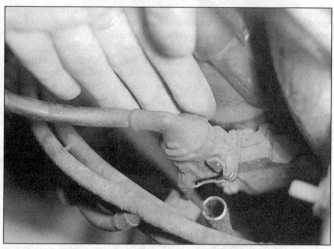

3.21 The distributor LT wiring multi-plug

8 Hold the distributor so that the punch marks on the distributor body and the offset drive dog are in approximate alignment, then insert the distributor into its recess.

9 Check that the drive components have engaged and then rotate the distributor until the punch marks on flange and head are in alignment. Insert the bolts and tighten to the specified torque.

10 Reconnect all the disconnected components.

New unit

11 Where a new distributor is being installed, its flange will obviously not have a punch mark and it must therefore be fitted in the following way.

12 Hold the distributor in approximately its fitted position and also ensure that the drive dog is in approximately the correct alignment to engage with the offset segments of the camshaft dog.

13 Locate the distributor on the cylinder head. When you are sure that the drive dogs are fully engaged, screw in the flange bolts so that they are not only positioned centrally in the flange slots, but still allow the distributor to be rotated stiffly.

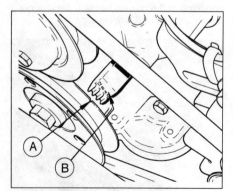

3.25 Ignition timing marks - 1986 on
A Crankshaft pulley notch
B Timing cover scale

14 Reconnect the distributor cap, the spark plug leads and the LT multi-plug.

15 Using a little quick-drying white paint, increase the contrast of the timing notch in the crankshaft pulley and the appropriate mark on the timing belt cover scale **(see illustration)**.

16 Connect a timing light (stroboscope) in accordance with the manufacturer's instructions.

17 Start the engine, allow it to idle and point the timing light at the timing marks. They should appear stationary and in alignment. If they are not, rotate the distributor as necessary to bring them into line and then tighten one of the distributor bolts.

18 Switch off the engine, remove the timing light and then tighten all the distributor mounting bolts to the specified torque.

19 Punch mark the distributor flange at a point exactly opposite the mark on the cylinder head. Future installation can then be carried out as described in paragraphs 1 to 10 of this Section.

1.0 and 1.1 litre models - 1986 onwards

Removal

20 Disconnect the leads from the spark plugs, spring back the retaining clips and lift off the distributor cap.

21 Disconnect the distributor LT wiring multi-plug **(see illustration)** and the vacuum hose at the distributor vacuum unit.

22 Remove No 1 spark plug (nearest the crankshaft pulley).

23 Place a finger over the plug hole and turn the crankshaft in thermal direction of rotation (clockwise viewed from the crankshaft pulley end) until pressure is felt in No 1 cylinder. This indicates that the piston is commencing its compression stroke. The crankshaft can be turned with a spanner on the pulley bolt.

24 Refer to the Specifications and look up the ignition timing setting for the engine being worked on.

25 Continue turning the crankshaft until the notch on the pulley is aligned with the correct setting on the scale located just above and to the right of the pulley. The "O" mark on the scale represents top dead centre (TDC) and the raised projections to the left of TDC are in increments of 4° BTDC **(see illustration)**.

26 Check that the rotor arm is pointing to the notch on the rim of the distributor body **(see illustration)**.

27 Make a mark on the distributor body and a corresponding mark on the cylinder block to aid refitting.

28 Undo the bolt securing the distributor clamp plate to the cylinder block, then withdraw the distributor from its location. As the distributor is removed, the rotor arm will move a few degrees clockwise. Note the new position of the rotor arm and make an alignment mark on the distributor body rim.

Refitting

29 Before installing the distributor make sure that the crankshaft is still positioned as previously described. If a new distributor is being fitted, transfer the markings made during removal to the new unit.

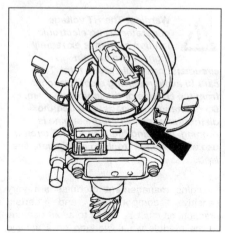

3.26 Rotor arm in alignment with distributor body rim notch

30 Hold the distributor over its hole in the cylinder block, with the mark made on the distributor body aligned with the mark made on the cylinder block.

31 Position the rotor arm so that it points to the mark made on the distributor rim after removal, and push the distributor fully home. As the skew gears mesh, the rotor arm will move clockwise and should align with the manufacturer's mark on the distributor rim.

32 With the distributor in place, turn the body slightly if necessary so that the arms of the trigger wheel and stator are aligned, then refit and tighten the clamp plate bolt.

33 Reconnect the LT wiring multi-plug and vacuum hose, then refit the distributor cap, spark plug and plug leads.

34 Adjust the ignition timing.

1.4 litre models

35 The procedure is the same as described in paragraphs 1 to 19 but additionally, disconnect the vacuum pipe at the distributor vacuum unit. When refitting the distributor, leave the vacuum pipe disconnected and plug its end when setting the distributor position. Refit the pipe on completion.

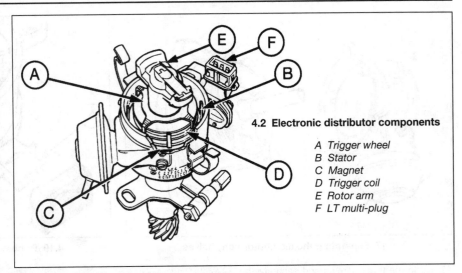

4.2 Electronic distributor components

A *Trigger wheel*
B *Stator*
C *Magnet*
D *Trigger coil*
E *Rotor arm*
F *LT multi-plug*

---

4   Distributor - overhaul

Note: Ensure that replacement parts are readily available before carrying out any overhaul or repair work on the distributor.

1.0 and 1.1 litre models - 1986 onwards

1 Remove the distributor from the engine.

2 Remove the rotor arm **(see illustration)**.

3 Extract the circlip securing the vacuum unit rod to the baseplate pivot post.

4 Undo the two vacuum unit retaining screws, tip the unit to release the rod from the pivot post and withdraw it from the distributor body.

5 Undo the two electronic amplifier module retaining screws and detach the module **(see illustration)**.

6 This is the limit of dismantling that can be undertaken. Should the distributor be worn or unserviceable in any other respect, renewal of the complete unit will be necessary.

7 Reassembly is the reversal of dismantling. Lubricate the baseplate pivot post with a high-melting-point grease and apply heat sink compound, available from Ford parts dealers, to the back of the amplifier module before refitting.

Bosch distributor (1.4 litre models)

8 Remove the distributor from the engine.

9 Remove the rotor arm and where fitted the plastic shield **(see illustration)**.

10 Undo the two screws securing the vacuum unit to the side of the distributor body **(see illustration)**. Tip the unit to release the rod from the baseplate pivot post and withdraw it from the distributor.

11 Undo the two screws securing the electronic amplifier module and remove the module **(see illustration)**.

12 This is the limit of dismantling that can be undertaken. Should the distributor be worn or unserviceable in any other respect, renewal of the complete unit will be necessary.

13 Reassembly is the reversal of dismantling. Lubricate the baseplate pivot post with a high-melting-point grease and apply heat sink compound, available from Ford parts dealers, to the back of the amplifier module before fitting.

Lucas distributor (1.4 litre models)

14 Remove the distributor from the engine.

15 Remove the rotor arm.

16 Undo the two electronic amplifier retaining screws and remove the amplifier.

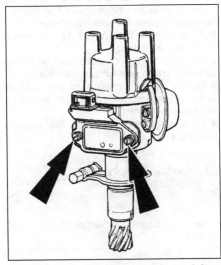

4.5 Electronic amplifier module retaining screws

4.9 Removing the rotor arm from the distributor

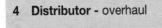

4.10 Vacuum unit left-hand retaining screw

4.11 Removing the amplifier module

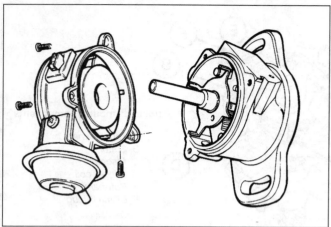

4.17 Separating the distributor body halves

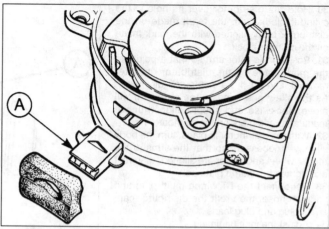

4.19 Rubber seal and trigger coil connector (A)

17 Undo the three screws and separate the two halves of the distributor body **(see illustration)**.

18 Withdraw the plastic spacer ring from the body upper half.

19 Withdraw the rubber seal, then pull the connection off the trigger coil terminals **(see illustration)**. Note the fitted direction of the connector to aid refitting.

20 Tip the trigger coil up and remove it from the body upper half.

21 Extract the stator retaining circlip and the upper shim **(see illustration)**.

22 Lift out the stator and the lower shim.

23 Slacken the vacuum unit retaining screw and remove the vacuum unit **(see illustration)**.

24 This is the limit of dismantling that can be undertaken. Should the distributor be worn or unserviceable in any other respect, renewal of the complete unit will be necessary.

25 Reassembly is the reversal of dismantling. Lubricate the vacuum unit peg with a high-melting-point grease and apply heat sink compound, available from Ford dealers, to the back of the amplifier module before refitting.

---

5 Ignition timing - adjustment

1.0, 1.1 and 1.4 litre models - 1986 onwards

1 On 1.0 and 1.1 litre models the procedure is the same as described in Chapter 5A but ignore all references to dwell angle checking, as this is not applicable to electronic ignition distributors.

2 On 1.4 litre models refer to the procedure contained in Section 3, paragraphs 1 to 19, but note that the distributor vacuum pipe must be disconnected and plugged during the checking operation.

Adjustments for unleaded fuel

3 In order to operate vehicles on 95 RON unleaded petrol, the ignition timing may need to be retarded to avoid pinking.

4 Ignition timing values for use with unleaded petrol are given in Specifications.

---

6 Ignition amplifier module - renewal

1 The ignition amplifier cannot be repaired and, if known to be defective, must be renewed as a unit. The vacuum advance characteristics of the module can be checked, but this is a task best entrusted to your Ford dealer.

2 To remove the module unit first disconnect the battery earth lead.

3 Detach the wiring connector from the module by pulling on the connector, not the leads.

4 Detach the vacuum hose from the module, undo and remove the single retaining screw and remove the module.

5 Refitting is a reversal of the removal procedure.

---

7 Ignition lock cylinder - removal and refitting

Refer to Chapter 5A, Section 11.

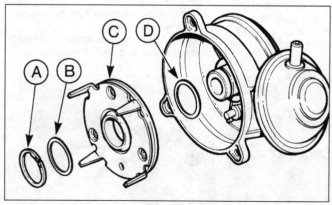

4.21 The distributor stator components

A Circlip   B Upper shim   C Stator   D Lower shim

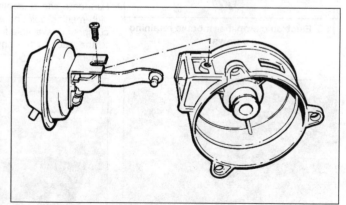
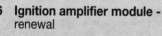

4.23 The distributor vacuum unit

Chapter 5 Part C:
Starting and charging systems

Contents

Degrees of difficulty

Easy, suitable for novice with little experience	Fairly easy, suitable for beginner with some experience	Fairly difficult, suitable for competent DIY mechanic	Difficult, suitable for experienced DIY mechanic	Very difficult, suitable for expert DIY or professional

Specifications

System type .... 12V negative earth, belt-driven alternator, pre-engaged starter motor

Battery
Type .... 12V, lead-acid
Charge condition:
   12.5V or above .... Satisfactory
   Below 12.5V .... Recharge

Bosch alternator
Rated output (13.5V at 6000 rpm) .... 45A (K1-45A) or 55A (K1-55A)
Maximum continuous speed .... 15000 rpm
Minimum brush length .... 5.0 mm
Regulator voltage at 4000 rpm (3 to 7A load) .... 13.7 to 14.6 volts
Stator winding resistance (ohms/phase) .... 0.09 to 0.099 (K1-45A) or 0.07 to 0.077 (K1-55A)
Rotor winding resistance at 20°C (ohms) .... 3.40 to 3.74 (K1-45A and K1-55A)

Lucas (type B) alternator
Rated output (13.5V at 6000 rpm) .... 45A (A133/45) or 55A (A133/55)
Maximum continuous speed .... 15 000 rpm
Minimum brush length .... 5.0 mm
Regulator voltage at 4000 rpm (3 to 7A load) .... 13.7 to 14.6 volts
Stator winding resistance (ohms/phase) .... 0.285 to 0.305* (A133/45) or 0.088 to 0.108† (A133/45) or 0.203 (A133/55)
Rotor winding resistance at 20°C (ohms) .... 3.04 to 3.36 (A133/45 and A133/55)
*Lucas Delta-type winding
†Lucas Star-type winding

Lucas (type D) alternator
Rated output (13.5V at 6000 rpm) .... 45A or 55A
Maximum continuous speed .... 15 000 rpm
Minimum brush length .... 5.0 mm
Regulator voltage at 4000 rpm (3 to 7A load) .... 13.7 to 14.6 volts
Stator winding resistance (ohms/phase) .... 0.229 to 0.254
Rotor winding resistance at 20°C (ohms) .... 3.04 to 3.36 (A127/45 and A127/55)

Motorola alternator
Rated output (13.5V at 6000 rpm) 45A (SD-45)
Maximum continuous speed .... 15 000 rpm
Minimum brush length .... 4.0 mm
Regulator voltage at 4000 rpm (3 to 7A load) .... 13.7 to 14.6 volts
Stator winding resistance (ohms/phase) .... 0.23 to 0.33 (SD-45)
Rotor winding resistance at 20°C (ohms) .... 3.8 to 4.2 (SD-45)

Mitsubishi alternator
Minimum brush length .... 5.0 mm

5C

Drivebelt tension

Using a belt tension gauge:
CVH engine:
   New belt .... 400 to 500N (90 to 113 lbf)
   Used belt .... 300 to 400N (68 to 90 lbf)
OHV engine:
   New belt .... 350 to 450N (79 to 101 lbf)
   Used belt .... 250 to 350N (56 to 79 lbf)
Using finger pressure:
   All types .... 4 mm deflection on longest run
A used belt is one which has been in operation for at least 10 minutes

Bosch long frame and Cajavec starter motors

Rating .... 0.85 kW or 0.95 kW
Number of brushes 4
Minimum brush length .... 8.0 mm
Minimum commutator diameter .... 32.8 mm
Armature endfloat .... 0.3 mm

Bosch short frame starter motor

Rating .... 1.7 kW or 0.8 kW
Number of brushes 4
Minimum brush length .... 8.0 mm
Minimum commutator diameter .... 32.8 mm
Armature endfloat .... 0.3 mm

Lucas starter motor

Rating .... 8M90 or 9M90
Number of brushes 4
Minimum brush length .... 8.0 mm
Armature endfloat .... 0.25 mm

Nippondenso starter motor

Rating .... 0.6 kW or 0.9 kW
Number of brushes 2
Minimum brush length .... 10.0 mm
Minimum commutator diameter .... 28.0 mm
Armature endfloat .... 0.6 mm

---

1 General information and precautions

General information

The electrical system is of the 12 volt negative earth type and comprises a 12 volt battery, alternator with integral voltage regulator, starter motor and related electrical accessories, components and wiring. The battery is charged by an alternator which is belt-driven.

The starter motor is of the pre-engaged type incorporating an integral solenoid. On starting, the solenoid moves the drive pinion into engagement with the flywheel ring gear before the starter motor is energised. Once the engine has started, a one-way clutch prevents the motor armature being driven by the engine until the pinion disengages from the flywheel.

Precautions

It is necessary to take extra care when working on the electrical system to avoid damage to semi-conductor devices (diodes and transistors), and to avoid the risk of personal injury. In addition to the precautions given in the *"Safety first!"* Section at the beginning of this manual, take note of the following points when working on the system:

Always remove rings, watches, etc before working on the electrical system. Even with the battery disconnected, capacitive discharge could occur if a component live terminal is earthed through a metal object. This could cause a shock or nasty burn.

Do not reverse the battery connections. Components such as the alternator or any other having semi-conductor circuitry could be irreparably damaged.

If the engine is being started using jump leads and a slave battery, connect the batteries positive to positive and negative to negative. This also applies when connecting a battery charger.

Never disconnect the battery terminals, or alternator multi-plug connector, when the engine is running.

The battery leads and alternator multi-plug must be disconnected before carrying out any electric welding on the car.

Never use an ohmmeter of the type incorporating a hand cranked generator for circuit or continuity testing.

2 Battery - removal and refitting

⚠️ *Warning: When reconnecting the battery, always connect the positive lead first and the negative lead last.*

1 Open the bonnet and support it on its stay.
2 The battery is mounted on the left-hand side in the engine compartment.

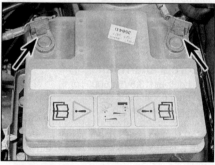

2.3 Battery lead terminals (arrowed)

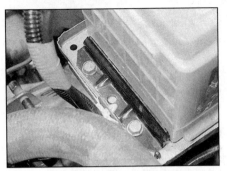

2.4 Battery retaining clamp

3 Disconnect the negative (earth) lead, followed by the positive lead **(see illustration)**.

4 Unbolt and remove the clamps from the nibs at the base of the battery casing **(see illustration)**.

5 Lift the battery from its location, taking care not to spill electrolyte on the paintwork.

6 Refitting is a reversal of removal.

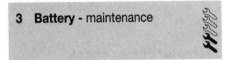

3 Battery - maintenance

Terminal check

1 To clean the battery terminals disconnect them, negative earth first, after having first removed the cover (where fitted). Use a wire brush or abrasive paper to clean the terminals. Bad corrosion should be treated with a solution of bicarbonate of soda, applied with an old toothbrush. Do not let this solution get into the battery.

2 Coat the battery terminals with petroleum jelly or a proprietary anti-corrosive compound before reconnecting them. Reconnect and tighten the positive (live) lead first, followed by the negative (earth) lead. Do not overtighten.

Electrolyte level check

3 The battery fitted as standard equipment is probably of the low maintenance type. However if a non-standard battery is fitted the following checks should be made.

4 Remove the cell covers and check that the plate separators in each cell are covered by approximately 6.0 mm of electrolyte. If the battery case is translucent, the cell covers need not be removed to check the level. Top-up if necessary with distilled or de-ionised water; do not overfill, and mop up any spillage at once (see "Weekly checks" illustration) .

Electrolyte replenishment

5 If the battery is in a fully charged state and one or more of the cells maintains a specific gravity reading which is 0.040 or more lower than the others, then it is likely that electrolyte has been lost from the cell at some time.

6 Top-up the cell with a solution of 1 part sulphuric acid to 2.5 parts of distilled water. If the cell is already topped up draw some electrolyte out of it with a pipette.

7 It is preferable to obtain ready mixed electrolyte: however, if the solution is to be mixed note the following:

 Warning: The water must never be added to the sulphuric acid otherwise it will explode. Always pour the acid slowly onto the water in a glass or plastic container.

General inspection

8 Wipe clean the top of the battery with a dry cloth to prevent the accumulation of dust and dampness which may cause the battery to become partially discharged over a period.

9 Check the battery clamp and platform for corrosion. If evident remove the battery and clean the deposits away. Then treat the affected metal with a proprietary anti-rust liquid and paint with the original colour.

10 Whenever the battery is removed it is worthwhile checking it for cracks and leakage. Cracks can be caused by topping-up the cells with distilled water in winter *after* instead of *before* a run. This gives the water no chance to mix with the electrolyte, so the former freezes and splits the battery case. If the case is fractured, it may be possible to repair it with a proprietary compound but this depends on the material used for the case.

Testing

11 If the car covers a small annual mileage it is worthwhile checking the specific gravity of the electrolyte every three months to determine the state of charge of the battery. Use a hydrometer to make the check and compare the results with the following table:

Ambient temperature 25°C (77°F):

	above	below
Fully charged	1.21 to 1.23	1.27 to 1.29
70% charged	1.17 to 1.19	1.23 to 1.25
Fully discharged	1.05 to 1.07	1.11 to 1.13

Note that the specific gravity readings assume an electrolyte temperature of 15°C (60°F); for every 10°C (18°F) below 15°C (60°F) subtract 0.007. For every 10°C (18°F) above 15°C (60°F) add 0.007.

12 If the battery condition is suspect, first check the specific gravity of electrolyte in each cell. A variation of 0.040 or more between any cells indicates loss of electrolyte or deterioration of the internal plates.

13 In cases where a sealed-for-life maintenance-free battery is fitted, topping-up and testing of the electrolyte in each cell is not possible. The condition of the battery type can therefore only be tested using a battery condition indicator or a voltmeter, as with a standard or low maintenance type battery.

14 If testing the battery using a voltmeter, connect it across the battery and compare the result with those given in the Specifications

under "charge condition". The test is only accurate if the battery has not been subject to any kind of charge for the previous six hours. If this is not the case switch on the headlights for 30 seconds then wait four to five minutes before testing the battery after switching off the headlights. All other electrical components must be switched off, so check that the doors and boot lid are fully shut when making the test.

15 If the voltage reading is less than the 12.2 volts then the battery is discharged, whilst a reading of 12.2 to 12.5 volts indicates a partially discharged condition.

16 If the battery is to be charged, remove it from the vehicle and charge it as follows:

Charging

17 In winter time when heavy demand is placed upon the battery, such as when starting from cold and much electrical equipment is continually in use, it is a good idea to have the battery occasionally fully charged from an external source.

Conventional and low maintenance batteries

18 Charge the battery at a rate of 3.5 to 4 amps and continue to charge the battery at this rate until no further rise in specific gravity is noted over a four hour period.

19 Alternatively, a trickle charger charging at a rate of 1.5 amps can be safely used overnight.

20 Specially rapid "boost" charges which are claimed to restore the power of the battery in 1 to 2 hours are not recommended as they can cause serious damage to the battery plates through overheating.

21 While charging the battery, note that the temperature of the electrolyte should never exceed 37.8°C (100°F).

Maintenance-free batteries

22 This battery type takes considerably longer to fully recharge than the conventional type, the time taken being dependent on the extent of discharge, but it can take anything up to three days.

23 A constant voltage type charger is required and this set, when connected, to 13.9 to 14.9 volts with a charger current below 25 amps. Using this method the battery should be useable within three hours, giving a voltage reading of 12.5 volts, but this is for a partially discharged battery and, as mentioned, full charging can take considerably longer.

24 If the battery is to be charged from a fully discharged state (condition reading less than 12.2 volts) have it recharged by your Ford dealer or local automotive electrician as the charge rate is higher and constant supervision during charging is necessary.

5C

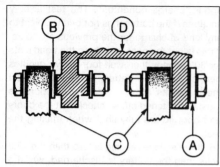

4.6 Alternator mounting components

A Large washer
B Small washer (where fitted)
C Mounting bracket
D Alternator mounting flanges

4 Alternator - removal and refitting

Removal

1 Disconnect the battery and disconnect the multi-plug or leads from the rear of the alternator.
2 Remove the head shield (where fitted).
3 Release the mounting and adjuster link bolts, push the alternator in towards the engine and slip the drivebelt from the pulley.
4 Unscrew and remove the mounting bolts and adjuster link bolt and withdraw the alternator from the engine.

5.2 Alternator adjusting strap bolt (arrowed)

5.4 Check drivebelt tension is correct

Refitting

5 Refit by reversing the removal operations, adjusting the drivebelt to the correct tension.
6 Note that it is important to ensure that the mounting bolt washers and spacers are fitted as shown **(see illustration)**. If this is not done it is possible to excessively strain or even break the alternator mounting flanges when the bolts are tightened.
7 The mountings should be tightened evenly and progressively in the following order - adjuster bolt, front mounting, rear mounting.

5 Alternator drivebelt - removal, refitting and tensioning

1 A conventional "V" drivebelt is used to drive the alternator, power being transmitted from a pulley on the front end of the crankshaft.
2 To remove a belt, slacken the alternator mounting bolts and the bolts on the adjuster link, push the alternator in towards the engine and slip the belt from the pulleys **(see illustration)**.
3 Fit the belt by slipping it over the pulley rims while the alternator is still loose on its mountings. Never be tempted to remove or fit a belt by prising it over a pulley without releasing the alternator. The pulley, and possibly the alternator, will be distorted or damaged.
4 To retension the belt, pull the alternator away from the engine until the belt is fairly taut and nip up the adjuster strap bolt. Check that the total deflection of the belt is as specified when tested on the longest belt run **(see illustration)**. A little trial and error may be required to obtain the correct tension. If the belt is too slack, it will slip and soon become glazed or burnt and the alternator will not perform correctly, with consequent low battery charge. If the belt is too tight, the bearings in the alternator will soon be damaged.
5 Do not lever against the body of the alternator to tension the belt, or damage may occur.

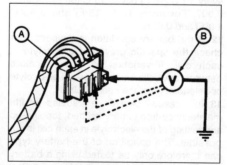

6.4 Alternator charging circuit continuity check

A Wiring multi-plug
B Voltmeter

6 Alternator - testing

1 The following in-vehicle alternator tests can be made irrespective of which type of alternator is fitted provided a 10 to 20 volt voltmeter, an ammeter (70 amp+) and a load rheostat are available. Alternatively a proprietary multimeter can be used.
2 Prior to undertaking any of the following tests, first check that the drivebelt tension is correct and that the battery is well charged.

Wiring continuity check

3 Detach the battery earth lead, then disconnect the wiring multiplug connector from the alternator.
4 Reconnect the earth lead, switch the ignition on and connect a voltmeter to a good earth point. Now check the voltage reading on each of the multi-plug terminals. A zero reading indicates an open circuit in the wiring whilst a battery voltage reading proves the wiring to be in good condition **(see illustration)**.

Alternator output check

5 Connect up the voltmeter, ammeter and rheostat, as shown **(see illustration)**.
6 Switch the headlights on, also the heater blower motor and heated rear window (where fitted). Start the engine and keep it running at 3000 rpm whilst varying the resistance to increase the current loading. The rated output should be achieved without the voltage dropping below 13 volts.
7 Complete the check by disconnecting the test instruments and switching off the ignition, headlights, blower motor and heated rear window.

Positive side voltage check

8 Connect up the voltmeter as shown **(see illustration)**. Switch on the headlamps then start the engine and note the voltage drop.

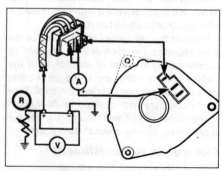

6.5 Alternator output check

A Ammeter
V Voltmeter
R Rheostat (30 amps rating resistor)

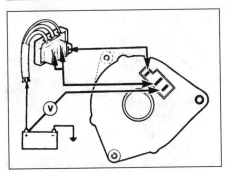

6.8 Alternator charge circuit voltage drop check - positive side

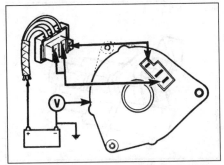

6.9 Alternator charge circuit voltage drop check - negative side

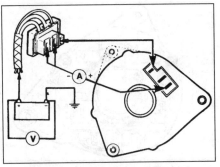

6.10 Alternator regulator control voltage check

Now run the engine at 3000 rpm. If the voltage shown is above 0.5 volt it is indicative of a high resistance in the positive side of the charge circuit, and this will need to be located and rectified. Switch the ignition and headlights off to complete.

Negative side voltage check

9 Proceed as described in paragraph 8 but connect the voltmeter as shown **(see illustration)**. A voltmeter reading in excess of 0.25 volts is indicative of a high resistance fault in the negative side wiring.

Regulator control voltage check

10 Connect up the voltmeter and ammeter as shown **(see illustration)** then start the engine and check the voltage reading.
11 Increase the engine speed to 3000 rpm

and note the ammeter reading. This should fall to between 3 and 5 amps at which point check the voltmeter which should read between 13.7 and 14.5 volts. Any readings given which are not within these limits indicate a fault in the voltage control regulator and this must be renewed.
12 Switch the ignition off and detach the test equipment. Disconnect the battery earth lead and reconnect the alternator multi-plug. Reconnect the battery earth lead to complete.

7 Alternator brushes and regulator - renewal

1 With the alternator removed from the engine, clean the external surfaces free from dirt.

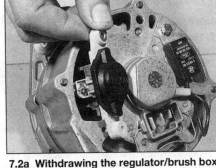

7.2a Withdrawing the regulator/brush box - Bosch alternator

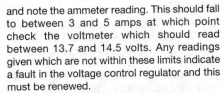

7.2b Compare the brush length with that shown in the Specifications - Bosch alternator

Bosch

2 Remove the regulator screws from the rear cover and withdraw the regulator **(see illustration)**. Check the length of each brush and renew if less than the specified minimum **(see illustration)**.
3 To remove the brushes, unsolder the wiring connectors and remove each brush with its spring **(see illustration)**.
4 Refit by reversing the removal operations.

Lucas type B

5 Remove the alternator rear cover.
6 Extract the brush box retaining screws and withdraw the brush assemblies from the brush box **(see illustration)**.
7 If the length of the brushes is less than the specified minimum, renew them. Refit by reversing the removal operations.
8 To remove the regulator, disconnect the wires from the unit and unscrew the retaining screw.
9 Refit by reversing the removal operations, but check that the small plastic spacer and the connecting link are correctly located.

Lucas type D

10 Proceed as described in paragraphs 5 and 6 **(see illustration)**.
11 If the brushes are worn beyond the minimum length specified, disconnect the field connector and renew the brush box/regulator complete as the brushes are not individually replaceable.
12 Refit in the reverse order to removal.

5C

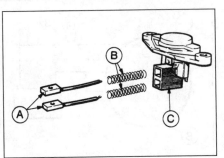

7.3 Brush box components - Bosch alternator

A Brushes   B Springs   C Brush box

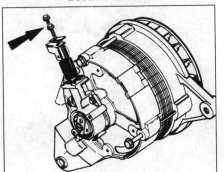

7.6 Brush box retaining screws - Lucas type B alternator

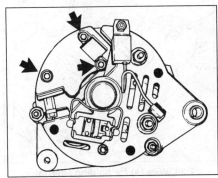

7.10 Brush box retaining screws - Lucas type D alternator

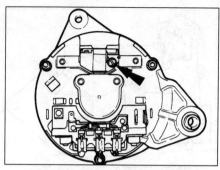

7.14a Brush box retaining screw - Motorola alternator

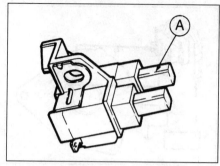

7.14b Brush box and brushes (A) - Motorola alternator

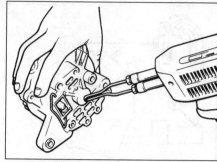

7.20 Heating alternator rear housing - Mitsubishi alternator

Motorola

13 Extract the two regulator securing screws, disconnect the two regulator leads and withdraw the unit.

14 Extract the brush box retaining screw and pull and tilt the brush box from its location, taking care not to damage the brushes during the process **(see illustrations)**.

15 If the brushes are worn beyond the specified length, unsolder the brush connections.

16 Fit the new brushes by reversing the removal operations.

Mitsubishi

17 Hold the alternator shaft against rotation and unscrew the pulley unit. Take off the spring washer, pulley, fan, large spacer and dust seal.

18 Scribe a line along the length of the alternator to facilitate reassembly of the housings and stator.

19 Unscrew the tie-bolts and remove the drive end housing.

20 Separate the rotor from the rear end housing and the stator. Before this can be done, the housing may have to be warmed using a soldering iron or hot air gun **(see illustration)**.

21 Check the brushes for wear. If they have worn below the minimum specified length, unscrew the four bolts and remove the rectifier and stator assembly from the rear housing.

22 Unsolder the stator connections from the rectifier pack terminals. Renew the brush box **(see illustration)**.

23 Resolder the new rectifier/brush pack leads and refit the pack and stator.

24 Hold the brushes in the retracted state with a piece of wire so that the brushes will pass over the slip rings **(see illustration)**.

25 Fit the rotor to the rear housing and then withdraw the temporary wire.

26 Fit the drive end housing (scribed line aligned) and secure with the tie-bolts.

27 Fit the dust seal, spacer, fan, pulley and spring washer. Tighten the pulley nut.

8 Starter motor - removal and refitting

1 Disconnect the battery.

2 Working from under the vehicle, disconnect the main starter motor cable and the two wires from the starter solenoid **(see illustration)**.

3 Unbolt the starter motor and withdraw it from its location.

4 Refit the starter motor by reversing the removal procedure.

9 Starter motor - testing

1 Check that the battery is fully charged.

Solenoid check

2 To test the solenoid, first disconnect the battery negative lead and both leads from the solenoid. Check the continuity of the solenoid windings by connecting a test lamp (12V with 2 to 3W bulb) between the starter spade terminal and the solenoid body **(see illustration)**. The lamp should light up.

3 Now make the test circuit as shown **(see illustration)**, using a higher wattage (18 to 21 W) bulb. Energise the solenoid by applying 12V between the spade terminal and the starter

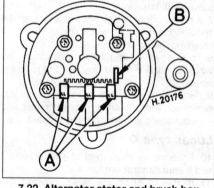

7.22 Alternator stator and brush box connections - Mitsubishi alternator

A Stator connections
B Brush box-to-rectifier terminal

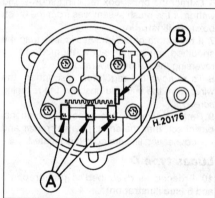

7.24 Wire (A) for holding alternator brushes in retracted position - Mitsubishi alternator

8.2 Starter motor cable connections (arrowed)

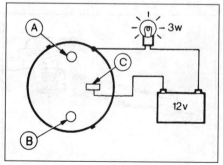

9.2 Starter motor solenoid winding check

A Battery terminal   *C Spade terminal*
B Feed terminal

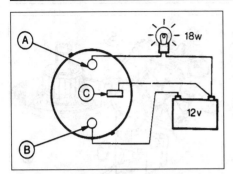

9.3 Starter motor solenoid continuity check

A Battery terminal   C Spade terminal
B Feed terminal

feed terminal. The solenoid should be heard to operate and the test bulb should light up, indicating that the solenoid contacts have closed.

On load voltage check

4 Connect a voltmeter between the battery terminals. Disconnect the positive LT lead from the ignition coil and operate the starter. The voltmeter should indicate not less than 10.5V.
5 Now connect the voltmeter between the starter main terminal and the body of the starter motor. Operate the starter, with the coil LT lead still disconnected. The reading on the voltmeter should be no more than 1.0V lower than that indicated during the test described in paragraph 4. If it is, check the battery-to-starter motor wiring.
6 Connect the voltmeter between the battery positive terminal and the starter motor main feed terminal. Operate the starter (with the LT coil positive lead disconnected) for two or three seconds and observe the meter readings. A reading of 12V should drop to less than 1.0V. If the reading is higher, a high resistance is indicated (refer to paragraph 7). If the reading is lower, refer to paragraph 8.
7 Connect the voltmeter between the two main stud terminals of the starter solenoid. With the positive LT lead disconnected from the coil, operate the starter for two or three seconds and note the meter readings. Battery voltage (12V) should be indicated first, followed by a voltage drop of less than 0.5V. If outside this tolerance, a faulty switch or

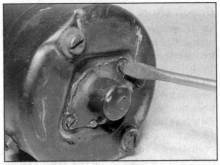

10.2 Remove the commutator end housing cap securing screws

connections may be the cause, or loose or corroded terminals in the circuit.
8 Connect a voltmeter between the battery negative terminal and the starter motor main casing. With the positive LT lead disconnected from the coil, operate the starter for two or three seconds. If the earth line is satisfactory, the reading should be less than 0.5V. If it is 0.6V or more then there is a high resistance in the earth return side of the circuit. This may be due to a loose or corroded connection either at the battery or at the engine block.

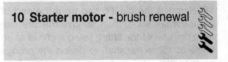

10 Starter motor - brush renewal

Bosch long frame and Cajavec

1 With the starter motor removed from the vehicle and cleaned, grip the unit in a vice fitted with soft jaw protectors.
2 Remove the two screws securing the commutator end housing cap, then remove the cap and rubber seal (see illustration).
3 Wipe any grease from the armature shaft, and remove the C-clip, or E-clip, as applicable, and shims from the end of the shaft (see illustrations).
4 Unscrew the two nuts and remove the washers, or remove the securing screws (as applicable), then lift off the commutator end housing (see illustrations).
5 Carefully prise the thrust retaining springs from their locations, then slide the brushes from the brush plate.

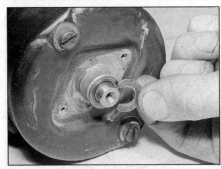

10.3a Remove the C-clip . . .

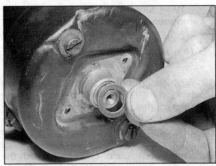

10.3b . . . and shims from the end of the armature shaft

6 If the brushes have worn to less than the specified minimum, renew them as a set. To renew the brushes, cut the leads at their midpoint and make a good soldered joint when connecting the new brushes.
7 The commutator face should be clean and free from burnt spots. Where necessary, burnish with fine glass paper (not emery) and wipe with a fuel-moistened cloth.
8 On starter motors where the commutator end housing is secured by nuts and washers, position the brush plate over the end of the armature, with the cut-outs in the brush plate aligned with the end housing securing studs.
9 On starter motors where the commutator end housing is secured by screws, position the brush plate over the end of the armature with the cut-outs in the brush plate aligned with the loops in the field windings (see illustration). The brush plate will be positively located when the commutator end housing screws are fitted.

5C

10.4a Remove the commutator end housing securing screws

10.4b Commutator end housing removed to expose brush plate

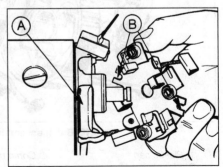

10.9 Align the cut-outs in the brush plate (B) with the loops in the field windings (A)

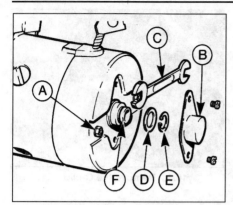

10.14 Commutator end housing components - Bosch short frame motor

A Securing screws   D Shims
B Housing cap   E C-clip
C Spanner   F Armature shaft

10 Position the brushes in their respective locations in the brush plate, and fit the brush retaining springs.
11 Guide the commutator end housing into position, at the same time sliding the rubber insulator into the cut-out in the housing. Secure the commutator end housing with the nuts and washers or screws, as applicable.
12 Fit sufficient shims to the end of the armature shaft to eliminate endfloat when the C-clip or E-clip, as applicable is fitted, then fit the clip.
13 Fit the armature shaft bearing seal to the commutator end housing, then apply a little lithium-based grease to the end of the armature shaft and refit the end housing cap, securing with the two screws.

Bosch short frame

14 To remove and refit the brush assembly, proceed as for the Bosch long frame except for the following **(see illustration)**.
15 Release the brush holders complete with brushes by pushing the brush holders towards the commutator and unclipping them from the brush plate. Withdraw the brush plate **(see illustration)**.
16 To renew the brushes, the leads must be unsoldered from the terminals on the brush plate, and the leads of the new brushes must be soldered to the terminals.
17 To refit the brush assembly, position the brush plate over the end of the armature shaft, then assemble the brush holders, brushes and springs, ensuring that the brush holder clips are securely located. The brush plate will be positively located when the commutator end housing screws are fitted.

Lucas

Note: *New star clips must be obtained for the armature shaft on reassembly.*
18 With the starter motor removed from the vehicle and cleaned, grip the unit in a vice fitted with soft jaw protectors.
19 Remove the plastic cap from the end of the armature shaft, then remove the star clip from the end of the shaft, using a chisel at an angle of 45° to the shaft to distort the prongs of the clip until it can be removed **(see illustration)**.
20 Unscrew the two securing nuts and remove the connector cable from the main feed terminal.

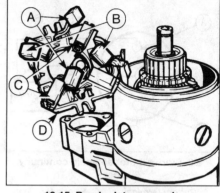

10.15 Brush plate removal - Bosch short frame motor

A Field brushes   C Brush plate
B Terminal brushes   D Brush holders

21 Extract the two commutator end plate securing screws, and carefully tap the end plate to free it. Lift the end plate clear to allow access to the two field brushes. Disconnect the two field brushes from the brush box to allow complete removal of the commutator end plate. Take care not to damage the gasket as the end plate is removed.
22 Remove the nut, washer and insulator from the main terminal stud on the commutator end plate, then push the stud and the second insulator through the end plate and unhook the brushes.
23 To remove the brush box, drill out the rivets securing the brush box to the end plate, then remove the brush box and gasket.
24 If the brushes have worn to less than the specified minimum, renew them as a set. To renew the brushes, cut the leads at their midpoint and make a good soldered joint when connecting the new brushes.
25 The commutator face should be clean and free from burnt spots. Where necessary, burnish with fine glass paper (not emery) and wipe with a fuel-moistened cloth.
26 Commence reassembly by positioning the brush box gasket on the commutator end plate, then position the brush box on the gasket and rivet the brush box to the end plate. Use a new gasket if necessary.
27 Fit the main terminal stud and insulator to the commutator end plate, then secure the stud with the remaining insulator, washer and nut. Fit the two brushes which are attached to the terminal stud into their respective locations in the brush box.
28 Fit the two field brushes into their locations in the brush box, then position the commutator end plate on the yoke and fit the two securing screws.
29 Fit a new star clip to the end of the armature shaft, ensuring that the clip is pressed home firmly to eliminate any endfloat in the armature **(see illustration)**. Fit the plastic cap over the end of the armature shaft.

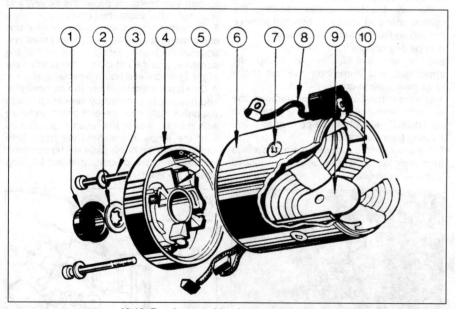

10.19 Brush assembly - Lucas starter motor

1 Plastic cap
2 Star clip
3 Commutator end plate
    securing screw
4 Commutator end plate
5 Brush box
6 Yoke
7 Pole securing screw
8 Solenoid connector link
9 Pole shoe
10 Field coils

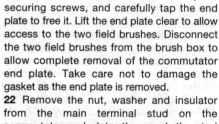

10.29 Using a soft faced hammer and socket to fit a new star clip to the end of the armature shaft - Lucas starter motor

Nippondenso

30 With the starter motor removed from the vehicle and cleaned, grip the unit in a vice fitted with soft jaw protectors.

31 Unscrew the retaining nut and washer and disconnect the wiring from the terminal on the solenoid.

32 Remove the two screws securing the commutator end housing cap and remove the cap **(see illustration)**.

33 Remove the C-clip from the groove in the armature shaft, and remove the spring.

34 Unscrew the two bolts and washers, and withdraw the commutator end housing.

35 Withdraw the two field brushes from the brush plate, then remove the brush plate.

36 If the brushes have worn to less than the specified minimum, renew them as a set. To renew the brushes, cut the leads at their midpoint and make a good soldered joint when connecting the new brushes.

37 The commutator face should be clean and free from burnt spots. Where necessary, burnish with fine glass paper (not emery) and wipe with a fuel-moistened cloth.

38 Position the brush plate over the end of the armature, aligning the cut-outs in the brush plate with the loops in the field windings. The brush plate will be positively located when the commutator end housing bolts are fitted.

39 Fit the brushes to their locations in the brush plate, and retain with the springs.

40 Fit the commutator end housing and secure with the two bolts and washers.

41 Fit the spring and the C-clip to the end of the armature shaft, then smear the end of the shaft with a little lithium-based grease, and refit the commutator end housing cap, securing with the two screws.

42 Reconnect the wiring to the solenoid terminal and fit the washer and retaining nut.

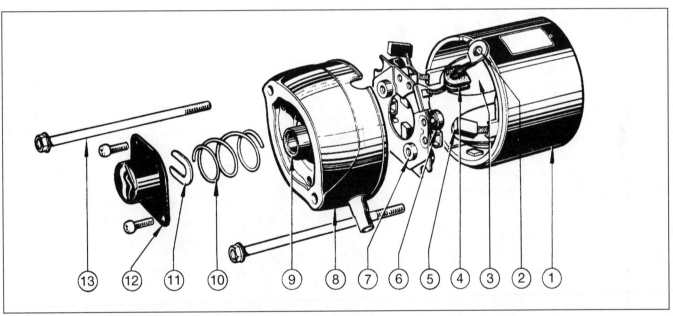

10.32 Brush assembly - Nippondenso starter motor

1 Yoke	6 Brush spring	11 C-clip
2 Solenoid connecting link	7 Brush plate	12 Commutator end housing cap
3 Pole shoe	8 Commutator end housing	13 Commutator end housing securing
4 Rubber grommet	9 Bush	bolt
5 Brush	10 Spring	

5C

Chapter 6
Clutch

Contents

Degrees of difficulty

Easy, suitable for novice with little experience	Fairly easy, suitable for beginner with some experience	Fairly difficult, suitable for competent DIY mechanic	Difficult, suitable for experienced DIY mechanic	Very difficult, suitable for expert DIY or professional

Specifications

Type	Single plate, diaphragm spring, operated by self-adjusting cable
Pedal stroke (nominal)	145 mm

Driven plate (disc)

Diameter:

1.0 and 1.1 litre	165 mm
1.3 and 1.6 litre	190 mm
All models (May 1988- on)	220 mm
Lining thickness	3.20 mm

Torque wrench settings	**Nm**	**lbf ft**
Pressure plate to flywheel:		
165 mm diameter	9 to 11	7 to 8
190 mm diameter	16 to 20	12 to 15
220 mm diameter	25 to 34	18 to 25
Release fork-to-shaft bolt:		
Up to May 1988	32	24
June 1988-on	38	28

6

1 General information and precautions

General information

The clutch is of a single dry plate type with a diaphragm spring pressure plate. Actuation is by cable and the pendant-mounted pedal incorporates a self-adjusting mechanism.

The release bearing is of the ball type and is kept in constant contact with the fingers of the diaphragm spring by the action of the pedal self-adjusting mechanism. In consequence, there is no pedal free movement adjustment required.

When the clutch pedal is released, the adjustment pawl is no longer engaged with the teeth on the pedal quadrant, the cable being tensioned, however, by the spring which is located between the pedal and the quadrant. When the pedal is depressed, the pawl engages in the nearest vee between the teeth. The particular tooth engagement position will gradually change as the components move to compensate for wear in the clutch disc (driven plate) and stretch in the cable.

The size of the clutch varies according to engine capacity (see Specifications).

Precautions

When renewing any clutch components on XR2 models built after May 1988, be aware that from that date, the clutch is of "low-lift" type, and earlier type clutch components should not be fitted. The correct components are marked "LOW-LIFT".

2 Clutch - removal, inspection and refitting

Removal

1 To remove the clutch it is necessary to disconnect the engine and transmission assembly. This can be done by either removing the engine and transmission complete, and then separating them on the bench, or by removing the transmission only.

2 Remove the clutch assembly by unscrewing the six bolts holding the pressure plate assembly to the rear face of the flywheel. Unscrew the bolts diagonally, half a turn at a time, to prevent distortion to the cover flange.

2.3 Withdraw the clutch pressure plate and disc from the flywheel. Note location dowels

2.10 Clutch disc (driven plate) marking

2.11 Refit the clutch cover assembly

3 With all the bolts and spring washers removed, lift the clutch assembly off the locating dowels **(see illustration)**. The clutch disc (driven plate) may fall out at this stage as it is not attached to either the clutch cover assembly or the flywheel.

Inspection

4 Examine the clutch disc friction lining for wear and loose rivets and the disc for rim distortion, cracks, broken hub springs and worn splines. The surface of the friction linings may be highly glazed but as long as the clutch material pattern can be clearly seen this is satisfactory. Compare the amount of lining wear with a new clutch disc at the stores in your local garage, and if the linings are more than three quarters worn renew the disc.

5 It is always best to renew the clutch as an assembly to preclude further trouble; an exchange unit will have been accurately set up and balanced to very fine limits.

6 Check the machined faces of the flywheel and the pressure plate. If either is grooved it should be machined until smooth or renewed.

7 If the pressure plate is cracked or split it is essential that an exchange unit is fitted, also if the pressure of the diaphragm spring is suspect.

8 Check the release bearing for smoothness of operation. There should be no harshness and no slackness in it. It should spin reasonably freely bearing in mind it has been pre-packed with grease.

Refitting

9 It is important that no oil or grease gets onto the clutch disc friction linings, or the pressure plate and flywheel faces during refitting. It is advisable to refit the clutch with clean hands and to wipe down the pressure plate and flywheel faces with a clean dry rag before reassembly begins.

10 Place the clutch (driven plate) against the flywheel, ensuring that it is the correct way round. The flywheel side of the disc is smooth. If the disc is fitted the wrong way round, it will be quite impossible to operate the clutch **(see illustration)**.

11 Refit the clutch cover assembly loosely on the dowels. Refit the six bolts and spring washers, and tighten them finger tight so that the disc is gripped but can still be moved **(see illustration)**.

12 The clutch disc must now be centralised so that when the engine and gearbox are mated, the gearbox input shaft splines will pass through the splines in the centre of the disc.

13 Centralisation can be carried out quite easily by inserting a round bar or long screwdriver through the hole in the centre of the clutch, so that the end of the bar rests in the small hole in the end of the crankshaft. Ideally an old input shaft should be used.

14 Using the hole in the end of the crankshaft as a fulcrum, moving the bar sideways or up and down will move the disc in the necessary direction to achieve centralisation.

15 Centralisation is easily judged by removing the bar and viewing the disc hub in relation to the hole in the centre of the clutch cover diaphragm spring. When the hub appears exactly in the centre of the hole all is correct. Alternatively, the input shaft will centre the clutch hub exactly obviating the need for visual alignment.

16 Tighten the clutch bolts firmly in a diagonal sequence to ensure that the cover plate is pulled down evenly and without distortion of the flange **(see illustration)**. Finally tighten the bolts down to the specified torque.

---

3 Clutch release bearing - renewal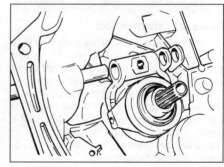

Pre May 1988 models

1 With the gearbox and engine separated to provide access to the clutch, attention can be given to the release bearing located in the bellhousing over the input shaft.

2 The release bearing is an important component and unless it is nearly new it is a mistake not to renew it during an overhaul of the clutch.

3 To remove the release bearing, first remove the bolt securing the release arm and pull out the shaft **(see illustrations)**.

4 The release fork and bearing can then be pulled off the input shaft.

2.16 Tightening the clutch cover (pressure) plate bolts. Note clutch disc centralising tool

3.3a Clutch release arm securing bolt - arrowed

3.3b Withdraw the shaft and remove the release bearing unit

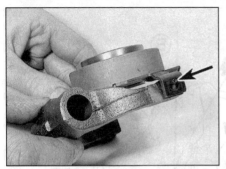

3.5 Clutch release bearing attachment to fork (roll pin arrowed)

4.2 Detach cable from clutch release lever fork

4.5 Withdraw cable from engine compartment side

5 To free the bearing from the release fork, simply unhook it **(see illustration)**.
6 Refitting is a reversal of this procedure.

All models May 1988 on

7 Note that models built after May 1988 have a release fork which cannot be detached from the shaft/lever, and neither can the shaft/lever be detached from the bellhousing, otherwise the procedure for bearing renewal is as described for the pre 1988 models.

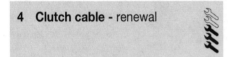

4 Clutch cable - renewal

1 Raise the clutch pedal and position a suitable block of wood underneath it to support it.
2 Raise and support the bonnet then grip the clutch inner cable as shown and disengage it from the clutch release lever **(see illustration)**.
3 Unclip and detach the dash lower insulating panel for access to the clutch pedal.
4 With the pedal raised, detach the pawl from the toothed segment, pivoting the segment forward.

5 Pivot the segment rearwards then remove the cable, passing it through the space between the pedal and the automatic adjustment unit. Withdraw the cable through the engine compartment **(see illustration)**.
6 To refit the cable, first raise and support the clutch pedal, as described in paragraph 1. Check that the adjustment unit pawl is disengaged from the segment then refit the clutch cable reversing the removal procedure **(see illustration)**.
7 When the cable is fitted, extract the support block from under the pedal then slowly operate the clutch to readjust the cable.
8 Refit the lower dash insulating panel to complete.

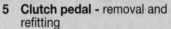

5 Clutch pedal - removal and refitting

Removal

1 Disconnect the clutch cable from the release lever and the pedal/self-adjustment unit.
2 On left-hand drive models, extract the spring clip from the pedal pivot shaft and withdraw the washers; keeping them in order

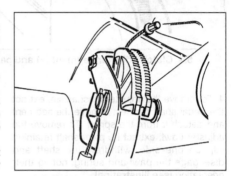

4.6 Reattach the clutch cable to the segment unit

for refitting. The pedal can then be removed sideways from the shaft.
3 On right-hand drive models the pedal is removed complete with the clutch/brake pedal support bracket. Disconnect the brake pedal-to-servo pushrod. Detach the brake stop-light switch wire multi-connector plug then unscrew and remove the four support bracket-to-bulkhead retaining nuts and the single bolt to the upper crash panel **(see illustrations)**. The pedal box support bracket can now be renewed and the clutch pedal removed, as described in paragraph 2.

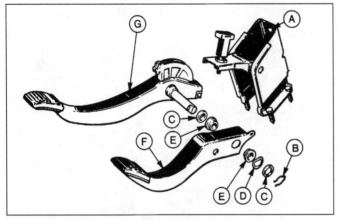

5.3a Brake and clutch pedal assembly components

A Mounting bracket
B Circlip
C Spacer
D Washer
E Bush
F Brake pedal
G Clutch pedal

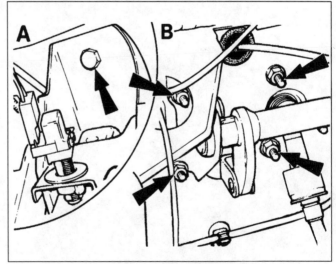

5.3b Clutch/brake pedal bracket retaining bolt (A) to crash panel and bulkhead bolts (B) - right-hand drive

6

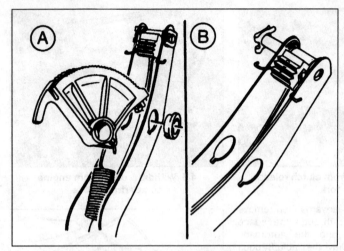

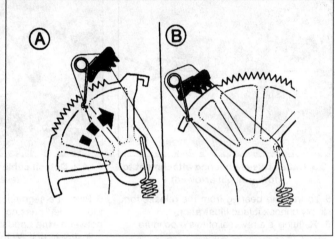

5.4 Clutch adjuster segment (A) and pawl (B) removal

5.6 Segment refitting: lift pawl (A) and rotate segment to position pawl as shown (B)

4 To remove the adjuster mechanism, extract the pedal shaft bushes, remove the segment and detach it from the spring. To remove the adjuster pawl, extract its pivot shaft retaining clip on one side, withdraw the shaft and disengage the pawl and spring, noting their orientation **(see illustration)**.

Refitting

5 Reassembly of the pedal and adjuster mechanism is a reversal of the removal procedure. Lubricate the pivot shafts prior to assembly with molybdenum grease.

6 When the pawl and segment are refitted to the pedal, lever up the pawl and turn the segment so that the pawl can be positioned clear of the segment teeth on the smooth section of the segment **(see illustration)**.

7 Refit the clutch pedal to the pivot shaft, locate the washers and securing clip and then attach the cable.

8 On right-hand drive models relocate the clutch/brake pedal bracket and secure with the retaining nuts and bolt.

9 Reconnect the clutch cable and adjust it.

10 Refit the dash lower insulating panel to complete, then check that the clutch operation is satisfactory.

Chapter 7
Manual gearbox

Contents

Degrees of difficulty

Easy, suitable for novice with little experience	Fairly easy, suitable for beginner with some experience	Fairly difficult, suitable for competent DIY mechanic	Difficult, suitable for experienced DIY mechanic	Very difficult, suitable for expert DIY or professional

Specifications

Type . . . . Four or five forward speeds and one reverse, synchromesh on all forward gears

Torque wrench settings	Nm	lbf ft
4-speed gearbox		
Gearbox-to-engine bolts	40	30
Starter motor bolts	40	30
Gearbox bearer	52	38
Gearbox bearer to gearbox	90	66
Spindle carrier to balljoint	80	59
Gearshift stabilizer to gearbox	55	41
Shift rod to selector shaft clamp bolt	15	11
Final drivegear to differential housing	115	85
Small to large housing	25	18
Housing cover	13	10
Selector shaft detent cap nut	27	20
Gearshift unit to floorpan	18	13
Oil filler plug	27	20
Reverse light switch	27	20
Selector gate stabilizer	6	4
Gearshift gaiter to body	2	1.5
Gearshift gate bolts (Feb 1987 on)	18 to 25	13 to 18
5-speed gearbox		
Gearbox-to-engine bolts	40	30
Starter motor bolts	40	30
Gearbox bearer to gearbox	90	66
Gearbox bearer to floor	52	38
Spindle carrier to balljoint	80	59
Gearshift stabilizer to gearbox	55	41
Gearshift gate bolts (Feb 1987 on)	18 to 25	13 to 18
Shift rod to selector shaft clamp bolt	16	12
Selector block to main selector shaft	14	10
Final drivegear to differential housing	115	85
Clutch housing to gearbox housing	25	18
Intermediate to gearbox housing	13	9
Fifth gear selector pin clamp bolt	17	13
Fifth gear selector plate to housing	30	22
Housing cover to intermediate housing	10	7
Selector shaft detent mechanism cap nut	30	22
Gearshift stabilizer to floor	18	13
Oil filler plug	27	20
Reverse light switch	27	20

1 General information

The 4-speed gearbox and differential are housed in a two section light alloy casting which is bolted to a transversely mounted engine. Drive from the engine/gearbox assembly is transmitted to the front roadwheels through open driveshafts.

The 5-speed gearbox is basically the same as the 4-speed version with the exception of a modified selector mechanism and an additional gear and synchro-hub contained in a housing attached to the side of the main gearbox casing.

The gearchange mechanisms of both types of gearbox were modified in early 1986 and again in February of 1987 - see text.

2 Gearchange mechanism - adjustment

1 This is not a routine operation and will normally only be required after dismantling, to compensate for wear or to overcome any "notchiness" evident during gear selection.

2 To set the linkage correctly, refer to Chapter 2A, Section 17.

3 Gearchange mechanism (4-speed) - removal, overhaul and refitting

Pre 1986 models

Removal

1 Before commencing removal operations, engage 4th gear.

2 Unscrew the gear lever knob, slide the rubber gaiter up to the lever and remove it **(see illustration)**.

3 If the vehicle is not over an inspection pit, jack it up and fit axle stands (see *"Jacking and vehicle support"*).

4 Unhook the tension spring which runs between the gearchange rod and the side-member.

5 Slacken the clamp bolt and pull the gearchange rod from the selector shaft which projects from the gearbox.

6 Unbolt the end of the stabilizer from the gearbox housing. Note the washer between the stabilizer trunnion and the gearbox.

7 Still working under the vehicle, unbolt the gearchange housing from the floor. Withdraw the housing/stabilizer from the vehicle.

Overhaul

8 To dismantle, unbolt the housing from the stabilizer and detach the gearchange lever with plastic cover and the stabilizer from the slide block.

9 Detach the gearchange rod from the slide block. This is done by unclipping the upper guide shell and withdrawing the rod.

10 The gear lever can be removed by prising off the rubber spring retaining clip and withdrawing the spring, half shell and plastic cover.

11 Renew any worn components and reassemble by reversing the dismantling procedure, but observe the following points.

12 If the stabilizer bush is in poor condition it can cause engine and gearbox noises to be transmitted to the vehicle interior. To renew the bush, press it out using a suitable bolt, nut and two washers, used together with a pair of suitable diameter sockets. During bush removal and refitting, do not pull down excessively on the stabilizer bar. Use sockets of different diameters so that one is the same as that of the bush housing and one the same diameter as the fitted bush.

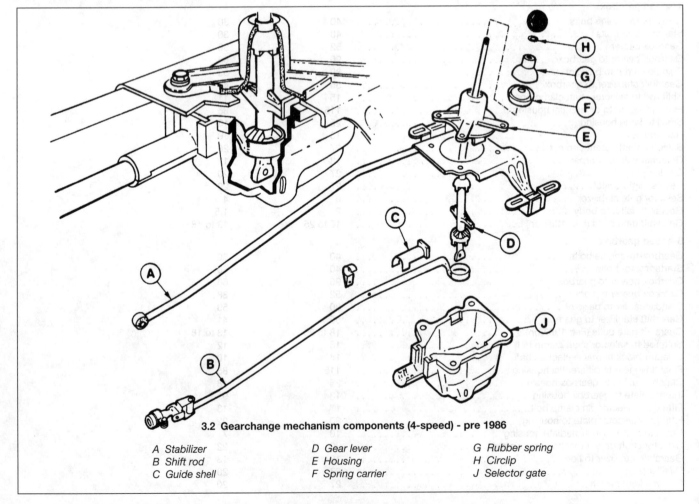

3.2 Gearchange mechanism components (4-speed) - pre 1986

A Stabilizer	D Gear lever	G Rubber spring
B Shift rod	E Housing	H Circlip
C Guide shell	F Spring carrier	J Selector gate

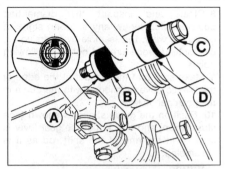

3.13 Gearshift stabilizer bush fitting method. Note the void positions in bush (inset)

A Washer   C Washer
B Bush   D Socket

13 Having withdrawn the old bush, insert the new one drawing it into position using the sockets, bolt, washers and nut. Position the voids in the bush as shown **(see illustration)** and take care during fitting not to damage or distort the bush.
14 Make sure that the cut-out at the edge of the plastic cover is aligned with the curve in the gearchange lever as shown **(see illustration)**.
15 The gear lever must locate in the shift rod cut-out.

Refitting

16 To install the gearchange mechanism to the vehicle, offer it up from below and loosely attach it to the floorpan **(see illustration)**.
17 Reconnect the stabilizer to the gearbox, remembering to fit the washer between the trunnion and the gearbox **(see illustration)**.
18 The mechanism should now be secured to the floorpan by tightening the nuts to the specified torque.
19 Reconnect the gearchange rod to the shaft at the gearbox, as described in Chapter 2A, Section 17.
20 Working inside the vehicle, refit the gaiter and the knob to the gear lever.
21 Lower the vehicle to the ground.

Models from early 1986

22 At the beginning of 1986 the remote control gearchange mechanism was modified on all 4-speed gearboxes **(see illustration)**.

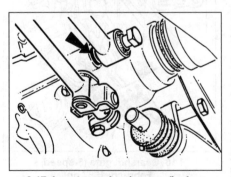

3.17 Locate washer (arrowed) when connecting the stabilizer

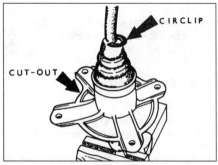

3.14 Circlip location and cut-out section of cover

23 Removal and refitting procedures are basically the same as described above, except that the gearchange housing is bolted directly to the floor and the four retaining nuts are accessible from inside the car.
24 Overhaul also follows the procedures described above.

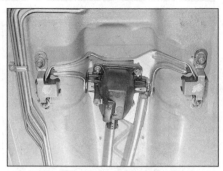

3.16 Gearchange mechanism floorpan mounting

Models from February 1987

25 As from February 1987, further modifications have been made to the gearchange mechanism, involving the gearshift gate, which will affect the overhaul procedure as follows.

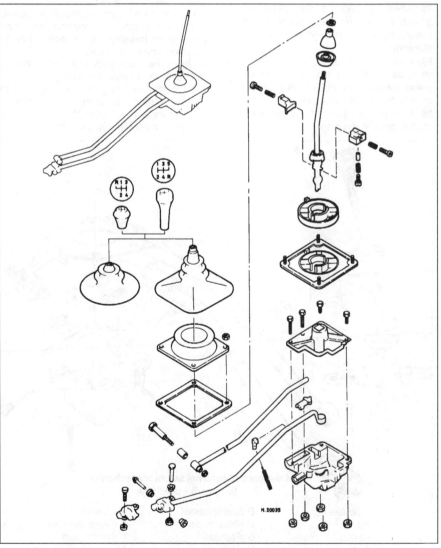

3.22 Gearchange mechanism components (4-speed) - early 1986 on

7

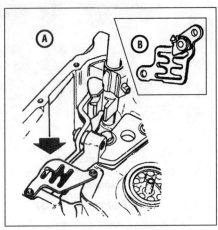

3.26 Gearshift gate (4-speed) - February 1987 on

A *4-speed assembly*
B *Reverse gear lock on underside of gate*

26 When dismantling for overhaul, the gearshift gate must be unbolted (two bolts) before removing the selector shaft **(see illustration)**.

27 When reassembling, the gearshift gate must be fitted after the selector shaft, but before the guide levers. Tighten the gate fixing bolts to the specified torque.

28 Note that the boss of the selector block must engage in the gate.

4 Gearchange mechanism (5-speed) - removal, overhaul and refitting

Pre 1986 models

Removal

1 Proceed as shown in paragraphs 1 to 3 of Section 3, but engage reverse gear instead of 4th.

2 Disconnect the exhaust pipe from the rubber mountings at the rear.

3 Proceed as shown in paragraphs 5 to 7 (Section 3).

Overhaul

4 To dismantle, unscrew and remove the three guide element spring retaining screws, one from each side of the selector housing, and one underneath (which also holds a lockpin). Extract the three springs and the lockpin **(see illustration)**.

5 Unscrew and remove the four selector housing-to-stabilizer mounting frame and gear lever housing cover bolts. Lift the gearlever and cover away.

6 Unclip the upper guide shell and lift the shift rod out of the selector housing.

7 To dismantle the gearlever prise off the rubber spring securing ring using a screwdriver and withdraw the rubber spring, the spring carrier and housing cover.

8 Clean and inspect the dismantled components. Renew any showing signs of excessive wear. Reassemble by reversing the dismantling procedure but note the following points.

9 Make sure that the cut-out at the edge of the plastic cover is aligned with the curve in the gearchange lever.

10 Position the guide shells as shown **(see illustration)** and check that the gear lever is located in the ring of the shift rod as it is assembled.

Refitting

11 Refit the gearchange mechanism to the vehicle, as described in paragraphs 16 to 21 of Section 3, and adjust as given for the 5-speed gearbox in Section 17, Chapter 2A.

Models from early 1986

12 At the beginning of 1986 the remote control gearchange mechanism was modified on all 5-speed gearboxes.

13 Removal and refitting procedures are basically the same as described above, except that the gearchange housing is bolted directly to the floor and the four retaining nuts are accessible from inside the car.

14 Overhaul also follows the procedures described above, but with reference to illustration 3.22.

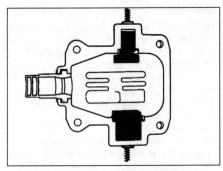

4.10 Guide shell and spring positioning

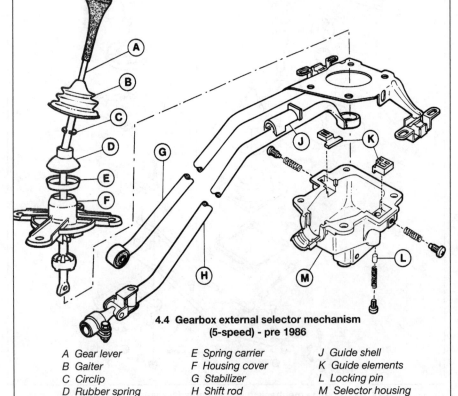

4.4 Gearbox external selector mechanism (5-speed) - pre 1986

A *Gear lever*	E *Spring carrier*	J *Guide shell*
B *Gaiter*	F *Housing cover*	K *Guide elements*
C *Circlip*	G *Stabilizer*	L *Locking pin*
D *Rubber spring*	H *Shift rod*	M *Selector housing*

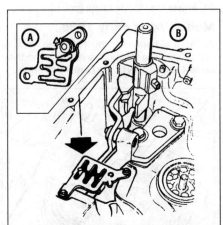

4.16 Gearshift gate (5-speed) - February 1987 on

A *Reverse gear lock*   B *5-speed assembly*

Models from February 1987

15 As from February 1987, further modifications have been made to the gearchange mechanism which affect the overhaul procedure as follows.

16 When dismantling for overhaul, the gearshift gate must be unbolted (two bolts) before removing the selector shaft **(see illustration)**.

17 When reassembling, the gearshift gate must be fitted after the selector shaft, but before the guide levers. Tighten the gate fixing bolts to the specified torque.

18 Note that the boss of the selector block must engage in the gate. The reverse gear lock must point downwards towards the selector shaft.

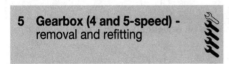

5 Gearbox (4 and 5-speed) - removal and refitting

All models

1 Disconnect the battery earth lead connector.

2 To ensure correct engagement of the selector mechanism during later operations, engage 4th gear on 4-speed models or reverse gear on 5-speed models.

3 Disconnect the speedometer cable from the gearbox after unscrewing the retaining nut **(see illustration)**.

4 Unhook the clutch cable from the release lever.

5 Unscrew and remove the top four bolts which hold the gearbox flange to the engine.

6 Release the gearbox breather tube from the side rail.

7 If the vehicle is not over an inspection pit, raise its front end and fit axle stands (see *"Jacking and vehicle support"*).

8 Support the weight of the engine either by using a jack and block of wood under the sump or by attaching a hoist.

9 Working under the vehicle, disconnect the leads from the starter motor and the reversing lamp switch.

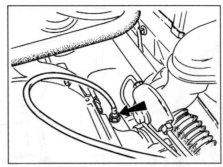

5.3 Speedometer drive cable retaining nut

10 Unbolt and remove the starter motor.

11 Unbolt and remove the cover plate from the lower face of the clutch housing **(see illustration)**.

12 Disconnect the gearchange rod from the gearbox selector shaft by releasing the clamp pinch-bolt and pulling the rod towards the rear of the vehicle. On 4-speed models, unhook the tension spring from the gearchange rod.

13 Unbolt the stabilizer rod from the side of the gearbox, noting that there is a washer between the trunnion of the rod and the gearbox casing.

14 Tie the gearchange rod and the stabilizer rod to the steering rack using a piece of wire.

15 Drain the oil from the gearbox into a suitable container. As a drain plug is not fitted, unscrew the selector shaft locking assembly which includes the nut, cap, spring and interlock pin **(see illustration)**.

16 On OHV models proceed as described in paragraphs 17 to 20 inclusive. On CVH models with driveshafts connected at their inner ends by socket-head bolts, proceed as described in paragraphs 21 to 23 inclusive.

OHV models

17 Unscrew and remove the balljoint retaining bolt from the outboard end of the right and left-hand suspension arms. The bolt is of Torx type, having a socket head, and, in the absence of the correct tool, an Allen key

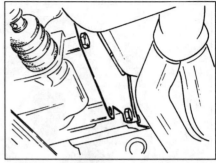

5.11 Unbolt and remove the clutch cover plate

may be used to stop the bolt turning while the nut is unscrewed. Unbolt and detach the suspension arms from their body mountings.

18 Unbolt and disconnect the left-hand side tie-bar, together with its bracket, from the body **(see illustration)**.

19 Disconnect the right- and left-hand driveshafts from the gearbox. Do this by inserting a lever between the constant velocity joint and the gearbox. With an assistant pulling the roadwheel outwards, strike the end of the lever to release the joint from the differential. In order to prevent the differential pinions from turning and obstructing the driveshaft holes, insert a plastic plug or similar.

20 Tie up the disconnected driveshaft to avoid putting any strain on the joints. **Note:** *When supported out of the way, the maximum angle imposed on the joints must not exceed 45° for the outer and 20° for the inner joint.*

CVH models

21 Disconnect the inner end of the left-hand assembly by unscrewing the socket-head bolts and removing them, together with the link washers. Suspend the driveshaft with wire so that it is out of the way observing the cautionary note in paragraph 20.

22 The right-hand intermediate shaft can be left in position during the removal of the gearbox. It is only necessary to unscrew and

7

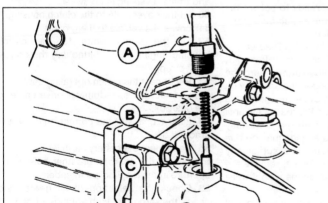

5.15 Selector shaft cap nut (A), spring (B) and interlock pin (C)

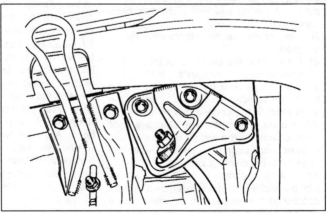

5.18 Tie-bar bracket and retaining bolts

5.38 Pinion gear displaced in differential

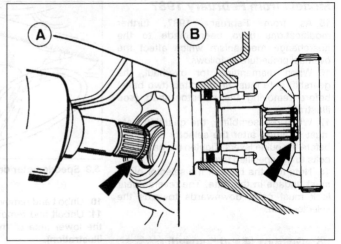

5.39 Snap-ring location on driveshaft (A) and when fitted (B)

remove the socket-head bolts with link washers and to suspend the driveshaft with wire out of the way, again observing the cautionary notes in paragraph 20.

23 If subsequently it is necessary to remove the intermediate driveshaft, refer to Chapter 8.

All models

24 Unscrew and remove the four bolts securing the engine/gearbox bearer to the body (two at the front and two at the rear).

25 Lower the engine as much as possible without overstraining the ancillary fittings and attachments (coolant hoses etc) so that the gearbox lower flange bolts can be unscrewed and removed. You may also need to loosen the engine mountings.

26 Withdraw the gearbox unit from the engine and carefully lower it (together with the bearer) and remove it from underneath the vehicle.

27 Unbolt and detach the bearer from the gearbox.

28 Before refitting the gearbox, lightly smear the splined part of the input shaft with a little grease, also the thrust bearing guide sleeve.

29 If the clutch has been dismantled, make sure that the disc (driven plate) has been centralised.

30 Refit the engine bearer to the underside of the gearbox.

31 Check that the engine adapter plate is correctly located on its dowels.

32 With the gearbox positioned on the floor below the vehicle, lift it up and engage the input shaft in the splined hub of the clutch driven plate. Obtain the help of an assistant for this work as the weight of the gearbox must not hang upon the input shaft while it is engaged in the driven plate.

33 Push the gearbox into full engagement with the engine and check that the unit sits on its locating dowels and that the adapter plate has not been displaced. Any reluctance for the gearbox to mate with the engine may be due to the splines of the input shaft and clutch

driven plate not engaging. Try swivelling the gearbox slightly, or have your assistant rotate the crankshaft by applying a spanner to the crankshaft pulley bolt.

34 Once the gearbox is fully engaged, screw in the lower retaining bolts to hold it to the engine.

35 Align the engine gearbox bearer bolt holes with the bolt holes in the body and fit the four retaining bolts. A trolley jack will be of assistance here to raise the engine/gearbox unit and support it whilst the bolts are inserted. Tighten the bolts to the specified torque setting once they are all located.

36 If the engine mounting bolts were loosened during removal, retighten them and remove the engine hoist or support device.

37 Insert the selector shaft interlock pin, spring and cap bolt, having smeared the threads of the bolt with jointing compound.

OHV models

38 Remove the temporary plastic plugs used to prevent displacement of the pinion gears in the differential. If plugs were not used, insert a finger into each driveshaft hole and align the pinion gear splined hole ready to accept the driveshaft. A mirror will assist in correct alignment **(see illustration)**.

39 Fit a new snap ring to the splined end of the left-hand driveshaft and insert the shaft into the gearbox **(see illustration)**. Turn the shaft as necessary to engage the splines with those on the pinion gear. Once engaged, have an assistant push hard on the roadwheel until the snap-ring engages, with the shaft fully home. Any reluctance to engage may be due to the driveshaft not being in a sufficiently horizontal attitude. In this event, remove the roadwheel in order to reduce the weight while the hub assembly is lifted.

40 Reconnect the suspension track control arm.

41 Repeat all the operations and refit the right-hand driveshaft.

42 Reconnect the left-hand tie-bar and bracket to its body mounting and tighten the three retaining bolts.

43 Reconnect the suspension arms to the body location on the inboard side, then reconnect the balljoint on the outer end of each arm to the spindle cover.

CVH models

44 If removed, reconnect the intermediate driveshaft assembly. Reconnect the left and right-hand driveshafts by aligning the bolt holes and fitting the socket-head bolts with the link washers.

All models

45 Connect the stabilizer rod to the gearbox, making sure to insert the washer between the trunnion of the rod and the gearbox casing.

46 Reconnect and adjust the gearchange rod.

47 Refit the gearchange rod tension spring (where applicable).

48 Refit the starter motor.

49 Connect the leads to the starter motor and to the reversing lamp switch.

50 Fit the cover plate to the clutch housing.

51 Lower the vehicle to the ground.

52 Fit the upper bolts to the clutch housing/engine flange (attaching the engine earth strap).

53 Reconnect the clutch operating cable.

54 Connect the speedometer drive cable to the gearbox.

55 Fill the unit with the correct quantity and grade of oil.

56 Reconnect the battery earth lead.

57 Locate the gearbox breather hole in the aperture in the longitudinal member.

58 Check the selection of all gears, and check the torque wrench settings of all nuts and bolts which were removed now that the weight of the vehicle is again on the roadwheels.

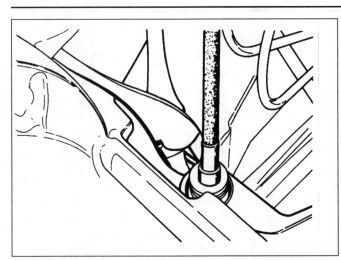

6.2 Extracting speedometer pinion retaining roll pin

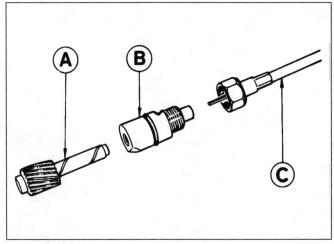

6.3 Speedometer driven gear (A), bearing (B) and drive cable (C)

6 Speedometer driven gear (4 and 5-speed gearbox) - removal and refitting

1 This work may be done without having to remove the gearbox from the vehicle.

2 Using a pair of side cutting pliers, lever out the roll pin which secures the speedometer drive pinion bearing in the gearbox housing **(see illustration)**.

3 Withdraw the pinion bearing, together with the speedometer drive cable **(see illustration)**. Separate the cable from the pinion by unscrewing the knurled ring.

4 Slide the pinion out of the bearing.

5 Always renew the O-ring on the pinion bearing before refitting.

6 Insert the pinion and bearing into the gearbox housing using a back-and-forth twisting motion to mesh the pinion teeth with those of the drivegear. Secure with the roll pin **(see illustration)**.

7 Reconnect the speedometer cable.

7 Gearbox overhaul - general information

Overhauling a gearbox is a difficult and involved job for the DIY home mechanic. In addition to dismantling and reassembling many small parts, clearances must be precisely measured and, if necessary, changed by selecting shims and spacers. Gearbox internal components are also often difficult to obtain and in many instances extremely expensive. Because of this, if the gearbox develops a fault or becomes noisy, the best course of action is to have the unit overhauled by a specialist or to obtain an exchange reconditioned unit.

Nevertheless, it is not impossible for the more experienced mechanic to overhaul a gearbox provided that the special tools are available and the job is done in a deliberate step-by-step manner so that nothing is overlooked.

The tools necessary for overhaul include internal and external circlip pliers, bearing pullers, a slide-hammer, a set of pin punches, a dial test indicator and possibly an hydraulic press. In addition, a large sturdy workbench and a vice will be required.

All work should be done in conditions of extreme cleanliness. When dismantling, make careful notes of how each component is fitted. This will facilitate accurate and straightforward reassembly.

Before dismantling the gearbox, it will help to have some idea of which component is malfunctioning. Certain problems can be related to specific areas in the gearbox which can in turn make component examination and replacement more straightforward. Refer to the Fault Finding Section at the end of this Manual for more information.

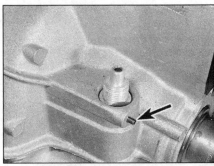

6.6 Speedometer driven gear unit located with new roll pin (arrowed)

7

Chapter 8
Driveshafts

Contents

Degrees of difficulty

Easy, suitable for novice with little experience	Fairly easy, suitable for beginner with some experience	Fairly difficult, suitable for competent DIY mechanic	Difficult, suitable for experienced DIY mechanic	Very difficult, suitable for expert DIY or professional

Specifications

Type . . . . Tubular, three section with inner and outer constant velocity (CV) joints. Additional intermediate driveshaft on 1.3 and 1.4 litre models on right-hand side.

Torque wrench settings	Nm	lbf ft
Driveshaft hub nut	230	170
Lower suspension arm pivot bolt	45	33
Lower suspension arm balljoint pinch-bolt	30	22
Tie-rod to mounting bracket	50	37
Driveshaft coupling flange bolts (1.3 and 1.4 litre models)	40	30
Intermediate driveshaft bearing housing to support bracket	20	15
Intermediate driveshaft support bracket to engine	68	50

1 General information and precautions

General information

Each driveshaft unit comprises three sections: the inboard end (namely a splined output shaft and constant velocity joint), the outboard end (being the splined front hub spindle and constant velocity joint) and a centre shaft with splined ends.

The inboard ends of the driveshaft are retained in the differential gears by the engagement of snap-rings. The outboard ends are secured to the hub by a nut which is staked after tightening. 1.3 and 1.4 litre models differ from other models in that they have driveshafts which are bolted at their inner ends to the transmission stub shaft on the left-hand side and the intermediate driveshaft on the right-hand side.

The intermediate shaft is a sliding fit into the right-hand transmission stub shaft and is supported on its outer end by a bearing and support bracket attached to the engine crankcase. The outboard end of the intermediate shaft and the inboard end of the right-hand driveshaft are attached by socket-head bolts.

Precautions

When removing the driveshafts or driveshaft joints from the transmission, some difficulty may be experienced in removing the selector shaft cap nut and locking assembly to drain the gearbox oil. This is due to the close proximity of the transmission mounting bracket making access to the cap nut awkward. This is of no great consequence as it is not absolutely necessary to drain the oil for these operations. Note however that a quantity of oil will be released when the driveshaft or driveshaft joint is released, so have a container at the ready.

2 Driveshaft joints - lubrication

1 When repacking joints with grease after overhaul or bellows renewal, use the following quantities of Ford special grease (Part no. 5003563) applied as shown **(see illustration)**. Refer to the following table:

	At A	At B
1.0 and 1.1 models:		
Outer joint	30 grammes	30 grammes
Inner joint	30 grammes	40 grammes
1.3, 1.4 and 1.6 models:		
Outer joint	40 grammes	40 grammes
Inner joint (except 1.6)	30 grammes	40 grammes
Inner joint (1.6)	35 grammes	80 grammes

3 Driveshaft oil seepage - rectification

1 On vehicles equipped with bolt-on type driveshaft joint flanges, it is possible for oil seepage to occur from the transmission oil supply. This can be rectified in the following way:

2 Remove the driveshaft and mark the alignment of the driveshaft in relation to the inner cup of the joint. Also mark the sheet metal cap in relation to the outer cup of the joint.

3 Extract the circlip and remove the joint from the sheet metal cap and the driveshaft.

4 Clean the mating surfaces of the sheet metal cap and joint and apply non-hardening sealer (jointing compound) to the area shown **(see illustration)**.

5 Reconnect the joint to the sheet metal cap and the driveshaft.

6 Refit the driveshaft, tightening the socket-headed bolts to a torque of 40 Nm (30 lbf ft).

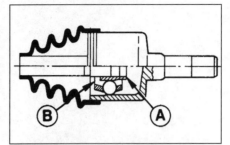

2.1 Sectional view of CV joint showing grease packing areas

4 Driveshaft inboard oil seal - renewal

1.0, 1.1 and 1.6 litre models

1 Raise and support the car at the front on safety stands (see *"Jacking and vehicle support"*).

2 Drain the gearbox oil by unscrewing the cap nut from the selector shaft locking mechanism, taking care not to lose the spring and interlock pin as they are ejected.

3 Disconnect the steering tie-rod balljoint by extracting the split pin and undoing the castellated nut. Release the tapered joint using a separator **(see illustration)**.

4 Unbolt and remove the pivot bolt from the inboard end of the suspension arm.

5 At the outboard end of the suspension arm, disengage the arm from the hub carrier by unscrewing and removing the pinch-bolt.

6 When the suspension arm is disconnected, take care not to strain the tie-bar at its body mounting at the front.

7 With an assistant pulling the roadwheel, insert a lever between the inboard constant velocity joint and the transmission. Strike the end of the lever, so prising the driveshaft out of the transmission **(see illustration)**. Tie the driveshaft to the steering rack housing to

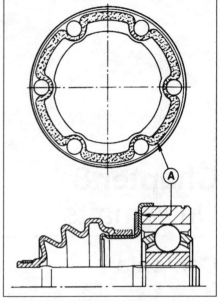

3.4 Driveshaft inboard joint sealant application area (A)

avoid strain on the CV joints caused by excessive deflection of the driveshaft.

8 Insert a suitable plug (an old driveshaft stub is ideal) into the transmission casing to prevent the differential gears being dislodged if both driveshafts are being removed.

9 Using a tool with a hook at its end, prise out the oil seal from the differential housing. Take care not to damage the seal housing.

10 Wipe out the oil seal seat, apply grease to the lips of a new oil seal and tap it into position using a piece of tubing or similar as a drift.

11 Using a mirror, check that the pinion gear within the differential is in correct alignment to receive the driveshaft. If not, insert the finger to align it.

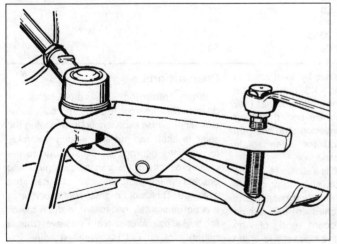

4.3 Balljoint separator detaching the steering tie-rod joint

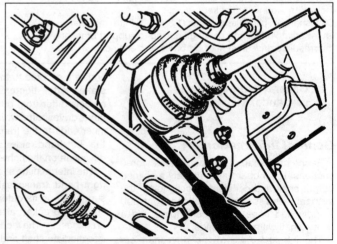

4.7 Lever the driveshaft free from the gearbox

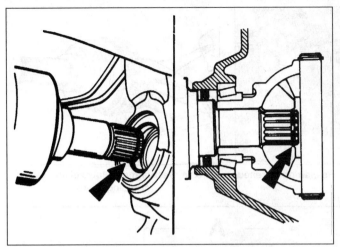
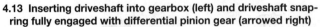

4.13 Inserting driveshaft into gearbox (left) and driveshaft snap-ring fully engaged with differential pinion gear (arrowed right)

4.18 Driveshaft flange joint socket-head bolts and link washers

12 Fit a new snap-ring to the driveshaft and then offer it up to engage it in the transmission.
13 Have your assistant push inwards on the roadwheel until the snap-ring is fully engaged **(see illustration)**. If any difficulty is experienced in pushing the driveshaft fully home, remove the roadwheel to reduce weight and lift the hub assembly until the driveshaft is in a more horizontal attitude.
14 Reconnect the suspension arm and tie-rod balljoint. Tighten the nuts and bolts to the specified torque when the weight of the car is again on its roadwheels.
15 Refit the interlock pin, spring and cap nut then top-up the gearbox oil level.

1.3 and 1.4 litre models

16 Raise the front of the car and support on safety stands.
17 Drain the gearbox oil by unscrewing the cap nut from the selector shaft locking mechanism. Take care not to lose the spring and interlock pin which will be ejected.
18 *Left-hand side seal:* Undo the six socket-head bolts and remove them, together with the three link washers from the driveshaft/stub shaft joint **(see illustration)**. Separate the driveshaft and support it by suspending out of the way with a length of wire or cord, but not at too great an angle.

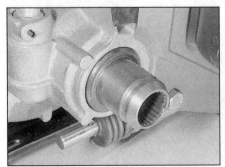

4.24 Right-hand stub shaft location in gearbox

19 *Right-hand side seal:* Remove the intermediate driveshaft.
20 The stub shaft on the side concerned can now be removed from the transmission housing. On the left-hand side, either carefully apply leverage between the transmission casing and the stub shaft flange or attach a slide hammer to the flange. On the right-hand side, tightly attach two worm-drive hose clips to the shaft so that their screw housings are radially opposite each other, then carefully apply leverage between the transmission casing and the worm-drive hose clip screw housings.
21 Using a tool with a hook at its end, prise out the oil seal from the differential housing. Take care not to damage the seal housing.
22 Wipe out the oil seal seat, apply grease to the lips of a new oil seal and tap it into position using a piece of tubing or similar as a drift.
23 Using a mirror, check that the pinion gear within the differential is in correct alignment to receive the stub shaft. If not, insert a finger to align it.

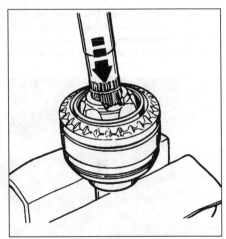

5.5 Inserting the driveshaft into the CV joint

24 Fit a new snap-ring to the stub shaft and then offer it up to engage it in the transmission and tap it home with a tube drift so that the snap-ring is felt to engage **(see illustration)**. On the right-hand stub shaft, if surface damage has occurred where the worm-drive clips were fitted, carefully remove any scoring with a fine file.
25 Reconnect the intermediate driveshaft on the right-hand side, then reconnect the driveshafts reversing the removal procedure.
26 Refit the interlock pin, spring and cap nut and top-up the gearbox oil level.

5 Driveshaft joint bellows - renewal

Note: *Refer to the information contained in Section 2 before proceeding.*

Inboard

1 For 1.0, 1.1 and 1.6 litre models, refer to Section 4 and proceed as described in paragraphs 1 to 6 inclusive. On 1.3 and 1.4 litre models, refer to Section 4 and proceed as described in paragraphs 16 and 18 to disconnect the right or left-hand driveshaft at the inner end (leaving the intermediate shaft in position).
2 Unclip and remove the bellows retaining clamps by prising open the looped section of the clamp with a screwdriver, then slide the bellows along the shaft to expose the CV (constant velocity) joint.
3 Wipe the surplus lubricant from the CV joint, then prise open the securing circlip and pull the shaft from the joint.
4 The bellows can now be withdrawn from the shaft.
5 Fit the new bellows into position on the shaft and repack the CV joint with grease. Insert the driveshaft back through the joint unit, pushing through until the circlip is felt to engage and secure it **(see illustration)**.

8

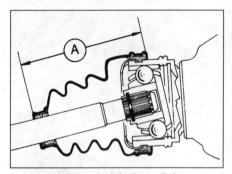

5.6 Driveshaft bellows fitting

*A On inner joint of shaft angle of 10° to 20° =
80 to 90 mm (3.1 to 3.5 in)*
*A On outer joint with shaft horizontal =
98 to 102 mm (3.8 to 4.0 in)*

6 Locate the new bellows into position over
the CV joint. The bellows positioning is
important. Check that, when in position with
the inner joint fully contracted and at an angle
of 10° to 20°, the full length of the bellows
clamps is as shown **(see illustration)**.
7 Fit and fasten the bellows clamps by
holding them round the bellows finger tight,
then clamp the pin into the next engagement
hole. Crimp the clamp to secure it **(see
illustration)**.
8 Reconnect the tie-rod joint and suspension
arm or driveshaft flange joint (as applicable).

Outboard

9 Unless the driveshaft is to be removed
completely for other repair work to be carried
out, the following method of bellows renewal
is recommended to avoid having to
disconnect the driveshaft from the hub carrier.
10 Remove the inboard joint bellows.
11 On the right-hand driveshaft, mark the
relative position of the torsional damper on
the shaft then unbolt and remove the damper
unit.
12 Release the clamps on the outboard joint
bellows and slide the bellows along the
driveshaft until they can be removed from the
inboard end of the shaft.
13 Thoroughly clean the driveshaft before
sliding on the new bellows. Replenish the
outboard joint with specified lubricant and
slide the bellows over the joint, setting its
overall length to the appropriate dimension
shown in illustration 5.6.
14 Fit and tighten the bellows clamps, but
make sure that the crimped part of the clamp
nearest the hub does not interfere with the
hub carrier as the driveshaft is rotated **(see
illustration)**.
15 Refit the inboard bellows and connect the
driveshaft to the transmission.
16 Refit the torsional damper to the right-
hand driveshaft and set it in the original
position marked during removal **(see
illustration)** before fully tightening the
retaining bolts.

5.7 Inboard joint bellows clamps fastened

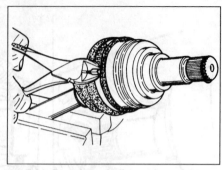

5.14 Securing a bellows clamp with
crimping pliers

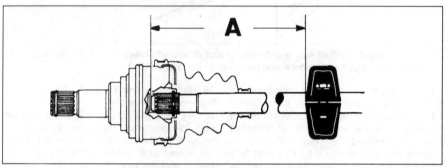

5.16 Torsional damper location on shaft
A = 308 to 312 mm (12.1 to 12.3 in)

6 Intermediate driveshaft (1.3 and 1.4 litre) - removal and refitting

Removal

1 Raise and support the front of the car on axle
stands (see *"Jacking and vehicle support"*).
2 Using an Allen key, unscrew and remove
the socket-head bolts and washers securing
the constant velocity joint to the intermediate
driveshaft. Tie the outer driveshaft away from
the work area.
3 Prise free and release the clamp securing
the intermediate driveshaft-to-stub shaft
gaiter **(see illustration)**.
4 Supporting the intermediate shaft, unscrew

the socket-head bolts and detach the bearing
housing from the support bracket.
5 Carefully slide the intermediate driveshaft
from the differential stub shaft **(see illustration)**.
6 Unbolt the support bracket from the engine.

Refitting

7 Before refitting the driveshaft, check that
the support bracket holes in the block are
clear to a depth of 16.0 mm and if necessary,
re-tap them.
8 Refit the support bracket to the engine and
insert the two bolts hand-tight.
9 Smear the intermediate driveshaft splines
with a molybdenum disulphide grease, and
insert the driveshaft into the differential.
10 Position the bearing housing on the
support bracket, insert the two socket-head
bolts and tighten them to the specified torque.

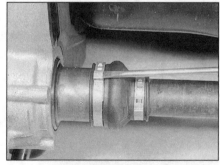

6.3 Releasing a gaiter clamp

6.5 Withdrawing the intermediate shaft
from the stub shaft

6.11 Intermediate shaft support bracket retaining bolts (arrowed)

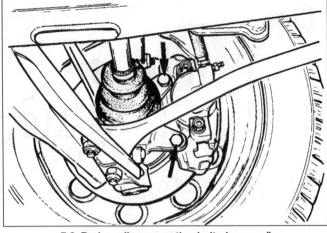

7.6 Brake caliper mounting bolts (arrowed)

11 Tighten the upper support bracket bolt to the specified torque, followed by the lower bolt. **Note:** *It is important to tighten them in this order* **(see illustration).**

12 Pack the end flange of the intermediate driveshaft with 30 grams (1 oz) of molybdenum disulphide grease.

13 Mate the intermediate and outer driveshafts, insert the socket-head bolts, and tighten them *in diagonal sequence* to the specified torque.

14 Note that if either of the support bracket or bearing housing bolts is subsequently loosened, the complete tightening sequence (paragraphs 8 to 11) must be followed in order to ensure correct position of the components.

15 Refit the intermediate shaft-to-stub shaft gaiter then locate the securing clamp, pushing it together finger tight, then clamp the pin into the next engagement hole. Crimp the clamp to secure it. Check that the gaiter is not twisted or stretched.

7 Driveshaft - removal and refitting

Removal

1 Slacken the roadwheel bolts and then raise the front of the vehicle (see *"Jacking and vehicle support"*).

2 Remove the roadwheel.

3 Refit two of the roadwheel bolts as a means of anchoring the disc when the hub nut is unscrewed (the disc retaining screw is not strong enough to stop the disc from rotating).

4 Have an assistant apply the footbrake and then unscrew the staked hub nut and remove it, together with the plain washer. The hub nut is particularly tight, and if you are unsure of the stability of the car on its stands, it is wise to refit the roadwheel(s) and slacken the hub nut when the car is on the ground.

5 Remove the temporary wheel bolts.

6 Unbolt the caliper and tie it up to the suspension strut to prevent strain on the flexible hose **(see illustration).**

7 Disconnect the inboard end of the driveshaft.

8 Support the driveshaft on a jack or tie it up.

9 Extract the small retaining screw and withdraw the brake disc from the hub.

10 It may now be possible to pull the hub from the driveshaft. If it does not come off easily, use a two-legged puller **(see illustration).**

11 Withdraw the driveshaft, complete with CV joints. If both driveshafts are being removed at the same time then the differential pinion gears must be retained in alignment with their transmission casing holes by inserting pieces of plastic tubing or, if available, an old stub shaft, but take care not to damage the oil seal within the transmission housing.

12 On 1.3 and 1.4 litre models, the left-hand side driveshaft inboard CV joint/stub shaft unit can be removed from the transmission as described in Section 4. On the right-hand side, the intermediate shaft assembly and inboard stub shaft can be removed if necessary by referring to Sections 6 and 4 respectively.

Refitting

13 To refit the driveshaft, first engage it in the splines of the hub carrier while supporting the shaft in a horizontal attitude to avoid strain on the CV joints.

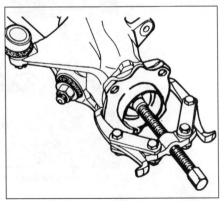

7.10 Hub withdrawal from driveshaft using a puller

14 Using the original nut and distance pieces of varying lengths, draw the driveshaft into the hub carrier.

15 Remove the old nut and distance pieces and fit the washer and a new nut, but only finger tight at this stage.

16 Fit the brake disc and caliper.

17 Connect the inboard end of the driveshaft and the suspension components.

18 Temporarily screw in two wheel bolts and then have an assistant apply the footbrake.

19 Tighten the hub nut to the specified torque. It is safer to leave the final tightening of the hub nut until the weight of the car is on the roadwheels. In the absence of a suitable torque wrench with a high enough range, full pressure on a knuckle bar or pipe extension about 457 mm (18 in) in length should give approximately the correct torque. Once tight, stake the nut into the shaft groove **(see illustration).** Fit the roadwheel and lower the vehicle.

20 Tighten the roadwheel bolts and then check the torque wrench settings of the other front suspension attachments now that the weight of the vehicle is on the roadwheels.

8

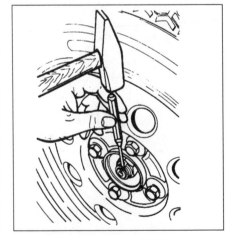

7.19 Stake the hub nut to secure

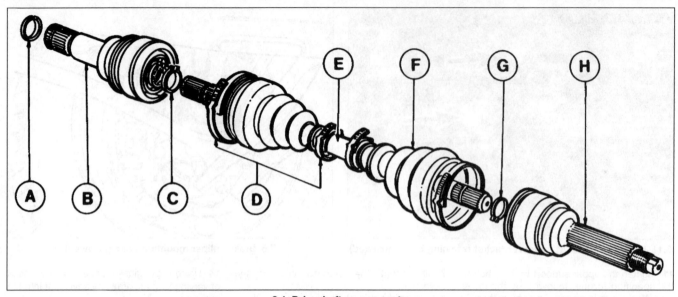

8.1 Driveshaft components

| A Snap-ring | C Circlip | E Driveshaft | G Circlip |
| B Inboard joint | D Bellows clamps | F Bellows | H Outboard joint |

8 Driveshaft - overhaul

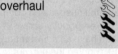

Note: *Refer to the information contained in Section 2 before proceeding.*

1 Remove the driveshaft **(see illustration).**

2 Clean away external dirt and grease, release the bellows clamps and slide the bellows from the CV joint.

3 Wipe away enough lubricant to be able to extract the circlip and then separate the CV joint with its splined shaft section from the main member of the driveshaft.

4 If removing the torsional damper from the right-hand driveshaft, mark its relative position on the shaft before unbolting it **(see illustration).**

5 Thoroughly clean the joint components and examine for wear or damage to the balls, cage, socket or splines. A repair kit may provide a solution to the problem, but, if the socket requires renewal, this will of course include the splined section of shaft and will prove expensive. If both joints require renewal of major components, then a new driveshaft or one which has been professionally reconditioned may prove to be more economical.

6 If the torsional damper was removed from the right-hand driveshaft, refit it in the position marked during its removal.

7 Reassemble the joint by reversing the dismantling operations. Use a new circlip if necessary and pack the joint with the specified quantity of lubricant. When fitting bellows, set their length in accordance with the information given in Section 5.

8 Refit the driveshaft.

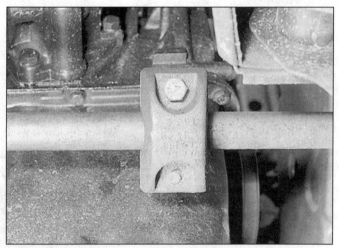

8.4 Torsional damper on right-hand driveshaft - mark position before removing

Chapter 9
Braking system

Contents

Degrees of difficulty

| Easy, suitable for novice with little experience | Fairly easy, suitable for beginner with some experience | Fairly difficult, suitable for competent DIY mechanic 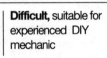 | Difficult, suitable for experienced DIY mechanic | Very difficult, suitable for expert DIY or professional 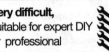 |

Specifications

System type . . . . Hydraulic, dual-circuit, discs at front (ventilated on XR2), drums at rear. Servo assistance. Mechanical handbrake to rear wheels only

Front (disc) brakes
Caliper type . . . . Single piston, sliding type
Disc diameter (outer):
  Standard . . . . 221 mm
  XR2 only . . . . 239 mm
Disc thickness (new):
  Standard . . . . 10 mm
  XR2 only . . . . 20 mm
Minimum allowable disc thickness:
  Standard . . . . 8.7 mm
  XR2 only . . . . 18.5 mm
Allowable disc run-out . . . . 0.15 mm
Minimum allowable pad thickness:
  Standard . . . . 1.5 mm
  XR2 only . . . . 1.5 mm

Rear (drum) brakes
Drum diameter:
  Standard . . . . 177.8 mm
  XR2 only . . . . 177.8 mm
Shoe width:
  Standard . . . . 30.0 mm
  XR2 only . . . . 38.0 mm
Wheel cylinder diameter:
  Standard . . . . 17.5 mm
  XR2 only . . . . 19.0 mm
Minimum allowable friction material thickness . . . . 1.0 mm

Torque wrench settings

	Nm	lbf ft
Disc caliper bracket to suspension unit	56	41
Caliper piston housing to bracket	23	17
Servo mounting nuts	23	17
Master cylinder-to-servo retaining nuts	24	18
Large bracket to bulkhead	23	17
Carrier plate to axle housing	23	17
Pressure control valve bracket (to chassis)	23	17
Hydraulic unions	14	10
Bleed valves	10	7

9

1 General information and precautions

General information

The braking system is of four-wheeled hydraulic type, with discs at the front and drums at the rear. The hydraulic system is of dual-circuit type, each circuit controls one front brake and one rear brake linked diagonally.

The front brake calipers are of single piston, sliding piston housing type. The rear brakes are of leading and trailing shoe design with a self adjusting mechanism. To compensate for the greater lining of wear of the leading shoe, its friction lining is thicker than that on the trailing shoe.

The master cylinder incorporates a reservoir cap which has a fluid level switch connected to a warning lamp on the instrument panel. A vacuum servo is standard on certain models. When fitted to RHD versions, because of the location of the servo/master cylinder on the left-hand side of the engine compartment, the brake pedal is operated through a transverse rod on the engine compartment rear bulkhead.

A brake pressure regulating control valve is fitted into the hydraulic circuit to prevent rear wheel locking under conditions of heavy braking.

The floor-mounted handbrake control lever operates through cables to the rear wheels only.

Precautions

⚠ **Warning 1: Hydraulic fluid is poisonous; wash off immediately and thoroughly in the case of skin contact and seek immediate medical advice if any fluid is swallowed or gets into the eyes. Certain types of hydraulic fluid are inflammable and may ignite when allowed into contact with hot components; when servicing any hydraulic system it is safest to assume that the fluid is inflammable and to take precautions against the risk of fire as though it is petrol that is being handled. Hydraulic fluid is also an effective paint stripper and will attack plastics; if any is spilt, it should be washed off immediately using copious quantities of fresh water. Finally, it is hygroscopic (it absorbs moisture from the air) - old fluid may be contaminated and unfit for further use. When topping-up or renewing the fluid, always use the recommended type and ensure that it comes from a freshly-opened sealed container.**
Warning 2: When working on the brake components, take care not to disperse brake dust into the air, or to inhale it, since it may contain asbestos which is injurious to health.

2 Hydraulic system - bleeding

Note: *Refer to Warning 1 in Section 1 before starting work.*

1 When a maintenance operation has only affected one circuit of the hydraulic system, then bleeding will normally only be required to that circuit (front and rear diagonally opposite). If the master cylinder or the pressure regulating valve have been disconnected and reconnected, then the complete system must be bled.
2 One of three methods can be used to bleed the system.

Bleeding - two-man method

3 Gather together a clean jar and a length of rubber or plastic bleed tubing which will fit the bleed screw tightly. The help of an assistant will be required.
4 Take great care not to spill onto the paintwork as it will act as a paint stripper. If any is spilled, wash it off at once with cold water.
5 Clean around the bleed screw on the front right-hand caliper and attach the bleed tube to the screw **(see illustration)**.
6 Check that the master cylinder reservoir is topped up and then destroy the vacuum in the brake servo (where fitted) by giving several applications of the brake foot pedal.
7 Immerse the open end of the bleed tube in the jar, which should contain 50 to 76 mm of hydraulic fluid. The jar should be positioned about 300 mm above the bleed nipple to prevent any possibility of air entering the system down the threads of the bleed screw when it is slackened.
8 Open the bleed screw half a turn and have your assistant depress the brake pedal slowly to the floor and then quickly remove his foot to allow the pedal to return unimpeded. Tighten the bleed screw at the end of each downstroke to prevent expelled air and fluid being drawn back into the system.
9 Observe the submerged end of the tube in the jar. When air bubbles cease to appear, fully tighten the bleed screw when the pedal is being held down by your assistant.
10 Top-up the fluid reservoir. It must be kept topped up throughout the bleeding operations. If the connecting holes in the master cylinder are exposed at any time due to low fluid level, then air will be drawn into the system and work will have to start all over again.
11 Repeat the operations on the left-hand rear brake **(see illustration)**, the left-hand front and the right-hand rear brake in that order (assuming that the whole system is being bled).
12 On completion, remove the bleed tube. Discard the fluid which has been bled from the system unless it is required for bleed jar purposes, *never* use it for filling the system.

2.5 Bleed tube attached to bleed screw on front brake

Bleeding - with one-way valve

13 There are a number of one-man brake bleeding kits currently available from motor accessory shops. It is recommended that one of these kits should be used whenever possible as they greatly simplify the bleeding operation and also reduce the risk of expelled air or fluid being drawn back into the system.
14 Connect the outlet tube of the bleeder device to the bleed screw and then open the screw half a turn. Depress the brake pedal to the floor and slowly release it. The one-way valve in the device will prevent expelled air from returning to the system at the completion of each stroke. Repeat this operation until clean hydraulic fluid, free from air bubbles, can be seen coming through the tube. Tighten the bleed screw and remove the tube.
15 Repeat the procedure on the remaining bleed nipples in the order described in paragraph 11. Remember to keep the master cylinder reservoir full.

Bleeding - with pressure bleeding kit

16 These are available from motor accessory shops and are usually operated by air pressure from the spare tyre.
17 By connecting a pressurised container to the master cylinder fluid reservoir, bleeding is then carried out by simply opening each bleed screw in turn and allowing the fluid to run out, rather like turning on a tap, until no air bubbles are visible in the fluid being expelled.

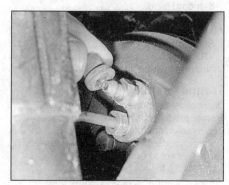

2.11 Rear brake bleed screw and protective cap

18 Using this system, the large reserve of fluid provides a safeguard against air being drawn into the master cylinder during the bleeding operations.

19 This method is particularly effective when bleeding "difficult" systems or when bleeding the entire system of routine fluid renewal.

All systems

20 On completion of bleeding, top-up the fluid level to the MAX mark on the reservoir. Check the feel of the brake pedal, which should be firm and free from any "sponginess" which would indicate air still being present in the system.

3.3 Prise free the retaining clip

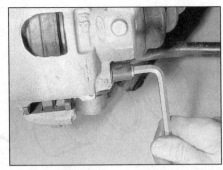

3.4 Undo the caliper anchor bracket bolts

3 Front disc pads - inspection, removal and refitting

Note: *Refer to Warning 2 in Section 1 before starting work.*

 Warning: Always support the vehicle on axle stands before removing the roadwheel to service brake assemblies.

Inspection

1 At the intervals specified in *"Routine Maintenance"*, place a mirror between the roadwheel and the caliper and check the thickness of the friction material of the disc pads. If the material has worn down to 1.5 mm or less, the pads must be renewed as an axle set (four pads).

Removal

2 Slacken the roadwheel bolts, raise the front of the vehicle, support with safety stands (see *"Jacking and vehicle support"*) and remove the roadwheel(s).

3 Using a screwdriver as shown, prise free the retaining clip from the caliper **(see illustration)**.

4 Using a 7 mm Allen key, unscrew the bolts until they can be withdrawn from the caliper anchor brackets **(see illustration)**.

5 Withdraw the piston housing and tie it up with a length of wire to prevent strain on the flexible hose **(see illustration)**.

6 Withdraw the inboard pad from the piston housing: the pad being secured to the piston by means of a spider-type spring clip.

7 Withdraw the outer pad which is secured in position by a piece of double-sided adhesive tape.

Refitting

8 Clean away all residual dust or dirt, *taking care not to inhale the dust,* as being asbestos based it is injurious to health.

9 Using a piece of flat wood, a tyre lever or similar, push the piston squarely into its bore. This is necessary in order to accommodate the new thicker pads when they are fitted.

10 Depressing the piston will cause the fluid level in the master cylinder reservoir to rise, so anticipate this by syphoning out some fluid using an old hydrometer or poultry baster. Take care not to drip hydraulic fluid onto the paintwork, it acts as an effective paint stripper.

11 Commence reassembly by fitting the inboard pad into the piston housing. Make sure that the spring clip on the back of the pad fits into the piston **(see illustration)**.

12 Peel back the protective paper covering from the adhesive surface of the new outboard pad and locate it in the jaws of the caliper anchor bracket.

13 Locate the caliper piston housing and screw in the Allen bolts to the specified torque.

14 Fit the retaining clip **(see illustration)**.

15 Repeat the operations on the opposite brake.

16 Apply the footbrake hard several times to position the pads against the disc and then check and top-up the fluid in the master cylinder reservoir.

17 Fit the roadwheel(s) and lower the vehicle.

18 Avoid heavy braking (if possible) for the first hundred miles or so when new pads have been fitted. This is to allow them to bed in and reach full efficiency.

4 Front caliper piston assembly - removal, overhaul and refitting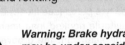

 Warning: Brake hydraulic fluid may be under considerable pressure in a pipeline, take care not to allow hydraulic fluid to spray into the face or eyes when loosening a connection.
Warning: Never refit old seals when reassembling brake system components.

Removal

1 Proceed as described in paragraphs 2 to 8 in the previous Section.

2 Disconnect the brake flexible hose from the caliper. This can be carried out in one of two ways. Either disconnect the flexible hose from the rigid hydraulic pipeline at the support bracket by unscrewing the union, or, once the caliper is detached, hold the end fitting of the hose in an open-ended spanner and unscrew the caliper from the hose. Do not allow the hose to distort an excessive amount.

3.5 Remove the caliper piston housing

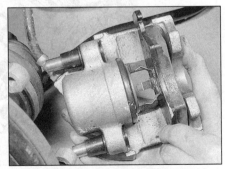

3.11 Inboard pad assembly to piston

3.14 Retaining clip refitted

9

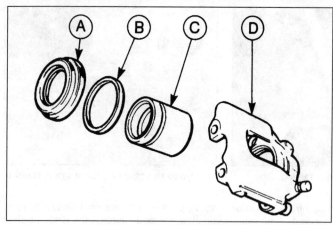

4.3 Caliper and piston components

A *Piston cover*   C *Piston*
B *Seal*   D *Housing*

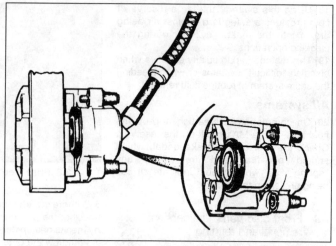

4.4 Caliper piston removal method with compressed air. Note wooden block fitted to avoid damaging the piston

Overhaul

3 Brush away all external dirt and pull off the piston dust-excluding cover **(see illustration)**.

4 Apply air pressure to the fluid inlet hole and eject the piston. Only low air pressure is needed for this, such as is produced by a foot-operated tyre pump **(see illustration)**.

5 Using a suitable hooked instrument, pick out the piston seal from the groove in the cylinder bore. Do not scratch the surface of the bore.

6 Examine the surfaces of the piston and the cylinder bore. If they are scored or show evidence of metal-to-metal rubbing, then a new piston housing will be required. Where the components are in good condition, discard the seal and obtain a repair kit.

7 Wash the internal components in clean brake hydraulic fluid or methylated spirit only, nothing else.

8 Using the fingers, manipulate the new seal into its groove in the cylinder bore.

9 Dip the piston in clean hydraulic fluid and insert it squarely into its bore.

10 Connect the rubber dust excluder between the piston and the piston housing and then depress the piston fully.

Refitting

11 Refit the caliper by reversing the removal operations.

12 When reconnecting the brake hose check that it is fitted and secured so that it is not distorted and will not interfere with any adjacent steering or suspension components.

13 Bleed the hydraulic circuit, then refit the roadwheel (s) and lower the vehicle.

14 If new pads have been fitted, heavy braking should be avoided where possible for the first hundred miles or so to allow them to bed in and reach full efficiency.

5 Front brake disc - examination, removal and refitting

Examination

1 Raise the front of the vehicle and remove the roadwheel.

2 Examine the surface of the disc. If it is deeply grooved or scored or if any small cracks are evident, it must either be refinished or renewed. Any refinishing must not reduce the thickness of the disc to below the specified minimum. Light scoring on a brake disc is normal and should be ignored.

3 If disc distortion is suspected, the disc can be checked for run-out using a dial gauge or feeler blades located between its face and a fixed point as the disc is rotated **(see illustration)**.

4 Where run-out exceeds the specified figure, renew the disc.

Removal

5 To remove a disc, unbolt the caliper, withdraw it and tie it up to the suspension strut to avoid strain on the flexible hose.

6 Extract the small disc retaining screw and pull the disc from the hub.

Refitting

7 If a new disc is being installed, clean its surfaces free from preservative before refitting the caliper. It will also be necessary to depress the piston and inner brake pad a small amount to accommodate the new thicker disc when assembling.

8 Refit the disc, its retaining screw, the caliper and the roadwheel and lower the vehicle to the floor.

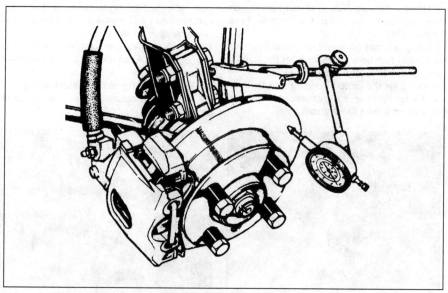

5.3 Checking the brake disc run-out using a dial gauge

6.7a Remove the dust cap . . .

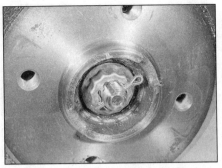

6.7b . . . the split pin and nut lock . . .

6.7c . . . the nut and thrustwasher

6 Rear brake linings - inspection, removal and refitting

Inspection

1 Inspection of the shoe linings can be carried out at the specified intervals by prising out the small inspection plug from the brake backplate and observing the linings through the hole using a mirror.

2 A minimum thickness of friction material must always be observed on the shoes; if it is worn down to this level, renew the shoes.

3 Do not attempt to re-line shoes yourself, but always obtain factory re-lined shoes.

4 Renew the shoes in an axle set (four shoes), even if only one is worn to the minimum.

6.9 Withdrawing the brake drum

Removal

5 Chock the front wheels. Slacken the roadwheel bolts, raise the rear of the vehicle and support it securely (see *"Jacking and vehicle support"*). Remove the roadwheels.

6 Release the handbrake fully.

7 Tap off the hub dust cap, remove the split pin, nut lock, nut and thrustwasher **(see illustrations)**.

8 Pull the hub/drum towards you and then push it back enough to be able to take the outer bearing from the spindle.

9 Remove the hub/drum **(see illustration)** and brush out any dust *taking care not to inhale it.*

10 Remove the shoe hold-down spring from the leading shoe **(see illustration)**. Do this by gripping the dished washer with a pair of pliers, depressing it and turning it through 90°. Remove the washer, spring and the hold-down post.

11 Note the locations of the leading and trailing shoes and also the upper and lower return springs. Unhook the brake shoes from the lower anchor plate and detach the lower return spring.

12 Detach the brake shoes from the wheel cylinder, manoeuvre them away from the backplate and disengage the handbrake cable from the relay arm **(see illustration)**.

13 The brake pull-off springs and adjuster strut can then be disconnected at the top end of the brake shoes. Again note orientation for refitting.

14 To detach the large ratchet and handbrake lever, remove the circlips.

Refitting

15 Prior to reassembly, wipe the carrier (back) plate clean and apply a light coating of brake grease (Thermopaul 1) to the brake shoe contact points indicated **(see illustration)**.

16 Refit the large ratchet to the leading brake shoe and the handbrake relay lever to the trailing brake shoe.

17 Relocate the pull-off springs into position between the top end of the leading and trailing shoe (as noted during removal).

18 Apply a small amount of brake grease to the large ratchet and handbrake relay lever contact surfaces, then reconnect the handbrake cable to the relay lever on the trailing shoe. Do not get any brake grease onto the brake linings.

19 Refit the brake shoes into position, prising open the leading edges to fit on the wheel cylinder at the top. Support in this position, relocate the lower brake pull-off spring then prise open the shoes at the bottom (trailing edges) and engage on the lower anchor plate **(see illustrations)**.

20 Centralise the shoes, by tapping them with the hand if necessary, then relocate the shoe hold-down pin, spring and dished washer. Depress and twist the washers through 90° to secure **(see illustration)**.

21 Before refitting the brake drum, check that the shoes are centralised, and release the automatic adjuster to fully contract the shoes.

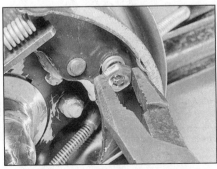

6.10 Brake hold-down spring and retainer removal

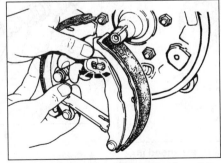

6.12 Disconnecting the handbrake cable from the relay arm

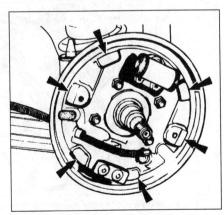

6.15 Lightly lubricate the brake shoe contact points (arrowed)

9

6.19a Brake shoe assembly at the top

6.19b Brake shoe assembly at the bottom

6.20 Rear brake shoes fully assembled

22 Lubricate the inboard bearing and oil seal lips in the brake drum/hub and fit the drum/hub onto the stub axle; taking care not to damage the oil seal lips.

23 Fit the outboard bearing and thrustwasher (lubricated with suitable wheel bearing grease) and screw the retaining nut into position.

24 Tightening the nut also sets the wheel bearing adjustment and it is therefore important that the correct procedure is followed. Refer to the information given in Chapter 10 on adjustment of the rear hub bearings.

25 With the wheel bearing adjustment completed and the nut retainer and split pin in position, refit the dust cap.

7.3 Rear wheel cylinder retaining bolts (arrowed)

26 Depress the brake pedal hard several times to actuate the self-adjusting mechanism and to bring the shoes up close to the drum.

27 Refit the roadwheel and lower the vehicle to the floor.

7 Rear wheel cylinder - removal, overhaul and refitting

Removal

1 Remove the brake drum.

2 Disconnect the fluid pipeline from the wheel cylinder and cap the end of the pipe to prevent loss of fluid. A bleed screw rubber dust cap is useful for this.

3 Unscrew the two bolts which hold the wheel cylinder to the brake backplate (see illustration).

4 To avoid removing the brake shoes when withdrawing the wheel cylinder, prise the shoes away from the cylinder (at the top) so that the automatic adjuster holds them clear of it. The cylinder can then be withdrawn (see illustration).

Overhaul

5 Clean away external dirt and then pull off the dust-excluding covers from the cylinder unit (see illustration).

6 The pistons will probably shake out. If they do not, apply air pressure (from a tyre pump) at the fluid inlet hole to eject them.

7 Examine the surfaces of the pistons and the cylinder bores for scoring or metal-to-metal rubbing areas. If evident, renew the complete cylinder assembly.

8 Where the components are in good condition, discard the rubber seals and dust excluders and obtain a repair kit.

9 Any cleaning should be done using hydraulic fluid or methylated spirit - nothing else.

10 Reassemble by dipping the first piston in clean hydraulic fluid and inserting it into the cylinder. Fit a dust excluder to it.

11 From the opposite end of the cylinder body, insert a new seal, spring, a second new seal, the second piston and the remaining dust excluder. Use only the fingers to manipulate the seals into position and make quite sure that the lips of the seals are the correct way round.

Refitting

12 Refit the cylinder to the backplate and secure with the two bolts and lockwashers.

13 Remove the plug and reconnect the hydraulic fluid pipe, taking care not to cross-thread the connection. Do not overtighten the union, but tighten it sufficiently to seal it. For the torque setting refer to Specifications.

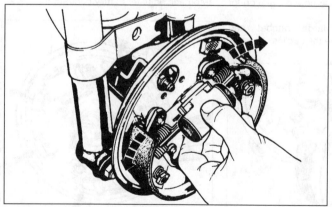

7.4 Rear wheel cylinder removal (brake shoes expanded in direction of arrows)

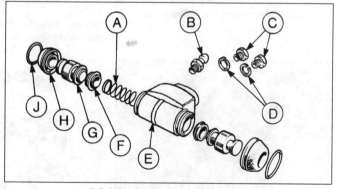

7.5 Wheel cylinder components

A Spring
B Bleed nipple
C Retaining bolts
D Lockwasher
E Piston housing
F Piston seal
G Piston
H Dust cover
J Gaiter springs

14 Relocate the brake shoes against the cylinder pistons by releasing the automatic adjuster.

15 Refit the brake drum and hub unit. Bleed the hydraulic circuit on completion.

8 Rear brake drum - inspection and renewal

1 Whenever a brake drum is removed, brush out dust from it, *taking care not to inhale it* as it contains asbestos which is injurious to health.
2 Examine the internal friction surface of the drum. If deeply scored, or so worn that the drum has become pocketed to the width of the shoes, then the drums must be renewed.
3 Regrinding is not recommended as the internal diameter will no longer be compatible with the shoe lining contact diameter.
4 If renewing the brake drum it is also advisable to renew the hub bearings and inner oil seal rather than transferring the old. The seal will need renewal in any case.

9 Master cylinder - removal, overhaul and refitting

Removal

1 Syphon out as much fluid as possible from the master cylinder reservoir using an old battery hydrometer or a poultry baster. Do not drip the fluid onto the paintwork or it will act as an effective paint stripper.

2 Disconnect the pipelines from the master cylinder by unscrewing the unions **(see illustration)**.
3 Disconnect the leads from the level warning switch in the reservoir cap. Remove the cap.
4 On models not fitted with a brake servo unit, unclip and remove the trim panel beneath the facia on the driver's side to give access to the brake pedal. Extract the brake pedal-to-pushrod clevis pin retaining clip and withdraw the pin.
5 Unbolt and remove the master cylinder. On non-servo models, remove the cylinder from the bulkhead whilst, on servo equipped models, the master cylinder is removed from the servo unit.

Overhaul

1.4 litre and XR2 models from early 1986

6 From the beginning of 1986, all XR2 models and 1.4 litre models are fitted with a brake master cylinder of a new design. The new master cylinder is identifiable by its small size and its smooth cylinder body appearance **(see illustration)**.
7 The overhaul procedure is as follows:
8 With the master cylinder removed from the car, drain the remaining brake fluid from the reservoir, then remove the reservoir from the cylinder body.
9 Using a screwdriver, lever off the primary piston fluid housing **(see illustration)** and withdraw the fluid housing and primary piston assembly from the master cylinder. Be prepared for some fluid spillage during this operation.

9.2 Master cylinder and hydraulic pipe connections

10 Separate the primary piston from the fluid housing and remove the fluid housing seal.
11 Tap the master cylinder on a block of wood to eject the secondary piston, then remove the secondary piston assembly from the master cylinder.
12 Prise off the fluid housing retaining ring and remove the O-ring seal from the cylinder body.
13 Extract the two reservoir seals from the master cylinder ports.
14 Carefully remove the two secondary piston return springs, the seal support ring, seal protecting ring and the fluid seals from each end of the piston.
15 Examine the cylinder bore for signs of scoring or wear ridges. If evident renew the master cylinder. If the cylinder appears satisfactory, obtain a repair kit which will contain new secondary piston and cylinder body seals and a complete new primary piston assembly.
16 Lubricate all the seals, the cylinder bore and the pistons with clean brake fluid, then reassemble as follows.
17 Refit the seals, support ring, protecting ring and springs to the secondary piston, then carefully insert the assembled piston into the master cylinder bore.
18 Fit the two new reservoir seals to the cylinder ports.
19 Fit a new seal to the fluid housing and fit the primary piston to the housing.
20 Fit a new O-ring to the end of the cylinder body, followed by the fluid housing retaining ring.

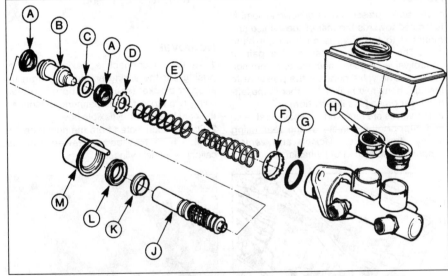

9.6 Exploded view of master cylinder - XR2 and 1.4 litre models, early 1986 on

A *Secondary piston seals*	F *Retaining ring*	K *Support ring*
B *Secondary piston*	G *O-ring seal*	L *Cap seal*
C *Protecting ring*	H *Reservoir seals*	M *Primary piston fluid*
D *Seal support ring*	J *Primary piston*	*housing*
E *Return springs*		

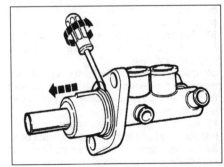

9.9 Levering off the primary piston fluid housing

9

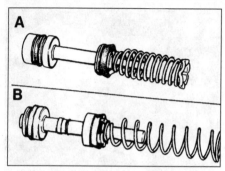

9.27 Master cylinder primary (A) and secondary (B) piston assemblies

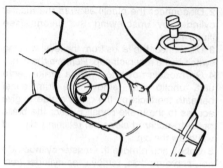

9.28 Master cylinder secondary piston stop pin

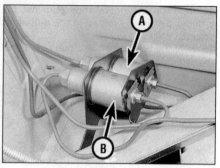

10.1 Brake pressure control valve

A Right-hand rear brake circuit valve
B Left-hand rear brake circuit valve

21 Carefully assemble the primary piston and fluid housing to the master cylinder, pushing the piston and housing in until the fluid housing is flush with the cylinder mounting flange.

22 Refit the master cylinder reservoir.

All other models

23 To overhaul the master cylinder fitted to these models, first clean away external dirt and then detach the fluid reservoir by tilting it sideways and gently pulling. Remove the two rubber seals.

24 Secure the master cylinder carefully in a vice fitted with jaw protectors.

25 Pull the dust excluder back from around the pushrod and using circlip pliers, extract the circlip which is now exposed.

26 Remove the pushrod, dust excluder and washer.

27 Withdraw the primary piston assembly, which will already have been partially ejected **(see illustration)**.

28 Using a small diameter rod, insert it into the end of the cylinder and push the secondary piston in so that the locking pin can be extracted **(see illustration)**.

29 Tap the end of the master cylinder on a block of wood and eject the secondary piston assembly.

30 Examine the pistons and cylinder bore surfaces for scoring or signs of metal-to-metal rubbing. If evident, renew the cylinder complete.

31 The primary piston unit cannot be dismantled and must be renewed as a unit.

32 Prise free and remove the secondary piston seals, noting their orientation. Once removed the seals must be discarded and a repair kit obtained for their renewal.

33 Cleaning of components should be done in brake hydraulic fluid or methylated spirit only - nothing else.

34 Using the new seals from the repair kit, assemble the secondary piston, making sure that the seal lips are the correct way round, as noted during dismantling.

35 Dip the piston assemblies in clean hydraulic fluid and fit them to the cylinder bore.

36 Fit the pushrod complete with new dust excluder and secure with a new circlip.

37 Engage the dust excluder with the master cylinder.

38 Depress the pushrod and locate the secondary piston lockpin.

39 Locate the two rubber seals and push the fluid reservoir into position.

40 It is recommended that a small quantity of fluid is now poured into the reservoir and the pushrod operated several times to prime it.

Refitting

41 Refit the master cylinder by reversing the removal operations.

42 Do not overtighten the hydraulic line unions and take care that they are clean and not cross-threaded when reconnecting. Refer to the specifications for the torque wrench setting.

43 Bleed the complete hydraulic system on completion of the work.

10 Brake pressure control valve - removal and refitting

Removal

1 The brake pressure control valve assembly is located towards the rear of the vehicle and mounted to the chassis on the right-hand side. The assembly consists of a pair of control valve cylinders mounted to a common bracket. One valve controls the pressure to the right-hand rear brake, the other to the left-hand rear brake **(see illustration)**.

2 The valves are removed as a pair. First raise and support the vehicle at the rear using safety stands (see *"Jacking and vehicle support"*). Chock the front wheels.

3 Clean the valves and connections externally, then unscrew the hydraulic line unions from the valves. Plug the disconnected lines to prevent excessive fluid leakage and the ingress of dirt.

4 Unscrew and remove the valve mounting bracket bolts and withdraw the valve assembly **(see illustration)**.

5 Each valve is secured to the bracket by means of a clip which can be prised free to release the valve from the bracket.

Refitting

6 Refitting is the reversal of the removal procedure. Check that the hydraulic line connections are clean before reconnecting, and take care not to cross-thread the unions.

7 Before lowering the vehicle at the rear, bleed the hydraulic system.

11 Brake hydraulic pipes - removal and refitting

Removal

1 Always disconnect a flexible hose by prising out the spring anchor clip from the support bracket **(see illustration)** and then, using two close-fitting spanners, disconnect the rigid line from the flexible hose.

2 Once disconnected from the rigid pipe, the flexible hose may be unscrewed from the caliper or wheel cylinder.

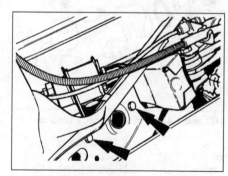

10.4 Brake pressure control valve securing bolts (arrowed)

11.1 Flexible-to-rigid brake pipe connection; spring anchor clip (arrowed)

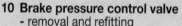

Refitting

3 When reconnecting pipeline or hose fittings, remember that all union threads are to metric sizes. No copper washers are used at unions and the seal is made at the swaged end of the pipe, so do not try to wind a union in if it is tight yet still stands proud of the surface into which it is screwed.

4 A flexible hose must never be installed twisted, but a slight "set" is permissible to give it clearance from an adjacent component. Do this by turning the hose slightly before inserting the bracket spring clip.

12 Vacuum servo unit - removal and refitting

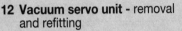

Removal

1 Using a suitable screwdriver as a lever, prise free the vacuum servo pipe connector from the servo unit **(see illustration)**.
2 Remove the master cylinder.
3 Unscrew and remove the four servo unit-to-mounting bracket retaining nuts.
4 Extract the spring clip from the connecting rod clevis pin using a pair of long-nosed pliers **(see illustration)**. Withdraw the clevis pin and remove the servo unit from the mounting bracket.

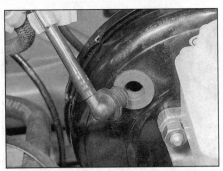

12.1 Vacuum servo pipe removal

5 The servo unit cannot be repaired and if defective must therefore be renewed.

Refitting

6 Refitting is a reversal of the removal procedure. Bleed the hydraulic system.
7 On completion, check the operation of the brake stop-light switch and, if necessary, readjust.

13 Handbrake - adjustment

Refer to Chapter 1, Section 19.

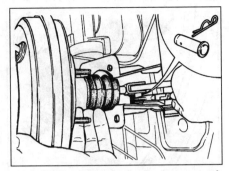

12.4 Clevis pin removal using long-nosed pliers

14 Handbrake cables - renewal

Pre September 1985 models

1 Chock the front wheels, then fully release the handbrake.
2 Raise and support the vehicle at the rear with safety stands (see *"Jacking and vehicle support"*).

Primary cable

3 Extract the spring clip and clevis pin and disconnect the primary cable from the equaliser **(see illustration)**.

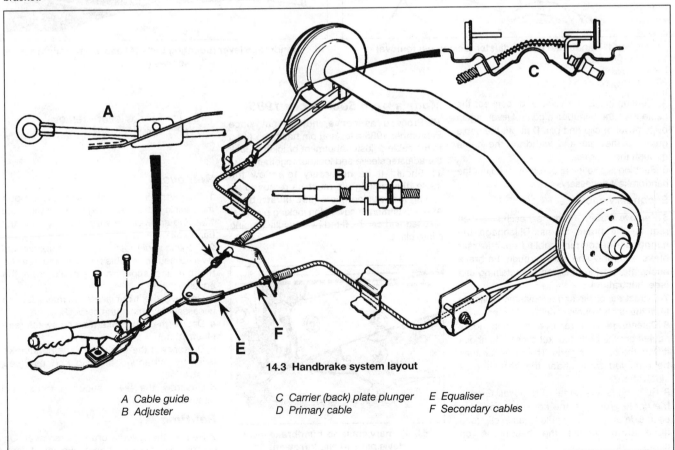

14.3 Handbrake system layout

A *Cable guide*
B *Adjuster*
C *Carrier (back) plate plunger*
D *Primary cable*
E *Equaliser*
F *Secondary cables*

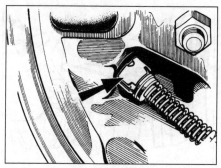

14.6 Handbrake cable-to-brake backplate securing clip

14.8 Secondary cable location bracket

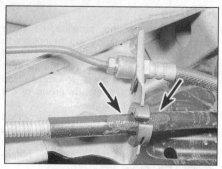

14.9 Lubricate each side of the cable location clip (arrowed)

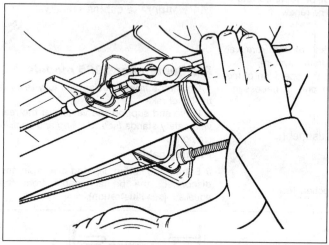

14.11 Handbrake cable adjuster locking pin removal

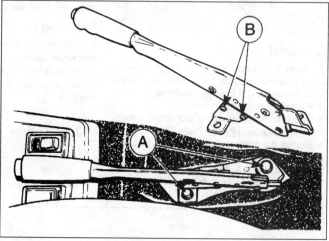

15.4 Handbrake lever mounting bolts (A) and warning light switch screws (B)

4 Working inside the vehicle, disconnect the cable from the handbrake control lever, again by removal of clip and pin. Drift out the cable guide to the rear and withdraw the cable through the floorpan.

5 Refitting is a reversal of removal. Adjust the handbrake if necessary.

Secondary cable

6 Remove the rear roadwheel each side then remove the brake drums. Disengage the handbrake secondary cable from the rear brake assembly and pass through the brake backplate, having released the retaining clip **(see illustration)**.

7 Extract the circlip and remove the clevis pin from the cable equaliser unit.

8 Disengage and remove the secondary cable from the body bracket clips and unhook it from the body supports. The cable can then be removed from under the vehicle **(see illustration)**.

9 Refitting is a reversal of removal. Grease the cable groove in the equaliser and also each side of the outer cable location clip **(see illustration)**. Adjust the handbrake on completion.

Models from September 1985

10 Proceed as above, noting that since September 1985 a locking pin has been fitted to the cable adjuster abutment bracket to lock the adjuster sleeve and locknut together.

11 Should it be necessary to renew the cable, the locking pin must be removed by pulling it out using pliers **(see illustration)**. After adjustment a new nylon locking pin must be used and can be fitted by carefully tapping it into place.

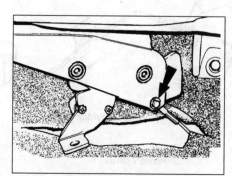

15.5 Primary cable-to-handbrake lever clevis pin and clip (arrowed)

15 Handbrake lever - removal and refitting

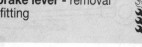

Removal

1 Chock the front wheels, raise and support the vehicle at the rear using safety stands (see *"Jacking and vehicle support"*). Release the handbrake.

2 Working underneath the vehicle, extract the lever-to-equaliser cable retaining clip, remove the pin and separate the cable from the equaliser.

3 Remove the front seats. It may also be necessary to remove the carpet.

4 Detach the handbrake warning switch **(see illustration)**.

5 Disconnect the cable from the handbrake lever by extracting the clip and pin **(see illustration)**.

6 Unscrew the lever securing bolts and remove the lever.

Refitting

7 Refit in the reverse order of removal. On completion, check the handbrake adjustment.

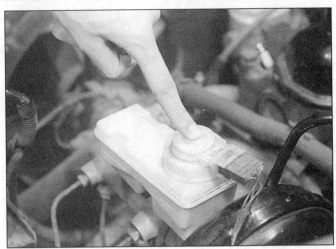

16.6 Depress the brake warning light switch plunger to test

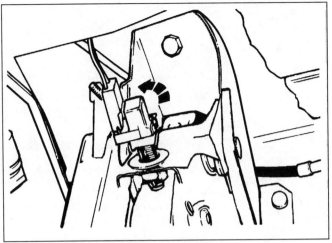

16.7 Brake stop-light switch removal

16 Brake warning lamps - renewal

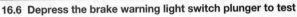

1 All models are fitted with a low fluid level warning switch in the master cylinder reservoir cap and a brake pedal stop-lamp switch.

2 Some models are also fitted with a handbrake ON warning lamp switch.

3 Warning indicator lamps are mounted on the instrument panel.

4 Access to the handbrake switch is obtained after removal of the front seats and floor carpets. The switch is secured to the lever by means of two retaining screws.

5 Whenever the switch is fully removed and refitted, check the operation of the switch and warning lamp with the ignition on prior to refitting the floor carpet and seats.

6 The low fluid level warning lamp switch operation can be checked by depressing the plunger in the top of the switch **(see illustration)**.

7 The stop-lamp switch is activated by brake pedal movement. To remove the switch, unclip and remove the facia underpanel, disconnect the multi-plug connector to the switch then turn the switch anti-clockwise to remove it **(see illustration)**.

8 To refit the switch, fit it into its lockring aperture, pressing inwards so that the switch barrel is in contact with the pedal, compensating for any free play that might exist in the pedal pivot. Twist the switch clockwise to lock it in this position then reattach the wiring connector.

9 On completion check the switch for satisfactory operation.

Chapter 10
Suspension and steering

Contents

Degrees of difficulty

| Easy, suitable for novice with little experience | Fairly easy, suitable for beginner with some experience | Fairly difficult, suitable for competent DIY mechanic 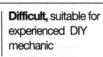 | Difficult, suitable for experienced DIY mechanic | Very difficult, suitable for expert DIY or professional |

Specifications

Suspension type
Front suspension . . . . Independent, MacPherson strut. Double-acting shock absorbers incorporated in the struts
Rear suspension . . . . Independent with coil spring and double-acting shock absorbers. Anti-roll bar on certain models

Steering
Type . . . . Rack and pinion with universally-jointed shaft and deformable column
Lubricant type . . . . To Ford specification SAM-1C-9106-A

Front wheel alignment
Toe setting (service check):
   All models . . . . Parallel to 6.0 mm toe-out
Toe-setting (setting if outside service check tolerance):
   All models . . . . 2.0 to 4.0 mm toe-out

Wheels
Type . . . . Pressed steel or alloy
Size:
   Standard 13x4.50J
   Sport and Ghia 13x5J
   XR2 . . . . 13x6J

Tyre sizes . . . . See Chapter 1 Specifications
Tyre pressures . . . . See end of "Weekly checks"

Torque wrench settings

	Nm	lbf ft
Front suspension		
Hub retaining nut	230	170
Lower arm inboard pivot bolt	45	33
Lower arm balljoint pinch-bolt	30	22
Balljoint lower arm/tie-bar	85	63
Strut to spindle carrier	93	69
Tie-bar to mounting bracket	50	37
Tie-bar mounting bracket to body	50	37
Top mounting locknut	50	37
Top mounting thrust bearing nut (plain)	50	37

Torque wrench settings (continued)

	Nm	lbf ft
Rear suspension		
Lower arm-to-body bolts	50	37
Lower arm-to-axle bolts	50	37
Shock absorber bottom mounting nuts	50	37
Shock absorber top mounting nuts	30	22
Panhard rod-to-body bolts	50	37
Panhard rod-to-axle bolts	50	37
Brake backplate bolts	23	17
Anti-roll bar-to-body nuts	23	17
Anti-roll bar-to-body screws	23	17
Steering		
Steering gear unit to bulkhead	40 to 50	30 to 37
Steering shaft to pinion coupling	45 to 56	33 to 41
Steering wheel to steering shaft nut	27 to 34	20 to 25
Steering column tube mounting nuts	20 to 25	15 to 18
Tie-rod end locknut	57 to 68	42 to 50
Tie-rod end to steering arm nut	24 to 30	18 to 22
Tie-rod inner balljoint (staked)	68 to 90	50 to 66
Tie-rod inner balljoint to rack (Loctite 270)	72 to 88	53 to 65
Pinion cover nut	60 to 70	44 to 52
Slipper plug	4 to 5	3 to 4
Wheels		
Roadwheel bolts	100	74

1 General information and precautions

General information

The front suspension is of independent type with MacPherson struts. The strut assembly on each side is controlled transversely by a fabricated lower (track control) arm whilst the fore and aft control is by means of a tie-bar connected between the lower arm and a mounting bracket on the chassis. The right-hand tie-bar on the XR2 model differs from that fitted to other models in the range.

The rear suspension is of five-point link type and consists of the axle beam, coil springs, double-acting telescopic shock absorbers, a Panhard rod and trailing arms. Certain models are also fitted with an anti-roll bar.

The steering is of rack and pinion type, with a safety steering column which incorporates a jointed lower shaft and a convoluted column tube.

2.1 Removing the steering wheel trim to reveal the steering wheel retaining nut

Precautions

When the front wheels are raised, avoid turning the steering wheel rapidly from lock-to-lock. This could cause hydraulic pressure build-up, with consequent damage to the bellows.

2 Steering wheel - removal and refitting

Removal

1 According to model, either pull off the steering wheel trim or prise out the insert which carries the Ford motif at the centre of the steering wheel **(see illustration)**. Insert the ignition key and turn it to position 1.

2 Prevent the steering wheel from turning with the front roadwheels in the straight-ahead attitude. Unscrew the steering wheel retaining nut using a socket with extension.

3 Scribe an alignment mark between the steering wheel and shaft end face to ensure correct realignment when refitting.

4 Remove the steering wheel from the shaft. No effort should be required to remove the steering wheel as it is located on a hexagonal section shaft which does not cause the binding associated with splined shafts.

5 Note the steering shaft direction indicator cam which has its peg uppermost.

Refitting

6 Refitting is a reversal of removal. Check that the roadwheels are still in the straight-ahead position and locate the steering wheel so that the alignment index marks made on the steering wheel and shaft end face correspond. Refit and tighten the steering wheel retaining nut to the specified torque setting. Refit the steering wheel trim.

3 Steering column - removal and refitting

Removal

1 Disconnect the battery earth lead then remove the steering wheel. Also remove the indicator cam from the steering shaft.

2 Unscrew and recover the steering column shroud retaining screws, then detach and remove the upper and lower column shrouds.

3 Extract the retaining clip from the bonnet release pivot pin, remove the lever and disconnect the cable.

4 Undo the four retaining screws and remove the column multifunction switches. Detach ignition switch wiring connector.

5 Unclip and withdraw the facia lever insulating panel on the driver's side.

6 Unscrew and remove the upper and lower column mounting clamp retaining nuts and washers **(see illustration)**, then slide free and withdraw the column tube and tolerance ring.

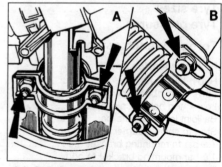

3.6 Steering column upper (A) and lower (B) mountings

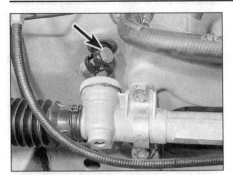

3.8 Pinion coupling clamp bolt (arrowed)

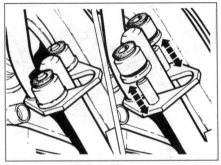

3.9a Steering column upper-to-lower shaft coupling

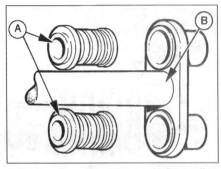

3.9b Steering column lower shaft coupling (B) and bushes (A)

7 Use a suitable screwdriver or implement to hook out the upper thrust bearing.

8 To remove the steering column shafts, unscrew and remove the lower shaft-to-pinion coupling clamp bolt **(see illustration)** then withdraw the upper and lower shafts as a unit. If any difficulty is experienced in separating the lower shaft from the pinion gear, prise the coupling open slightly with a screwdriver.

9 The upper and lower shafts can be separated and the bushes renewed if necessary **(see illustrations)**.

Refitting

10 Refit the shafts reversing the removal procedure and check that the bulkhead seal is not disturbed or distorted when the shaft is refitted.

11 Reconnect the lower shaft to the steering gear pinion shaft and loosely engage the clamp for the moment.

12 The steering column tube assembly can now be fitted.

13 With the upper thrust bearing located in the column, fit the column tube over the shaft, align the mounting clamp holes with the fixing studs then engage and fit the washers and retaining nuts, but do not fully tighten them yet. Semi-tighten the nuts so that the column tube is supported as far up as possible.

14 Locate the upper column shroud and then adjust the column so that the shroud and instrument panel (facia) are not in contact **(see illustration)** and tighten the column retaining nuts to the specified torque wrench setting. When tightened, check that the upper and lower steering shaft coupling pins and bushes are still fully engaged.

15 The upper shroud is now removed again to allow the ignition switch multi-plug to be reconnected and the steering column switches to be relocated and secured with the four screws.

16 Secure the wiring looms of the switches to the column with a plastic strap clip.

17 Locate and secure the bonnet release catch and cable.

18 Locate and secure the upper and lower column shrouds.

19 Relocate the bearing tolerance ring then refit the direction indicator arm.

20 Refit the steering wheel.

21 Recheck that the upper and lower steering shaft coupling pegs and bushes are still fully engaged, then tighten the lower shaft-to-pinion clamp bolt to the specified torque wrench setting.

22 Refit the facia lower insulating panel.

23 To complete, check that the steering action is satisfactory, reconnect the battery earth lead and check that the column multi-function switches, ignition switch and steering lock are operational.

4 Steering gear bellows - renewal

1 At the first indication of a split or grease leakage from the bellows, renew them.

2 The tie-rod diameter will be 11.8 mm or 13.3 mm. It is important to identify which type is fitted in order that the correct bellows replacement kit is obtained.

3 Raise the front of the vehicle and support it securely. Remove the front roadwheels. Turn each hub slowly to full lock to gain access to each tie-rod balljoint.

4 Prior to undoing a tie-rod end locknut, make a relative alignment mark across the faces of the tie-rod and balljoint to ensure correct alignment on refitting **(see illustration)**. Release the tie-rod end locknut, but only unscrew it one quarter of a turn.

5 Extract the split pin and remove the nut from the balljoint taper pin.

6 Using a suitable balljoint extractor, separate the balljoint taper pin from the eye of the steering arm **(see illustration)**.

7 Unscrew the balljoint from the end of the tie-rod.

8 Release the clips from both ends of the damaged bellows and slide them from the rack and the tie-rod.

9 Turn the steering wheel gently to expel as much lubricant as possible from the rack housing. It is recommended that the bellows on the opposite side be released by detaching their inboard clip, turning the bellows back and clearing the lubricant as it is also ejected at this end of the rack housing.

10 Smear the narrow neck of the new bellows with the specified grease and slide them over the tie-rod into position on the rack housing.

11 If new bellows are being fitted to the pinion end of the rack, leave both ends of the bellows unclamped at this stage.

12 If the bellows are being fitted to the rack support bush end of the rack housing, clamp only the inner end of the bellows and leave the outer end unfastened.

3.14 Set column to give small clearance at (X) between the shrouds and facia panel

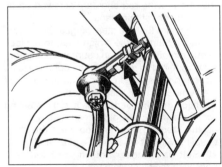

4.4 Mark relative positions of balljoint and tie rod (arrowed)

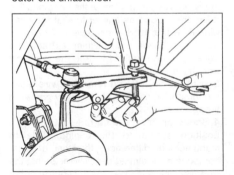

4.6 Detaching the balljoint with a separator tool

10

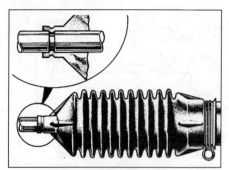

4.15a **Bellows must engage in rod groove (inset)**

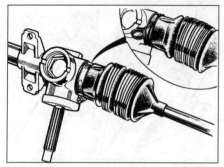

4.15b **Discard original wire type bellows retaining clip (inset) and use new worm drive type**

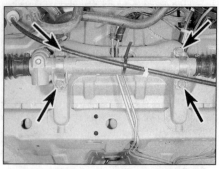

6.6 **Steering gear unit securing bolts (arrowed)**

13 Screw on the tie-rod end until the locknut requires only 1/4 turn to lock it.

14 Connect the tie-rod end balljoint to the steering arm, tighten the nut to the specified torque and insert a new split pin.

15 Lubricate the support bush end of the rack by applying 50 cc of the specified lubricant into the bellows at that end. Check that the bellows are correctly engaged in the groove at the tie-rod end, then secure using a new clip **(see illustrations)**.

16 Repeat this procedure with the pinion end of the rack but apply 70 cc of lubricant.

17 Tighten the tie-rod end locknut against the tie-rod end and check that the alignment marks correspond. Refit the roadwheels and lower the vehicle.

18 If the position of the tie-rod locknut was not altered from its original setting, the front wheel alignment (toe) will not have altered, but it is recommended that the alignment be checked at the earliest opportunity.

5 Tie-rod end balljoint - renewal

1 If, as the result of inspection, the tie-rod end balljoints are found to be worn, remove them as described in the preceding Section.

2 When the balljoint nuts are unscrewed, it is sometimes found that the balljoint taper pin turns in the eye of the steering arm to prevent the nut from unscrewing. Should this happen, apply pressure to the top of the balljoint using a length of wood as a lever to seat the taper pin while the nut is unscrewed. When this condition is met, a balljoint extractor is unlikely to be required to free the taper pin from the steering arm.

3 With the tie-rod end removed, wire brush the threads of the tie-rod and apply grease to them.

4 Screw on the new tie-rod to take up a position similar to the original. Due to manufacturing differences, the fitting of a new component will almost certainly mean that the front wheel alignment will require some adjustment.

5 Connect the balljoint to the steering arm.

6 Steering gear - removal and refitting

Removal

1 Set the front roadwheels in the straight-ahead position.

2 Raise the front of the vehicle and fit safety stands (see *"Jacking and vehicle support"*).

3 Working under the bonnet, remove the pinch-bolt from the coupling at the base of the steering column shaft.

4 Extract the split pins from the tie-rod balljoint taper pin nuts, unscrew the nuts and remove them.

5 Separate the balljoints from the steering arms using a suitable tool.

6 Flatten the locktabs on the steering gear securing bolts and unscrew and remove the bolts **(see illustration)**. Withdraw the steering gear downwards to separate the coupling from the steering shaft and then take it out from under the front wing.

Refitting

7 Refitting is a reversal of removal. If a new rack and pinion assembly is being installed, the tie-rod ends will have to be removed from the original unit and screw onto the new tie-rods to approximately the same setting. If a note was not made of the position of the original tie-rod ends on their rods, inspection of the threads will probably indicate their original location. In any event it is important that the new tie-rod ends are screwed on an equal amount at this stage.

8 Make sure that the steering gear is centred. Do this by turning the pinion shaft to full lock in one direction and then count the number of turns required to rotate it to the opposite lock. Now turn the splined pinion shaft through half the number of turns just counted.

9 Check that the roadwheels and the steering wheel are in the straight-ahead attitude, offer up the steering gear and connect the shaft coupling without inserting the pinch-bolt.

10 Bolt up the gear housing and lock the bolts with their lockplate tabs.

11 Reconnect the tie-rod ends to the steering arms. Use new split pins.

12 Tighten the coupling pinch-bolt to the specified torque. Lower the vehicle to the floor.

13 If the tie-rod ends were disturbed or if a new assembly was installed, check and adjust the front wheel alignment.

7 Steering angles and wheel alignment

1 When reading this Section, reference should also be made in respect of front and rear suspension arrangement.

2 Accurate front wheel alignment is essential to good steering and for even tyre wear. Before considering the steering angles, check that the tyres are correctly inflated, that the roadwheels are not buckled, the hub bearings are not worn or incorrectly adjusted and that the steering linkage is in good order.

3 Wheel alignment consists of four factors:

Camber is the angle at which the roadwheels are set from the vertical when viewed from the front or rear of the vehicle. Positive camber is the angle (in degrees) that the wheels are tilted outwards at the top, from the vertical.

Castor is the angle between the steering axis and a vertical line when viewed from each side of the vehicle. Positive castor is indicated when the steering axis is inclined towards the rear of the vehicle at its upper end.

Steering axis inclination is the angle, when viewed from the front or rear of the vehicle, between the vertical and an imaginary line drawn between the upper and lower suspension swivel balljoints or upper and lower strut mountings.

Toe is the amount by which the distance between the front inside edges of the roadwheel differs from that between the rear inside edges. If the distance at the front is less than that at the rear, the wheels are said to toe-in. If the distance at the front inside edges is greater than that at the rear, the wheels toe-out.

4 Due to the need for precision gauges to measure the small angles of the steering and suspension settings, it is preferable to leave this work to your dealer. Camber and castor angles are set in production and are not adjustable. If these angles are ever checked and found to be outside specification then either the suspension components are damaged or distorted, or wear has occurred in the bushes at the attachment point.

5 If you wish to check front wheel alignment yourself, first make sure that the lengths of both tie-rods are equal when the steering is in the straight-ahead position. This can be measured reasonably accurately by counting the number of exposed threads on the tie-rod adjacent to the balljoint assembly.

6 Adjust if necessary by releasing the locknut from the balljoint assembly and the clamp at the small end of the bellows.

7 Obtain a tracking gauge. These are available in various forms from accessory stores, or one can be fabricated from a length of steel tubing, suitably cranked to clear the sump and bellhousing, and having a set screw and locknut at one end.

8 With the gauge, measure the distance between the two inner rims of the roadwheels (at hub height) at the rear of the wheel. Push the vehicle forward to rotate the wheel through 180° (half a turn) and measure the distance between the wheel inner rims, again at hub height, at the front of the wheel. This last measurement should differ from the first one by the specified toe-in/toe-out (see Specifications).

9 Where the toe setting is found to be incorrect, release the tie-rod balljoint locknuts and turn the tie-rods by an equal amount. Only turn them through a quarter turn at a time before rechecking the alignment. Do not grip the threaded part of the tie-rod during adjustment and make sure that the bellows outboard clip is released, otherwise the bellows will twist as the tie-rod is rotated. When each tie-rod is viewed from the rack housing, turning the rods clockwise will increase the toe-out. Always turn the tie-rods in the same direction when viewed from the centre of the vehicle, otherwise they will become unequal in length. This would cause the steering wheel spoke alignment to alter and also cause problems on turning with tyre scrubbing.

10 After adjustment of the tie-rods check that the exposed thread portion of each is equal and does not exceed 28 mm. Also check that the steering wheel position is centralised, with the front roadwheels in the straight-ahead position.

11 If the steering wheel angular position is incorrect, but the tracking alignment of the front roadwheels is correct, proceed as follows:

12 Where the steering wheel misalignment is less than 30° then the wheel can be left in position.

13 Where the steering wheel is misaligned by more than 60°, turn the steering onto full lock then move it back to centralise it in the centre point of the lock-to-lock travel. You will now

need to remove the steering wheel and refit it in the correct alignment position.

14 To correct further misalignment between the position of the steering wheel and the roadwheels when in the straight-ahead position, you will need to raise and support the front of the vehicle on safety stands (see "Jacking and vehicle support").

15 Mark the relative positions of the tie-rods to joints, loosen the locknut and the outer steering bellows clip, then rotate each tie-rod an equivalent amount in the same direction to correct the steering wheel misalignment. Note that 30° of tie-rod rotation equals 1° of steering wheel angular correction. Rotate the rods clockwise (viewed from the left-hand side of the car) to correct a clockwise misalignment of the steering wheel. Rotate the tie-rods anti-clockwise to correct an anti-clockwise misalignment (also viewed from the left-hand side of the vehicle).

16 After the steering wheel and tie-rod adjustment is complete, recheck the wheel alignment (paragraphs 5 to 9 inclusive) and retighten the locknuts without altering the positional settings of the tie-rods. Hold the balljoint assembly at the mid-point of its arc of travel (flats are provided on it for a spanner) while the locknuts are tightened.

17 Finally, tighten the bellows clamps.

18 Rear wheel alignment is set in production and is not adjustable, but when dismantling any part, it is essential that all washers are refitted in their original positions as they control the wheel setting for the life of the vehicle.

8 Front hub bearings - inspection, removal and renewal

Inspection

1 All models are fitted with non-adjustable front hub bearings, the bearing play being set when the hub nut is tightened to its specified setting during initial assembly or overhaul.

2 To check the bearings for excessive wear, raise and support the vehicle at the front end so that the roadwheels are clear of the ground.

3 Grip the roadwheel tyre at the top and bottom and use a rocking motion to check for play of the bearings.

4 A small amount of endfloat may be detected when checking for play (even after fitting new bearings) but when the wheel is spun there should be no sign of roughness, binding or vibration caused by the bearings.

5 If the hub bearings are suspect or obviously worn beyond an acceptable level they must be renewed.

Removal

6 Before removing the roadwheel(s) the vehicle must be suitably supported on safety stands at the front (see "Jacking and vehicle support").

7 Get an assistant to apply the footbrake then undo the roadwheel bolts and remove the wheel.

8 Refit two of the roadwheel bolts as a means of anchorage for the disc when the hub nut is unscrewed.

9 Have an assistant apply the footbrake and then unscrew the staked hub nut and remove it, together with the plain washer. This nut is very tight so, if you are unsure of the raised car's stability, refit the roadwheel(s) and undo the hub nut with the car on the ground.

10 Remove the wheel and/or wheel bolts.

11 Unbolt the brake caliper and tie it up to the suspension strut to avoid strain on the flexible hose (see illustration).

12 Withdraw the hub/disc. If it is tight, use a two-legged puller.

13 Extract the split pin and unscrew the castellated nut from the tie-rod end balljoint.

14 Using a suitable balljoint splitter, separate the balljoint from the steering arm (see illustration).

15 Unscrew and remove the special Torx pinch-bolt which holds the lower arm balljoint to the stub axle carrier (see illustration).

16 Support the driveshaft on a block of wood and remove the bolts which hold the stub axle carrier to the base of the suspension strut.

17 Using a suitable lever, separate the carrier from the strut by prising open the clamp jaws.

18 Support the driveshaft at the outboard CV joint and pull the stub axle carrier clear of the driveshaft.

8.11 Brake caliper retaining bolts (arrowed)

8.14 Separate the balljoint

10

8.15 Lower arm balljoint and stub axle carrier Torx bolt (arrowed)

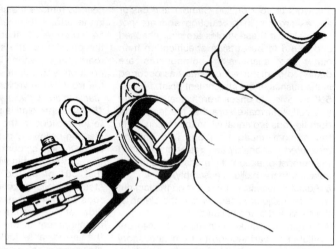

8.23 Bearing track removal from stub axle carrier

19 Remove the stub axle carrier and grip it in a vice fitted with jaw protectors.
20 Using pliers, pull out the dust shield from the groove in the stub axle carrier.
21 Prise out the inner and outer oil seals.
22 Lift out the bearings.
23 With a suitable drift, drive out the bearing tracks **(see illustration)**.
24 Clean away all the old grease from the stub axle carrier.

Renewal

25 Drive the new bearing tracks squarely into their seats using a piece of suitable diameter tubing or press tool **(see illustration)**.
26 Liberally pack grease into the bearings, making sure to work plenty into the spaces between the rollers.
27 Install the bearing to one side of the carrier, then fill the lips of the new oil seal with grease and tap it squarely into position.
28 Fit the bearing and its seal to the opposite side in a similar way.

29 Fit the dust shield by tapping it into position using a block of wood.
30 Smear the driveshaft splines with grease, then install the carrier over the end of the driveshaft.
31 Connect the carrier to the suspension strut and tighten the bolt to the specified torque.
32 Reconnect the suspension lower arm balljoint to the carrier and secure by passing the pinch-bolt through the groove in the balljoint stud **(see illustration)**.
33 Reconnect the tie-bar to the steering arm, tighten the castellated nut and secure with a new split pin.
34 Install the hub/disc and push it on to the driveshaft as far as it will go using hand pressure.
35 In the absence of the special hub installer tool (14-022), draw the hub/disc onto the driveshaft by using a two or three-legged puller with legs engaged behind the carrier. On no account try to knock the hub/disc into position using hammer blows or the CV joint will be damaged.

36 Grease the threads at the end of the driveshaft, fit the plain washer and screw on a new nut, finger tight.
37 Fit the brake caliper, tightening the mounting bolts to the specified torque (see Chapter 9 Specifications).
38 Screw in two wheel bolts and have an assistant apply the footbrake.
39 Tighten the hub nut to the specified torque. This is a high torque and if a suitably calibrated torque wrench is not available, use a socket with a knuckle bar 457.2 mm in length. Applying maximum leverage to the knuckle bar should tighten the nut to very close to its specified torque. For safety it is probably better to leave the final tightening of the hub nut until the car is on its wheels.
40 Stake the nut into the driveshaft groove, if applicable **(see illustration)**.
41 Remove the temporary roadwheel bolts.
42 Fit the roadwheel and lower the vehicle to the floor. Fully tighten the roadwheel bolts and hub nut (if applicable). If necessary stake the hub nut.

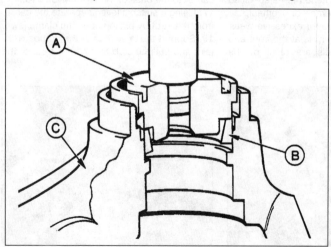

8.25 Bearing track installation
A Press tool   B Bearing track   C Stub axle carrier

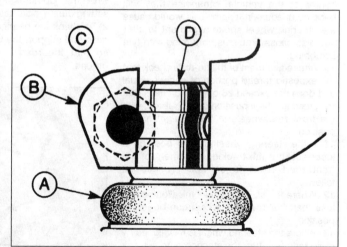

8.32 Balljoint pinch-bolt location
A Balljoint   B Carrier   C Pinch-bolt   D Balljoint stud

8.40 Stake the hub nut to secure

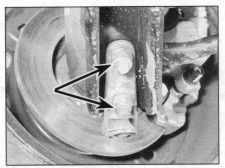

9.4 Tie-bar-to-lower suspension arm retaining nuts (arrowed)

10.2 Tie-bar and mounting bracket
Note that the XR2 differs slightly from that fitted to other models

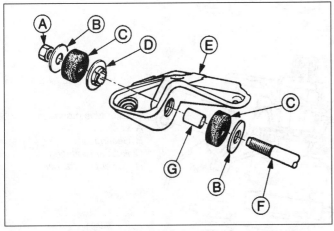

10.4 Tie-bar mounting bracket and bush components

A Retaining nut	D Bearing	F Tie-bar
B Washer	E Bracket	G Bush sleeve
C Bush		

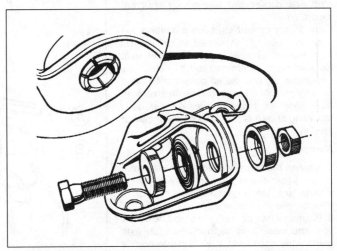

10.5 Tie-bar bush renewal, using draw bolt and cupped washers

9 Front suspension lower arm - removal, bush replacement and refitting

1 Raise the front of the vehicle and support it securely on safety stands (see *"Jacking and vehicle support"*).
2 Unbolt and remove the pivot bolt from the inboard end of the suspension arm.
3 At the outboard end of the suspension arm, disengage the arm from the hub carrier by unscrewing and removing the pinch-bolt.
4 Unscrew the tie-bar-to-lower arm attachment nuts and withdraw the lower arm **(see illustration)**.
5 Renewal of the pivot bush at the inboard end of the suspension arm is possible using a nut and bolt, or a vice, and suitable distance pieces. Apply some brake hydraulic fluid to facilitate installation of the new bush. If the balljoint is worn or corroded, renew the suspension arm complete.
6 Refitting the arm is a reversal of removal. Tighten all nuts and bolts to the specified torque when the weight of the vehicle is again on the roadwheels.

10 Front tie-bar - removal and refitting

Removal

1 Jack up the front of the vehicle and support securely on axle stands (see *"Jacking and vehicle support"*).
2 Unscrew and remove the nut which holds the tie-bar to the large pressed steel mounting bracket. Take off the dished washer and the rubber insulator **(see illustration)**.
3 Unscrew and remove the tie-bar-to-lower arm retaining nuts then push the tie-bar upwards and clear of the arm.
4 Remove the tie-bar, together with the remaining bush and washer **(see illustration)**.
5 Where necessary, the bush in the pressed-steel mounting bracket can be renewed if the old bush is drawn out using a bolt, nut and suitable distance pieces **(see illustration)**.
6 Lubricate the bush-to-bracket contact faces before inserting the replacement items.

Refitting

7 Refitting the tie-bar is a reversal of removal. The shouldered face of the tie-bar must face upwards when fitted **(see illustration)**. Finally tighten all nuts and bolts to the specified torque only when the weight of the vehicle is again on its roadwheels.

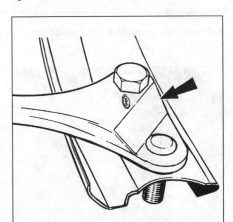

10.7 Shouldered face of tie-bar must face top when fitted

10

11 Front suspension strut -
removal, overhaul and refitting

Note 1: *At the beginning of 1986, a revised type of bolt was introduced to secure the front stub axle carrier to the suspension strut. These bolts are precision ground and provide more positive and accurate location of the stub axle carrier and strut, thus reducing the possibility of a change in suspension and steering angles when the two components are dismantled and reassembled. It is recommended by Ford that this latest bolt should be used on pre-1986 models if the stub axle carrier and suspension strut are separated.*

Note 2: *A modified strut top mounting has been progressively introduced on XR2 models from November 1984 onwards to eliminate isolated cases of premature tyre wear. This later mounting and related parts can be fitted to early models if required (see illustration). Note that the nylon spacer on the early mounting shown is not used on the modified version.*

Removal

1 Slacken the roadwheel bolts, raise the front of the vehicle and support it securely on stands (see *"Jacking and vehicle support"*), then remove the roadwheel.

2 Position a jack beneath the stub axle carrier unit and raise it to support the stub axle carrier, driveshaft and CV joints in their normal positions to ensure that they are not damaged.

3 Undo the retaining nuts and withdraw the two bolts securing the suspension strut to the stub axle carrier **(see illustration)**.

4 Detach the brake hose and location grommet from the strut bracket.

5 Working at the top end of the strut, detach the cover and then unscrew the strut retaining nut **(see illustration)**.

6 Withdraw the complete strut assembly from under the front wing.

Overhaul

7 Clean away external dirt and mud from the strut.

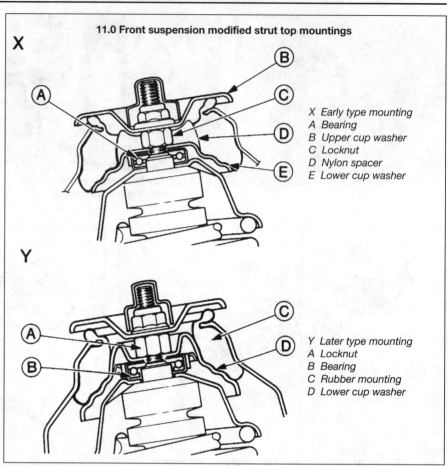

11.0 Front suspension modified strut top mountings

X

Y

X Early type mounting
A Bearing
B Upper cup washer
C Locknut
D Nylon spacer
E Lower cup washer

Y Later type mounting
A Locknut
B Bearing
C Rubber mounting
D Lower cup washer

8 If the strut has been removed due to oil leakage or to lack of damping, then it should be renewed with a new or factory reconditioned unit. Dismantling of the original strut is not recommended and internal components are not generally available.

9 Before the strut is exchanged, the coil spring will have to be removed. To do this, a spring compressor or compressors will be needed. These are generally available from tool hire centres or they can be purchased at most motor accessory shops.

10 Engage the compressors over at least three coils of the spring and compress the spring sufficiently to release spring tension from the top mounting **(see illustration)**.

11 Once the spring is compressed, unscrew and remove the nut from the end of the piston rod which retains the top mounting. As there will be a tendency for the piston rod to turn while the nut is unscrewed, provision is made at the end of the rod to insert a 6 mm Allen key to hold the rod still.

12 Remove the top mounting and lift off the spring and compressor.

13 The compressor need not be released if the spring is to be fitted immediately to a new strut. If the compressor is to be released from the spring, make sure that you do it slowly and progressively.

14 The top mounting can be dismantled by sliding off the thrust bearing and withdrawing the spring upper seat, gaiter spring and, where fitted, insulator. Also if fitted, slide the bump stop from the piston rod.

11.3 Suspension strut-to-stub axle carrier retaining bolts

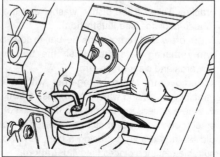

11.5 Strut top mounting nut removal
Note Allen key to prevent rod from turning

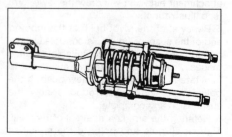

11.10 Typical spring compressor in position

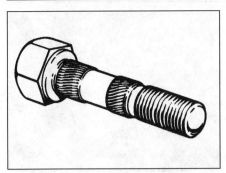

11.21 Special service bolts for attaching strut to carrier

15 Renew any worn or damaged components. If the front strut and/or coil spring is to be renewed then it is advisable also to renew the equivalent assembly on the other side.
16 Fit the spring to the strut, making sure that the ends of the coils locate correctly in the shaped parts of the spring seats.
17 Fit the top mounting components, being very careful to maintain the correct order of assembly of the individual components.
18 Gently release and remove the spring compressor.
19 With the spring compressor removed, check that the ends of the spring are fully located in the shaped sections of the spring seatings.

Refitting

20 Refit the strut unit reversing the removal procedure.
21 The suspension strut-to-stub axle carrier fitting position is critical and, during manufacture, this is set using a jig and normal production bolts fitted. When reassembling the stub axle carrier and strut, two new Ford special service bolts must be used to ensure

that the correct carrier-to-strut fitting position is restored. These bolts can be identified by their knurled shank **(see illustration)**.
22 Lower the vehicle so that it is free-standing before tightening the top mounting nuts to its specified wrench setting, then refit the plastic cover.

12 Rear hub bearings - removal, refitting and adjustment

Removal

1 Remove the brake drum **(see illustration)**.
2 With the drum removed the bearings and inner hub can be cleaned and inspected, but avoid getting grease onto the braking surface of the drum.
3 Use a suitable tool and hook out the grease retainer from the inner hub.
4 Extract the inner bearing cone.
5 Using a suitable punch, drive out the bearing outer tracks, taking care not to burr the bearing seats.

Refitting

6 If new bearings are being fitted to both hubs do not mix up the bearing components, but keep them in their individual packs until required.
7 Drive the new bearing tracks squarely into their hub recesses.
8 Pack both bearings with a lithium-based grease, working plenty into the rollers. Be generous, but there is no need to fill the cavity between the inner and outer bearings.
9 Locate the inboard bearing and then grease the lips of a new oil seal (grease retainer) and tap it into position.

10 Fit the brake drum/hub onto the stub axle, taking care not to catch the oil seal (grease retainer) lips.
11 Fit the outboard bearing and the thrustwasher and screw the retaining nut into position. Adjust the bearing endfloat and lower the vehicle to complete.

Adjustment

12 Raise and support the rear of the vehicle on safety stands (see *"Jacking and vehicle support"*). Release the handbrake.
13 This adjustment will normally only be required if, when the top and bottom of the roadwheel are gripped and "rocked", excessive movement can be detected in the bearings. Slight movement is essential.
14 Remove the roadwheels. Using a hammer and cold chisel, tap off the dust cap from the end of the hub.
15 Extract the split pin and take off the nut retainer.
16 Tighten the hub nut to a torque of between 20 and 25 Nm (15 and 18 lbf ft), at the same time rotating the roadwheel in an anti-clockwise direction **(see illustration)**.
17 Unscrew the nut one half a turn and then tighten it only finger tight.
18 Fit the nut retainer so that two of its slots line up with the split pin hole. Insert a new split pin, bending the end *around* the nut, not over the end of the stub axle.
19 Tap the dust cap into position.
20 Recheck the play as described in paragraph 13. A fractional amount of wheel movement *must* be present.
21 Repeat the operations on the opposite hub, refit the roadwheels and lower the vehicle to the floor.

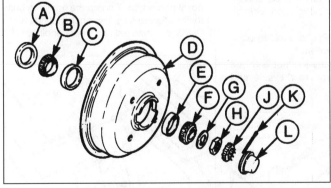

12.1 Rear hub/drum components

A Grease retainer
B Tapered roller bearing (inner)
C Bearing track
D Hub/drum
E Bearing track
F Tapered roller bearing (outer)
G Thrustwasher
H Nut
J Nut lock
K Split pin
L Grease cap

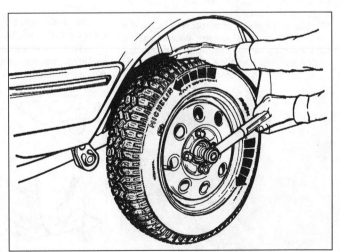

12.16 Rear wheel bearing adjustment

10

13 Rear shock absorber -
removal, testing and refitting

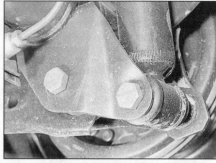

Removal

1 Slacken the rear roadwheel bolts, raise and support the rear of the vehicle using safety stands (see *"Jacking and vehicle support"*). Remove the roadwheel.
2 Position a jack beneath the rear axle for support.
3 Raise the tailgate and, from within the vehicle at the rear, prise free the plastic cap covering the top end of the rear shock absorber on the side concerned.
4 Unscrew and remove the shock absorber upper mounting locknut, washer and insulator **(see illustration)**.
5 Unscrew and remove the shock absorber lower mounting locknut **(see illustration)**. Withdraw the bolt then lever the shock absorber unit upwards to disengage it from its location peg **(see illustrations)**.

Testing

6 To test the shock absorber, grip its lower mounting in a vice so that the unit is vertical.
7 Fully extend and extract the shock absorber ten or twelve times. Any lack of resistance in either direction will indicate the need for renewal, as will evidence of leakage of fluid.

Refitting

8 Refitting is a reversal of removal, but if a new unit is being installed, prime it first in a similar way to that described for testing.
9 To ease the fitting of the shock absorber lower arm onto the location peg, lubricate the bush and peg with a solution of soapy water. Locate a suitable section of tubing or a socket on the top face of the shock absorber location arm bush and lever it down into position on the peg.
10 Locate the lower mounting bolt and loosely fit the locknut.
11 Extend the shock absorber and locate it at the top end fitting the insulator, washer and nut.
12 Lower the vehicle and when free-standing tighten the upper and lower mounting nuts to the specified torque wrench settings.

13.4 Rear suspension shock absorber top mounting

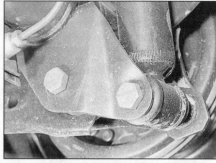

13.5a Rear suspension shock absorber lower mounting

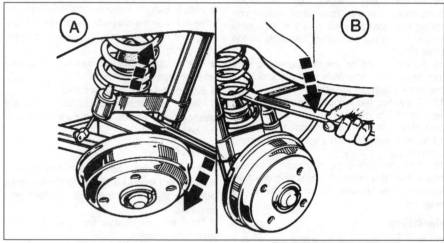

13.5b Lever rear shock absorber clear of locating peg to remove it from the peg (A) or position on the peg (B) when refitting

14 Panhard rod - removal, bush renewal and refitting

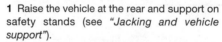

1 Raise the vehicle at the rear and support on safety stands (see *"Jacking and vehicle support"*).
2 Undo and remove the Panhard rod-to-body retaining bolt **(see illustration)**.
3 Unscrew and remove the locknut and bolt retaining the Panhard rod to the axle and remove the rod.

4 Renewal of the Panhard rod bushes can be accomplished by using sockets or distance pieces and applying pressure in the jaws of a vice **(see illustration)**. Lubricate the new bushes with paraffin to ease fitting.
5 Refit the Panhard rod by reversing the removal procedure. Tighten the retaining bolts to their specified torque wrench settings when the vehicle is lowered and free-standing.

13.5c Rear suspension shock absorber location peg

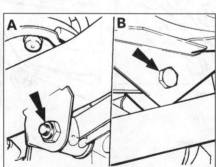

14.2 Panhard rod mounting to axle (A) and body (B)

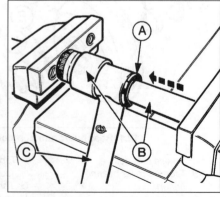

14.4 Panhard rod bush removal method

A Bush   C Panhard rod
B Sockets

15.3 Rear anti-roll bar to body mounting

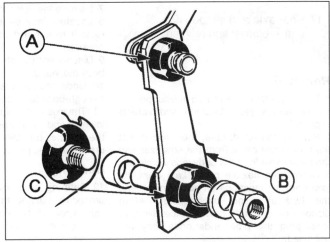

15.4 Rear anti-roll bar connecting link (B) with upper (A) and lower (C) bush assemblies

15 Rear anti-roll bar - removal, bush renewal and refitting

1 Loosen the roadwheel bolts on each side at the rear, raise the rear of the vehicle, support on safety stands and remove the rear wheels (see *"Jacking and vehicle support"*).

2 Unscrew and remove the shock absorber lower mounting bolt nuts, but *do not* withdraw the bolt.

3 Unscrew and remove the anti-roll bar-to-body mounting bracket nuts. Withdraw the mounting bush clamps **(see illustration)**.

4 The anti-roll bar and connecting link assembly can now be disengaged from the lower shock absorber mounting and the bar removed **(see illustration)**.

5 To remove the body mounting bushes prise them open by levering within the split on their rear face.

6 To detach the connecting links from the anti-roll bar press free the upper bush. This

bush can be renewed if worn or defective, but the lower bush cannot and it will therefore be necessary to renew the complete link if this is defective.

7 If the anti-roll bar is damaged or distorted it must be renewed.

8 Refitting is a reversal of the removal procedure. When refitting the connecting link to the anti-roll bar ensure that the longer tube end faces towards the centre of the vehicle.

9 Do not fully tighten the anti-roll bar location and mounting nuts until the vehicle is lowered and free-standing.

16 Rear coil spring - removal and refitting

Removal

1 Slacken the roadwheel bolts, raise the rear of the vehicle and support it securely with safety stands (see *"Jacking and vehicle support"*).

2 Locate a jack under the rear axle and raise it to support (not lift) the axle.

3 Remove the retaining nut and disconnect the shock absorber at its upper mounting.

4 Unscrew and remove the lower arm through-bolt from the axle.

5 Slowly lower the jack under the axle to release the spring tension and allow its removal. Remove the insulator ring **(see illustration)**.

6 If required, the bump stop rubber can be prised free from its location hole in the axle. When refitting the bump stop, press it down firmly into its location hole and turn it so that its lower section is felt to snap into position **(see illustration)**.

Refitting

7 Refitting is a reversal of the removal procedure. Do not tighten the lower arm and shock absorber retaining nuts until after the vehicle is lowered and is free-standing.

16.5 Rear coil spring and insulator ring (arrowed)

16.6 Rear suspension coil spring and bump stop rubber

10

17 Rear axle and suspension unit - removal and refitting

Removal

1 Raise the rear of the vehicle and support on safety stands (see *"Jacking and vehicle support"*).

2 Release the handbrake, then disconnect the handbrake cable from the equalizer and the outer cable from the body location clips.

3 Detach the flexible brake liner from the lower arm connections on each side. Clean the hydraulic line connections before disconnecting and, to prevent excessive fluid loss, plug the pipe ends once they are detached.

4 Undo the Panhard rod-to-axle pivot bolt and retaining nut and withdraw the bolt.

5 Unbolt and detach the exhaust downpipe at the flange connection.

6 Unbolt and remove the Panhard rod from the body.

7 Remove the rear anti-roll bar (where fitted).

8 Locate a jack beneath the rear axle and raise it to support the axle (trolley type, if possible).

9 Disconnect the shock absorber at its top body mounting.

10 Undo and remove the lower arm-to-body through-bolts **(see illustration)**.

11 The axle and suspension unit can now be lowered and withdrawn from the underside of the vehicle, but take care not to snag the brake hydraulic pipes.

Refitting

12 Refitting is a reversal of the removal procedure, but note the following:

a) *Do not fully tighten the chassis and suspension fastening until after the vehicle is lowered and is free-standing. The respective torque wrench settings are given in the Specifications.*

b) *Reconnect and adjust the handbrake cable. When the brake lines are reconnected, top-up the hydraulic fluid level and bleed the hydraulic circuit.*

18 Rear axle unit - removal and refitting

Removal

1 Proceed as described in the previous Section, paragraphs 1 to 8 inclusive.

2 Referring to Section 13, disconnect the shock absorber on each side at its lower end.

3 The axle tube and coil spring assemblies can now be lowered and withdrawn from the underside of the vehicle. Take care not to snag the brake hydraulic lines when removing.

Refitting

4 Refitting is a direct reversal of the removal procedure.

5 Reconnect the shock absorbers at their lower mountings.

6 Note that the special remarks made in paragraph 12 of the previous Section also apply when refitting the axle unit.

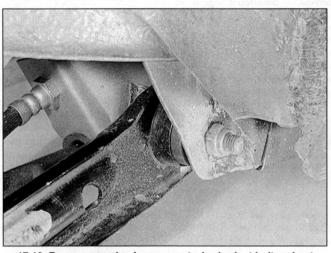

17.10 Rear suspension lower arm-to-body pivot bolt and nut

Chapter 11
Bodywork and fittings

Contents

Degrees of difficulty

| **Easy,** suitable for novice with little experience | **Fairly easy,** suitable for beginner with some experience | **Fairly difficult,** suitable for competent DIY mechanic | **Difficult,** suitable for experienced DIY mechanic | **Very difficult,** suitable for expert DIY or professional |

Specifications

Torque wrench settings

	Nm	**lbf ft**
All seat belt anchor bolts	29 to 41	21 to 30
Front belt stalk-to-seat frame screws	25 to 30	18 to 22
Bumper retaining nuts	11 to 13	8 to 10

1 General information

The body is of a monocoque all-steel, welded construction with impact absorbing front and rear sections. There are two side doors and a full-length lifting tailgate for easy access to the rear compartment. The side doors are fitted with antiburst locks. The tailgate hinges are bolted to the underside of the roof panel and welded to the tailgate. Gas-filled dampers support the tailgate in the open position; when closed it is fastened by a key-operated lock.

Wrap-around polycarbonate bumpers are fitted front and rear, and further body protection is given by side mouldings which are also manufactured in this material.

Rust and corrosion protection is applied to all new vehicles and includes zinc phosphate dipping and wax injection of the box sections and door interiors.

2 Maintenance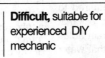

Bodywork and underframe

The general condition of a vehicle's bodywork is the one thing that significantly affects its value. Maintenance is easy but needs to be regular. Neglect, particularly after minor damage, can lead quickly to further deterioration and costly repair bills. It is important also to keep watch on those parts of the vehicle not immediately visible, for instance the underside, inside all the wheel arches and the lower part of the engine compartment.

The basic maintenance routine for the bodywork is washing preferably with a lot of water, from a hose. This will remove all the loose solids which may have stuck to the vehicle. It is important to flush these off in such a way as to prevent grit from scratching the finish. The wheel arches and underframe need washing in the same way to remove any accumulated mud which will retain moisture and tend to encourage rust. Paradoxically enough, the best time to clean the underframe and wheel arches is in wet weather when the mud is thoroughly wet and soft. In very wet weather the underframe is usually cleaned of large accumulations automatically and this is a good time for inspection.

Periodically, except on vehicles with a wax-based underbody protective coating, it is a good idea to have the whole of the underframe of the vehicle steam cleaned, engine compartment included, so that a thorough inspection can be carried out to see what minor repairs and renovations are necessary. Steam cleaning is available at many garages and is necessary for removal of the accumulation of oily grime which sometimes is allowed to become thick in certain areas. If steam cleaning facilities are not available, there are one or two excellent

11

grease solvents available. The dirt can then be simply hosed off. Note that these methods should not be used on vehicles with wax-based underbody protective coating or the coating will be removed. Such vehicles should be inspected annually, preferably just prior to winter, when the underbody should be washed down and any damage to the wax coating repaired. Ideally, a completely fresh coat should be applied. It would also be worth considering the use of such wax-based protection for injection into door panels, sills, box sections, etc, as an additional safeguard against rust damage where such protection is not provided by the vehicle manufacturer.

After washing paintwork, wipe off with a chamois leather to give an unspotted clear finish. A coat of clear protective wax polish will give added protection against chemical pollutants in the air. If the paintwork sheen has dulled or oxidised, use a cleaner/polisher combination to restore the brilliance of the shine. This requires a little effort, but such dulling is usually caused because regular washing has been neglected. Care needs to be taken with metallic paintwork, as special nonabrasive cleaner/polisher is required to avoid damage to the finish. Always check that the door and ventilator opening drain holes and pipes are completely clear so that water can be drained out. Bright work should be treated in the same way as paint work. Windscreens and windows can be kept clear of the smeary film which often appears, by the use of a proprietary glass cleaner. Never use any form of wax or other body or chromium polish on glass.

Upholstery and carpets

Mats and carpets should be brushed or vacuum cleaned regularly to keep them free of grit. If they are badly stained remove them from the vehicle for scrubbing or sponging and make quite sure they are dry before refitting. Seats and interior trim panels can be kept clean by wiping with a damp cloth. If they do become stained (which can be more apparent on light coloured upholstery) use a little liquid detergent and a soft nail brush to scour the grime out of the grain of the material. Do not forget to keep the headlining clean in the same way as the upholstery. When using liquid cleaners inside the vehicle do not over-wet the surfaces being cleaned. Excessive damp could get into the seams and padded interior causing stains, offensive odours or even rot. If the inside of the vehicle gets wet accidentally it is worthwhile taking some trouble to dry it out properly, particularly where carpets are involved. Do not leave oil or electric heaters inside the vehicle for this purpose.

3 Minor body damage - repair

Repair of minor scratches in bodywork

If the scratch is very superficial, and does not penetrate to the metal of the bodywork, repair is very simple. Lightly rub the area of the scratch with a paintwork renovator, or a very fine cutting paste to remove loose paint from the scratch and to clear the surrounding bodywork of wax polish. Rinse the area with clean water.

Apply touch-up paint or a paint film to the scratch using a fine paint brush; continue to apply fine layers of paint until the surface of the paint in the scratch is level with the surrounding paintwork. Allow the new paint at least two weeks to harden: then blend it into the surrounding paintwork by rubbing the scratch area with a paintwork renovator or a very fine cutting paste. Finally, apply wax polish.

Where the scratch has penetrated right through to the metal of the bodywork, causing the metal to rust, a different repair technique is required. Remove any loose rust from the bottom of the scratch with a penknife, then apply rust inhibiting paint to prevent the formation of rust in the future. Using a rubber or nylon applicator fill the scratch with bodystopper paste. If required, this paste can be mixed with cellulose thinners to provide a very thin paste which is ideal for filling narrow scratches. Before the stopper-paste in the scratch hardens, wrap a piece of smooth cotton rag around the top of a finger. Dip the finger in cellulose thinners and then quickly sweep it across the surface of the stopper-paste in the scratch; this will ensure that the surface of the stopper-paste is slightly hollowed. The scratch can now be painted over as described earlier in this Section.

Repair of dents in bodywork

When deep denting of the vehicle's bodywork has taken place, the first task is to pull the dent out, until the affected bodywork almost attains its original shape. There is little point in trying to restore the original shape completely, as the metal in the damaged area will have stretched on impact and cannot be reshaped fully to its original contour. It is better to bring the level of the dent up to a point which is about 1/8 in (3 mm) below the level of the surrounding bodywork. In cases where the dent is very shallow anyway, it is not worth trying to pull it out at all. If the underside of the dent is accessible, it can be hammered out gently from behind, using a mallet with a wooden or plastic head. Whilst doing this, hold a suitable block of wood firmly against the outside of the panel to absorb the impact from the hammer blows and thus prevent a large area of the bodywork from being "belled-out".

Should the dent be in a section of the bodywork which has a double skin or some other factor making it inaccessible from behind, a different technique is called for. Drill several small holes through the metal inside the area particularly in the deeper section. Then screw long self-tapping screws into the holes just sufficiently for them to gain a good purchase in the metal. Now the dent can be pulled out by pulling on the protruding heads of the screws with a pair of pliers.

The next stage of the repair is the removal of the paint from the damaged area, and from an inch or so of the surrounding "sound" bodywork. This is accomplished most easily by using a wire brush or abrasive pad on a power drill, although it can be done just as effectively by hand using sheets of abrasive paper. To complete the preparation for filling, score the surface of the bare metal with a screwdriver or the tang of a file, or alternatively, drill small holes in the affected area. This will provide a really good "key" for the filler paste.

To complete the repair see the Section on filling and re-spraying.

Repair of rust holes or gashes in bodywork

Remove all paint from the affected area and from an inch or so of the surrounding "sound" bodywork, using an abrasive pad or a wire brush on a power drill. If these are not available a few sheets of abrasive paper will do the job just as effectively. With the paint removed you will be able to gauge the severity of the corrosion and therefore decide whether to renew the whole panel (if this is possible) or to repair the affected area. New body panels are not as expensive as most people think and it is often quicker and more satisfactory to fit a new panel than to attempt to repair large areas of corrosion.

Remove all fittings from the affected area except those which will act as a guide to the original shape of the damaged bodywork (eg headlamp shells etc). Then, using tin snips or a hacksaw blade, remove all loose metal and any other metal badly affected by corrosion. Hammer the edges of the hole inwards in order to create a slight depression for the filler paste.

Wire brush the affected area to remove the powdery rust from the surface of the remaining metal. Paint the affected area with rust inhibiting paint; if the back of the rusted area is accessible treat this also.

Before filling can take place it will be necessary to block the hole in some way. This can be achieved by the use of aluminium or plastic mesh, or aluminium tape.

Aluminium or plastic mesh or glass fibre matting, is probably the best material to use for a large hole. Cut a piece to the approximate size and shape of the hole to be filled, then position it in the hole so that its edges are below the level of the surrounding bodywork. It can be retained in position by several blobs of filler paste around its periphery.

Aluminium tape should be used for small or very narrow holes. Pull a piece off the roll and trim it to the approximate size and shape required, then pull off the backing paper (if used) and stick the tape over the hole; it can be overlapped if the thickness of one piece is insufficient. Burnish down the edges of the tape with the handle of a screwdriver or similar, to ensure that the tape is securely attached to the metal underneath.

Bodywork repairs - filling and re-spraying

Before using this Section, see the Sections on dent, deep scratch, rust holes and gash repairs.

Many types of bodyfiller are available, but generally speaking those proprietary kits which contain a tin of filler paste and a tube of resin hardener are best for this type of repair. A wide, flexible plastic or nylon applicator will be found invaluable for imparting a smooth and well contoured finish to the surface of the filler.

Mix up a little filler on a clean piece of card or board - measure the hardener carefully (follow the maker's instructions on the pack) otherwise the filler will set too rapidly or too slowly. Using the applicator apply the filler paste to the prepared area; draw the applicator across the surface of the filler to achieve the correct contour and to level the filler surface. As soon as a contour that approximates to the correct one is achieved, stop working the paste - if you carry on too long the paste will become sticky and begin to "pick up" on the applicator. Continue to add thin layers of filler paste at twenty-minute intervals until the level of the filler is just proud of the surrounding bodywork.

Once the filler has hardened, excess can be removed using a metal plane or file. From then on, progressively finer grades of abrasive paper should be used, starting with a 40 grade production paper and finishing with 400 grade wet-and-dry paper. Always wrap the abrasive paper around a flat rubber, cork, or wooden block - otherwise the surface of the filler will not be completely flat. During the smoothing of the filler surface the wet-and-dry paper should be periodically rinsed in water. This will ensure that a very smooth finish is imparted to the filler at the final stage.

At this stage the "dent" should be surrounded by a ring of bare metal, which in turn should be encircled by the finely "feathered" edge of the good paintwork. Rinse the repair area with clean water, until all of the dust produced by the rubbing-down operation has gone.

Spray the whole repair area with a light coat of primer - this will show up any imperfections in the surface of the filler. Repair these imperfections with fresh filler paste or bodystopper, and once more smooth the surface with abrasive paper. If bodystopper is used, it can be mixed with cellulose thinners to form a really thin paste which is ideal for filling small holes. Repeat this spray and repair procedure until you are satisfied that the surface of the filler, and the feathered edge of the paintwork are perfect. Clean the repair area with clean water and allow to dry fully.

The repair area is now ready for final spraying. Paint spraying must be carried out in a warm, dry, windless and dust free atmosphere. This condition can be created artificially if you have access to a large indoor working area, but if you are forced to work in the open, you will have to pick your day very carefully. If you are working indoors, dousing the floor in the work area with water will help to settle the dust which would otherwise be in the atmosphere. If the repair area is confined to one body panel, mask off the surrounding panels; this will help to minimise the effects of a slight mis-match in paint colours. Bodywork fittings (eg chrome strips, door handles etc) will also need to be masked off. Use genuine masking tape and several thicknesses of newspaper for the masking operations.

Before commencing to spray, agitate the aerosol can thoroughly, then spray a test area (an old tin, or similar) until the technique is mastered. Cover the repair area with a thick coat of primer; the thickness should be built up using several thin layers of paint rather than one thick one. Using 400 grade wet-and-dry paper, rub down the surface of the primer until it is really smooth. While doing this, the work area should be thoroughly doused with water, and the wet-and-dry paper periodically rinsed in water. Allow to dry before spraying on more paint.

Spray on the top coat, again building up the thickness by using several thin layers of paint. Start spraying in the centre of the repair area and then work outwards, with a side-to-side motion, until the whole repair area and about 2 inches of the surrounding original paintwork is covered. Remove all masking material 10 to 15 minutes after spraying on the final coat of paint.

Allow the new paint at least two weeks to harden, then, using a paintwork renovator or a very fine cutting paste, blend the edges of the paint into the existing paintwork. Finally, apply wax polish.

Plastic components

With the use of more and more plastic body components by the vehicle manufacturers (eg bumpers, spoilers, and in some cases major body panels), rectification of more serious damage to such items has become a matter of either entrusting repair work to a specialist in this field, or renewing complete components. Repair of such damage by the DIY owner is not really feasible owing to the cost of the equipment and materials required for effecting such repairs. The basic technique involves making a groove along the line of the crack in the plastic using a rotary burr in a power drill. The damaged part is then welded back together by using a hot air gun to heat up and fuse a plastic filler rod into the groove. Any excess plastic is then removed and the area rubbed down to a smooth finish. It is important that a filler rod of the correct plastic is used, as body components can be made of a variety of different types (eg polycarbonate, ABS, polypropylene).

Damage of a less serious nature (abrasions, minor cracks etc) can be repaired by the DIY owner using a two-part epoxy filler repair material. Once mixed in equal proportions, this is used in similar fashion to the bodywork filler used on metal panels. The filler is usually cured in twenty to thirty minutes, ready for sanding and painting.

If the owner is renewing a complete component himself, or if he has repaired it with epoxy filler, he will be left with the problem of finding a suitable paint for finishing which is compatible with the type of plastic used. At one time the use of a universal paint was not possible owing to the complex range of plastics encountered in body component applications. Standard paints, generally speaking, will not bond to plastic or rubber satisfactorily. However, it is now possible to obtain a plastic body parts finishing kit which consists of a pre-primer treatment, a primer and coloured top coat. Full instructions are normally supplied with a kit, but basically the method of use is to first apply the pre-primer to the component concerned and allow it to dry for up to 30 minutes. Then the primer is applied and left to dry for about an hour before finally applying the special coloured top coat. The result is a correctly coloured component where the paint will flex with the plastic or rubber, a property that standard paint does not normally possess.

4 Major body damage - repair

Where serious damage has occurred or large areas need renewal due to neglect, it means certainly that completely new sections or panels will need welding in and this is best left to professionals. If the damage is due to impact, it will also be necessary to completely check the alignment of the bodyshell structure. Due to the principle of construction, the strength and shape of the whole car can be affected by damage to one part. In such instances the services of a Ford agent with specialist checking jigs are essential. If a body is left misaligned, it is first of all dangerous as the car will not handle properly, and secondly uneven stresses will be imposed on the steering, engine and transmission, causing abnormal wear or complete failure. Tyre wear may also be excessive.

11

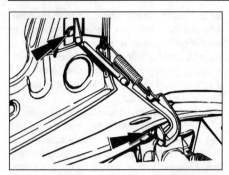

5.2 Bonnet stay retaining bolts (arrowed)

5 Bonnet - removal and refitting

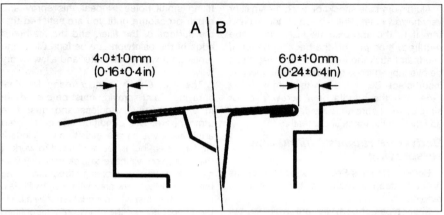

5.7 Bonnet surround clearance to wing (A) and to the cowl panel (B)

Removal

1 Open the bonnet and support it by using a prop or have an assistant hold it.

2 Undo and remove the bolt which secures the stay at one end **(see illustration)**.

3 Remove the radiator grille.

4 Mark an outline around the hinge plates to aid realignment of the bonnet when refitting it, then undo the four hinge bolts and lift the bonnet clear.

Refitting

5 Refit by reversing the removal operations. If a new bonnet is being installed, position it so that an equal gap is provided at each side when it is being closed.

6 The bonnet should close smoothly and positively without excessive pressure. If it does not, carry out the following adjustment.

7 Loosen the bolts retaining the bonnet lock unit on the bulkhead plenum chamber cover, then locate the bonnet so that the clearance between it and the cowl panel is as shown **(see illustration)**. Align the bonnet so that the gap between it and the wing panels is even and set at the clearance shown.

8 Lower or raise the lock unit so that the bonnet is level with the cowl panel and wings. Tighten the securing bolts and recheck the bonnet alignment and release unit for satisfactory operation.

6 Bonnet components - removal and refitting

Release cable

1 Working inside the vehicle, extract the three screws and remove the steering column shroud. Open the bonnet. Releasing the bonnet when the cable is broken is not easy: support the car securely on axle stands or ramps. Reach up between the bulkhead and remove the bolts securing the lock unit to the plenum chamber cover plate. The bonnet should be free to lift.

2 Draw the cable sideways and disengage the inner cable nipple from the release lever.

3 On the engine compartment side of the bulkhead, detach the cable grommet from the location bracket on the bonnet lock unit, and disconnect the cable from the lock **(see illustration)**.

4 Withdraw the cable through the bulkhead and into the car interior for removal.

5 Refitting is a reversal of the removal procedure. On completion check the operation of the release mechanism before shutting the bonnet and again afterwards.

Lock

6 Open and support the bonnet.

7 Detach the cable grommet from the location bracket on the lock unit and disconnect the cable from the lock.

8 Undo the two retaining bolts and withdraw the lock unit from the plenum chamber cover plate.

9 Refit by reversing the removal procedure. If necessary adjust the position of the lock unit prior to fully tightening the retaining bolts.

7 Radiator grille - removal and refitting

1 Grip each end of the radiator grille and pull it upwards to detach it from its lower support **(see illustration)**, then withdraw it and disconnect it from the three top fasteners.

2 Refitting is the reversal of removal.

6.3 Bonnet release cable-to-lock attachment

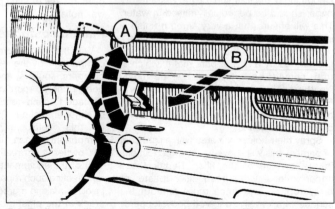

7.1 Radiator grille removal; pull up (A), pull out (B) and then swing the grille downwards

8.5 Tailgate hinge retaining nuts (arrowed)

8 Tailgate - removal and refitting

1 Open the tailgate fully and disconnect the leads from the heated rear window and the wiper (where fitted).
2 From the top edge of the tailgate aperture, remove the weatherstrip and then peel back the headlining.
3 With an assistant supporting the tailgate, unbolt and remove the struts. The strut balljoint is released by prising out the small plastic peg.
4 Make an outline marking around the hinge mounting positions to provide an alignment guide when refitting the tailgate.

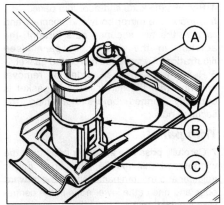

9.3 Tailgate lock barrel clip (A), cylinder (B) and retainer (C)

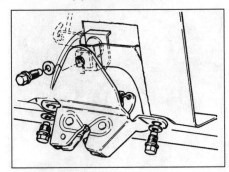

9.7 Tailgate latch and securing screws

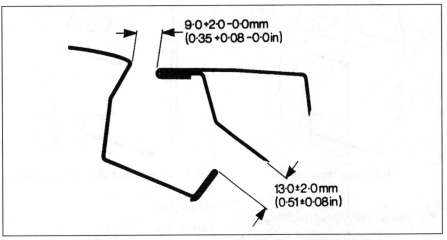

8.7 Tailgate-to-roof alignment clearance and to weatherstrip flange

9.0 +2.0 -0.0mm (0.35 +0.08 -0.0in)

13.0 ±2.0mm (0.51 ±0.08in)

5 Unscrew the hinge nuts (see illustration), remove them with the washers and lift the tailgate from the vehicle.
6 The tailgate lock and (if fitted) the wiper motor are accessible for removal once the trim panel has been released from its securing clips.
7 Refitting is a reversal of removal, but do not fully tighten the hinge screws until the tailgate has been adjusted to give the correct alignment (see illustration).

9 Tailgate components - removal and refitting

Lock barrel
1 Open and support the tailgate.
2 Unclip and detach the tailgate trim panel.
3 Unclip and detach the rod from the plastic lever (see illustration).
4 Slide the lock retainer along so that its exposed large aperture aligns with the lock barrel, then remove the retainer and extract the lock unit and pad from the tailgate.
5 Refitting is a reversal of the removal procedure.

Latch
6 Proceed as described in paragraphs 1 to 3.
7 Undo the three screws and remove the latch unit, together with the lever and rod (see illustration).
8 Refit reversing the removal procedure. Check that the latch is fitted so that the rod and lever are in alignment with the end of the lock barrel.

Latch remote release
9 A remotely controlled, electrically operated tailgate release is fitted to certain later models. The main component is a solenoid/thermal switch assembly, which is only supplied complete (even though only one section of the assembly to be renewed may be faulty).

10 Remove the latch assembly.
11 Remove the solenoid fixing screws and unhook the operating rod, then withdraw the solenoid assembly.
12 Refitting is a reversal of removal, but make sure that the operating rod is securely engaged in the nylon actuator.

Striker
13 Open and support the tailgate.
14 Make an outline marking around the striker to provide an alignment guide when refitting it.
15 Undo the two retaining bolts and remove them, together with the washers, then withdraw the striker.
16 Refit in the reverse order to removal. Check that the striker is correctly aligned with the previously made outline marking before fully tightening the retaining bolts.

Strut (damper unit)
17 Open the tailgate and support it with a prop or get an assistant to support it.
18 Using a screwdriver as shown (see illustration), prise free and release the strut retaining peg at each end and remove the strut by pulling it free from the joints.
19 Refit in the reverse order to removal.

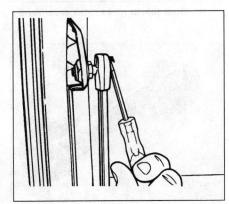

9.18 Tailgate damper strut detachment

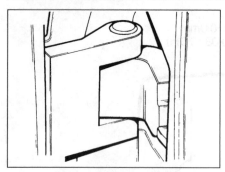

10.2a Door hinge roll pin

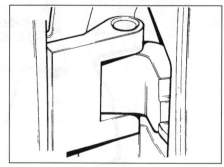

10.2b Door hinge solid pin (permanent)

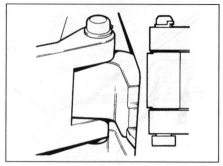

10.2c Upper door hinge solid pin (removable)

10 Doors - removal and refitting

1 Open the door fully and support its lower edge on a jack or blocks covered with a pad of rag.

2 Three different types of hinge pins have been used in production **(see illustrations)** and the particular method of removal for each type is given in the following paragraphs:

Roll pins

3 Detach and remove the plastic plugs from the hinge pins.

4 Using a suitable length of rod or, if available, Ford special tool 41.002, drift out the hinge pins: knocking them downwards. Get an assistant to support and steady the door during this operation.

Solid pins

Permanent

5 Where these pins are used, door removal is only possible after unbolting the hinges from the body. The fixing nuts can be reached after removing the side trim panel at the footwell and the facia panel lower cover.

Removable

6 This type of hinge pin can be removed after extracting the circlip and prising or tapping the pin downwards. The lower hinge pin cannot be removed and the hinge must be unbolted.

Both types

7 Lift the door clear of the stubs and remove it.

8 Refit the door reversing the removal procedure. Lubricate the hinges and pins as they are fitted and ensure that the hinge pin holes are correctly aligned when drifting the new hinge pins into position.

11 Door components - removal and refitting

Mirror and glass

1 To renew the glass, prise free the retainer from the mirror body using a coin or similar suitable lever and remove the glass **(see illustration)**.

2 Locate the new glass into position and press the new retainer evenly around its perimeter onto the body. Check that the retainer is fully engaged on completion.

3 To remove the mirror unit complete, prise free the plastic cover from the adjustment knob using a suitable screwdriver.

4 Remove the knob and door trim panel.

5 Support the mirror body and unscrew and remove the two securing nuts through the aperture in the door inner panel **(see illustration)**. Remove the mirror and gasket.

6 Refit in the reverse order of removal ensuring that the mirror-to-body gasket is correctly aligned before tightening the securing nuts.

Trim panel

7 Carefully prise free the cover pads from the window winder handle, the door mirror adjuster and the trim panel (one at the forward edge and one at the lower edge in the centre) **(see illustrations)**.

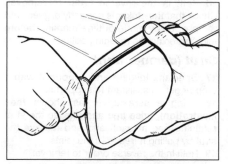

11.1 Door mirror glass retainer removal

11.5 Door mirror attachment nuts (arrowed)

11.7a Remove cover pad from the window regulator handle . . .

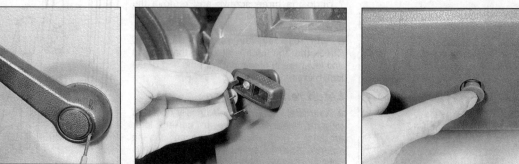

11.7b . . . the door mirror adjuster . . .

11.7c . . . and the trim panel

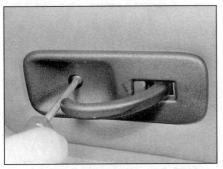

11.8a Remove retaining screws . . .

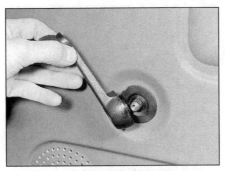

11.8b . . . and withdraw the regulator handle

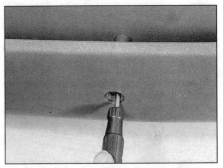

11.8c Remove the trim panel retaining screws

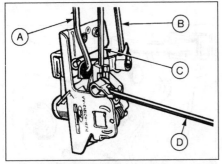

11.9 Remove the door control handle bezel screw

11.11 Prise free the door panel and locating clips

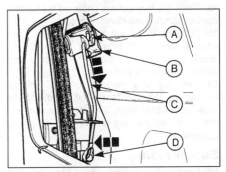

11.15 Door lock barrel (A), retainer (B), lock rod (C) and clip (D)

8 With the pads removed, unscrew and remove the retaining screws **(see illustrations)**.

9 Undo and remove the door control handle bezel retaining screw and withdraw the bezel **(see illustration)**.

10 Remove the door pull/armrest which is secured by two screws.

11 Carefully prise free and remove the panel from the door **(see illustration)**.

12 Withdraw the insulating washer from the window winder handle shaft then carefully peel back the plastic insulating screen from the door for access to the components within the door cavity.

13 Refit the panel in the reverse order of removal.

Lock

14 Remove the door trim panel and insulation screen.

15 Detach the lock rod from the latch then pull the retainer from the door cylinder **(see illustration)**.

16 Withdraw the lock cylinder, together with the lock rod, from the door.

17 Refitting is a reversal of the removal procedure. When inserting the lock cylinder, ensure that the cylinder lever points towards the front of the car and check that the lock barrel is correctly aligned before fitting the retainer.

Latch unit

18 Remove the door trim panel and insulation screen.

19 Unclip and detach the remote control rod, the exterior handle rod and the lock cylinder rods from the latch levers **(see illustration)**.

20 Undo the three screws and remove the latch unit, manoeuvring it free from the rear of the glass rim extension **(see illustration)**.

21 Detach the private lock rod from the latch then the retaining clips and black bush from the levers **(see illustration)**.

22 Refitting is a reversal of the removal procedure. To ease refitting of the black bush and sliding clip soak them in hot water prior to fitting. When fitting the latch unit into position it must be in its closed position. Check that all control rod securing clips are secure before refitting the door trim assembly.

Remote control handle

23 Remove the door trim panel and insulation screen.

24 Unclip and detach the remote control rod from the latch then push free the anti-rattle retainer from the door.

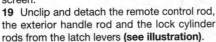

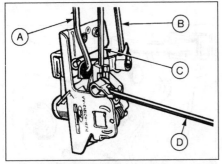

11.19 Door latch and rod attachments

A *Private lock rod and bush*
B *Lock rod (exterior)*
C *Exterior handle rod*
D *Remote control rod*

11.20 Door latch

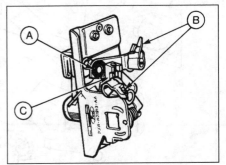

11.21 Latch lever black bush (A), fixed clips (B) and sliding clip (C)

11

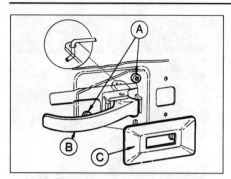

11.25 Door remote control handle (B), retaining screws (A) and bezel (C)

11.28 Door striker

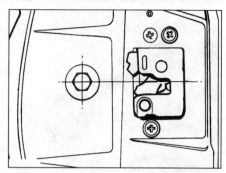

11.30 Adjust striker position to align with the latch throat centre line

25 Undo the two screws securing the remote control handle (see illustration).
26 Fully raise the window, manoeuvre the handle and rod into the door cavity, disconnect the rod from the handle and extract the handle and rod.
27 Refitting is a reversal of the removal procedure. When refitting the handle to the inner door panel move it as far as possible to the rear before tightening the retaining screws.

Striker plate

28 Loosen the striker locknut then unscrew and remove the striker, together with washer, from the door pillar (see illustration).
29 To refit the striker, locate the washer onto the threaded end of the striker so that the cone apex is adjacent to the nut face. Screw the striker into position, but do not fully tighten it yet.
30 Close and open the door and align the striker with the latch (see illustration). When the door shuts in a satisfactory manner open it and retighten the locknut to set the striker in the required position.

Exterior handle

31 Remove the door trim panel and insulation screen.
32 Detach the lock rod from the latch nut then unscrew and remove the handle retaining screws (see illustration). Remove the handle and lock rod from the door.
33 Refit in the reverse order of removal. When inserting the lock rod into the handle the rod latch end must face to the rear. Smear the end of the rod with Vaseline to ease assembly.

Window regulators

34 Remove the door trim panel and insulation screen.
35 Adjust the window position so that the regulator and bracket are accessible through the lower aperture in the door inner panel (see illustration).
36 Use a suitable bit and drill through the four window regulator-to-inner panel securing rivets (see illustration).
37 Press the regulator into the door cavity, then slide the regulator arm to the rear and disengage it from the slide.

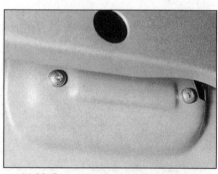

11.32 Door exterior handle retaining screws viewed from within the door

38 Push the window upwards into the closed position, support it with a prop and then carefully withdraw the window regulator from the door cavity.
39 Refit in the reverse order of removal, but note the following:
40 Locate the regulator into its approximate position with the winder shaft resting on door panel aperture; then, with the window lowered to align its bracket with the aperture in the door inner panel, re-engage the regulator arm. Align the regulator unit rivet holes and using a pop rivet gun, secure the regulator with four pop-rivets.
41 Check the window regulator operation prior to refitting the door trim panel and insulating screen.

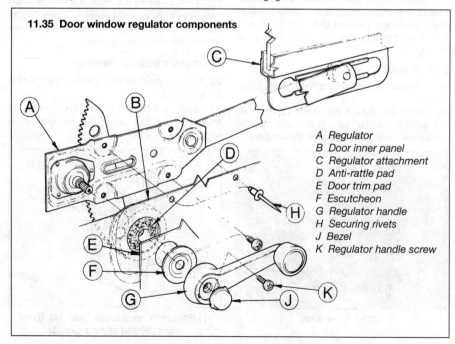

11.35 Door window regulator components

A Regulator
B Door inner panel
C Regulator attachment
D Anti-rattle pad
E Door trim pad
F Escutcheon
G Regulator handle
H Securing rivets
J Bezel
K Regulator handle screw

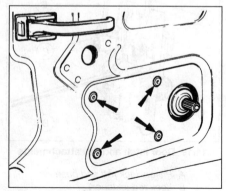

11.36 Window regulator-to-door panel securing rivets

12.2a Inner door belt weatherstrip removal

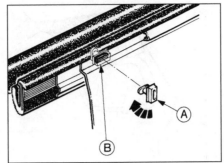

12.2b Outer door belt weatherstrip removal

A Retaining clip   B Clip installed

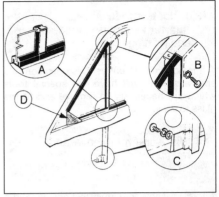

12.3 Quarter window channel (A), upper fixing (B), lower fixing (C) and adhesive pad (D)

12 Door windows - removal and refitting

Quarter windows

Fixed type

1 Lower the door window then remove the door trim panel and insulation screen.
2 Carefully prise free and remove the inner and outer door belt weatherstrips **(see illustrations)**.

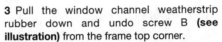

Note: remove bright external moulding on L and GLS models

3 Pull the window channel weatherstrip rubber down and undo screw B **(see illustration)** from the frame top corner.
4 Undo the lower retaining screw, pull the channel rearwards to an angle of 45° and remove it.
5 Carefully prise free the triangular weatherstrip from its adhesive pad and retaining clips which untwist for removal.
6 Prise free the weatherstrip and glass from the door, then detach the weatherstrip from the glass (if required).
7 Refit in the reverse order of removal. Lubricate the weatherstrip with soapy water to ease its fitting to the glass. When refitting the glass and weatherstrip to the door insert as far forwards as possible. Clean off all soapy water from the weatherstrip prior to peeling off the backing paper from the adhesive pad and pressing it into position. If a new pad is not being fitted stick some double-sided adhesive tape to the old pad before fitting.

Opening type

8 Proceed as described in paragraphs 1 and 2 in the previous Section.
9 Pull the window channel weatherstrip downwards and undo the retaining screw from the top end of the frame.

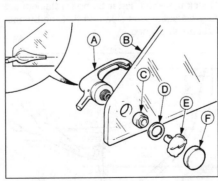

12.11b Quarter window catch components

A Handle   D Seal washer
B Glass   E End cap screw
C Bush   F End cap

10 Detach the clips from the triangular portion of the weatherstrip and peel it away from the door frame to which it is retained by adhesive.
11 Prise free (taking care) the quarter window and channel, final removal of the channel being achieved by drilling out the two pop rivets **(see illustrations)**.
12 Refit in the reverse order of removal.
13 Ease refitting of the weatherstrip by applying soapy water to it. Avoid getting the soapy water onto the adhesive pad.
14 When fitting the window and channel check that the glass is located in the channel. Insert and, if required, push the weatherstrip vertical section upwards to get the window to fit correctly at the top corner.
15 When fitted, adjust the channel by loosening the upper and lower retaining screws so that the glass does not tilt in its frame, then retighten the screws.

Main windows

16 Remove the door quarter window.
17 Slide the door glass forward to detach the regulator arm from the glass bracket/slide **(see illustration)**.
18 Support the glass, holding it towards the innermost edge of the window opening, and withdraw it from the door.
19 Refit in the reverse order of removal. Tilt the glass down at the front end when inserting it into the door. Lubricate the regulator slide and check window operation prior to refitting the door trim panel.

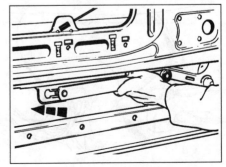

12.17 Door window regulator arm detachment

12.11a Quarter window (opening) attachments

A Upper screw   D Glass retaining
B Rivets   screw
C Lower screw   E Seal washer

11

13 Tailgate and fixed rear quarter windows - removal and refitting

1 It is advisable to entrust this operation to a specialist who will have the special tools which are necessary to remove and fit the glass to vehicle body seals.

14 Windscreen - removal and refitting

1 It is advisable to entrust this operation to a specialist who will have the special tools which are necessary to remove and fit the glass to vehicle body seals.

15 Interior mirror - removal and refitting

1 The interior mirror is bonded to the windscreen glass. If it must be removed, use a length of thin nylon cord (see illustration) to break the adhesive bond between the stem of the mirror and the windscreen patch.
2 When refitting the mirror, the following preliminary work must first be carried out.
3 Remove existing adhesive from the windscreen glass using a suitable solvent. Allow the solvent to evaporate. The location of the mirror base is marked on the glass with a black patch, so that there should not be any chance of an error when fitting.
4 If the original mirror is being refitted, clean away all the old adhesive from the mirror mounting base, and apply a new adhesive patch to it.
5 If a new windscreen is being installed, peel off the protective layer from the black patch, which is pre-coated with adhesive.
6 Peel off the protective layer from the mirror adhesive patch and locate the mirror precisely onto the black patch on the screen. Hold it in position for at least two minutes.
7 For best results, the fitting of a bonded type mirror should be carried out in an ambient temperature of 70°C (158°F). The careful use

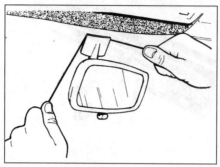

15.1 Break adhesive bond of mirror to windscreen using cord

of a blower heater on both the glass and mirror should achieve this temperature level. Take necessary precautions to avoid burns.

16 Bumpers - removal and refitting

Front bumper

Metal centre section type

1 From underneath each front wing, undo and remove the two bumper retaining nuts (see illustration).
2 Disengage the quarter bumper retainer each side then, from the front of the car, grip the bumper and pull it free.
3 Refit reversing the removal procedure. Check that the quarter bumper retainers are fully engaged each side and that the bumper is aligned correctly.

All moulded type

4 From underneath each front wing, undo and remove the bumper retaining nuts.
5 Open the bonnet and unscrew the bumper retaining nut beneath each headlamp unit (see illustration).
6 Disengage the quarter bumper retainer each side, then, from the front of the car, grip the bumper and pull it free.
7 Refit reversing the removal procedure. Check that the quarter bumper retainers are fully engaged each side and that the bumper is correctly aligned.

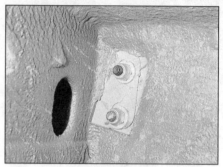

16.1 Bumper retaining nuts under wing panel

Front quarter bumpers

Metal centre section type

8 Use a pair of suitable pliers and detach the quarter bumper retaining tangs, as shown (see illustration).
9 Once removed the quarter bumper must be renewed.
10 Refit by pushing the quarter bumper into position on the metal section.

All moulded type

11 Prise out and remove the moulding strip from the quarter bumper to expose the retainer heads.
12 Use a chisel and remove the rivet heads from the upper retainer, then press out the rivets.
13 Prise open and detach the bumper-to-quarter bumper retaining clips (see illustration), then remove the quarter bumper.
14 Clean the moulding recess out with methylated spirit to remove the adhesive.
15 Align and fit the quarter bumper to the main bumper and locate the securing clips and rivets.
16 Using a blowlamp, or similar, very carefully heat the new moulding so that it is warm to the touch then detach the backing paper from the moulding and locate the moulding into the quarter bumper channel recess, pressing it firmly into position.

Rear bumper

17 Open the tailgate and lift out the floor cover and tool tray from the luggage compartment.

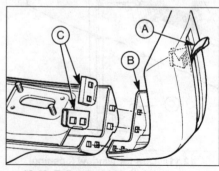

16.13 Fully moulded quarter bumper attachments

A Moulding   C Retaining clips
B Quarter bumper

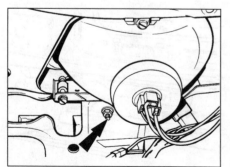

16.5 Bumper retaining nut in engine compartment

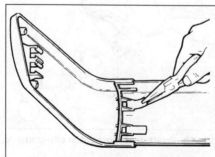

16.8 Quarter bumper retaining tang removal

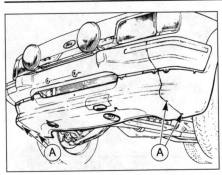

17.1 Front spoiler attachment screw positions (A)

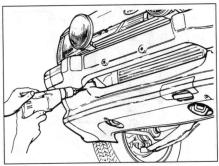

17.2 Drill out the front spoiler retaining rivets

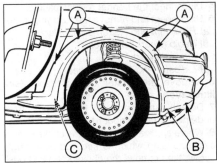

17.6 Front wheel arch spoiler retaining nuts (A), joint screws (B) and rear lower corner (C)

18 Detach the number plate wiring.

19 Undo the bumper retaining nuts from the rear face of the floor area on each side, then grip the bumper and withdraw it, simultaneously disengaging the quarter bumpers each side.

20 Refit in the reverse order to removal. Renew the rubber seal washers on the bumper retaining studs if they are perished or in poor condition. Ensure that the quarter bumper retainers fully engage when fitting.

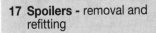

17 Spoilers - removal and refitting

Front

1 Undo and remove the front spoiler retaining screws, two each side, from the positions indicated (**see illustration**).

2 The spoiler is further attached to the front panel by rivets, nine at the front and one at the top leading edge of the wheel arch spider each side. Use a suitable drill (4.5 mm diameter) and drill out the rivets (**see illustration**).

3 The spoiler can now be withdrawn.

4 Refitting is a reversal of the removal procedure, but use the proper Ford rivets to secure the spoiler as they have a plastic body coating to protect against corrosion.

Wheel arches

Front

5 Raise and support the vehicle at the front. Remove the roadwheel on the side concerned for access to the underside of the spoiler.

6 Undo and remove the five retaining nuts and two retaining screws from the positions indicated (**see illustration**).

7 Use a 4.5 mm diameter drill and drill out the seven securing rivets from the locations indicated (**see illustration**).

8 Detach the spoiler retaining studs from the wheel arch, then grip the spoiler on its lower corner and pull it to disengage it from the pushfit fasteners.

9 To remove the plastic fasteners from the sill panel and wing edge, insert a self-tapping screw into them and pull them free.

10 Refitting is a reversal of the removal procedure.

Rear

11 Raise and support the rear of the vehicle on safety stands, remove the wheel on the side concerned for access to the spoiler underside.

12 Remove the rear bumper.

13 Undo and remove the two retaining screws from the wheel arch flange.

14 The spoiler is secured by five rivets (**see illustration**). Carefully drill out the rivets using a 4.5 mm diameter drill.

15 Remove the two screws from the wheel arch and rear panel moulding joint.

16 Grip the moulding at the rear and pull it free from the wheel arch/rocker panel and push-fit fasteners. The moulding is additionally secured by means of adhesive tape to the bodywork, and the bond between the two must be broken carefully.

17 Remove the plastic fasteners from the wheel arch and rocker panel by inserting a self-tapping screw and pulling them free (**see illustration**). Remove any adhesive tape remaining in position on the bodywork or moulding.

18 Clean the areas of contact for the adhesive tape with methylated spirits. Insert new plastic fasteners in place of those removed.

19 Carefully warm up the spoiler tape channel until it is warm to the touch. (Use a blow lamp, or similar, but take great care).

20 Apply primer and the new length of adhesive tape to the spider, then fit the spoiler front edge under the sill panel moulding, detach the protector film from the tape and

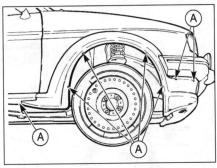

17.7 Front wheel arch spoiler rivet positions (A)

locate the spoiler pressing firmly home into the push-in fasteners. Smooth the spider down and check that its top edge contacts the body along its full length.

21 Refitting is now a reversal of the removal procedure. Use Ford special rivets to secure the spoiler and leave tightening the retaining screws until after the rivets are fitted.

18 Facia crash padding and vents - removal and refitting

Removal

1 Disconnect the battery earth lead.

2 Remove the steering wheel.

3 Remove the steering column shrouds and combination switches.

17.14 Rear wheel arch spoiler flange screw (A) and rivet positions

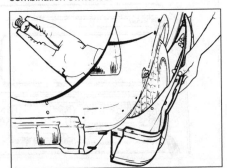

17.17 Rear wheel arch removal
Inset shows method of withdrawing the plastic fasteners

4 Disconnect the bonnet release handle.
5 Disconnect and remove the following items:
a) *Facia trim and instrument cluster unit*
b) *Radio (where applicable)*
c) *Fuse/relay box*
d) *Indicator and facia switches*
6 Remove the heater control panel **(see illustration)**.
7 Detach and remove the carpet from underneath the dashboard.
8 Where applicable, remove the choke control cable housing which is secured by a single screw, then remove the choke knob and push the choke cable and switch forwards through the crash pad **(see illustration)**.

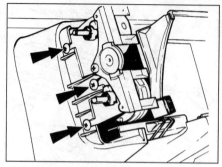

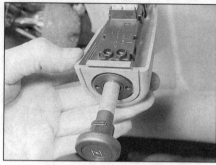

18.6 Heater control panel retaining screws

18.8 Choke control unit removal

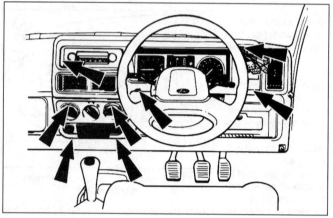

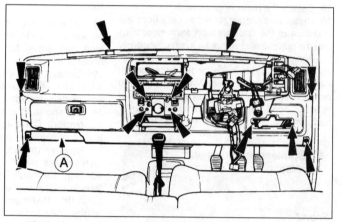
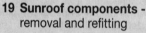

18.9 Heater control panel and facia panel retaining screw positions

18.10 Heater control panel and crash pad retaining screw positions
Note position of strengthening bar (A)

9 Undo the heater control panel mounting screws **(see illustration)**. Push the bulb holders forwards to the underside of the crash pad.
10 Detach the screw covers from the top of the crash pad **(see illustration)**.
11 Detach the glovebox light wires and pull the wires through to the underside of the crash pad.
12 Undo and remove the six crash pad retaining screws and carefully withdraw the crash pad facia. The strengthening bar at the base can be removed as the facia crash pad is withdrawn.
13 The centre and side vents can be detached from the facia crash pad by undoing the retaining screws **(see illustrations)**.

Refitting

14 Refit in the reverse order of removal. Ensure that all electrical connections are correctly and securely made. On completion, check the operation of the various instruments and controls.

19 Sunroof components - removal and refitting

Panel

1 Compress the sunroof catch each side to disengage the handle pins from the bracket. Lift the roof panel, detach the stop clip and remove the panel **(see illustration)**.

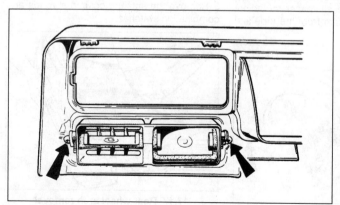

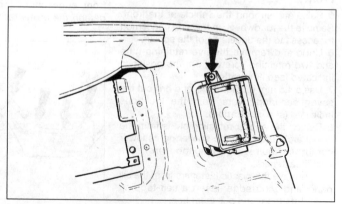
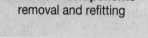

18.13a Central vent retaining screws

18.13b Side vent retaining screw

19.1 Glass sunroof components

A Screw
B Hinge plate
C Pedestal block
D Handle screw block
E Shim
F Spacer
G Pivot block
H Handle

2 If the sunroof panel is being renewed, undo the hinge plate retaining screws and remove it from the pedestal block. Remove the handle pivot retainers in a similar manner and withdraw the adjusting washer(s) from the handle screw block, then detach the block from the panel. Pull free the seal and pedestal block covers from the panel.

3 Refitting is a reversal of the removal procedure, but note the following:

4 When fitting a new seal to the roof tray flange, the seal ends must abut in the centre of the rear flange. Cut the seal to length as required **(see illustration)**.

5 When assembling the handle screw block to the panel, locate the shim, fit the block legs into their holes in the glass and then fit the washer onto each block leg.

6 If necessary, the hinge plates can be adjusted **(see illustration)**.

7 When the panel is fitted and closed, check the height of the roof tray and adjust, if required, by adding or subtracting washers under the handle so that the roof line is flush to the panel **(see illustration)**.

Handle bracket

8 Remove the sunroof panel then undo and remove the handle cap securing screw. Lower and remove the handle cup.

9 Undo the two bracket retaining bolts and remove the bracket. Collect and note any adjustment washers **(see illustration)**.

10 Refit in the reverse order of removal and adjust it as described in paragraph 7.

Hinge retainer

11 Remove the sunroof panel and then carefully prise free and remove the roof aperture weatherstrip.

12 Detach the headlining securing clips from the aperture flange and then pull down the headlining (with care) to expose the retainer and its securing screws.

13 Undo the retainer securing screws and withdraw it, together with its seal **(see illustration)**.

14 Refit in the reverse order of removal, but fit a new retainer seal.

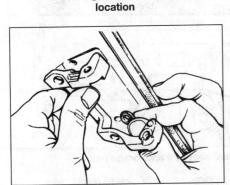

19.4 Sunroof glass weatherstrip joint location

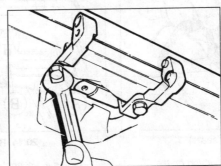

19.6 Hinge plate adjustment direction

19.7 Adjust roof panel height position by inserting (or removing) washers as required

19.9 Undo the bracket retaining bolts

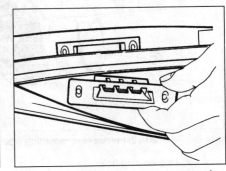

19.13 Sunroof hinge retainer removal

11

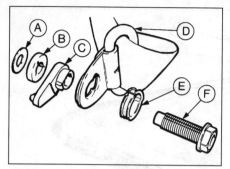

20.2 Seat belt upper anchor components

A Paper washer   D Anchor
B Spacer   E Bush
C Anti-rotation   F Bolt
   spacer

20 Seat belts - removal and refitting

Belts and stalks - front

1 Undo the lower anchor bar retaining bolt and remove the bar rear end from the mounting panel.
2 Remove the cover from the upper anchor and disconnect the upper anchor **(see illustration)**.
3 From the rear quarter panel trim, remove the belt webbing guide and let the belt retract onto its reel.
4 Detach and withdraw the quarter trim panel.
5 Undo the inertia reel unit retaining bolt and remove the reel unit **(see illustration)**.
6 The stalk and buckle unit can be detached by unscrewing the single retaining bolt, but note the locations of the washer, spacer and paper washer as they are removed **(see illustration)**.

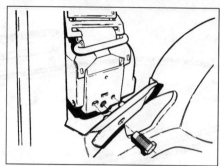

20.5 Seat belt inertia reel retaining bolt

7 Refitting is a reversal of the removal procedure, but note the following special points:
8 When fitting the inertia reel unit check that the locating pegs engage fully.
9 When fitting the upper anchorage check that the webbing does not get twisted and also that the anti-rotation peg engages fully into the pillar.
10 Tighten the retaining bolts to the specified torque wrench settings.
11 Check the seat belt for satisfactory operation when the seats are readjusted to their normal positions.

Belts - rear

12 Prise free and pivot up the inertia reel unit cover (if fitted) then undo and remove the retaining bolt **(see illustration)**.
13 Remove the rear seat cushion and push the buckles through the cushion slit as it is withdrawn.
14 Unscrew the six buckle and lower anchor retaining screws **(see illustration)**.
15 Remove the C pillar anchor point covers and disconnect the upper anchors.
16 Prise free the webbing guides from the package tray supports and remove the guides whilst letting the webbing wind into the reel.

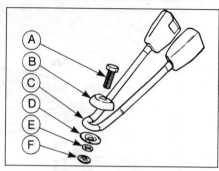

20.6 Seat belt stalk and buckle components

A Bolt   D Washer
B Cover   E Spacer
C Stalk and buckles F Paper washer

17 Refitting is a reversal of removal. When fitting the reel unit to the quarter panel check that the location peg engages fully into its hole. Check that the webbing does not get twisted during refitting. Tighten the retaining bolts to the specified torque wrench setting.
18 On completion check that the belt operation is satisfactory.

21 Seats - removal and refitting

Front seat

1 Slide the seat as far forward as it will go.
2 Unscrew and remove the bolts which retain the rear of the seat slides to the floorpan.
3 Slide the seat as far to the rear as it will go and remove the bolts which secure the front ends of the slides to the floor.
4 Remove the seat from the vehicle interior.
5 If the seat slides must be detached from the seat, invert the seat and remove the two bolts from each side. Detach the cross-rod and clips.

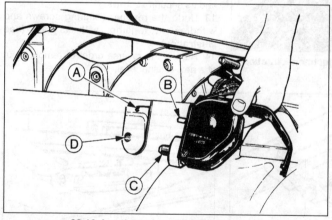

20.12 Inertia reel mounting (rear seats)

A Peg locating hole   C Mounting bolt
B Locating peg   D Mounting

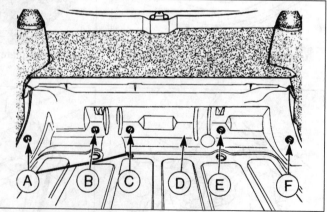

20.14 Rear seat belt anchorage points

A Inertia reel anchor points   D Inertia reel buckles
B Centre lap belt   E Centre lap buckle
C Inertia reel buckles   F Inertia reel anchor point

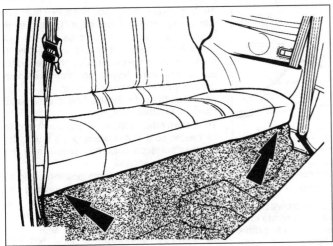

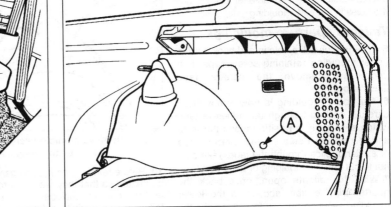

21.7 Rear seat cushion securing screw positions

22.4 Wheel arch side panel fasteners (A)

6 Refitting is a reversal of removal. Tighten the front bolts before the rear ones to ensure that the seat is located evenly on the floorpan.

Rear seat

Cushion

7 Undo the two cushion retaining screws from the positions indicated **(see illustration)**.
8 Disengage the cushion from the retainer hooks at the rear then lift out the cushion.
9 Refit in the reverse order to removal.

Backrest

10 Hinge the rear seat panel forwards then unscrew and remove the four rear panel retaining screws. Lift out the panel.
11 Where both rear seat panels and also the centre hinge are to be removed, first remove the panels then mark the outline of the hinge around its periphery to ensure correct realignment when refitting it. Undo the retaining bolts and withdraw the hinge.
12 Refit in the reverse order of removal. Align

the hinge correctly before tightening the retaining screws. Check that the panel engages with its retaining catch on completion.

22 Rear wheel arch cover - removal and refitting

1 Open the tailgate and lift out the luggage compartment floor covers.
2 Detach the rear shock absorber upper mounting cover.
3 Pivot the seat panel forwards and then remove the seat striker and cover.
4 Detach the side panel fasteners **(see illustration)**, then pull out the panel at the rear end and detach the interior lamp wiring.
5 Detach the panel cover at the top edge, beneath the parcel shelf support, move the cover rearwards and disconnect it from the quarter panel trim. Lift the panel out of the car.

6 Refit in the reverse order to removal. If necessary adjust the position of the rear seat striker on completion.

23 Body mouldings - removal and refitting

Body side mouldings

1 Using a thin-bladed screwdriver, prise away the moulding insert strip, carefully levering from the lower edge.
2 The moulding is secured by rivets and these can be drilled out using a 3.0 mm drill. With the rivets drilled through, the moulding can be removed **(see illustration)**.
3 Refitting is a reversal of the removal procedure, but you will need a pop-rivet gun and supply of suitable rivets to secure the moulding. Check its alignment as the moulding is secured in position.

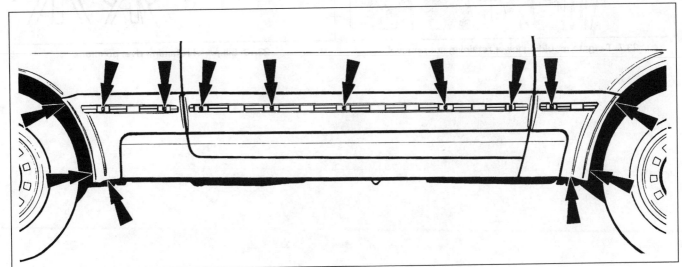

23.2 Body side moulding rivet locations (except XR2)

11

4 Where a new moulding is being fitted you will need to first drill the rivet holes in it. Use the old moulding as a suitable template to drill the holes in the new moulding.

Tailgate aperture mouldings

5 Prise free or drill a hole in and hook out the upper moulding retaining screw caps then undo and remove the screws **(see illustration)**.

6 The upper moulding is now removed by carefully cutting through the adhesive tape which secures it in position along the front and rear edges. Use a soft-edge razor blade or similar to slice through the tape. Take care not to cut into the moulding or paintwork.

7 With the tailgate open, prise back the quarter trim to gain access to the lower moulding securing nut. Undo and remove the nut **(see illustration)**.

8 Gripping the moulding at its top end, pull it away from the body panel so that the adhesive bond is broken, and remove the moulding.

9 Remove any adhesive tape still remaining on the body panel, wiping it off with a rag dipped in methylated spirit.

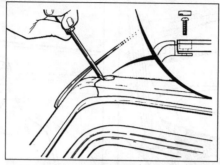

23.5 Remove moulding screw cap for access to screw

10 Before refitting, the mouldings will need to be heated so that they are warm to the touch and the contact surfaces coated in primer, followed by the adhesive tape.

11 Refitting is otherwise now a reversal of the removal procedure.

Sill panel moulding

12 Raise and support the car at the front end (see *"Jacking and vehicle support"*).

13 Use a 4.5 mm drill and drill out the moulding-to-sill rivets from the positions indicated **(see illustration)**.

14 Grip the moulding and pull it free from the car, pulling from its lower edge. The top edge is secured in position by press fit retainers and adhesive tape and should just pull free. If the top edge of the sill is reluctant to separate, carefully slit the adhesive tape along its length using a safe-edge razor or similar.

15 Clean the old adhesive from the sill panel using methylated spirit.

16 Before refitting the moulding it will need to be heated so that it is warm to the touch, the contact surfaces coated in primer and the adhesive tape applied.

17 Press the moulding into position along its top edge, ensuring that it is fully secured and correctly located in the retainers. Press and smooth the moulding down to ensure that it adheres to the sill along the full length.

18 Using a suitable pop-rivet gun, insert pop-rivets to secure the panel along its lower edge, but use only the special plastic capped type rivets supplied by Ford.

19 On completion lower the vehicle to the ground.

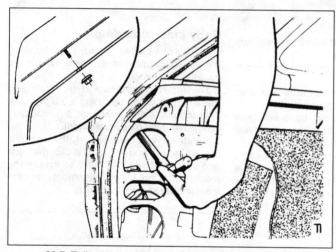

23.7 Tailgate moulding lower retaining nut removal

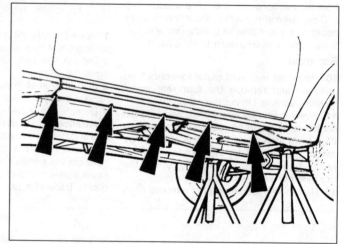

23.13 Sill panel retaining rivet positions

Chapter 12
Body electrical systems

Contents

Degrees of difficulty

Easy, suitable for novice with little experience	Fairly easy, suitable for beginner with some experience	Fairly difficult, suitable for competent DIY mechanic	Difficult, suitable for experienced DIY mechanic	Very difficult, suitable for expert DIY or professional

Specifications

System type . . . . 12V negative earth

Wipers
Wiper blades (front and rear) . . . . Champion X-4103
Wiper arms (front and rear) . . . . Champion CCA5

Bulbs
Headlamp:
   Halogen 55/60W
   Tungsten 40/45W
Parking lamp 5W
Stop/tail lamp 21/5W
Reversing lamp 21W
Rear number plate lamp 10W
Rear foglamp 21W
Direction indicator lamps (front and rear) 21W
Instrument warning lamps . . . . 1.3 or 2.6W
Panel illumination lamps . . . . 1.3 or 2.6W
Glovebox lamp 4W
Interior lamps 10W
Cigar lighter illumination lamp 1.4W

Fuses

Circuits	Fuse number	Fuse rating (amp)
Hazard flasher, horn, remote luggage compartment release	1	30
Interior light, clock, windscreen washer	2	15
Wiper motor (front/rear), rear window washer and reversing lamp	4	20
Heater blower motor	5	20
Cooling fan (engine)	6	20
Heated rear window	7	30
Direction indicators, brake lights, fuel gauge	8	10
Sidelamps (left), number plate lights, instrument panel lamps, cigar lighter, heater control switch, glovebox lamp	9	10
Sidelamps (right), illumination for switches	10	10
Dipped beam (left) and rear foglamp	11	10
Dipped beam (right)	12	10
Main beam (left)	13	10
Main beam (right)	14	10
Additional in-line or relay fuse circuits	(a) Radio	
	(b) Remote tailgate release switch	
	(c) Auxiliary driving lights	

Relays (on fusebox)

I	Ignition switch (yellow)
II	Heated rear window and heated door mirror (with auto cut-out) (grey)
III	Remote tailgate release (yellow)
IV	Intermittent wiper motor (red)
V	Headlamp washers (if fitted) (blue)
VI	Direction indicators (black)

1 General information and precautions

General information

The electrical system is of the 12-volt negative earth type. Electricity is generated by an alternator, belt-driven from the crankshaft pulley. A lead-acid storage battery provides a reserve of power for starting and when the demands of the system temporarily exceed the alternator output.

The battery negative terminal is connected to "earth" (vehicle metal) and most electrical system components are wired so that they only receive a positive feed, the current returning via vehicle metal. This means that the component mounting forms part of the circuit. Loose or corroded mountings can therefore cause apparent electrical faults.

From October 1986, models covered by this manual were progressively equipped with a dim-dip lighting system which became a legal requirement in the UK for all cars registered from April 1st, 1987 onwards. The system provides the headlamps with a brightness level between that of the sidelamps and the normal dipped headlamp beam. The purpose of this legislation is to prevent cars being driven on sidelamps only. The electrical control of the system is by three additional relays located in the fuse unit. Circuit changes are shown in the applicable wiring diagrams at the end of this Chapter.

Although some repair procedures are given in this Chapter, renewal of a well-used item will sometimes prove more satisfactory. The reader whose interests extend beyond component renewal should obtain a copy of the "Automobile Electrical Manual", available from the publishers of this book.

Precautions

It is necessary to take extra care when working on the electrical system to avoid damage to semi-conductor devices (diodes and transistors), and to avoid the risk of personal injury. In addition to the precautions given in the "Safety first!" Section at the beginning of this manual, take note of the following points when working on the system.

Always remove rings, watches, etc before working on the electrical system. Even with the battery disconnected, capacitive discharge could occur if a component live terminal is earthed through a metal object. This could cause a shock or nasty burn.

Do not reverse the battery connections. Components such as the alternator or any other having semi-conductor circuitry could be irreparably damaged.

If the engine is being started using jump leads and a slave battery, connect the batteries positive to positive and negative to negative. This also applies when connecting a battery charger.

Never disconnect the battery terminals, or alternator multi-plug connector, when the engine is running.

The battery leads and alternator multi-plug must be disconnected before carrying out any electric welding on the car.

Never use an ohmmeter of the type incorporating a hand cranked generator for circuit or continuity testing.

2 Electrical fault finding - general information

Note 1: *A short-circuit that occurs in the wiring between a circuit's battery supply and its fuse will not cause the fuse in that particular circuit to blow. This part of the circuit is unprotected - bear this in mind when fault-finding on the vehicle's electrical system.*

Note 2: *Refer to the precautions given in "Safety first!" and in Section 1 of this Chapter before starting work. The following tests relate to testing of the main electrical circuits, and should not be used to test delicate electronic circuits (such as anti-lock braking systems), particularly where an electronic control unit (ECU) is involved.*

General

1 A typical electrical circuit consists of an electrical component, any switches, relays, motors, fuses, fusible links or circuit breakers related to that component, and the wiring and connectors which link the component to both the battery and the chassis. To help to pinpoint a problem in an electrical circuit, wiring diagrams are included at the end of this Chapter.

2 Before attempting to diagnose an electrical fault, first study the appropriate wiring diagram, to obtain a more complete understanding of the components included in the particular circuit concerned. The possible sources of a fault can be narrowed down by noting whether other components related to the circuit are operating properly. If several components or circuits fail at one time, the

problem is likely to be related to a shared fuse or earth connection.

3 Electrical problems usually stem from simple causes, such as loose or corroded connections, a faulty earth connection, a blown fuse, a melted fusible link, or a faulty relay. Visually inspect the condition of all fuses, wires and connections in a problem circuit before testing the components. Use the wiring diagrams to determine which terminal connections will need to be checked, in order to pinpoint the trouble-spot.

4 The basic tools required for electrical fault finding include: a circuit tester or voltmeter (a 12-volt bulb with a set of test leads can also be used for certain tests), a self-powered test light (sometimes known as a continuity tester), an ohmmeter (to measure resistance), a battery and set of test leads, and a jumper wire, preferably with a circuit breaker or fuse incorporated, which can be used to bypass suspect wires or electrical components. Before attempting to locate a problem with test instruments, use the wiring diagram to determine where to make the connections.

5 To find the source of an intermittent wiring fault (usually due to a poor or dirty connection, or damaged wiring insulation), an integrity test can be performed on the wiring, which involves moving the wiring by hand, to see if the fault occurs as the wiring is moved. It should be possible to narrow down the source of the fault to a particular section of wiring. This method of testing can be used in conjunction with any of the tests described in the following sub-Sections.

6 Apart from problems due to poor connections, two basic types of fault can occur in an electrical circuit - open-circuit, or short-circuit.

7 Open-circuit faults are caused by a break somewhere in the circuit, which prevents current from flowing. An open-circuit fault will prevent a component from working, but will not cause the relevant circuit fuse to blow.

8 Short-circuit faults are caused by a "short" somewhere in the circuit, which allows the current flowing in the circuit to "escape" along an alternative route, usually to earth. Short-circuit faults are normally caused by a breakdown in wiring insulation, which allows a feed wire to touch either another wire, or an earthed component such as the bodyshell. A short-circuit fault will normally cause the relevant circuit fuse to blow.

Finding an open-circuit

9 To check for an open-circuit, connect one lead of a circuit tester or voltmeter to either the negative battery terminal or a known good earth.

10 Connect the other lead to a connector in the circuit being tested, preferably nearest to the battery or fuse.

11 Switch on the circuit, bearing in mind that some circuits are live only when the ignition switch is moved to a particular position.

12 If voltage is present (indicated either by the tester bulb lighting or a voltmeter reading, as applicable), this means that the section of the circuit between the relevant connector and the battery is problem-free.

13 Continue to check the remainder of the circuit in the same fashion.

14 When a point is reached at which no voltage is present, the problem must lie between that point and the previous test point with voltage. Most problems can be traced to a broken, corroded or loose connection.

Finding a short-circuit

15 To check for a short-circuit, first disconnect the load(s) from the circuit (loads are the components which draw current from a circuit, such as bulbs, motors, heating elements, etc).

16 Remove the relevant fuse from the circuit, and connect a circuit tester or voltmeter to the fuse connections.

17 Switch on the circuit, bearing in mind that some circuits are live only when the ignition switch is moved to a particular position.

18 If voltage is present (indicated either by the tester bulb lighting or a voltmeter reading, as applicable), this means that there is a short-circuit.

19 If no voltage is present, but the fuse still blows with the load(s) connected, this indicates an internal fault in the load(s).

Finding an earth fault

20 The battery negative terminal is connected to "earth" - the metal of the engine/transmission and the car body - and most systems are wired so that they only receive a positive feed, the current returning via the metal of the car body. This means that the component mounting and the body form part of that circuit. Loose or corroded mountings can therefore cause a range of electrical faults, ranging from total failure of a circuit, to a puzzling partial fault. In particular, lights may shine dimly (especially when another circuit sharing the same earth point is in operation), motors (eg wiper motors or the radiator cooling fan motor) may run slowly, and the operation of one circuit may have an apparently-unrelated effect on another. Note that on many vehicles, earth straps are used between certain components, such as the engine/transmission and the body, usually where there is no metal-to-metal contact between components, due to flexible rubber mountings, etc.

21 To check whether a component is properly earthed, disconnect the battery, and connect one lead of an ohmmeter to a known good earth point. Connect the other lead to the wire or earth connection being tested. The resistance reading should be zero; if not, check the connection as follows.

22 If an earth connection is thought to be faulty, dismantle the connection, and clean back to bare metal both the bodyshell and the wire terminal, or the component's earth connection mating surface. Be careful to remove all traces of dirt and corrosion, then use a knife to trim away any paint, so that a clean metal-to-metal joint is made. On reassembly, tighten the joint fasteners securely; if a wire terminal is being refitted, use serrated washers between the terminal and the bodyshell, to ensure a clean and secure connection. When the connection is remade, prevent the onset of corrosion in the future by applying a coat of petroleum jelly or silicone-based grease, or by spraying on (at regular intervals) a proprietary ignition sealer or a water-dispersant lubricant.

---

3 Fuses, relays and circuit breakers - location and renewal

Fuses

1 Fuses are combined in one unit under the facia panel (see illustration).

2 The fuses are numbered to identify the circuit which they protect and the circuits are represented by symbols on the plastic cover of the box.

3 When an accessory or other electrical component or system fails, always check the fuse first. The fuses are coloured red (10A), blue (15A), yellow (20/25A) or green (30A). Never replace a fuse with one of higher rating or bypass it with tinfoil, and, if the new fuse blows immediately, check the reason before renewing again. The most common cause of a fuse blowing is faulty insulation creating a short-circuit.

4 An in-line fuse is used on models fitted with a radio (without cassette) and this is of 2 or 2.5 amp rating. On models with a radio/cassette, the fuse will be integral in, or at the rear of, the unit case; the fuse being of 2.5, 3.15 or 6.3 amp rating, depending on car model. Earlier electronic ignition models with a radio/cassette will also have a line fuse of 0.5 amp rating.

5 Spare fuses are carried in the fusebox lid.

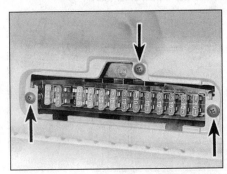

3.1 Fuse unit (cover removed). Note three unit retaining screws (arrowed)

3.6 Fuse unit removed from facia for access to relays

4.2a Steering column multi-function switch retaining screws (arrowed)

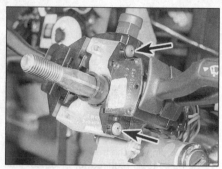

4.2b Windscreen wash/wipe retaining screws (arrowed)

Relays

6 Relays are of the plug-in type **(see illustration)**. The circuits they serve are listed in the Specifications.

7 Should it be necessary to remove or refit a relay, it is necessary to lower the fuse unit to gain access as follows.

8 Remove the lower panel under the facia.

9 Remove the fuse unit plastic cover and undo the three fuse unit retaining screws.

10 The fuse unit will now drop down behind the facia. Press in the legs of the relay retaining cage and remove the cage. Withdraw the relevant relay from its location.

Circuit breaker

11 A fusible link is incorporated into the battery feed. If failure of this link occurs, it will probably be due to a major electrical fault, in which case the problem should be referred to a Ford dealer for further advice.

---

4   Switches - removal and refitting

Note: *Disconnect the battery before removing any switches.*

Steering column combination switches

1 Both the indicator and light switch can be removed in the same manner. First undo the recessed retaining screws and carefully remove the upper and lower steering column shrouds. Guide the lower shroud over the bonnet release lever when removing it.

2 Undo the two screws of the switch concerned and withdraw the switch from the column. Disconnect the wiring at the multi-plug **(see illustrations)**.

3 Refit in the reverse order of removal, but check the switch for satisfactory operation before refitting the column shrouds.

Courtesy light switch

4 Open the door on the side concerned, unscrew the switch retaining screw **(see illustration)** and withdraw the switch and wiring so that the wire connector is accessible. Disconnect the wiring at the connector to fully withdraw the switch.

5 Refit in the reverse order of removal locating the switch in the rubber shroud in the pillar aperture.

Heater motor rocker switch (low series)

6 This switch can simply be prised free from the dash panel using a suitable flat-bladed screwdriver **(see illustration)**. Locate a piece of cardboard or similar between the panel and the screwdriver as a protector pad when levering.

7 Withdraw the switch and disconnect the wiring multi-plug.

8 Refit in the reverse order to removal.

Heater motor switch (high series)

9 Pull free the three heater control knobs, undo the four screws then remove the bulb holders and the heater facia.

4.4 Remove the courtesy light switch retaining screw

10 Reach behind the switch, depress the two retaining tabs and withdraw the switch and wiring. Disconnect the wiring at the multiplug **(see illustration)**.

11 Refit in the reverse order to removal.

Facia panel "tab" switches

12 Insert a small thin-edged screwdriver between the edge of the switch (on the left-hand side) and the panel and carefully prise it free **(see illustration)**. To avoid possible damage to the facia position a piece of cardboard or similar as a pad between the screwdriver and panel.

13 Withdraw the switch and disconnect the multi-plug **(see illustration)**.

14 Refit in the reverse order of removal.

Handbrake warning light switch

15 Remove the handbrake lever, undo the two switch retaining screws, disconnect the wiring multi-plug and remove the switch.

4.6 Low series heater motor rocker switch removal

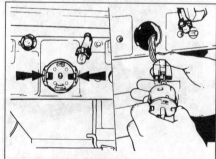

4.10 High series heater motor switch removal

4.12 Prise at point shown . . .

4.13 . . . to release and withdraw the tab switch

4.18 Econolight switch location and securing screws (arrowed)

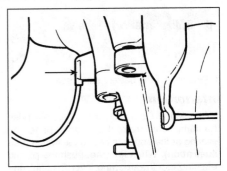

4.20 Reversing light switch location on gearbox

16 Refit in the reverse order of removal. Check the switch for satisfactory operation on completion.

Stop-light switch

17 Refer to Chapter 9.

Econolights switch

18 These are located in the engine compartment and are mounted on the bulkhead. To remove a switch, detach the vacuum line, disconnect the wiring connector and undo the switch retaining screws (**see illustration**).

19 Refit in the reverse order to removal. Restart the engine on completion and check the instrument lights for correct operations.

Reversing light switch

20 This is accessible from the engine compartment. Disconnect the switch wiring

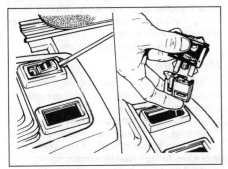

4.21 Luggage compartment lid release switch removal

connector then unscrew and remove the switch from its location on the side of the gearbox (**see illustration**).

Luggage compartment switch (lid release)

21 This is a rocker type switch and is fitted to the central floor console. It can be removed in the same manner as that described for the heater motor switch (**see illustration**).

5 Clock - removal and refitting

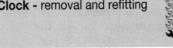

Facia-mounted

1 Detach the battery earth lead.

2 Use a suitable thin-bladed screwdriver as a lever and prise free the clock from the facia. Position a small piece of cardboard between the facia and the screwdriver blade to avoid the possibility of damage to the facia.

3 Withdraw the clock and disconnect the wiring multi-plug (**see illustration**).

4 Refit in the reverse order to removal.

Roof-mounted

5 Disconnect the battery earth lead.

6 Undo the two screws securing the clock unit to the header panel (**see illustration**), withdraw the clock/courtesy lamp unit and disconnect the wiring multi-plug.

7 Refitting is a reversal of the removal procedure.

6 Cigar lighter - removal and refitting

1 Disconnect the battery earth lead.

2 Carefully withdraw the cigar lighter element.

3 Pull out the body and ring from the bezel.

4 Detach the wiring multi-plug and illumination bulb.

5 To renew the lighter elements, depress the knob so that the coil locknut is accessible. Grip the shaft with some thin nose pliers, unscrew the locknut (**see illustration**) and remove the coil.

6 Fit the new coil and refit the cigar lighter by reversing the removal procedure.

7 Manual choke knob illuminating bulb - renewal

1 Extract the choke knob retaining clip and withdraw the knob and sleeve.

2 Press the bulb fully home into its holder (against spring tension) then simultaneously use a thin-bladed screwdriver and push the bulb base holder downwards to remove the bulb.

3 To refit the bulb, press it into its holder and push the base holder upwards to secure. Slide the sleeve into position, refit the knob and locate its retaining clip.

5.3 Facia-mounted clock removal

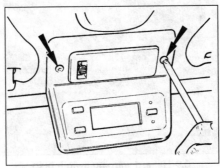

5.6 Roof-mounted clock retaining screws (arrowed)

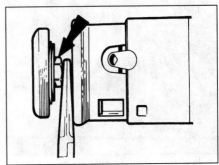

6.5 Cigar lighter coil retaining nut (arrowed)

12

8 Bulbs (interior) - renewal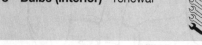

1 Disconnect the battery earth lead.

Interior lamp

2 Check that the switch is off. Carefully prise the lamp unit from the header panel by levering at the opposite end to the switch **(see illustration)**. When levering, push the plastic retaining clip inwards and lever the light unit away.
3 The bulb is now accessible for inspection and replacement, if necessary. If required, completely remove the unit by disconnecting the wire at the multi-plug.

Glovebox lamp

4 With the glovebox lid opened, press the lamp holder out of the latch unit. The bulb can now be removed from its holder for inspection and replacement **(see illustration)**.

Heater control illumination bulbs

High series

5 Pull free the three control knobs then undo the four heater panel retaining screws and remove the facia panel **(see illustration)**.
6 Untwist the bulb holders from the facia panel and pull free the bulbs **(see illustration)**.

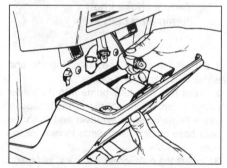

8.6 Heater control bulb removal - high series

8.8 Heater control illumination bulb replacement - low series

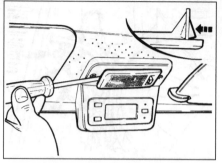

8.2 Interior lamp removal - high series

Low series

7 Remove the instrument panel surround.
8 Untwist the bulb holder and withdraw it, then pull the bulb from the holder for inspection/replacement **(see illustration)**.

Hazard warning bulb

9 Pull the switch cover upwards and remove it to expose the bulb, then pull the bulb free from its holder **(see illustration)**.

Luggage compartment bulb

10 Using a thin-bladed screwdriver, prise free the lamp from the trim panel.
11 The festoon bulb can then be unclipped from its holder for inspection/replacement.

Clock (roof-mounted) bulb

12 This procedure applies to vehicles fitted with a clock made in France or W. Germany, with the part number suffix "FA" or later **(see illustration)**.
13 Remove the clock/courtesy lamp assembly.
14 Using a screwdriver with a small blade, prise down the tabs at the back of the clock, and remove the back.
15 Remove the bulb by turning it through 90°.

All bulbs

16 Refitting is the reversal of removal for all lamp assemblies. Check their operation is satisfactory on completion.

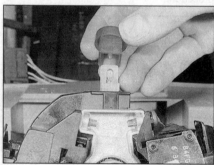

8.9 Hazard warning switch bulb replacement

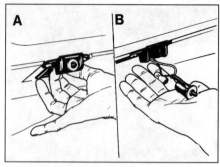

8.4 Press out glovebox lamp holder (A) and remove bulb (B)

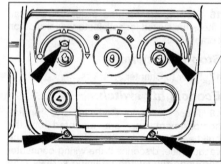

8.5 Heater panel retaining screws (arrowed) - high series

9 Bulbs (exterior) - renewal

Caution: Avoid touching the glass envelope of a headlamp or auxiliary driving lamp bulb. Failure to do this may result in premature bulb failure.
1 Disconnect the battery earth lead.

Headlamp

2 Open the bonnet and, working from the engine compartment side, disconnect the wiring multi-plug from the rear of the headlamp concerned **(see illustration)**.
3 Remove the rubber gaiter and rotate the bulb securing clip or extract the spring clip according to type **(see illustrations)**.
4 Withdraw the bulb **(see illustration)**.

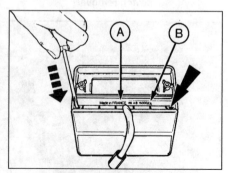

8.12 Roof-mounted clock unit
A Country of manufacture
B Part number suffix

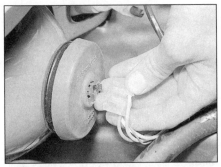

9.2 Detach lead connector from rear of headlight . . .

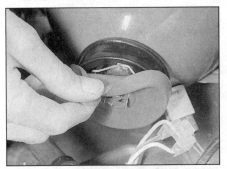

9.3a . . . prise free the gaiter . . .

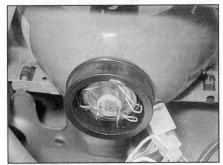

9.3b . . . release the clips . . .

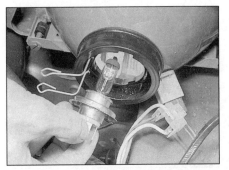

9.4 . . . and withdraw the bulb

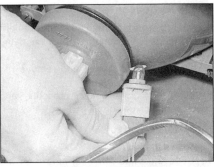

9.6 Sidelamp removal

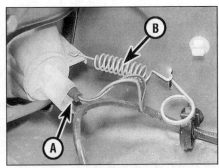

9.7 Front indicator bulb holder (A). Note indicator unit retaining spring (B)

5 Fit the bulb, avoiding handling it with the fingers. If you have touched it, wipe the bulb with a pad moistened in methylated spirit.

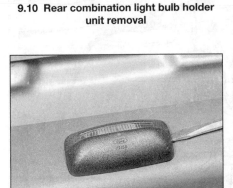

9.10 Rear combination light bulb holder unit removal

Front parking lamp (sidelamp)

6 The operations are similar to those just described for the headlamp bulb. Twist the parking lamp bulb holder from the headlamp unit **(see illustration)**.

Front indicator lamp

7 Working inside the engine compartment, twist the bulb holder from the rear of the lamp **(see illustration)**.
8 Remove the bulb from the holder.

Rear lamps

9 Remove the spare wheel cover from the luggage compartment, then carefully detach and withdraw the rear side trim panel on the side concerned for access to the lamp unit.
10 Push the bulb holder unit retaining clip upwards to release and remove the unit **(see illustration)**. The bulb(s) can now be

untwisted and removed from the holder, as required.

Rear number plate lamp

11 Using a suitable thin-bladed screwdriver, prise free the light unit from the bumper and withdraw the unit **(see illustration)**.
12 Prise open the retaining clips on each side and withdraw the lens from the unit body **(see illustration)**. The bulb can then be removed from the holder unit by pressing and untwisting it.

Rear foglamp

13 With the tailgate opened, remove the lockable compartment lid (if fitted) and the load compartment box. Detach the wiring multi-plug.
14 Undo the plastic retainer knobs, then withdraw the foglamp unit from under the rear bumper **(see illustrations)**.

9.11 Prise free the number plate lamp unit . . .

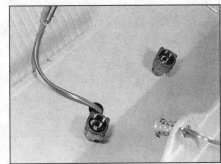

9.12 . . . and separate the lens and body for access to the bulb

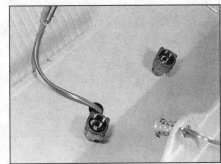

9.14a Foglamp unit retaining knobs

12

9.14b Remove the foglight . . .

9.15 . . . and separate lens from body for access to the bulb

10.3 Headlight unit retaining bolt removal

15 Depress the securing tangs and separate the reflector from the unit for access to the bulb which can be removed by pressing and untwisting from its holder **(see illustration)**.

All lamps

16 Refitting of the bulb and associated components is a reversal of the removal procedure in all cases. Check the bulb for satisfactory operation on completion.

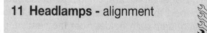

10 Exterior lamp units - removal and refitting

1 Disconnect the battery earth lead.

Headlamp

2 Raise the bonnet then disconnect the wiring multi-plug at the rear of the headlamp unit.
3 Undo the retaining bolt at the top of the unit **(see illustration)**.
4 Unclip the vertical adjustment screw unit from the top of the lamp and withdraw the lamp, lifting it from the lower location lugs **(see illustration)**.
5 Refitting is a reversal of the removal procedure, but on completion check the operation of the light unit and adjust it.

Front indicator lamp

6 Working from the engine compartment side, disengage the lamp unit retaining spring by pulling to the rear.
7 Untwist the bulb holder and remove the lamp unit **(see illustration)**.
8 Refit reversing the removal procedure and check operation on completion.

Rear lamp unit

9 Remove the bulb holder.
10 Undo the three retaining nuts from the inside and withdraw the unit.
11 Refit in reverse order to removal and check operation of all lights on completion.

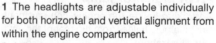

11 Headlamps - alignment

1 The headlights are adjustable individually for both horizontal and vertical alignment from within the engine compartment.
2 Adjustments should not normally be necessary and, if their beam alignment is suspect, they should be checked by a Ford garage with optical alignment equipment.

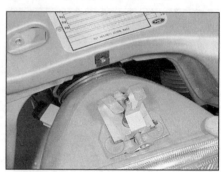

10.4 Detach headlight unit adjuster at the top

3 A temporary adjustment can be made by turning the vertical and/or horizontal adjuster screws at the rear of each headlight unit **(see illustration)**. When making an alignment check, the car tyre pressure must be correct and the car standing unladen on level ground.
4 To assist in making an alignment check/adjustment the accompanying diagram shows the provisional headlamp beam alignment with the vehicle parked a distance of 10 m from a wall or aiming board **(see illustration)**. The headlamps are "dipped".

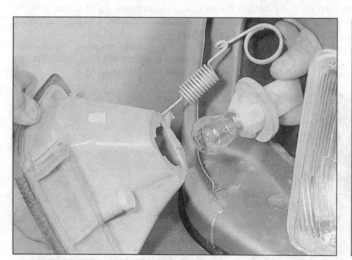

10.7 Front indicator lamp unit removal

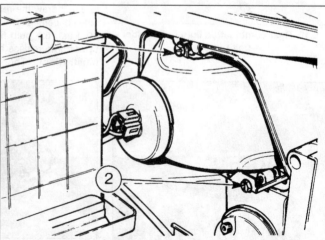

11.3 Headlamp vertical (1) and horizontal (2) adjuster screws

11.4 Headlamp beam alignment diagram

Left-hand drive shown. Transpose 15° beam inclination angle to the left for right-hand drive.
A *Distance between headlamp centres*
B *Light/dark boundary*
C *Dipped beam centre*
D *Dipped beam pattern*
H *Height from ground to centre of headlamps*
X *10 to 12 cm, preferably with full tank*
OO *Vehicle centre line*

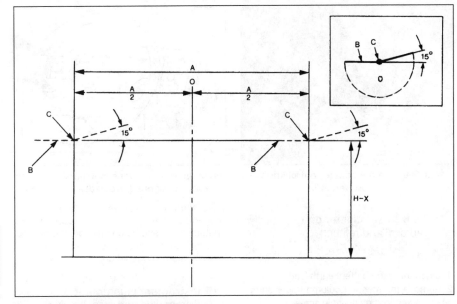

12 Auxiliary driving lamps - bulb renewal

1 Undo and remove the lens retaining screw from the lower edge of the light unit **(see illustration)**.
2 Prise free the lens from the light bowl, starting at the lower edge. When free, detach the wiring connectors, release the bulb retaining clip and withdraw the bulb from the holder in the reflector. Avoid touching the bulb with the fingers **(see illustration)**.
3 Refit in the reverse order to removal.

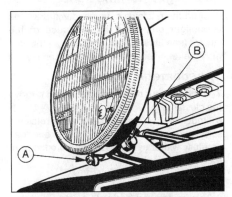

12.1 Auxiliary lamp lens securing screw (A) and unit securing nut (B)

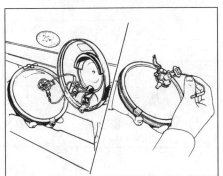

12.2 Bulb replacement - auxiliary lamp

13 Auxiliary driving lamps - removal, refitting and adjustment

1 Disconnect the battery earth lead.
2 Detach the lamp wire from its main loom connector.
3 Unscrew and remove the mounting bolt and nut, withdraw the bolt and remove the light unit.
4 Refit in the reverse order to removal and check alignment before fully tightening the mounting bolt and nut.
5 As with the headlamps, the auxiliary driving lamps should be adjusted using optical beam setting equipment and this task is best entrusted to your Ford dealer. However, to assist when making initial adjustments, reference should be made to the accompanying diagram which shows a beam setting pattern with the vehicle parked on level ground at a distance of 10 m from a wall or aiming board. The wall should be marked accordingly to enable the beams to be set as required **(see illustration)**.

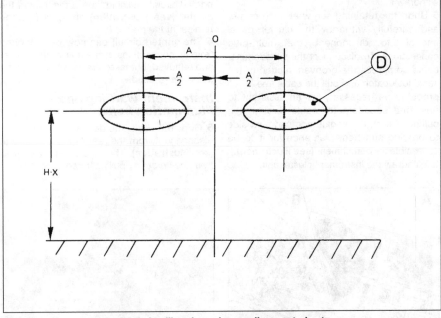

13.5 Auxiliary lamp beam alignment chart

A *Lamp centre distance*
D *Area of maximum light intensity*
H *Lamp centre line to ground distance*
O *Centre line of vehicle*
X *18 cm (7.1 in)*

12

14.3 Remove the heater control knobs - low series

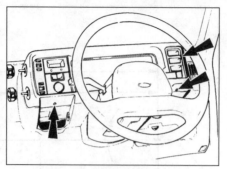

14.4a Instrument panel surround securing screw locations (arrowed) - low series

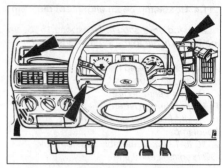

14.4b Instrument panel surround securing screw locations (arrowed) - high series

14 Instrument cluster unit - removal and refitting

1 Disconnect the battery earth lead.
2 Remove the steering column upper shroud which is secured by a single screw.
3 On low series models, pull free the heater control knobs **(see illustration)**.
4 Undo and remove the panel surround retaining screws **(see illustrations)**. Note that the lower left-hand screw on high series models is obscured by the heater control panel, which must first be removed for access to the mounting. Carefully withdraw the surround. On low series models pivot the surround from the right, reach to the rear of the clock, depress the retaining tabs and withdraw the clock, then remove the surround to the left to clear the heater controls and withdraw it.
5 Undo the retaining screw at each corner and carefully withdraw the cluster panel enough to disconnect the multi-plug connections. To disconnect the speedometer cable compress the grooved section of the cable lock catch and pull the cable free. It will probably be necessary for an assistant to push the speedometer cable through the bulkhead from the engine compartment side to provide sufficient clearance for it to be accessible for detachment **(see illustration)**.
6 Withdraw the instrument cluster unit.

7 Refitting is a reversal of the removal procedure. Take care not to damage the printed circuit and its connections on the rear face of the unit. Check operation of instruments on completion.

15 Instrument cluster unit - dismantling and reassembly

Note: *With the instrument cluster removed, its various components can be removed individually or collectively as required. When handling the instrument cluster and its components care must be taken not to knock or damage them in any way.*

Printed circuit

1 Remove the tachometer unit and the fuel/temperature gauge.
2 Undo the four screws and remove the lens.
3 Using a suitable implement, press the printed circuit retaining tabs at the front of the cluster **(see illustration)** and pull free the retainer at the rear.
4 The printed circuit can now be detached from its connections at the rear of the cluster and removed, but take care not to damage it if it is to be re-used.

Instrument warning and illumination bulbs

5 Grip the bulb holder and twist it to disengage it from the rear of the cluster unit **(see illustration)**. The bulb can be removed from the holder by pulling it free.

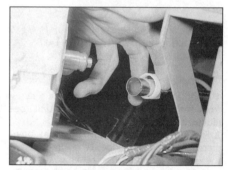

14.5 Disconnect the speedometer cable

Econolight warning light

6 Undo the retaining screw and withdraw the econolight unit from the rear face of the cluster **(see illustration)**. If defective, this unit must be renewed as a complete assembly.

Speedometer head

7 Undo the four retaining screws and remove the cluster lens.
8 Undo the two speedometer head retaining screws from the rear face of the unit and then carefully withdraw the head unit from the front **(see illustration)**.

Tachometer

9 This is removed in a similar manner to that of the speedometer head except that it is secured by three nuts and washers.

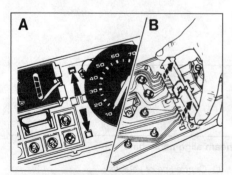

15.3 Press tabs arrowed (A) and withdraw printed circuit retainer (B)

15.5 Bulb and holder removed from instrument cluster panel

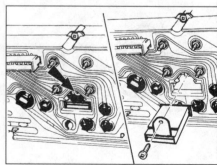

15.6 Undo screw (arrowed) and withdraw the econolight unit

Fuel/temperature gauge

10 This is removed in a similar manner to that described for the speedometer head except that it is secured by four nuts and washers **(see illustration)**.

Cluster reassembly

11 Refitting of components is a reversal of the removal procedure. When refitting the lens to the front face, position it on the cluster body with the two engagement pegs protruding through on each top corner; the lugs on the lower edge of the body must correspondingly engage in the cut-outs in the cluster body.

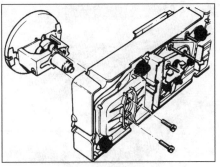

15.8 Speedometer unit removal - low series

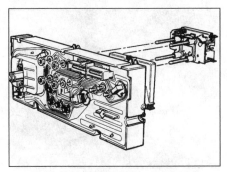

15.10 Fuel/temperature gauge unit removal - high series

16 Speedometer cable - removal and refitting
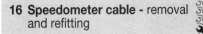
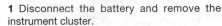

1 Disconnect the battery and remove the instrument cluster.
2 Disconnect the cable from the transmission and release it from its clips and grommets.
3 Withdraw the cable through the bulkhead.
4 Refitting is a reversal of removal. The cable is supplied as a complete assembly.

17 Horn(s) - removal and refitting
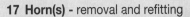

1 The horn(s) are located in the left-hand front corner of the engine compartment. Before removing, disconnect the battery.

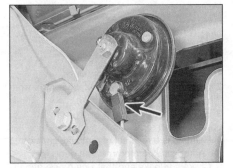

17.2 Horn support bracket and lead connection (arrowed)

18.3 Wiper arm retaining nut

2 Disconnect the lead from the horn **(see illustration)**.
3 Unscrew the single bolt and remove the horn and bracket.
4 Refitting is a reversal of removal.

18 Windscreen wiper blades and arms - removal and refitting
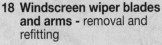

1 Pull the wiper arm away from the glass until it locks.
2 Depress the small clip on the blade and slide the blade out of the hooked part of the arm **(see illustration)**.
3 Before removing the wiper arms it is worthwhile marking their parked position on the glass with a strip of masking tape as an aid to refitting. Raise the plastic nut cover **(see illustration)**.

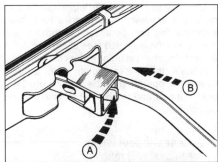

18.2 Press clip (A) and slide arm (B) through blade holder to release

20.2a Remove plastic cover . . .

4 Unscrew the nut which holds the arm to the pivot shaft and pull the arm from the shaft splines.
5 Refit by reversing the removal operations.

19 Wiper blade rubber - renewal

Refer to "Weekly checks".

20 Windscreen wiper motor - removal and refitting

1 Disconnect the battery earth lead.
2 Pull free the plastic cover from the wiper motor which is mounted on the bulkhead **(see illustrations)**.
3 Detach the wiring multi-plug from the wiper motor.
4 Undo the three retaining bolts and withdraw the wiper motor and mounting plate.
5 The wiper motor can now be disconnected from the arm and connecting link. Take care not to bend the link arm or damage the bush and ball.
6 Unscrew and remove the three securing bolts and detach the wiper motor from the mounting plate.
7 Refit in the reverse order of removal. Lubricate the bush and ball with grease prior to assembling and, when fitting the mounting plate to the bulkhead, check that the foam seal strip is in position between the mating surfaces.

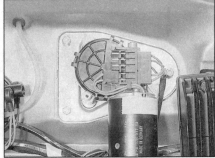

20.2b . . . for access to wiper motor unit (windscreen)

12

21.2a Undo the retaining bolts . . .

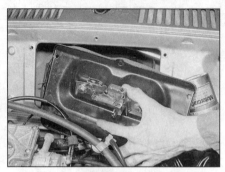

21.2b . . . and withdraw the mounting plate/lock unit

21.3 Heater blower motor location. Note retaining clip positions (arrowed)

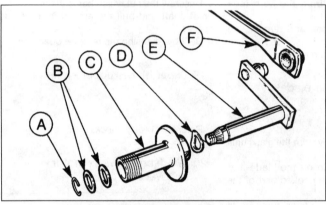

21.4a Wiper pivot shaft components (front)

A Circlip
B Shim washer
C Bearing and housing
D Wave washers
E Pivot shaft
F Link arm

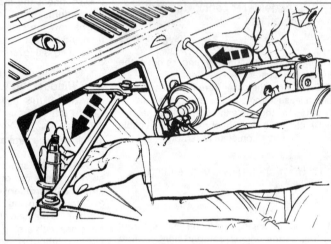

21.4b Wiper motor linkage withdrawal

21 Windscreen wiper linkage - removal and refitting

1 Remove the windscreen wiper motor and the wiper arms and blades.
2 Undo the six bolts which secure the bonnet lock mounting plate to the bulkhead **(see illustration)**, disconnect the actuating cable to the lock and remove the mounting plate/lock unit **(see illustration)**.
3 Unclip and remove the heater blower motor from its recess then disconnect the motor wiring at the multi-plug connectors **(see illustration)**.

4 Unscrew and remove the wiper spindle arm nuts and washers **(see illustration)**, then withdraw the linkage assembly through the aperture in the bulkhead **(see illustration)**.
5 Refit in the reverse order to removal. Lubricate the linkage joints with grease. Check the operation of the wiper motor, the blower motor and the bonnet release lock on completion.

22 Rear window wiper motor - removal and refitting

1 Disconnect the battery earth lead.
2 Remove the rear wiper arm and blade.
3 Undo the nut retaining the wiper arm pivot shaft.
4 Open and raise the tailgate and carefully detach the inner trim panel by prising free the securing clips.
5 Undo the two wiper motor bracket-to-tailgate retaining bolts **(see illustration)**.
6 Detach the earth lead which is retained by a screw to the tailgate. Disconnect the wiring multi-plug then withdraw the wiper motor and operating linkage from the tailgate cavity.
7 Refit in the reverse order of removal and check operation prior to refitting the tailgate trim panel.

23 Windscreen washer pump - removal and refitting

1 Drain the washer fluid container.
2 Disconnect the lead and washer pipe from the pump unit **(see illustration)**.
3 Ease the washer pump away from the fluid container and remove it.
4 Refitting is a reversal of removal; check that the pump sealing grommet is a good fit.
5 Check for leaks and that pump operation is satisfactory on completion.

22.5 Rear window wiper motor location and retaining bolts (arrowed)

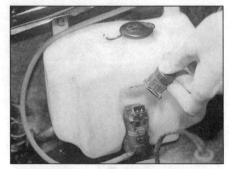

23.2 Remove the multi-plug from the windscreen washer pump

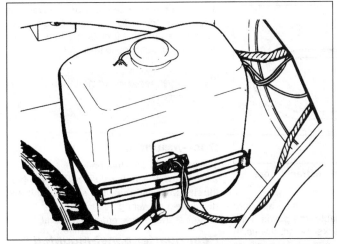

24.1 Rear housing window washer pump and reservoir

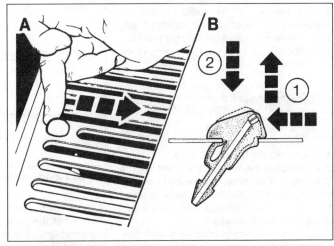

25.1 Windscreen washer nozzle removal (A) and fitting (B)

24 Rear window washer pump - removal and refitting

1 The rear window washer pump is attached to the reservoir in the luggage compartment **(see illustration)**.
2 Unhook the rubber securing band retaining the reservoir in position.
3 Drain the contents of the reservoir, disconnect the wiring connector to the pump unit at the top and the washer pipe at the bottom.
4 Carefully ease the washer pump away from the reservoir.
5 Refit in the reverse order to removal. Check that the pump seal grommet is a good fit.
6 Check for leaks and that pump operation is satisfactory on completion.

25 Windscreen washer nozzle and pipe - removal and refitting

1 To remove the nozzle(s), push the nozzle to the rear whilst pulling it up on its front edge. When the nozzle is clear of its location hole detach the fluid feed pipe **(see illustration)**.

2 If the pipe is to be removed, disconnect it at the pump end and pull it clear through the plenum chamber.
3 Refit in the reverse order to removal. Ensure that the feed pipe is located in rubber grommets where it passes through body panels.
4 On completion check for satisfactory operation of the washers and, if necessary, adjust the nozzles for jet spray direction by inserting a pin into the nozzle and moving it in the required direction.

26 Rear window washer nozzle and pipe - removal and refitting

1 Open the tailgate, then carefully prise down the headlining at its rear edge for access to the underside of the nozzle. The weatherstrip will have to be prised free to allow the headlining to be detached, so take care not to damage it.
2 Pull free the feed pipe from the washer nozzle, undo the retaining nut, withdraw the shakeproof washer and seal then remove the nozzle.
3 To remove the hose, detach it from the reservoir pump and pull it through the body

channels. To ease refitting of the hose, attach a length of cord to the end of the hose before removal. The cord can be left in position and tied to the new hose to ease refitting.
4 Refit in the reverse order to removal.

27 In-car entertainment equipment - general information

1 The following Sections cover radio/cassette player equipment fitted during production which is of Ford manufacture.
2 When fitted during production, the radio will be located in the lower centre console (low series variants) or in the instrument panel directly above the central air vents (high series variants).
3 Production fitted speakers will be mounted in the passenger door (mono system) or one in each door and one in each rear quarter trim panel (stereo system). On all models and for all systems the aerial is mounted in the front wing panel on the driver's side. Note that only manual aerials are fitted in production.

28 Radio - removal and refitting

1 Disconnect the battery.
2 Remove the radio control knobs and withdraw the tuning knob spacer and the tone control lever.
3 Unscrew and remove the facia plate retaining nuts and washers, then withdraw the facia plate **(see illustration)**.
4 The radio retaining tangs can now be pulled inwards (towards the centre of the radio) and the radio withdrawn from its aperture **(see illustration)**.
5 With the radio withdrawn, disconnect the power lead, the speaker plug, earth lead, the aerial cable and feed.

28.3 Radio facia plate retaining nut (arrowed) with control knob removed

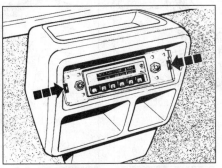

28.4 Press securing tangs inwards to remove radio

12

6 From the rear of the radio remove the plastic support bracket and locating plate, then remove the radio from the front bracket.

7 Refitting is the reversal of the removal procedure.

29 Radio/cassette player - removal and refitting

1 Disconnect the battery earth lead.

2 To withdraw the radio/cassette unit from its aperture, you will need to fabricate U-shaped extractor tools from wire rod of suitable gauge to insert into the withdrawal slots on each side of the unit **(see illustration)**.

3 Insert the withdrawal tools as shown, then pushing each outwards simultaneously, pull them evenly to withdraw the radio/cassette unit. It is important that an equal pressure is applied to each tool as the unit is withdrawn **(see illustrations)**.

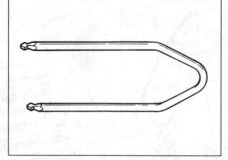

29.2 Radio/cassette extractor tool

4 Once withdrawn from its aperture disconnect the aerial cable, the power lead, the aerial feed, the speaker plugs, the earth lead and the light and memory feed (where applicable).

5 Push the retaining clips inwards to remove the removal tool from each side **(see illustration)**.

6 Refit in the reverse order of removal. The withdrawal tools do not have to be used, simply push the unit into its aperture until the securing clips engage in their slots.

30 Loudspeaker - removal and refitting

Door-mounted

1 Remove the door trim panel.

2 Unscrew the four retaining screws **(see illustration)**, withdraw the speaker unit and disconnect the wiring.

3 Refit in the reverse order to removal.

Rear quarter panel-mounted

4 Remove the rear seat cushion and the seat backrest.

5 Detach and remove the rear quarter lower trim panel. To avoid disconnecting the seat

29.3a Insert removal tool into radio/cassette

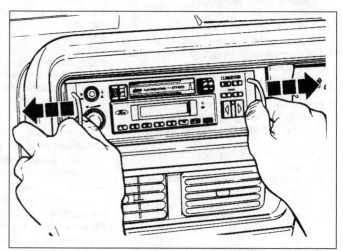

29.3b Radio cassette withdrawal

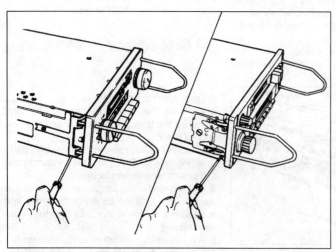

29.5 Releasing the removal tool

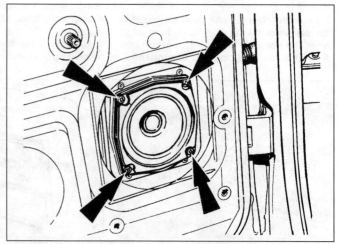

30.2 Door-mounted speaker unit and securing screws (arrowed)

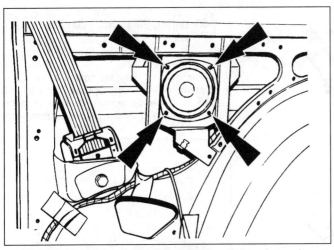

30.6 Rear quarter panel speaker unit location and securing screws (arrowed)

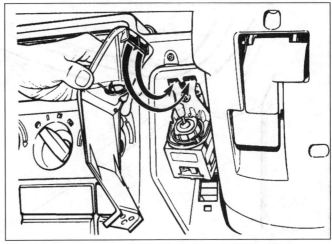

31.2 Speaker joystick bezel removal - high series

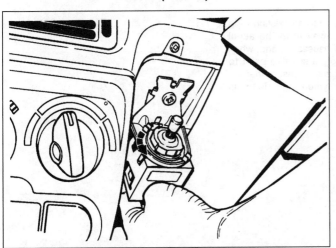

31.3 Speaker joystick removal - high series

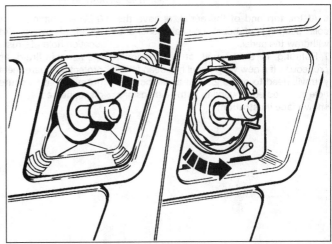

31.5 Speaker joystick removal - low series

belt anchor, slide the panel up the belt and position out of the way to provide access to the speaker.

6 Undo the four retaining screws, remove the speaker and detach the leads **(see illustration)**.

7 Refit in reverse order to removal.

31 Speaker fader joystick - removal and refitting

1 Disconnect the battery earth lead.

High series variant

2 Unscrew and remove the single bezel retaining screw, lower the bezel and slide it away and detach from the upper bracket **(see illustration)**.

3 Rotate the joystick retaining clip anti-clockwise **(see illustration)**, remove the clip and withdraw the joystick from the bracket. Detach the wiring multi-plug.

4 Refit in the reverse order to removal.

Low series variant

5 Use a flat-bladed screwdriver to prise free the bezel and pivot the bezel upwards at the lower edge to disengage it from the bracket at the top edge **(see illustration)**.

6 Rotate the joystick retaining clip anti-clockwise, remove the clip and withdraw the joystick from its mounting bracket. Detach the wiring multi-plug.

7 Refit in the reverse order to removal.

32 Aerial - removal and refitting

1 Unclip and remove the lower insulating panel from the dash panel on the driver's side.

2 Reach up behind the radio and disconnect the aerial lead.

3 Detach and remove the dirt guard on the trailing edge under the front wing on the

driver's side. To ease access, raise and support the front of the vehicle and remove the front roadwheels on that side.

4 Undo and remove the aerial mounting bracket bolt from the inner wing **(see illustration)**.

5 Carefully pull the aerial lead down through the body panel, removing the grommet if necessary.

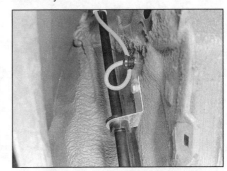

32.4 Wing-mounted aerial viewed from wing underside

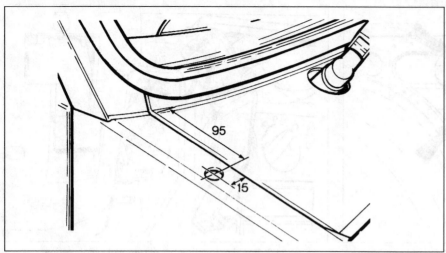

32.7 Aerial location hole position in wing panel
Dimensions shown in mm

33 Wiring diagrams - general information

Each wiring diagram covers a particular system of the appropriate vehicle; as indicated in each caption. Carefully read the Key to each diagram before commencing work.

6 At the top end of the aerial, remove the collar securing nut, bezel and seal washer and withdraw the aerial.

7 Refitting is a reversal of the removal procedure. If a new wing panel has been fitted you will need to drill a 22 mm aerial location hole in its top edge working to the dimensions shown **(see illustration)**.

8 When refitting the aerial to an existing wing panel, clean any dirt away from the aerial location hole (de-rust if necessary) and, when the aerial is fitted, apply a suitable paint to protect any bare metal areas. Ensure that the grommet is secure when the lead is disconnected.

Key to Wiring diagrams

Item	Description	Diagram/ grid ref	Item	Description	Diagram/ grid ref
1	Alternator	1/A3	55	Luggage comp lamp	3/L7
2	Auto trans inhibitor switch	1/A3	56	Luggage comp switch	3/M2
3	Auto trans selector illumination	1/L5	57	Multifunction switch	2/K5
4	Auxiliary air valve	1/C5			3/K5
5	Battery	1/C7	58	Oil pressure switch	1/B5
6	Choke on light and switch	1/K3	59	Radiator cooling fan	1/A6
7	Cigar lighter	3/H5	60	Rear foglamp	2/M4
8	Clock	3/H4	61	Rear foglamp switch	2/K1
9	Cold running valve	1/C6	62	Rear light cluster LH	2/M7
10	Cooling fan switch	1/B6			3/M7
11	Dim-dip relay V	2/A4	63	Rear light cluster RH	2/M1
12	Dim-dip relay X	2/A4	64	Rear washer pump	3/L8
13	Dip beam relay III	2/A5	65	Rear window control relay	3/B4
14	Distributor	1/E2	66	Rear window wash/wipe switch	2/H1
		1/E4			3/H1
		1/E5	67	Rear window wiper motor	3/M5
		1/E6	68	Reversing lamp switch	2/K5
		1/E7	69	Side mark flasher lamp LH	2/B8
15	Door switch LH	3/G8	70	Side mark flasher lamp RH	2/C1
16	Door switch RH	3/G1	71	Spark plugs	1/F2
17	Econogauge	1/K3			1/F4
18	Econolight switch (red)	1/H7			1/F5
19	Econolight switch (amber)	1/G7			1/F6
20	EGR system control	1/C2			1/F7
21	EGR system vacuum switch	1/C3	72	Spot lamp relay	2/C3
22	EGR system valve	1/D2	73	Starter auto trans relay	1/B3
23	Filter (suppressor)	1/H8	74	Starter motor	1/A4
24	Flasher lamp LH	2/A8	75	Stop-lamp switch	1/H2
25	Flasher lamp RH	2/A1			2/F3
26	Flasher relay	2/C4	76	Tailgate release actuator	3/M4
27	Fuel sender	1/M7	77	Tailgate release relay	3/B4
28	Fuel shut-off valve	1/F3	78	Tailgate release switch	3/G3
		1/C3	79	Thermal switch	1/C6
		1/C5	80	Water temp sender	1/A5
		1/C6	81	Windscreen washer pump	3/E3
		1/C7	82	Wiper intermittent relay	3/C6
29	Glovebox switch/lamp	2/H6	83	Wiper motor	3/C6
30	Handbrake warning switch	1/L5			
31	Headlamp unit LH	2/A7			
32	Headlamp unit RH	2/A2			
33	Headlamp washer pump	3/C1			
34	Headlamp washer relay	3/B4			
35	Heated rear window	3/M3			
36	Heated rear window switch	2/J1			
		3/J1			
37	Heater blower motor	3/F5			
38	Heater blower switch	3/E6			
39	Heater blower switch illum.	2/D6			
40	High beam relay VIII	2/B6			
41	Horn	3/A6			
42	Idle speed control relay	1/B2			
43	Idle speed control valve	1/B1			
44	Ignition coil	1/D2			
		1/D4			
		1/E5			
		1/E6			
		1/E7			
45	Ignition module 3D mapped	1/C4			
46	Ignition switch	1/H1			
47	Ignition switch relay	1/G4			
48	Instrument cluster	1/K4			
		2/G5			
		3/G5			
49	Interior lamp/switch	3/H4			
50	Licence plate lamp	2/M6			
51	Light/wiper switch	2/K4			
		3/K4			
52	Long range lamp LH	2/A6			
53	Long range lamp RH	2/A3			
54	Low brake fluid switch	1/B6			

Wire colours

B	Blue	Rs	Pink
Bk	Black	S	Grey
Bn	Brown	V	Violet
Gn	Green	W	White
R	Red	Y	Yellow

Notes

Diagrams are based on 1983 to 86 model. Alternative connections for 1986-on are shown as dashed lines.

Brackets show how the circuit can be connected in more than one way.

Feed wires are coloured red (black when switched), and all earths are brown.

12

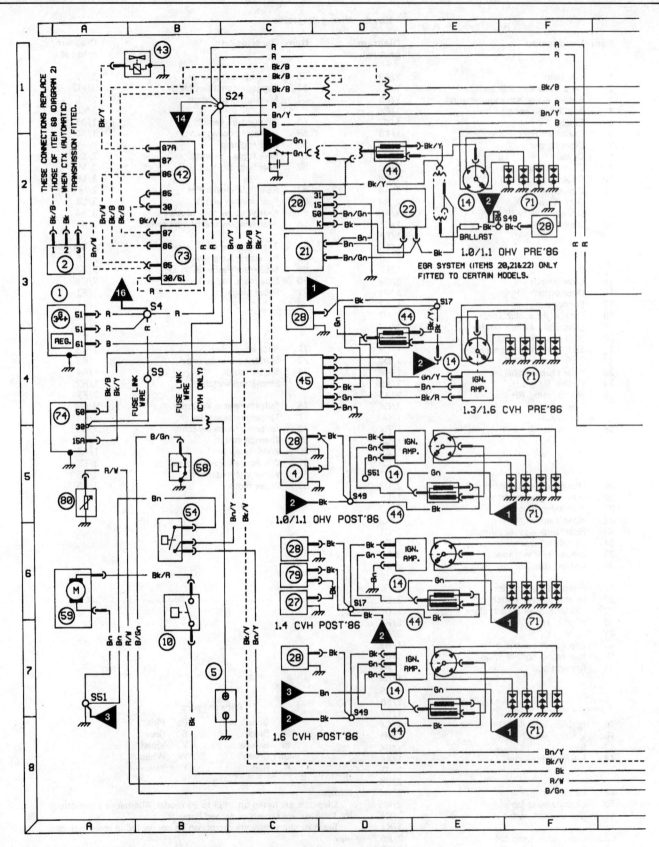

Diagram 1: Starting, charging and ignition - All models

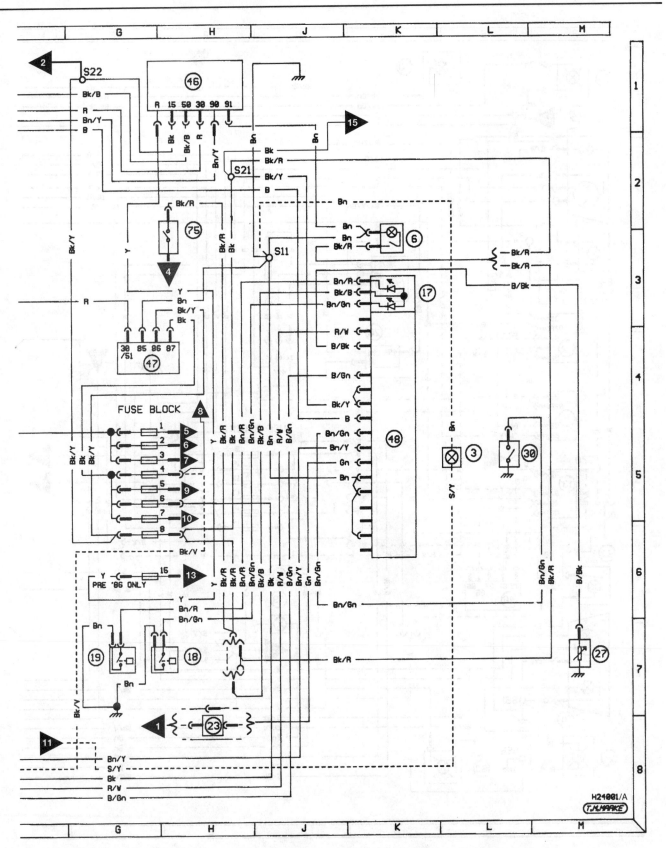

Diagram 1 (continued): Starting, charging and ignition - All models

H24001/A

T.J.MARKE

12

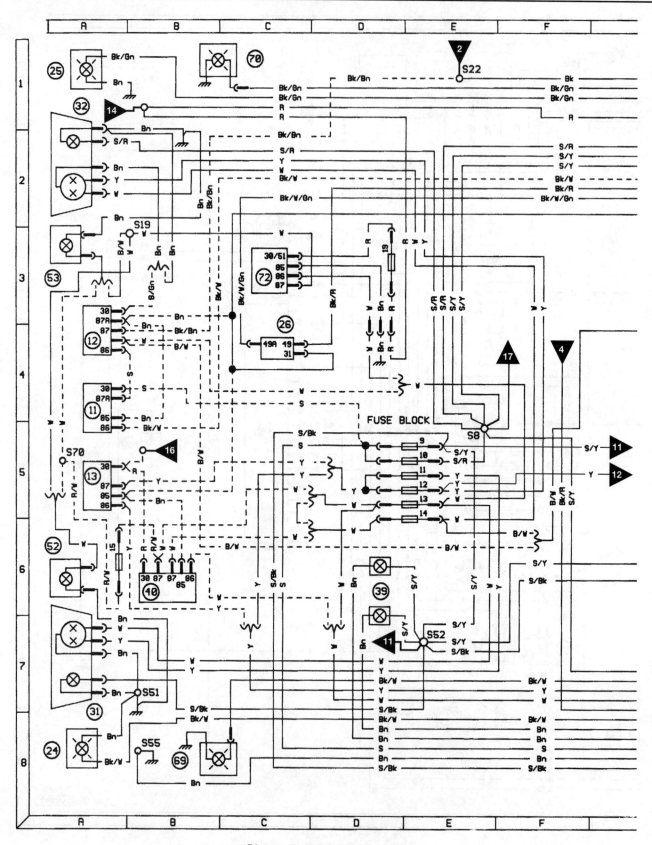

Diagram 2: Lighting - All models

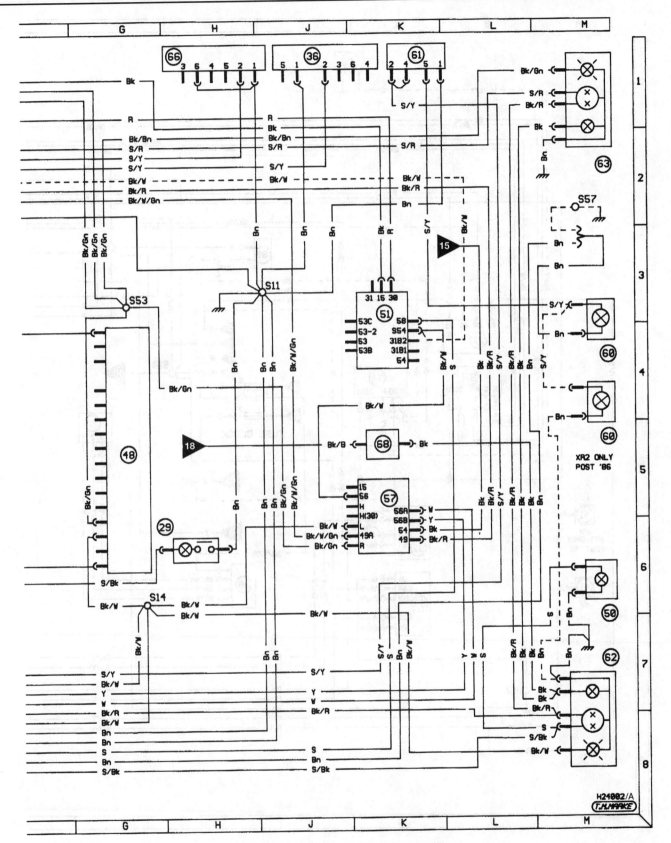

Diagram 2 (continued): Lighting - All models

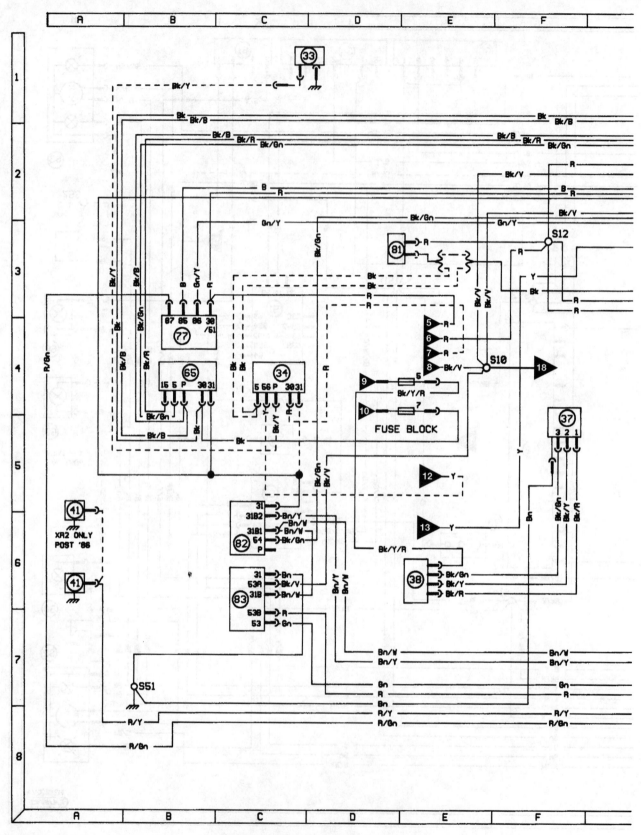

Diagram 3: Ancillary circuits - All models

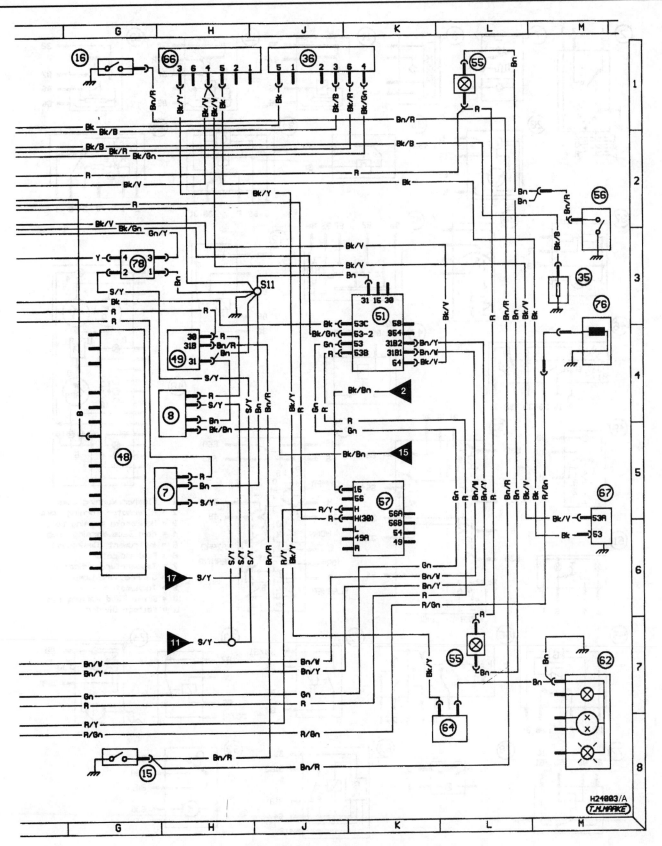

Diagram 3 (continued): Ancillary circuits - All models

H24003/A
T.H.MAAKE

12

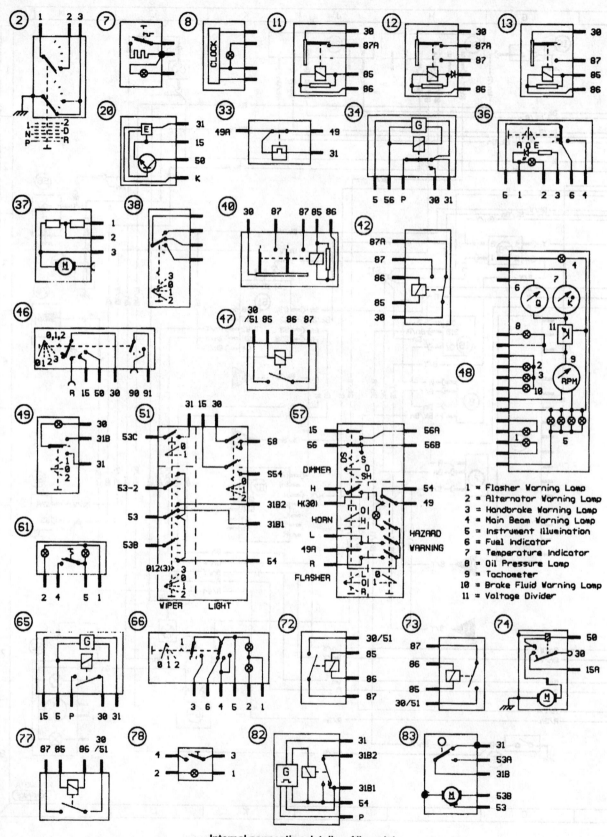

1 = Flasher Warning Lamp
2 = Alternator Warning Lamp
3 = Handbrake Warning Lamp
4 = Main Beam Warning Lamp
5 = Instrument Illumination
6 = Fuel Indicator
7 = Temperature Indicator
8 = Oil Pressure Lamp
9 = Tachometer
10 = Brake Fluid Warning Lamp
11 = Voltage Divider

Internal connection details - All models

Dimensions and Weights

Dimensions

	Saloons and Van	XR2
Overall length:		
Without overriders	3648 mm (143.7 in)	-
With overriders	3695 mm (145.6 in) or 3712 mm (146.3 in)	3712 mm (146.3 in)
Overall width	1585 mm (62.4 in)	1620 mm (63.8 in)
Overall height:		
Maximum	1334 mm (52.6 in)	1334 mm (52.6 in)
Minimum	1316 mm (51.9 in)	1310 mm (51.6 in)
Wheelbase	2288 mm (90.1 in)	2288 mm (90.1 in)
Track:		
Front	1367 mm (53.9 in)	1385 mm (54.6 in)
Rear	1321 mm (52.0 in)	1339 mm (52.8 in)

Weights

Basic kerb weight:	
1.0, 1.1 Base, L and Van	765.0 kg (1687 lb)
1.1 Ghia	780.0 kg (1720 lb)
1.1S (option)	797.5 kg (1758 lb)
1.3 and 1.4 Base, L, Ghia	800.0 kg (1764 lb)
1.3 and 1.4 S (option)	812.5 kg (1791 lb)
1.6 XR2	851.0 kg (1876 lb)
Gross vehicle weight:	
1.0 and 1.1 litre	1200 kg (2646 lb)
1.3 and 1.4 litre	1225 kg (2701 lb)
1.6 litre	1275 kg (2811 lb)

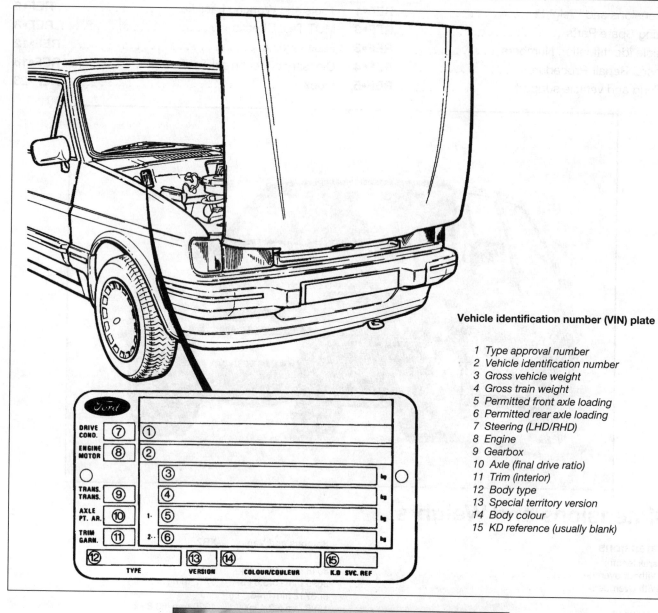

Vehicle identification number (VIN) plate

1 Type approval number
2 Vehicle identification number
3 Gross vehicle weight
4 Gross train weight
5 Permitted front axle loading
6 Permitted rear axle loading
7 Steering (LHD/RHD)
8 Engine
9 Gearbox
10 Axle (final drive ratio)
11 Trim (interior)
12 Body type
13 Special territory version
14 Body colour
15 KD reference (usually blank)

Alternative VIN plate location to the rear of the right-hand headlight

Buying spare parts

Spare parts are available from many sources, including maker's appointed garages, accessory shops, and motor factors. To be sure of obtaining the correct parts, it will sometimes be necessary to quote the vehicle identification number. If possible, it can also be useful to take the old parts along for positive identification. Items such as starter motors and alternators may be available under a service exchange scheme - any parts returned should always be clean.

Our advice regarding spare part sources is as follows.

Officially-appointed garages

This is the best source of parts which are peculiar to your car, and which are not otherwise generally available (eg badges, interior trim, certain body panels, etc). It is also the only place at which you should buy parts if the vehicle is still under warranty.

Accessory shops

These are very good places to buy materials and components needed for the maintenance of your car (oil, air and fuel filters, spark plugs, light bulbs, drivebelts, oils and greases, brake pads, touch-up paint, etc). Components of this nature sold by a reputable shop are of the same standard as those used by the car manufacturer.

Besides components, these shops also sell tools and general accessories, usually have convenient opening hours, charge lower prices, and can often be found not far from home. Some accessory shops have parts counters where the components needed for almost any repair job can be purchased or ordered.

Motor factors

Good factors will stock all the more important components which wear out comparatively quickly, and can sometimes supply individual components needed for the overhaul of a larger assembly (eg brake seals and hydraulic parts, bearing shells, pistons, valves, alternator brushes). They may also handle work such as cylinder block reboring, crankshaft regrinding and balancing, etc.

Tyre and exhaust specialists

These outlets may be independent, or members of a local or national chain. They frequently offer competitive prices when compared with a main dealer or local garage, but it will pay to obtain several quotes before making a decision. When researching prices, also ask what "extras" may be added - for instance, fitting a new valve and balancing the wheel are both commonly charged on top of the price of a new tyre.

Other sources

Beware of parts or materials obtained from market stalls, car boot sales or similar outlets. Such items are not invariably sub-standard, but there is little chance of compensation if they do prove unsatisfactory. In the case of safety-critical components such as brake pads, there is the risk not only of financial loss but also of an accident causing injury or death.

Second-hand components or assemblies obtained from a car breaker can be a good buy in some circumstances, but this sort of purchase is best made by the experienced DIY mechanic.

Vehicle identification numbers

Modifications are a continuing and unpublicised process in vehicle manufacture, quite apart from major model changes. Spare parts lists are compiled upon a numerical basis, the individual vehicle identification numbers being essential to correct identification of the component concerned.

When ordering spare parts, always give as much information as possible. Quote the car model, year of manufacture, body and engine numbers, as appropriate.

The Vehicle Identification Number (*VIN*) is located on the plate found in the engine compartment either on the bulkhead or on the front cross panel directly to the rear of the right-hand headlamp unit **(see illustrations)**. The VIN plate also carries information concerning paint colour, final drive ratio, etc.

The engine number on OHV variants is located on the exhaust side at the flywheel end of the engine. On CVH engines the number is located at the timing case end on the exhaust side **(see illustrations)**.

Other identification numbers or codes are stamped on major items such as the gearbox, final drive housing, distributor etc. These numbers are unlikely to be needed by the home mechanic.

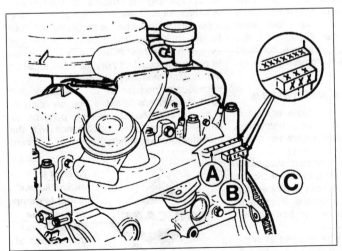

Engine number location - OHV engine

A Engine number   C Engine build date
B Engine code

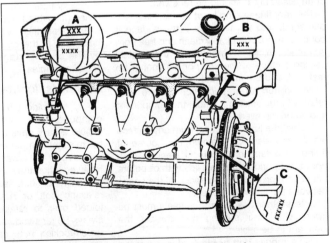

Engine number location - CVH engine

A Engine number   C Engine number for
B Engine code   repair reference

Whenever servicing, repair or overhaul work is carried out on the car or its components, observe the following procedures and instructions. This will assist in carrying out the operation efficiently and to a professional standard of workmanship.

Joint mating faces and gaskets

When separating components at their mating faces, never insert screwdrivers or similar implements into the joint between the faces in order to prise them apart. This can cause severe damage which results in oil leaks, coolant leaks, etc upon reassembly. Separation is usually achieved by tapping along the joint with a soft-faced hammer in order to break the seal. However, note that this method may not be suitable where dowels are used for component location.

Where a gasket is used between the mating faces of two components, a new one must be fitted on reassembly; fit it dry unless otherwise stated in the repair procedure. Make sure that the mating faces are clean and dry, with all traces of old gasket removed. When cleaning a joint face, use a tool which is unlikely to score or damage the face, and remove any burrs or nicks with an oilstone or fine file.

Make sure that tapped holes are cleaned with a pipe cleaner, and keep them free of jointing compound, if this is being used, unless specifically instructed otherwise.

Ensure that all orifices, channels or pipes are clear, and blow through them, preferably using compressed air.

Oil seals

Oil seals can be removed by levering them out with a wide flat-bladed screwdriver or similar implement. Alternatively, a number of self-tapping screws may be screwed into the seal, and these used as a purchase for pliers or some similar device in order to pull the seal free.

Whenever an oil seal is removed from its working location, either individually or as part of an assembly, it should be renewed.

The very fine sealing lip of the seal is easily damaged, and will not seal if the surface it contacts is not completely clean and free from scratches, nicks or grooves. If the original sealing surface of the component cannot be restored, and the manufacturer has not made provision for slight relocation of the seal relative to the sealing surface, the component should be renewed.

Protect the lips of the seal from any surface which may damage them in the course of fitting. Use tape or a conical sleeve where possible. Lubricate the seal lips with oil before fitting and, on dual-lipped seals, fill the space between the lips with grease.

Unless otherwise stated, oil seals must be fitted with their sealing lips toward the lubricant to be sealed.

Use a tubular drift or block of wood of the appropriate size to install the seal and, if the seal housing is shouldered, drive the seal down to the shoulder. If the seal housing is unshouldered, the seal should be fitted with its face flush with the housing top face (unless otherwise instructed).

Screw threads and fastenings

Seized nuts, bolts and screws are quite a common occurrence where corrosion has set in, and the use of penetrating oil or releasing fluid will often overcome this problem if the offending item is soaked for a while before attempting to release it. The use of an impact driver may also provide a means of releasing such stubborn fastening devices, when used in conjunction with the appropriate screwdriver bit or socket. If none of these methods works, it may be necessary to resort to the careful application of heat, or the use of a hacksaw or nut splitter device.

Studs are usually removed by locking two nuts together on the threaded part, and then using a spanner on the lower nut to unscrew the stud. Studs or bolts which have broken off below the surface of the component in which they are mounted can sometimes be removed using a stud extractor. Always ensure that a blind tapped hole is completely free from oil, grease, water or other fluid before installing the bolt or stud. Failure to do this could cause the housing to crack due to the hydraulic action of the bolt or stud as it is screwed in.

When tightening a castellated nut to accept a split pin, tighten the nut to the specified torque, where applicable, and then tighten further to the next split pin hole. Never slacken the nut to align the split pin hole, unless stated in the repair procedure.

When checking or retightening a nut or bolt to a specified torque setting, slacken the nut or bolt by a quarter of a turn, and then retighten to the specified setting. However, this should not be attempted where angular tightening has been used.

For some screw fastenings, notably cylinder head bolts or nuts, torque wrench settings are no longer specified for the latter stages of tightening, "angle-tightening" being called up instead. Typically, a fairly low torque wrench setting will be applied to the bolts/nuts in the correct sequence, followed by one or more stages of tightening through specified angles.

Locknuts, locktabs and washers

Any fastening which will rotate against a component or housing during tightening should always have a washer between it and the relevant component or housing.

Spring or split washers should always be renewed when they are used to lock a critical component such as a big-end bearing retaining bolt or nut. Locktabs which are folded over to retain a nut or bolt should always be renewed.

Self-locking nuts can be re-used in non-critical areas, providing resistance can be felt when the locking portion passes over the bolt or stud thread. However, it should be noted that self-locking stiffnuts tend to lose their effectiveness after long periods of use, and should then be renewed as a matter of course.

Split pins must always be replaced with new ones of the correct size for the hole.

When thread-locking compound is found on the threads of a fastener which is to be re-used, it should be cleaned off with a wire brush and solvent, and fresh compound applied on reassembly.

Special tools

Some repair procedures in this manual entail the use of special tools such as a press, two or three-legged pullers, spring compressors, etc. Wherever possible, suitable readily-available alternatives to the manufacturer's special tools are described, and are shown in use. In some instances, where no alternative is possible, it has been necessary to resort to the use of a manufacturer's tool, and this has been done for reasons of safety as well as the efficient completion of the repair operation. Unless you are highly-skilled and have a thorough understanding of the procedures described, never attempt to bypass the use of any special tool when the procedure described specifies its use. Not only is there a very great risk of personal injury, but expensive damage could be caused to the components involved.

Environmental considerations

When disposing of used engine oil, brake fluid, antifreeze, etc, give due consideration to any detrimental environmental effects. Do not, for instance, pour any of the above liquids down drains into the general sewage system, or onto the ground to soak away. Many local council refuse tips provide a facility for waste oil disposal, as do some garages. If none of these facilities are available, consult your local Environmental Health Department, or the National Rivers Authority, for further advice.

With the universal tightening-up of legislation regarding the emission of environmentally-harmful substances from motor vehicles, most vehicles have tamperproof devices fitted to the main adjustment points of the fuel system. These devices are primarily designed to prevent unqualified persons from adjusting the fuel/air mixture, with the chance of a consequent increase in toxic emissions. If such devices are found during servicing or overhaul, they should, wherever possible, be renewed or refitted in accordance with the manufacturer's requirements or current legislation.

OIL CARE
FOLLOW THE CODE

OIL BANK LINE
0800 66 33 66

Note: It is antisocial and illegal to dump oil down the drain. To find the location of your local oil recycling bank, call this number free.

The jack provided with the vehicle is designed primarily for emergency wheel changing, and its use for servicing and overhaul work on the vehicle is best avoided (see "Wheel changing"). Instead, a more substantial workshop jack (trolley jack or similar) should be used. Whichever type is employed, it is essential that additional safety support is provided by means of axle stands designed for this purpose. Never use makeshift means such as wooden blocks or piles of house bricks, as these can easily topple or, in the case of bricks, disintegrate under the weight of the vehicle.

When using the jack supplied with the vehicle, the jacking point on each side of the car is centrally positioned beneath the door sill. Check that the jack is fully engaged before raising the vehicle.

When using a trolley or other type of workshop jack, it can be located beneath the longitudinal engine/transmission support member at the front or under the axle beam at the rear (see illustration). In the latter case, care must be taken not to damage the Panhard rod; to prevent this, it is advisable to make up a suitable distance block incorporating a V-shaped cut-out in its top face to accommodate the axle beam. The block is then fitted between the jack head and the axle beam.

If raising the vehicle completely, raise the rear end first. Axle stands must **only** be located under double-skinned side or chassis members (see illustrations).

If removal of the wheels is not required, the use of drive-on ramps is recommended. Caution should be exercised to ensure that they are correctly aligned with the wheels, and that the vehicle is not driven too far along them so that it promptly falls off the other ends, or tips the ramps.

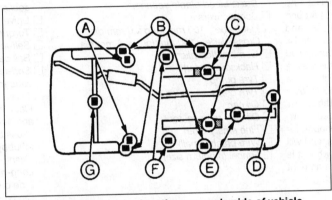

Jacking and support locations on underside of vehicle

A, B and C* Support locations only
D Front jacking location (except XR2)
E Front jacking location for XR2 only
F Side jacking locations
G Rear jacking location
*Note: At location "C" it is important that the vehicle is only supported on the double skinned portion of the longitudinal member (see tinted area on "C")

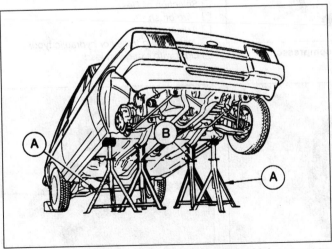

Axle stand location points at front of vehicle
A Body sill   B Chassis runner

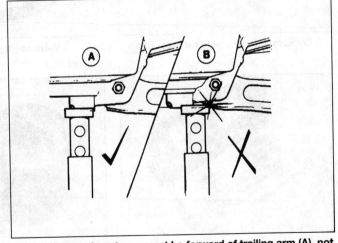

Axle stand location at rear must be forward of trailing arm (A), not under it (B)

Introduction

A selection of good tools is a fundamental requirement for anyone contemplating the maintenance and repair of a motor vehicle. For the owner who does not possess any, their purchase will prove a considerable expense, offsetting some of the savings made by doing-it-yourself. However, provided that the tools purchased meet the relevant national safety standards and are of good quality, they will last for many years and prove an extremely worthwhile investment.

To help the average owner to decide which tools are needed to carry out the various tasks detailed in this manual, we have compiled three lists of tools under the following headings: *Maintenance and minor repair*, *Repair and overhaul*, and *Special*. Newcomers to practical mechanics should start off with the *Maintenance and minor repair* tool kit, and confine themselves to the simpler jobs around the vehicle. Then, as confidence and experience grow, more difficult tasks can be undertaken, with extra tools being purchased as, and when, they are needed. In this way, a *Maintenance and minor repair* tool kit can be built up into a *Repair and overhaul* tool kit over a considerable period of time, without any major cash outlays. The experienced do-it-yourselfer will have a tool kit good enough for most repair and overhaul procedures, and will add tools from the *Special* category when it is felt that the expense is justified by the amount of use to which these tools will be put.

Maintenance and minor repair tool kit

The tools given in this list should be considered as a minimum requirement if routine maintenance, servicing and minor repair operations are to be undertaken. We recommend the purchase of combination spanners (ring one end, open-ended the other); although more expensive than open-ended ones, they do give the advantages of both types of spanner.

☐ *Combination spanners:*
   Metric - 8 to 19 mm inclusive
☐ *Adjustable spanner - 35 mm jaw (approx.)*
☐ *Spark plug spanner (with rubber insert) - petrol models*
☐ *Spark plug gap adjustment tool - petrol models*
☐ *Set of feeler gauges*
☐ *Brake bleed nipple spanner*
☐ *Screwdrivers:*
   Flat blade - 100 mm long x 6 mm dia
   Cross blade - 100 mm long x 6 mm dia
☐ *Combination pliers*
☐ *Hacksaw (junior)*
☐ *Tyre pump*
☐ *Tyre pressure gauge*
☐ *Oil can*
☐ *Oil filter removal tool*
☐ *Fine emery cloth*
☐ *Wire brush (small)*
☐ *Funnel (medium size)*

Repair and overhaul tool kit

These tools are virtually essential for anyone undertaking any major repairs to a motor vehicle, and are additional to those given in the *Maintenance and minor repair* list. Included in this list is a comprehensive set of sockets. Although these are expensive, they will be found invaluable as they are so versatile - particularly if various drives are included in the set. We recommend the half-inch square-drive type, as this can be used with most proprietary torque wrenches.

The tools in this list will sometimes need to be supplemented by tools from the *Special* list:

☐ *Sockets (or box spanners) to cover range in previous list (including Torx sockets)*
☐ *Reversible ratchet drive (for use with sockets)*
☐ *Extension piece, 250 mm (for use with sockets)*
☐ *Universal joint (for use with sockets)*
☐ *Torque wrench (for use with sockets)*
☐ *Self-locking grips*
☐ *Ball pein hammer*
☐ *Soft-faced mallet (plastic/aluminium or rubber)*
☐ *Screwdrivers:*
   Flat blade - long & sturdy, short (chubby), and narrow (electrician's) types
   Cross blade – Long & sturdy, and short (chubby) types
☐ *Pliers:*
   Long-nosed
   Side cutters (electrician's)
   Circlip (internal and external)
☐ *Cold chisel - 25 mm*
☐ *Scriber*
☐ *Scraper*
☐ *Centre-punch*
☐ *Pin punch*
☐ *Hacksaw*
☐ *Brake hose clamp*
☐ *Brake/clutch bleeding kit*
☐ *Selection of twist drills*
☐ *Steel rule/straight-edge*
☐ *Allen keys (inc. splined/Torx type)*
☐ *Selection of files*
☐ *Wire brush*
☐ *Axle stands*
☐ *Jack (strong trolley or hydraulic type)*
☐ *Light with extension lead*

Sockets and reversible ratchet drive

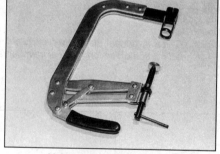

Valve spring compressor

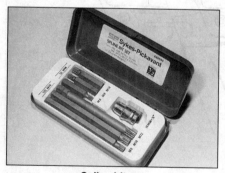

Spline bit set

Piston ring compressor

Clutch plate alignment set

Special tools

The tools in this list are those which are not used regularly, are expensive to buy, or which need to be used in accordance with their manufacturers' instructions. Unless relatively difficult mechanical jobs are undertaken frequently, it will not be economic to buy many of these tools. Where this is the case, you could consider clubbing together with friends (or joining a motorists' club) to make a joint purchase, or borrowing the tools against a deposit from a local garage or tool hire specialist. It is worth noting that many of the larger DIY superstores now carry a large range of special tools for hire at modest rates.

The following list contains only those tools and instruments freely available to the public, and not those special tools produced by the vehicle manufacturer specifically for its dealer network. You will find occasional references to these manufacturers' special tools in the text of this manual. Generally, an alternative method of doing the job without the vehicle manufacturers' special tool is given. However, sometimes there is no alternative to using them. Where this is the case and the relevant tool cannot be bought or borrowed, you will have to entrust the work to a dealer.

☐ Valve spring compressor
☐ Valve grinding tool
☐ Piston ring compressor
☐ Piston ring removal/installation tool
☐ Cylinder bore hone
☐ Balljoint separator
☐ Coil spring compressors (where applicable)
☐ Two/three-legged hub and bearing puller
☐ Impact screwdriver
☐ Micrometer and/or vernier calipers
☐ Dial gauge
☐ Stroboscopic timing light
☐ Dwell angle meter/tachometer
☐ Universal electrical multi-meter
☐ Cylinder compression gauge
☐ Hand-operated vacuum pump and gauge
☐ Clutch plate alignment set
☐ Brake shoe steady spring cup removal tool
☐ Bush and bearing removal/installation set
☐ Stud extractors
☐ Tap and die set
☐ Lifting tackle
☐ Trolley jack

Buying tools

Reputable motor accessory shops and superstores often offer excellent quality tools at discount prices, so it pays to shop around.

Remember, you don't have to buy the most expensive items on the shelf, but it is always advisable to steer clear of the very cheap tools. Beware of 'bargains' offered on market stalls or at car boot sales. There are plenty of good tools around at reasonable prices, but always aim to purchase items which meet the relevant national safety standards. If in doubt, ask the proprietor or manager of the shop for advice before making a purchase.

Care and maintenance of tools

Having purchased a reasonable tool kit, it is necessary to keep the tools in a clean and serviceable condition. After use, always wipe off any dirt, grease and metal particles using a clean, dry cloth, before putting the tools away. Never leave them lying around after they have been used. A simple tool rack on the garage or workshop wall for items such as screwdrivers and pliers is a good idea. Store all normal spanners and sockets in a metal box. Any measuring instruments, gauges, meters, etc, must be carefully stored where they cannot be damaged or become rusty.

Take a little care when tools are used. Hammer heads inevitably become marked, and screwdrivers lose the keen edge on their blades from time to time. A little timely attention with emery cloth or a file will soon restore items like this to a good finish.

Working facilities

Not to be forgotten when discussing tools is the workshop itself. If anything more than routine maintenance is to be carried out, a suitable working area becomes essential.

It is appreciated that many an owner-mechanic is forced by circumstances to remove an engine or similar item without the benefit of a garage or workshop. Having done this, any repairs should always be done under the cover of a roof.

Wherever possible, any dismantling should be done on a clean, flat workbench or table at a suitable working height.

Any workbench needs a vice; one with a jaw opening of 100 mm is suitable for most jobs. As mentioned previously, some clean dry storage space is also required for tools, as well as for any lubricants, cleaning fluids, touch-up paints etc, which become necessary.

Another item which may be required, and which has a much more general usage, is an electric drill with a chuck capacity of at least 8 mm. This, together with a good range of twist drills, is virtually essential for fitting accessories.

Last, but not least, always keep a supply of old newspapers and clean, lint-free rags available, and try to keep any working area as clean as possible.

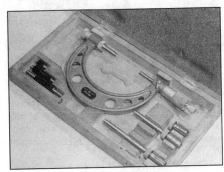

Micrometer set

Dial test indicator ("dial gauge")

Stroboscopic timing light

Compression tester

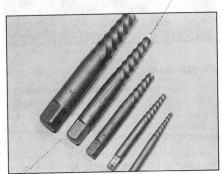

Stud extractor set

This is a guide to getting your vehicle through the MOT test. Obviously it will not be possible to examine the vehicle to the same standard as the professional MOT tester. However, working through the following checks will enable you to identify any problem areas before submitting the vehicle for the test.

Where a testable component is in borderline condition, the tester has discretion in deciding whether to pass or fail it. The basis of such discretion is whether the tester would be happy for a close relative or friend to use the vehicle with the component in that condition. If the vehicle presented is clean and evidently well cared for, the tester may be more inclined to pass a borderline component than if the vehicle is scruffy and apparently neglected.

It has only been possible to summarise the test requirements here, based on the regulations in force at the time of printing. Test standards are becoming increasingly stringent, although there are some exemptions for older vehicles. For full details obtain a copy of the Haynes publication Pass the MOT! (available from stockists of Haynes manuals).

An assistant will be needed to help carry out some of these checks.

The checks have been sub-divided into four categories, as follows:

1 Checks carried out **FROM THE DRIVER'S SEAT**

2 Checks carried out **WITH THE VEHICLE ON THE GROUND**

3 Checks carried out **WITH THE VEHICLE RAISED AND THE WHEELS FREE TO TURN**

4 Checks carried out on **YOUR VEHICLE'S EXHAUST EMISSION SYSTEM**

---

1 Checks carried out **FROM THE DRIVER'S SEAT**

Handbrake

☐ Test the operation of the handbrake. Excessive travel (too many clicks) indicates incorrect brake or cable adjustment.

☐ Check that the handbrake cannot be released by tapping the lever sideways. Check the security of the lever mountings.

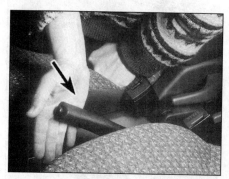

Footbrake

☐ Depress the brake pedal and check that it does not creep down to the floor, indicating a master cylinder fault. Release the pedal, wait a few seconds, then depress it again. If the pedal travels nearly to the floor before firm resistance is felt, brake adjustment or repair is necessary. If the pedal feels spongy, there is air in the hydraulic system which must be removed by bleeding.

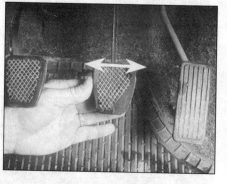

☐ Check that the brake pedal is secure and in good condition. Check also for signs of fluid leaks on the pedal, floor or carpets, which would indicate failed seals in the brake master cylinder.

☐ Check the servo unit (when applicable) by operating the brake pedal several times, then keeping the pedal depressed and starting the engine. As the engine starts, the pedal will move down slightly. If not, the vacuum hose or the servo itself may be faulty.

Steering wheel and column

☐ Examine the steering wheel for fractures or looseness of the hub, spokes or rim.

☐ Move the steering wheel from side to side and then up and down. Check that the steering wheel is not loose on the column, indicating wear or a loose retaining nut. Continue moving the steering wheel as before, but also turn it slightly from left to right.

☐ Check that the steering wheel is not loose on the column, and that there is no abnormal

movement of the steering wheel, indicating wear in the column support bearings or couplings.

Windscreen and mirrors

☐ The windscreen must be free of cracks or other significant damage within the driver's field of view. (Small stone chips are acceptable.) Rear view mirrors must be secure, intact, and capable of being adjusted.

290mm

Seat belts and seats

Note: *The following checks are applicable to all seat belts, front and rear.*

☐ Examine the webbing of all the belts (including rear belts if fitted) for cuts, serious fraying or deterioration. Fasten and unfasten each belt to check the buckles. If applicable, check the retracting mechanism. Check the security of all seat belt mountings accessible from inside the vehicle.

☐ The front seats themselves must be securely attached and the backrests must lock in the upright position.

Doors

☐ Both front doors must be able to be opened and closed from outside and inside, and must latch securely when closed.

2 Checks carried out WITH THE VEHICLE ON THE GROUND

Vehicle identification

☐ Number plates must be in good condition, secure and legible, with letters and numbers correctly spaced – spacing at (A) should be twice that at (B).

☐ The VIN plate and/or homologation plate must be legible.

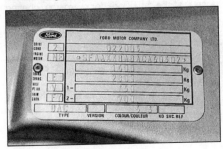

Electrical equipment

☐ Switch on the ignition and check the operation of the horn.

☐ Check the windscreen washers and wipers, examining the wiper blades; renew damaged or perished blades. Also check the operation of the stop-lights.

☐ Check the operation of the sidelights and number plate lights. The lenses and reflectors must be secure, clean and undamaged.

☐ Check the operation and alignment of the headlights. The headlight reflectors must not be tarnished and the lenses must be undamaged.

☐ Switch on the ignition and check the operation of the direction indicators (including the instrument panel tell-tale) and the hazard warning lights. Operation of the sidelights and stop-lights must not affect the indicators - if it does, the cause is usually a bad earth at the rear light cluster.

☐ Check the operation of the rear foglight(s), including the warning light on the instrument panel or in the switch.

Footbrake

☐ Examine the master cylinder, brake pipes and servo unit for leaks, loose mountings, corrosion or other damage.

☐ The fluid reservoir must be secure and the fluid level must be between the upper (A) and lower (B) markings.

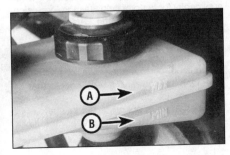

☐ Inspect both front brake flexible hoses for cracks or deterioration of the rubber. Turn the steering from lock to lock, and ensure that the hoses do not contact the wheel, tyre, or any part of the steering or suspension mechanism. With the brake pedal firmly depressed, check the hoses for bulges or leaks under pressure.

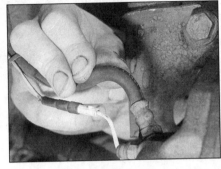

Steering and suspension

☐ Have your assistant turn the steering wheel from side to side slightly, up to the point where the steering gear just begins to transmit this movement to the roadwheels. Check for excessive free play between the steering wheel and the steering gear, indicating wear or insecurity of the steering column joints, the column-to-steering gear coupling, or the steering gear itself.

☐ Have your assistant turn the steering wheel more vigorously in each direction, so that the roadwheels just begin to turn. As this is done, examine all the steering joints, linkages, fittings and attachments. Renew any component that shows signs of wear or damage. On vehicles with power steering, check the security and condition of the steering pump, drivebelt and hoses.

☐ Check that the vehicle is standing level, and at approximately the correct ride height.

Shock absorbers

☐ Depress each corner of the vehicle in turn, then release it. The vehicle should rise and then settle in its normal position. If the vehicle continues to rise and fall, the shock absorber is defective. A shock absorber which has seized will also cause the vehicle to fail.

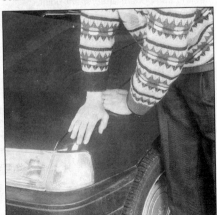

Exhaust system

☐ Start the engine. With your assistant holding a rag over the tailpipe, check the entire system for leaks. Repair or renew leaking sections.

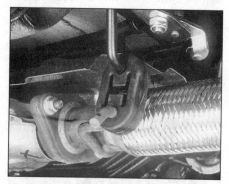

3 Checks carried out
WITH THE VEHICLE RAISED AND THE WHEELS FREE TO TURN

Jack up the front and rear of the vehicle, and securely support it on axle stands. Position the stands clear of the suspension assemblies. Ensure that the wheels are clear of the ground and that the steering can be turned from lock to lock.

Steering mechanism

☐ Have your assistant turn the steering from lock to lock. Check that the steering turns smoothly, and that no part of the steering mechanism, including a wheel or tyre, fouls any brake hose or pipe or any part of the body structure.
☐ Examine the steering rack rubber gaiters for damage or insecurity of the retaining clips. If power steering is fitted, check for signs of damage or leakage of the fluid hoses, pipes or connections. Also check for excessive stiffness or binding of the steering, a missing split pin or locking device, or severe corrosion of the body structure within 30 cm of any steering component attachment point.

Front and rear suspension and wheel bearings

☐ Starting at the front right-hand side, grasp the roadwheel at the 3 o'clock and 9 o'clock positions and shake it vigorously. Check for free play or insecurity at the wheel bearings, suspension balljoints, or suspension mountings, pivots and attachments.
☐ Now grasp the wheel at the 12 o'clock and 6 o'clock positions and repeat the previous inspection. Spin the wheel, and check for roughness or tightness of the front wheel bearing.

☐ If excess free play is suspected at a component pivot point, this can be confirmed by using a large screwdriver or similar tool and levering between the mounting and the component attachment. This will confirm whether the wear is in the pivot bush, its retaining bolt, or in the mounting itself (the bolt holes can often become elongated).

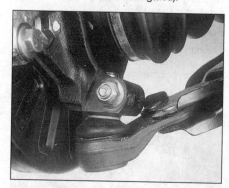

☐ Carry out all the above checks at the other front wheel, and then at both rear wheels.

Springs and shock absorbers

☐ Examine the suspension struts (when applicable) for serious fluid leakage, corrosion, or damage to the casing. Also check the security of the mounting points.
☐ If coil springs are fitted, check that the spring ends locate in their seats, and that the spring is not corroded, cracked or broken.
☐ If leaf springs are fitted, check that all leaves are intact, that the axle is securely attached to each spring, and that there is no deterioration of the spring eye mountings, bushes, and shackles.

☐ The same general checks apply to vehicles fitted with other suspension types, such as torsion bars, hydraulic displacer units, etc. Ensure that all mountings and attachments are secure, that there are no signs of excessive wear, corrosion or damage, and (on hydraulic types) that there are no fluid leaks or damaged pipes.
☐ Inspect the shock absorbers for signs of serious fluid leakage. Check for wear of the mounting bushes or attachments, or damage to the body of the unit.

Driveshafts (fwd vehicles only)

☐ Rotate each front wheel in turn and inspect the constant velocity joint gaiters for splits or damage. Also check that each driveshaft is straight and undamaged.

Braking system

☐ If possible without dismantling, check brake pad wear and disc condition. Ensure that the friction lining material has not worn excessively, (A) and that the discs are not fractured, pitted, scored or badly worn (B).

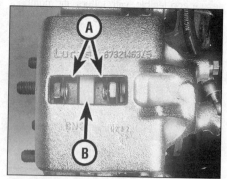

☐ Examine all the rigid brake pipes underneath the vehicle, and the flexible hose(s) at the rear. Look for corrosion, chafing or insecurity of the pipes, and for signs of bulging under pressure, chafing, splits or deterioration of the flexible hoses.
☐ Look for signs of fluid leaks at the brake calipers or on the brake backplates. Repair or renew leaking components.
☐ Slowly spin each wheel, while your assistant depresses and releases the footbrake. Ensure that each brake is operating and does not bind when the pedal is released.

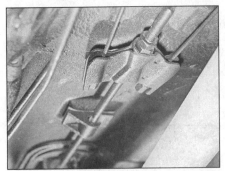

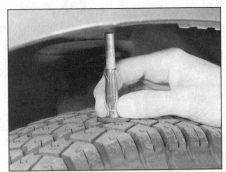

□ Examine the handbrake mechanism, checking for frayed or broken cables, excessive corrosion, or wear or insecurity of the linkage. Check that the mechanism works on each relevant wheel, and releases fully, without binding.

□ It is not possible to test brake efficiency without special equipment, but a road test can be carried out later to check that the vehicle pulls up in a straight line.

Fuel and exhaust systems

□ Inspect the fuel tank (including the filler cap), fuel pipes, hoses and unions. All components must be secure and free from leaks.

□ Examine the exhaust system over its entire length, checking for any damaged, broken or missing mountings, security of the retaining clamps and rust or corrosion.

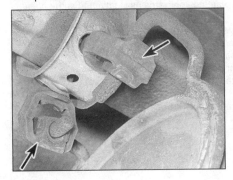

Wheels and tyres

□ Examine the sidewalls and tread area of each tyre in turn. Check for cuts, tears, lumps, bulges, separation of the tread, and exposure of the ply or cord due to wear or damage. Check that the tyre bead is correctly seated on the wheel rim, that the valve is sound and

properly seated, and that the wheel is not distorted or damaged.

□ Check that the tyres are of the correct size for the vehicle, that they are of the same size and type on each axle, and that the pressures are correct.

□ Check the tyre tread depth. The legal minimum at the time of writing is 1.6 mm over at least three-quarters of the tread width. Abnormal tread wear may indicate incorrect front wheel alignment.

Body corrosion

□ Check the condition of the entire vehicle structure for signs of corrosion in load-bearing areas. (These include chassis box sections, side sills, cross-members, pillars, and all suspension, steering, braking system and seat belt mountings and anchorages.) Any corrosion which has seriously reduced the thickness of a load-bearing area is likely to cause the vehicle to fail. In this case professional repairs are likely to be needed.

□ Damage or corrosion which causes sharp or otherwise dangerous edges to be exposed will also cause the vehicle to fail.

4 Checks carried out on YOUR VEHICLE'S EXHAUST EMISSION SYSTEM

Petrol models

□ Have the engine at normal operating temperature, and make sure that it is in good tune (ignition system in good order, air filter element clean, etc).

□ Before any measurements are carried out, raise the engine speed to around 2500 rpm, and hold it at this speed for 20 seconds. Allow

the engine speed to return to idle, and watch for smoke emissions from the exhaust tailpipe. If the idle speed is obviously much too high, or if dense blue or clearly-visible black smoke comes from the tailpipe for more than 5 seconds, the vehicle will fail. As a rule of thumb, blue smoke signifies oil being burnt (engine wear) while black smoke signifies unburnt fuel (dirty air cleaner element, or other carburettor or fuel system fault).

□ An exhaust gas analyser capable of measuring carbon monoxide (CO) and hydrocarbons (HC) is now needed. If such an instrument cannot be hired or borrowed, a local garage may agree to perform the check for a small fee.

CO emissions (mixture)

□ At the time of writing, the maximum CO level at idle is 3.5% for vehicles first used after August 1986 and 4.5% for older vehicles. From January 1996 a much tighter limit (around 0.5%) applies to catalyst-equipped vehicles first used from August 1992. If the CO level cannot be reduced far enough to pass the test (and the fuel and ignition systems are otherwise in good condition) then the carburettor is badly worn, or there is some problem in the fuel injection system or catalytic converter (as applicable).

HC emissions

□ With the CO emissions within limits, HC emissions must be no more than 1200 ppm (parts per million). If the vehicle fails this test at idle, it can be re-tested at around 2000 rpm; if the HC level is then 1200 ppm or less, this counts as a pass.

□ Excessive HC emissions can be caused by oil being burnt, but they are more likely to be due to unburnt fuel.

Diesel models

□ The only emission test applicable to Diesel engines is the measuring of exhaust smoke density. The test involves accelerating the engine several times to its maximum unloaded speed.

Note: *It is of the utmost importance that the engine timing belt is in good condition before the test is carried out.*

□ Excessive smoke can be caused by a dirty air cleaner element. Otherwise, professional advice may be needed to find the cause.

Engine

- ☐ Engine fails to rotate when attempting to start
- ☐ Starter motor turns engine slowly
- ☐ Engine rotates, but will not start
- ☐ Engine difficult to start when cold
- ☐ Engine difficult to start when hot
- ☐ Starter motor noisy or excessively-rough in engagement
- ☐ Engine starts, but stops immediately
- ☐ Engine idles erratically
- ☐ Engine misfires at idle speed
- ☐ Engine misfires throughout the driving speed range
- ☐ Engine hesitates on acceleration
- ☐ Engine stalls
- ☐ Engine lacks power
- ☐ Engine backfires
- ☐ Oil pressure warning light illuminated with engine running
- ☐ Engine runs-on after switching off
- ☐ Engine noises

Cooling system

- ☐ Overheating
- ☐ Overcooling
- ☐ External coolant leakage
- ☐ Internal coolant leakage
- ☐ Corrosion

Fuel and exhaust systems

- ☐ Excessive fuel consumption
- ☐ Fuel leakage and/or fuel odour
- ☐ Excessive noise or fumes from exhaust system

Clutch

- ☐ Pedal travels to floor - no pressure or very little resistance
- ☐ Clutch fails to disengage (unable to select gears)
- ☐ Clutch slips (engine speed increases, with no increase in vehicle speed)
- ☐ Judder as clutch is engaged
- ☐ Noise when depressing or releasing clutch pedal

Gearbox

- ☐ Noisy in neutral with engine running
- ☐ Noisy in one particular gear
- ☐ Difficulty engaging gears
- ☐ Jumps out of gear
- ☐ Vibration
- ☐ Lubricant leaks

Driveshafts

- ☐ Clunking or knocking noise on turns
- ☐ Vibration when accelerating or decelerating

Braking system

- ☐ Vehicle pulls to one side under braking
- ☐ Noise (grinding or high-pitched squeal) when brakes applied
- ☐ Excessive brake pedal travel
- ☐ Brake pedal feels spongy when depressed
- ☐ Excessive brake pedal effort required to stop vehicle
- ☐ Judder felt through brake pedal or steering wheel when braking
- ☐ Brakes binding
- ☐ Rear wheels locking under normal braking

Steering and Suspension

- ☐ Vehicle pulls to one side
- ☐ Wheel wobble and vibration
- ☐ Excessive pitching and/or rolling around corners, or during braking
- ☐ Wandering or general instability
- ☐ Excessively-stiff steering
- ☐ Excessive play in steering
- ☐ Tyre wear excessive

Electrical system

- ☐ Battery will not hold a charge for more than a few days
- ☐ Ignition/no-charge warning light remains illuminated with engine running
- ☐ Ignition/no-charge warning light fails to come on
- ☐ Lights inoperative
- ☐ Instrument readings inaccurate or erratic
- ☐ Horn inoperative, or unsatisfactory in operation
- ☐ Windscreen/tailgate wipers inoperative, or unsatisfactory in operation
- ☐ Windscreen/tailgate washers inoperative, or unsatisfactory in operation

Introduction

The vehicle owner who does his or her own maintenance according to the recommended service schedules should not have to use this section of the manual very often. Modern component reliability is such that, provided those items subject to wear or deterioration are inspected or renewed at the specified intervals, sudden failure is comparatively rare. Faults do not usually just happen as a result of sudden failure, but develop over a period of time. Major mechanical failures in particular are usually preceded by characteristic symptoms over hundreds or even thousands of miles. Those components which do occasionally fail without warning are often small and easily carried in the vehicle.

With any fault-finding, the first step is to decide where to begin investigations. Sometimes this is obvious, but on other occasions, a little detective work will be necessary. The owner who makes half a dozen haphazard adjustments or replacements may be successful in curing a fault (or its symptoms), but will be none the wiser if the fault recurs, and ultimately may have spent more time and money than was necessary. A calm and logical approach will be found to be more satisfactory in the long run. Always take into account any warning signs or abnormalities that may have been noticed in the period preceding the fault - power loss, high or low gauge readings, unusual smells, etc - and remember that failure of components such as fuses or spark plugs may only be pointers to some underlying fault.

The pages which follow provide an easy-reference guide to the more common problems which may occur during the operation of the vehicle. These problems and their possible causes are grouped under headings denoting various components or systems, such as Engine, Cooling system, etc. The Chapter and/or Section which deals with the problem is also shown in brackets. Whatever the fault, certain basic principles apply. These are as follows:

Verify the fault. This is simply a matter of being sure that you know what the symptoms are before starting work. This is particularly important if you are investigating a fault for someone else, who may not have described it very accurately.

Don't overlook the obvious. For example, if the vehicle won't start, is there fuel in the tank? (Don't take anyone else's word on this particular point, and don't trust the fuel gauge either!) If an electrical fault is indicated, look for loose or broken wires before digging out the test gear.

Cure the disease, not the symptom. Substituting a flat battery with a fully-charged one will get you off the hard shoulder, but if the underlying cause is not attended to, the new battery will go the same way. Similarly, changing oil-fouled spark plugs for a new set will get you moving again, but remember that the reason for the fouling (if it wasn't simply an incorrect grade of plug) will have to be established and corrected.

Don't take anything for granted. Particularly, don't forget that a "new" component may itself be defective (especially if it's been rattling around in the boot for months), and don't leave components out of a fault diagnosis sequence just because they are new or recently-fitted. When you do finally diagnose a difficult fault, you'll probably realise that all the evidence was there from the start.

Engine

Engine fails to rotate when attempting to start

☐ Battery terminal connections loose or corroded (Chapter 1).
☐ Battery discharged or faulty (Chapter 5C).
☐ Broken, loose or disconnected wiring in the starting circuit (Chapter 5C).
☐ Defective starter solenoid or switch (Chapter 5C).
☐ Defective starter motor (Chapter 5C).
☐ Starter pinion or flywheel/driveplate ring gear teeth loose or broken (Chapters 2 or 5).
☐ Engine earth strap broken or disconnected.

Starter motor turns engine slowly

☐ Partially-discharged battery (recharge, use jump leads, or push start) (Chapter 5C).
☐ Battery terminals loose or corroded (Chapter 1).
☐ Battery earth to body defective (Chapter 5C).
☐ Engine earth strap loose.
☐ Starter motor (or solenoid) wiring loose (Chapter 5C).
☐ Starter motor internal fault (Chapter 5C).

Engine rotates, but will not start

☐ Fuel pump defective (Chapter 4).
☐ Fuel tank empty.
☐ Battery discharged (engine rotates slowly) (Chapter 5C).
☐ Battery terminal connections loose or corroded (Chapter 1).
☐ Ignition components damp or damaged (Chapters 1 and 5).
☐ Broken, loose or disconnected wiring in the ignition circuit (Chapters 1 and 5A or B).
☐ Worn, faulty or incorrectly-gapped spark plugs (Chapters 1 and 5A or B).
☐ Major mechanical failure (eg broken timing chain) (Chapter 2).

Engine difficult to start when cold

☐ Battery discharged (Chapter 5C).
☐ Battery terminal connections loose or corroded (Chapter 1).
☐ Worn, faulty or incorrectly-gapped spark plugs (Chapters 1 and 5A or B).
☐ Other ignition system fault (Chapters 1 and 5A or B).
☐ Low cylinder compressions (Chapter 2).

Engine difficult to start when hot

☐ Air filter element dirty or clogged (Chapter 1).
☐ Low cylinder compressions (Chapter 2).

Starter motor noisy or excessively-rough in engagement

☐ Starter pinion or flywheel/driveplate ring gear teeth loose or broken (Chapters 2 or 5).
☐ Starter motor mounting bolts loose or missing (Chapter 5C).
☐ Starter motor internal components worn or damaged (Chapter 5C).

Engine starts, but stops immediately

☐ Loose or faulty electrical connections in the ignition circuit (Chapters 1 and 5A or B).
☐ Vacuum leak at the throttle body or inlet manifold (Chapter 4).

Engine idles erratically

☐ Carburettor stepper motor plunger dirty (where fitted).
☐ Incorrectly-adjusted idle speed (Chapter 4).
☐ Air filter element clogged (Chapter 1).
☐ Vacuum leak at the throttle body, inlet manifold or associated hoses (Chapter 4).
☐ Worn, faulty or incorrectly-gapped spark plugs (Chapters 1 and 5A or B).
☐ Uneven or low cylinder compressions (Chapter 2).
☐ Camshaft lobes worn (Chapter 2B).

Engine misfires at idle speed

☐ Worn, faulty or incorrectly-gapped spark plugs (Chapters 1 and 5A or B).
☐ Faulty spark plug HT leads (Chapter 5A or B).
☐ Vacuum leak at the throttle body, inlet manifold or associated hoses (Chapter 4).
☐ Distributor cap cracked or tracking internally, where applicable (Chapter 5A or B).
☐ Uneven or low cylinder compressions (Chapter 2).
☐ Disconnected, leaking, or perished crankcase ventilation hoses (Chapter 4).

Engine misfires throughout the driving speed range

☐ Fuel filter choked (where fitted).
☐ Fuel pump faulty, or delivery pressure low (Chapter 4).
☐ Fuel tank vent blocked, or fuel pipes restricted (Chapter 4).
☐ Vacuum leak at the throttle body, inlet manifold or associated hoses (Chapter 4).
☐ Worn, faulty or incorrectly-gapped spark plugs (Chapters 1 and 5A or B).
☐ Faulty spark plug HT leads (Chapter 5A or B).
☐ Distributor cap cracked or tracking internally, where applicable (Chapter 5A or B).
☐ Faulty ignition coil (Chapter 5B).
☐ Uneven or low cylinder compressions (Chapter 2).

Engine hesitates on acceleration

☐ Worn, faulty or incorrectly-gapped spark plugs (Chapters 1 and 5A or B).
☐ Vacuum leak at the throttle body, inlet manifold or associated hoses (Chapter 4).

Engine stalls

☐ Vacuum leak at the throttle body, inlet manifold or associated hoses (Chapter 4).
☐ Fuel filter choked (where fitted).
☐ Fuel pump faulty, or delivery pressure low (Chapter 4).
☐ Fuel tank vent blocked, or fuel pipes restricted (Chapter 4).

Engine lacks power

☐ Fuel filter choked (where fitted).
☐ Fuel pump faulty, or delivery pressure low (Chapter 4).
☐ Uneven or low cylinder compressions (Chapter 2).
☐ Worn, faulty or incorrectly-gapped spark plugs (Chapters 1 and 5A or B).

Engine lacks power (continued)

- [ ] Vacuum leak at the throttle body, inlet manifold or associated hoses (Chapter 4).
- [ ] Brakes binding (Chapters 1 and 9).
- [ ] Clutch slipping (Chapter 6).

Engine backfires

- [ ] Vacuum leak at the throttle body, inlet manifold or associated hoses (Chapter 4).

Oil pressure warning light illuminated with engine running

- [ ] Low oil level, or incorrect oil grade (*"Weekly checks"*).
- [ ] Faulty oil pressure sensor (Chapter 2).
- [ ] Worn engine bearings and/or oil pump (Chapter 2).
- [ ] Excessively high engine operating temperature (Chapter 3).
- [ ] Oil pressure relief valve defective (Chapter 2).
- [ ] Oil pick-up strainer clogged (Chapter 2).

Note: *Low oil pressure in a high-mileage engine at tickover is not necessarily a cause for concern. Sudden pressure loss at speed is far more significant. In any event, check the gauge or warning light sender before condemning the engine.*

Engine runs-on after switching off

- [ ] Excessive carbon build-up in engine (Chapter 2).
- [ ] Excessively high engine operating temperature (Chapter 3).

Engine noises

Pre-ignition (pinking) or knocking during acceleration or under load

- [ ] Ignition timing incorrect/ignition system fault (Chapters 1 and 5A or B).
- [ ] Incorrect grade of spark plug (Chapters 1 and 5A or B).
- [ ] Incorrect grade of fuel.
- [ ] Vacuum leak at throttle body, inlet manifold or associated hoses (Chapter 4).
- [ ] Excessive carbon build-up in engine (Chapter 2).

Whistling or wheezing noises

- [ ] Leaking inlet manifold or throttle body gasket (Chapter 4).
- [ ] Leaking exhaust manifold gasket (Chapter 4).
- [ ] Leaking vacuum hose (Chapters 4 and 9).
- [ ] Blowing cylinder head gasket (Chapter 2).

Tapping or rattling noises

- [ ] Worn valve gear, timing chain or camshaft (Chapter 2).
- [ ] Ancillary component fault (water pump, alternator, etc) (Chapters 3, 5C, etc).

Knocking or thumping noises

- [ ] Worn big-end bearings (regular heavy knocking, perhaps less under load) (Chapter 2).
- [ ] Worn main bearings (rumbling and knocking, perhaps worsening under load) (Chapter 2).
- [ ] Piston slap (most noticeable when cold) (Chapter 2).
- [ ] Ancillary component fault (water pump, alternator, etc) (Chapters 3, 5C, etc).

Cooling system

Overheating

- [ ] Auxiliary drivebelt broken or incorrectly adjusted (Chapter 1).
- [ ] Insufficient coolant in system (*"Weekly checks"*).
- [ ] Thermostat faulty (Chapter 3).
- [ ] Radiator core blocked, or grille restricted (Chapter 3).
- [ ] Electric cooling fan or thermostatic switch faulty (Chapter 3).
- [ ] Ignition timing incorrect, or ignition system fault (Chapters 1 and 5A or B).
- [ ] Inaccurate temperature gauge sender unit (Chapter 3).
- [ ] Airlock in cooling system (Chapter 3).

Overcooling

- [ ] Thermostat faulty (Chapter 3).
- [ ] Inaccurate temperature gauge sender unit (Chapter 3).

External coolant leakage

- [ ] Deteriorated or damaged hoses or hose clips (Chapters 1 and 3).
- [ ] Radiator core or heater matrix leaking (Chapter 3).
- [ ] Pressure cap faulty (Chapter 3).
- [ ] Water pump internal seal leaking (Chapter 3).
- [ ] Water pump-to-block seal leaking (Chapter 3).
- [ ] Boiling due to overheating (Chapter 3).
- [ ] Core plug leaking (Chapter 2).

Internal coolant leakage

- [ ] Leaking cylinder head gasket (Chapter 2).
- [ ] Cracked cylinder head or cylinder block (Chapter 2).

Corrosion

- [ ] Infrequent draining and flushing (Chapter 1).
- [ ] Incorrect coolant mixture or inappropriate coolant type (*"Weekly checks"*).

Fuel and exhaust systems

Excessive fuel consumption

- [ ] Air filter element dirty or clogged (Chapter 1).
- [ ] Ignition timing incorrect or ignition system fault (Chapters 1 and 5A or B).
- [ ] Brakes binding (Chapter 9).
- [ ] Tyres under-inflated (*"Weekly checks"*).

Fuel leakage and/or fuel odour

- [ ] Damaged fuel tank, pipes or connections (Chapters 1 and 4).

Excessive noise or fumes from exhaust system

- [ ] Leaking exhaust system or manifold joints (Chapters 1 and 4).
- [ ] Leaking, corroded or damaged silencers or pipe (Chapters 1 and 4).
- [ ] Broken mountings causing body or suspension contact (Chapter 4).

Clutch

Pedal travels to floor - no pressure or very little resistance

☐ Badly stretched or broken cable (Chapter 6).
☐ Stripped pawl on pedal (Chapter 6).
☐ Broken clutch release bearing or arm (Chapter 6).
☐ Broken diaphragm spring in clutch pressure plate (Chapter 6).

Clutch fails to disengage (unable to select gears)

☐ Cable free play excessive (Chapter 6).
☐ Clutch driven plate sticking on gearbox input shaft splines (Chapter 6).
☐ Clutch driven plate sticking to flywheel or pressure plate (Chapter 6).
☐ Faulty pressure plate assembly (Chapter 6).
☐ Clutch release mechanism worn or incorrectly assembled (Chapter 6).

Clutch slips (engine speed increases, with no increase in vehicle speed)

☐ Clutch driven plate linings excessively worn (Chapter 6).

☐ Clutch driven plate linings contaminated with oil or grease (Chapter 6).
☐ Faulty pressure plate or weak diaphragm spring (Chapter 6).

Judder as clutch is engaged

☐ Clutch driven plate linings contaminated with oil or grease (Chapter 6).
☐ Clutch driven plate linings excessively worn (Chapter 6).
☐ Faulty or distorted pressure plate or diaphragm spring (Chapter 6).
☐ Worn or loose engine or gearbox mountings (Chapter 2).
☐ Clutch driven plate hub or gearbox input shaft splines worn (Chapter 6).

Noise when depressing or releasing clutch pedal

☐ Worn clutch release bearing (Chapter 6).
☐ Worn or dry clutch pedal pivot (Chapter 6).
☐ Faulty pressure plate assembly (Chapter 6).
☐ Pressure plate diaphragm spring broken (Chapter 6).
☐ Broken clutch driven plate cushioning springs (Chapter 6).

Gearbox

Noisy in neutral with engine running

☐ Input shaft bearings worn (noise apparent with clutch pedal released, but not when depressed) (Chapter 7).*
☐ Clutch release bearing worn (noise apparent with clutch pedal depressed, possibly less when released) (Chapter 6).

Noisy in one particular gear

☐ Worn, damaged or chipped gear teeth (Chapter 7).*

Difficulty engaging gears

☐ Clutch fault (Chapter 6).
☐ Worn or damaged gear linkage (Chapter 7).
☐ Worn synchroniser units*

Jumps out of gear

☐ Worn or damaged gear linkage (Chapter 7).
☐ Worn synchroniser units*
☐ Worn selector forks*

Vibration

☐ Lack of oil (Chapter 1).
☐ Worn bearings (Chapter 7).*

Lubricant leaks

☐ Leaking oil seal (Chapter 7).
☐ Leaking housing joint (Chapter 7).*

*Although the corrective action necessary to remedy the symptoms described is beyond the scope of the home mechanic, the above information should be helpful in isolating the cause of the condition, so that the owner can communicate clearly with a professional mechanic.

Driveshafts

Clunking or knocking noise on turns (at slow speed on full lock)

☐ Worn outer constant velocity (CV) joints (Chapter 8).
☐ Lack of CV joint lubrication, possibly due to damaged gaiter (Chapter 8).

Vibration when accelerating or decelerating

☐ Worn inboard joint (Chapter 8).
☐ Bent or distorted shaft (Chapter 8).

Braking system

Note: *Before assuming that a brake problem exists, make sure that the tyres are in good condition and correctly inflated, that the front wheel alignment is correct, and that the vehicle is not loaded with weight in an unequal manner. Apart from checking the condition of all pipe and hose connections, any faults occurring on the anti-lock braking system should be referred to a Ford dealer for diagnosis.*

Vehicle pulls to one side under braking

☐ Worn, defective, damaged or contaminated front or rear brake pads on one side (Chapters 1 and 9).
☐ Seized or partially-seized front or rear brake caliper piston (Chapter 9).
☐ A mixture of brake pad lining materials fitted between sides (Chapter 9).
☐ Brake caliper mounting bolts loose (Chapter 9).
☐ Worn or damaged steering or suspension components (Chapters 1 and 10).

Noise (grinding or high-pitched squeal) when brakes applied

☐ Brake pad friction lining material worn down to metal backing (Chapters 1 and 9).
☐ Excessive corrosion of brake disc - may be apparent after the vehicle has been standing for some time (Chapters 1 and 9).

Excessive brake pedal travel

☐ Faulty master cylinder (Chapter 9).
☐ Air in hydraulic system (Chapter 9).
☐ Faulty vacuum servo unit (Chapter 9).

Brake pedal feels spongy when depressed

☐ Air in hydraulic system (Chapter 9).

☐ Deteriorated flexible rubber brake hoses (Chapters 1 and 9).
☐ Master cylinder mountings loose (Chapter 9).
☐ Faulty master cylinder (Chapter 9).

Excessive brake pedal effort required to stop vehicle

☐ Faulty vacuum servo unit (Chapter 9).
☐ Disconnected, damaged or insecure brake servo vacuum hose (Chapters 1 and 9).
☐ Primary or secondary hydraulic circuit failure (Chapter 9).
☐ Seized brake caliper piston(s) (Chapter 9).
☐ Brake pads incorrectly fitted (Chapter 9).
☐ Incorrect grade of brake pads fitted (Chapter 9).
☐ Brake pads contaminated (Chapter 9).

Judder felt through brake pedal or steering wheel when braking

☐ Excessive run-out or distortion of brake disc(s) (Chapter 9).
☐ Brake pad linings worn (Chapters 1 and 9).
☐ Brake caliper mounting bolts loose (Chapter 9).
☐ Wear in suspension or steering components or mountings (Chapters 1 and 10).

Brakes binding

☐ Seized brake caliper piston(s) (Chapter 9).
☐ Incorrectly-adjusted handbrake mechanism (Chapter 9).
☐ Faulty master cylinder (Chapter 9).

Rear wheels locking under normal braking

☐ Seized brake caliper piston(s) (Chapter 9).
☐ Faulty brake pressure regulator (Chapter 9).

Steering and suspension

Note: *Before diagnosing suspension or steering faults, be sure that the trouble is not due to incorrect tyre pressures, mixtures of tyre types, or binding brakes.*

Vehicle pulls to one side

☐ Defective tyre (*"Weekly checks"*).
☐ Excessive wear in suspension or steering components (Chapters 1 and 10).
☐ Incorrect front wheel alignment (Chapter 10).
☐ Accident damage to steering or suspension components (Chapters 1 and 10).

Wheel wobble and vibration

☐ Front roadwheels out of balance (vibration felt mainly through the steering wheel) (Chapter 10).
☐ Rear roadwheels out of balance (vibration felt throughout the vehicle) (Chapter 10).
☐ Roadwheels damaged or distorted (Chapter 10).
☐ Faulty or damaged tyre (*"Weekly checks"*).
☐ Worn steering or suspension joints, bushes or components (Chapters 1 and 10).
☐ Wheel bolts loose (Chapter 10).

Excessive pitching and/or rolling around corners, or during braking

☐ Defective shock absorbers (Chapters 1 and 10).
☐ Broken or weak coil spring and/or suspension component (Chapters 1 and 10).
☐ Worn or damaged anti-roll bar or mountings (Chapter 10).

Wandering or general instability

☐ Incorrect front wheel alignment (Chapter 10).
☐ Worn steering or suspension joints, bushes or components (Chapters 1 and 10).
☐ Roadwheels out of balance (Chapter 10).
☐ Faulty or damaged tyre (*"Weekly checks"*).
☐ Wheel bolts loose (Chapter 10).
☐ Defective shock absorbers (Chapters 1 and 10).

Excessively-stiff steering

☐ Lack of steering gear lubricant (Chapter 10).
☐ Seized track rod end balljoint or suspension balljoint (Chapters 1 and 10).
☐ Broken or incorrectly adjusted auxiliary drivebelt (Chapter 1).
☐ Incorrect front wheel alignment (Chapter 10).
☐ Steering rack or column bent or damaged (Chapter 10).

Excessive play in steering

☐ Worn steering column universal joint(s) (Chapter 10).
☐ Worn steering track rod end balljoints (Chapters 1 and 10).
☐ Worn rack-and-pinion steering gear (Chapter 10).
☐ Worn steering or suspension joints, bushes or components (Chapters 1 and 10).

Tyre wear excessive

Tyres worn on inside or outside edges

☐ Tyres under-inflated (wear on both edges) (*"Weekly checks"*).
☐ Incorrect camber or castor angles (wear on one edge only) (Chapter 10).

□ Worn steering or suspension joints, bushes or components (Chapters 1 and 10).
□ Excessively-hard cornering.
□ Accident damage.

Tyre treads exhibit feathered edges

□ Incorrect toe setting (Chapter 10).

Tyres worn in centre of tread

□ Tyres over-inflated ("Weekly checks").

Tyres worn on inside and outside edges

□ Tyres under-inflated ("Weekly checks").
□ Worn shock absorbers (Chapters 1 and 10).

Tyres worn unevenly

□ Tyres out of balance ("Weekly checks").
□ Excessive wheel or tyre run-out ("Weekly checks").
□ Worn shock absorbers (Chapters 1 and 10).
□ Faulty tyre ("Weekly checks").

Electrical system

Note: For problems associated with the starting system, refer to the faults listed under "Engine" earlier in this Section.

Battery will not hold a charge for more than a few days

□ Battery defective internally (Chapter 5C).
□ Battery electrolyte level low - where applicable ("Weekly checks").
□ Battery terminal connections loose or corroded (Chapter 1).
□ Auxiliary drivebelt worn - or incorrectly adjusted, where applicable (Chapter 1).
□ Alternator not charging at correct output (Chapter 5C).
□ Alternator or voltage regulator faulty (Chapter 5C).
□ Short-circuit causing continual battery drain (Chapters 5C and 12).

Ignition/no-charge warning light remains illuminated with engine running

□ Auxiliary drivebelt broken, worn, or incorrectly adjusted (Chapter 1).
□ Alternator brushes worn, sticking, or dirty (Chapter 5C).
□ Alternator brush springs weak or broken (Chapter 5C).
□ Internal fault in alternator or voltage regulator (Chapter 5C).
□ Broken, disconnected, or loose wiring in charging circuit (Chapter 5C).

Ignition/no-charge warning light fails to come on

□ Warning light bulb blown (Chapter 12).
□ Broken, disconnected, or loose wiring in warning light circuit (Chapter 12).
□ Alternator faulty (Chapter 5C).

Lights inoperative

□ Bulb blown (Chapter 12).
□ Corrosion of bulb or bulbholder contacts (Chapter 12).
□ Blown fuse (Chapter 12).
□ Faulty relay (Chapter 12).
□ Broken, loose, or disconnected wiring (Chapter 12).
□ Faulty switch (Chapter 12).

Instrument readings inaccurate or erratic

Instrument readings increase with engine speed

□ Faulty voltage regulator (Chapter 12).

Fuel or temperature gauges give no reading

□ Faulty gauge sender unit (Chapter 4).
□ Wiring open-circuit (Chapter 12).
□ Faulty gauge (Chapter 12).

Fuel or temperature gauges give continuous maximum reading

□ Faulty gauge sender unit (Chapter 4).
□ Wiring short-circuit (Chapter 12).
□ Faulty gauge (Chapter 12).

Horn inoperative, or unsatisfactory in operation

Horn operates all the time

□ Horn contacts permanently bridged or horn push stuck down (Chapter 12).

Horn fails to operate

□ Blown fuse (Chapter 12).
□ Cable or cable connections loose, broken or disconnected (Chapter 12).
□ Faulty horn (Chapter 12).

Horn emits intermittent or unsatisfactory sound

□ Cable connections loose (Chapter 12).
□ Horn mountings loose (Chapter 12).
□ Faulty horn (Chapter 12).

Windscreen/tailgate wipers inoperative, or unsatisfactory in operation

Wipers fail to operate, or operate very slowly

□ Wiper blades stuck to screen, or linkage seized or binding (Chapters 1 and 12).
□ Blown fuse (Chapter 12).
□ Cable or cable connections loose, broken or disconnected (Chapter 12).
□ Faulty relay (Chapter 12).
□ Faulty wiper motor (Chapter 12).

Wiper blades sweep over too large or too small an area of the glass

□ Wiper arms incorrectly positioned on spindles (Chapter 1).
□ Excessive wear of wiper linkage (Chapter 12).
□ Wiper motor or linkage mountings loose or insecure (Chapter 12).

Wiper blades fail to clean the glass effectively

□ Wiper blade rubbers worn or perished ("Weekly checks").
□ Wiper arm tension springs broken, or arm pivots seized (Chapter 12).
□ Insufficient windscreen washer additive to adequately remove road film ("Weekly checks").

Windscreen/tailgate washers inoperative, or unsatisfactory in operation

One or more washer jets inoperative

□ Blocked washer jet (Chapter 12).
□ Disconnected, kinked or restricted fluid hose (Chapter 12).
□ Insufficient fluid in washer reservoir ("Weekly checks").

Washer pump fails to operate

□ Broken or disconnected wiring or connections (Chapter 12).
□ Blown fuse (Chapter 12).
□ Faulty washer switch (Chapter 12).
□ Faulty washer pump (Chapter 12).

Washer pump runs for some time before fluid is emitted from jets

□ Faulty one-way valve in fluid supply hose (Chapter 12).

A

ABS (Anti-lock brake system) A system, usually electronically controlled, that senses incipient wheel lockup during braking and relieves hydraulic pressure at wheels that are about to skid.

Air bag An inflatable bag hidden in the steering wheel (driver's side) or the dash or glovebox (passenger side). In a head-on collision, the bags inflate, preventing the driver and front passenger from being thrown forward into the steering wheel or windscreen.

Air cleaner A metal or plastic housing, containing a filter element, which removes dust and dirt from the air being drawn into the engine.

Air filter element The actual filter in an air cleaner system, usually manufactured from pleated paper and requiring renewal at regular intervals.

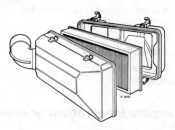

Air filter

Allen key A hexagonal wrench which fits into a recessed hexagonal hole.

Alligator clip A long-nosed spring-loaded metal clip with meshing teeth. Used to make temporary electrical connections.

Alternator A component in the electrical system which converts mechanical energy from a drivebelt into electrical energy to charge the battery and to operate the starting system, ignition system and electrical accessories.

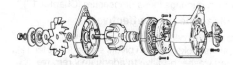

Alternator (exploded view)

Ampere (amp) A unit of measurement for the flow of electric current. One amp is the amount of current produced by one volt acting through a resistance of one ohm.

Anaerobic sealer A substance used to prevent bolts and screws from loosening. Anaerobic means that it does not require oxygen for activation. The Loctite brand is widely used.

Antifreeze A substance (usually ethylene glycol) mixed with water, and added to a vehicle's cooling system, to prevent freezing of the coolant in winter. Antifreeze also contains chemicals to inhibit corrosion and the formation of rust and other deposits that would tend to clog the radiator and coolant passages and reduce cooling efficiency.

Anti-seize compound A coating that reduces the risk of seizing on fasteners that are subjected to high temperatures, such as exhaust manifold bolts and nuts.

Anti-seize compound

Asbestos A natural fibrous mineral with great heat resistance, commonly used in the composition of brake friction materials. Asbestos is a health hazard and the dust created by brake systems should never be inhaled or ingested.

Axle A shaft on which a wheel revolves, or which revolves with a wheel. Also, a solid beam that connects the two wheels at one end of the vehicle. An axle which also transmits power to the wheels is known as a live axle.

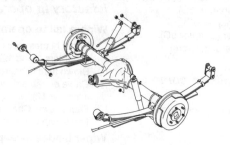

Axle assembly

Axleshaft A single rotating shaft, on either side of the differential, which delivers power from the final drive assembly to the drive wheels. Also called a driveshaft or a halfshaft.

B

Ball bearing An anti-friction bearing consisting of a hardened inner and outer race with hardened steel balls between two races.

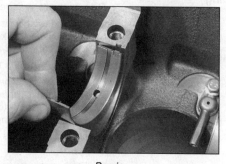

Bearing

Bearing The curved surface on a shaft or in a bore, or the part assembled into either, that permits relative motion between them with minimum wear and friction.

Big-end bearing The bearing in the end of the connecting rod that's attached to the crankshaft.

Bleed nipple A valve on a brake wheel cylinder, caliper or other hydraulic component that is opened to purge the hydraulic system of air. Also called a bleed screw.

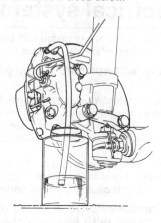

Brake bleeding

Brake bleeding Procedure for removing air from lines of a hydraulic brake system.

Brake disc The component of a disc brake that rotates with the wheels.

Brake drum The component of a drum brake that rotates with the wheels.

Brake linings The friction material which contacts the brake disc or drum to retard the vehicle's speed. The linings are bonded or riveted to the brake pads or shoes.

Brake pads The replaceable friction pads that pinch the brake disc when the brakes are applied. Brake pads consist of a friction material bonded or riveted to a rigid backing plate.

Brake shoe The crescent-shaped carrier to which the brake linings are mounted and which forces the lining against the rotating drum during braking.

Braking systems For more information on braking systems, consult the *Haynes Automotive Brake Manual*.

Breaker bar A long socket wrench handle providing greater leverage.

Bulkhead The insulated partition between the engine and the passenger compartment.

C

Caliper The non-rotating part of a disc-brake assembly that straddles the disc and carries the brake pads. The caliper also contains the hydraulic components that cause the pads to pinch the disc when the brakes are applied. A caliper is also a measuring tool that can be set to measure inside or outside dimensions of an object.

Camshaft A rotating shaft on which a series of cam lobes operate the valve mechanisms. The camshaft may be driven by gears, by sprockets and chain or by sprockets and a belt.

Canister A container in an evaporative emission control system; contains activated charcoal granules to trap vapours from the fuel system.

Canister

Carburettor A device which mixes fuel with air in the proper proportions to provide a desired power output from a spark ignition internal combustion engine.

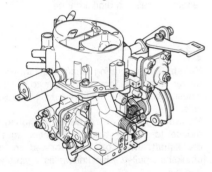

Carburettor

Castellated Resembling the parapets along the top of a castle wall. For example, a castellated balljoint stud nut.

Castellated nut

Castor In wheel alignment, the backward or forward tilt of the steering axis. Castor is positive when the steering axis is inclined rearward at the top.

Catalytic converter A silencer-like device in the exhaust system which converts certain pollutants in the exhaust gases into less harmful substances.

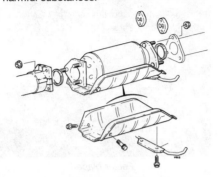

Catalytic converter

Circlip A ring-shaped clip used to prevent endwise movement of cylindrical parts and shafts. An internal circlip is installed in a groove in a housing; an external circlip fits into a groove on the outside of a cylindrical piece such as a shaft.

Clearance The amount of space between two parts. For example, between a piston and a cylinder, between a bearing and a journal, etc.

Coil spring A spiral of elastic steel found in various sizes throughout a vehicle, for example as a springing medium in the suspension and in the valve train.

Compression Reduction in volume, and increase in pressure and temperature, of a gas, caused by squeezing it into a smaller space.

Compression ratio The relationship between cylinder volume when the piston is at top dead centre and cylinder volume when the piston is at bottom dead centre.

Constant velocity (CV) joint A type of universal joint that cancels out vibrations caused by driving power being transmitted through an angle.

Core plug A disc or cup-shaped metal device inserted in a hole in a casting through which core was removed when the casting was formed. Also known as a freeze plug or expansion plug.

Crankcase The lower part of the engine block in which the crankshaft rotates.

Crankshaft The main rotating member, or shaft, running the length of the crankcase, with offset "throws" to which the connecting rods are attached.

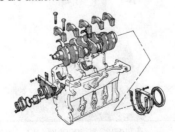

Crankshaft assembly

Crocodile clip See Alligator clip

D

Diagnostic code Code numbers obtained by accessing the diagnostic mode of an engine management computer. This code can be used to determine the area in the system where a malfunction may be located.

Disc brake A brake design incorporating a rotating disc onto which brake pads are squeezed. The resulting friction converts the energy of a moving vehicle into heat.

Double-overhead cam (DOHC) An engine that uses two overhead camshafts, usually one for the intake valves and one for the exhaust valves.

Drivebelt(s) The belt(s) used to drive accessories such as the alternator, water pump, power steering pump, air conditioning compressor, etc. off the crankshaft pulley.

Accessory drivebelts

Driveshaft Any shaft used to transmit motion. Commonly used when referring to the axleshafts on a front wheel drive vehicle.

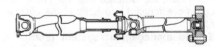

Driveshaft

Drum brake A type of brake using a drum-shaped metal cylinder attached to the inner surface of the wheel. When the brake pedal is pressed, curved brake shoes with friction linings press against the inside of the drum to slow or stop the vehicle.

Drum brake assembly

E

EGR valve A valve used to introduce exhaust gases into the intake air stream.

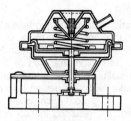

EGR valve

Electronic control unit (ECU) A computer which controls (for instance) ignition and fuel injection systems, or an anti-lock braking system. For more information refer to the *Haynes Automotive Electrical and Electronic Systems Manual*.

Electronic Fuel Injection (EFI) A computer controlled fuel system that distributes fuel through an injector located in each intake port of the engine.

Emergency brake A braking system, independent of the main hydraulic system, that can be used to slow or stop the vehicle if the primary brakes fail, or to hold the vehicle stationary even though the brake pedal isn't depressed. It usually consists of a hand lever that actuates either front or rear brakes mechanically through a series of cables and linkages. Also known as a handbrake or parking brake.

Endfloat The amount of lengthwise movement between two parts. As applied to a crankshaft, the distance that the crankshaft can move forward and back in the cylinder block.

Engine management system (EMS) A computer controlled system which manages the fuel injection and the ignition systems in an integrated fashion.

Exhaust manifold A part with several passages through which exhaust gases leave the engine combustion chambers and enter the exhaust pipe.

Exhaust manifold

F

Fan clutch A viscous (fluid) drive coupling device which permits variable engine fan speeds in relation to engine speeds.

Feeler blade A thin strip or blade of hardened steel, ground to an exact thickness, used to check or measure clearances between parts.

Feeler blade

Firing order The order in which the engine cylinders fire, or deliver their power strokes, beginning with the number one cylinder.

Flywheel A heavy spinning wheel in which energy is absorbed and stored by means of momentum. On cars, the flywheel is attached to the crankshaft to smooth out firing impulses.

Free play The amount of travel before any action takes place. The "looseness" in a linkage, or an assembly of parts, between the initial application of force and actual movement. For example, the distance the brake pedal moves before the pistons in the master cylinder are actuated.

Fuse An electrical device which protects a circuit against accidental overload. The typical fuse contains a soft piece of metal which is calibrated to melt at a predetermined current flow (expressed as amps) and break the circuit.

Fusible link A circuit protection device consisting of a conductor surrounded by heat-resistant insulation. The conductor is smaller than the wire it protects, so it acts as the weakest link in the circuit. Unlike a blown fuse, a failed fusible link must frequently be cut from the wire for replacement.

G

Gap The distance the spark must travel in jumping from the centre electrode to the side

Adjusting spark plug gap

electrode in a spark plug. Also refers to the spacing between the points in a contact breaker assembly in a conventional points-type ignition, or to the distance between the reluctor or rotor and the pickup coil in an electronic ignition.

Gasket Any thin, soft material - usually cork, cardboard, asbestos, or soft metal - installed between two metal surfaces to ensure a good seal. For instance, the cylinder head gasket seals the joint between the block and the cylinder head.

Gasket

Gauge An instrument panel display used to monitor engine conditions. A gauge with a movable pointer on a dial or a fixed scale is an analogue gauge. A gauge with a numerical readout is called a digital gauge.

H

Halfshaft A rotating shaft that transmits power from the final drive unit to a drive wheel, usually when referring to a live rear axle.

Harmonic balancer A device designed to reduce torsion or twisting vibration in the crankshaft. May be incorporated in the crankshaft pulley. Also known as a vibration damper.

Hone An abrasive tool for correcting small irregularities or differences in diameter in an engine cylinder, brake cylinder, etc.

Hydraulic tappet A tappet that utilises hydraulic pressure from the engine's lubrication system to maintain zero clearance (constant contact with both camshaft and valve stem). Automatically adjusts to variation in valve stem length. Hydraulic tappets also reduce valve noise.

I

Ignition timing The moment at which the spark plug fires, usually expressed in the number of crankshaft degrees before the piston reaches the top of its stroke.

Inlet manifold A tube or housing with passages through which flows the air-fuel mixture (carburettor vehicles and vehicles with throttle body injection) or air only (port fuel-injected vehicles) to the port openings in the cylinder head.

J

Jump start Starting the engine of a vehicle with a discharged or weak battery by attaching jump leads from the weak battery to a charged or helper battery.

L

Load Sensing Proportioning Valve (LSPV) A brake hydraulic system control valve that works like a proportioning valve, but also takes into consideration the amount of weight carried by the rear axle.

Locknut A nut used to lock an adjustment nut, or other threaded component, in place. For example, a locknut is employed to keep the adjusting nut on the rocker arm in position.

Lockwasher A form of washer designed to prevent an attaching nut from working loose.

M

MacPherson strut A type of front suspension system devised by Earle MacPherson at Ford of England. In its original form, a simple lateral link with the anti-roll bar creates the lower control arm. A long strut - an integral coil spring and shock absorber - is mounted between the body and the steering knuckle. Many modern so-called MacPherson strut systems use a conventional lower A-arm and don't rely on the anti-roll bar for location.

Multimeter An electrical test instrument with the capability to measure voltage, current and resistance.

N

NOx Oxides of Nitrogen. A common toxic pollutant emitted by petrol and diesel engines at higher temperatures.

O

Ohm The unit of electrical resistance. One volt applied to a resistance of one ohm will produce a current of one amp.

Ohmmeter An instrument for measuring electrical resistance.

O-ring A type of sealing ring made of a special rubber-like material; in use, the O-ring is compressed into a groove to provide the sealing action.

O-ring

Overhead cam (ohc) engine An engine with the camshaft(s) located on top of the cylinder head(s).

Overhead valve (ohv) engine An engine with the valves located in the cylinder head, but with the camshaft located in the engine block.

Oxygen sensor A device installed in the engine exhaust manifold, which senses the oxygen content in the exhaust and converts this information into an electric current. Also called a Lambda sensor.

P

Phillips screw A type of screw head having a cross instead of a slot for a corresponding type of screwdriver.

Plastigage A thin strip of plastic thread, available in different sizes, used for measuring clearances. For example, a strip of Plastigage is laid across a bearing journal. The parts are assembled and dismantled; the width of the crushed strip indicates the clearance between journal and bearing.

Plastigage

Propeller shaft The long hollow tube with universal joints at both ends that carries power from the transmission to the differential on front-engined rear wheel drive vehicles.

Proportioning valve A hydraulic control valve which limits the amount of pressure to the rear brakes during panic stops to prevent wheel lock-up.

R

Rack-and-pinion steering A steering system with a pinion gear on the end of the steering shaft that mates with a rack (think of a geared wheel opened up and laid flat). When the steering wheel is turned, the pinion turns, moving the rack to the left or right. This movement is transmitted through the track rods to the steering arms at the wheels.

Radiator A liquid-to-air heat transfer device designed to reduce the temperature of the coolant in an internal combustion engine cooling system.

Refrigerant Any substance used as a heat transfer agent in an air-conditioning system. R-12 has been the principle refrigerant for many years; recently, however, manufacturers have begun using R-134a, a non-CFC substance that is considered less harmful to the ozone in the upper atmosphere.

Rocker arm A lever arm that rocks on a shaft or pivots on a stud. In an overhead valve engine, the rocker arm converts the upward movement of the pushrod into a downward movement to open a valve.

Rotor In a distributor, the rotating device inside the cap that connects the centre electrode and the outer terminals as it turns, distributing the high voltage from the coil secondary winding to the proper spark plug. Also, that part of an alternator which rotates inside the stator. Also, the rotating assembly of a turbocharger, including the compressor wheel, shaft and turbine wheel.

Runout The amount of wobble (in-and-out movement) of a gear or wheel as it's rotated. The amount a shaft rotates "out-of-true." The out-of-round condition of a rotating part.

S

Sealant A liquid or paste used to prevent leakage at a joint. Sometimes used in conjunction with a gasket.

Sealed beam lamp An older headlight design which integrates the reflector, lens and filaments into a hermetically-sealed one-piece unit. When a filament burns out or the lens cracks, the entire unit is simply replaced.

Serpentine drivebelt A single, long, wide accessory drivebelt that's used on some newer vehicles to drive all the accessories, instead of a series of smaller, shorter belts. Serpentine drivebelts are usually tensioned by an automatic tensioner.

Serpentine drivebelt

Shim Thin spacer, commonly used to adjust the clearance or relative positions between two parts. For example, shims inserted into or under bucket tappets control valve clearances. Clearance is adjusted by changing the thickness of the shim.

Slide hammer A special puller that screws into or hooks onto a component such as a shaft or bearing; a heavy sliding handle on the shaft bottoms against the end of the shaft to knock the component free.

Sprocket A tooth or projection on the periphery of a wheel, shaped to engage with a chain or drivebelt. Commonly used to refer to the sprocket wheel itself.

Starter inhibitor switch On vehicles with an

automatic transmission, a switch that prevents starting if the vehicle is not in Neutral or Park.

Strut See MacPherson strut.

T

Tappet A cylindrical component which transmits motion from the cam to the valve stem, either directly or via a pushrod and rocker arm. Also called a cam follower.

Thermostat A heat-controlled valve that regulates the flow of coolant between the cylinder block and the radiator, so maintaining optimum engine operating temperature. A thermostat is also used in some air cleaners in which the temperature is regulated.

Thrust bearing The bearing in the clutch assembly that is moved in to the release levers by clutch pedal action to disengage the clutch. Also referred to as a release bearing.

Timing belt A toothed belt which drives the camshaft. Serious engine damage may result if it breaks in service.

Timing chain A chain which drives the camshaft.

Toe-in The amount the front wheels are closer together at the front than at the rear. On rear wheel drive vehicles, a slight amount of toe-in is usually specified to keep the front wheels running parallel on the road by offsetting other forces that tend to spread the wheels apart.

Toe-out The amount the front wheels are closer together at the rear than at the front. On front wheel drive vehicles, a slight amount of toe-out is usually specified.

Tools For full information on choosing and using tools, refer to the *Haynes Automotive Tools Manual.*

Tracer A stripe of a second colour applied to a wire insulator to distinguish that wire from another one with the same colour insulator.

Tune-up A process of accurate and careful adjustments and parts replacement to obtain the best possible engine performance.

Turbocharger A centrifugal device, driven by exhaust gases, that pressurises the intake air. Normally used to increase the power output from a given engine displacement, but can also be used primarily to reduce exhaust emissions (as on VW's "Umwelt" Diesel engine).

U

Universal joint or U-joint A double-pivoted connection for transmitting power from a driving to a driven shaft through an angle. A U-joint consists of two Y-shaped yokes and a cross-shaped member called the spider.

V

Valve A device through which the flow of liquid, gas, vacuum, or loose material in bulk may be started, stopped, or regulated by a movable part that opens, shuts, or partially obstructs one or more ports or passageways. A valve is also the movable part of such a device.

Valve clearance The clearance between the valve tip (the end of the valve stem) and the rocker arm or tappet. The valve clearance is measured when the valve is closed.

Vernier caliper A precision measuring instrument that measures inside and outside dimensions. Not quite as accurate as a micrometer, but more convenient.

Viscosity The thickness of a liquid or its resistance to flow.

Volt A unit for expressing electrical "pressure" in a circuit. One volt that will produce a current of one ampere through a resistance of one ohm.

W

Welding Various processes used to join metal items by heating the areas to be joined to a molten state and fusing them together. For more information refer to the *Haynes Automotive Welding Manual.*

Wiring diagram A drawing portraying the components and wires in a vehicle's electrical system, using standardised symbols. For more information refer to the *Haynes Automotive Electrical and Electronic Systems Manual.*

Note: *References throughout this index are in the form - "Chapter number"•"page number"*

Preserving Our Motoring Heritage

< *The Model J Duesenberg Derham Tourster. Only eight of these magnificent cars were ever built – this is the only example to be found outside the United States of America*

Almost every car you've ever loved, loathed or desired is gathered under one roof at the Haynes Motor Museum. Over 300 immaculately presented cars and motorbikes represent every aspect of our motoring heritage, from elegant reminders of bygone days, such as the superb Model J Duesenberg to curiosities like the bug-eyed BMW Isetta. There are also many old friends and flames. Perhaps you remember the 1959 Ford Popular that you did your courting in? The magnificent 'Red Collection' is a spectacle of classic sports cars including AC, Alfa Romeo, Austin Healey, Ferrari, Lamborghini, Maserati, MG, Riley, Porsche and Triumph.

A Perfect Day Out

Each and every vehicle at the Haynes Motor Museum has played its part in the history and culture of Motoring. Today, they make a wonderful spectacle and a great day out for all the family. Bring the kids, bring Mum and Dad, but above all bring your camera to capture those golden memories for ever. You will also find an impressive array of motoring memorabilia, a comfortable 70 seat video cinema and one of the most extensive transport book shops in Britain. The Pit Stop Cafe serves everything from a cup of tea to wholesome, home-made meals or, if you prefer, you can enjoy the large picnic area nestled in the beautiful rural surroundings of Somerset.

> *John Haynes O.B.E., Founder and Chairman of the museum at the wheel of a Haynes Light 12.*

< *Graham Hill's Lola Cosworth Formula 1 car next to a 1934 Riley Sports.*

The Museum is situated on the A359 Yeovil to Frome road at Sparkford, just off the A303 in Somerset. It is about 40 miles south of Bristol, and 25 minutes drive from the M5 intersection at Taunton.

Open 9.30am - 5.30pm (10.00am - 4.00pm Winter) 7 days a week, *except Christmas Day, Boxing Day and New Years Day*

Special rates available for schools, coach parties and outings Charitable Trust No. 292048